Relations and Functions within and around Language

Open Linguistics Series

Series Editor: Robin Fawcett, University of Cardiff

This series is 'open' in two related ways. First, it is not confined to works associated with any one school of linguistics. For almost two decades the series has played a significant role in establishing and maintaining the present climate of 'openness' in linguistics, and we intend to maintain this tradition. However, we particularly welcome works which explore the nature and use of language through modelling its potential for use in social contexts, or through a cognitive model of language – or indeed a combination of the two.

The series is also 'open' in the sense that it welcomes works that open out 'core' linguistics in various ways: to give a central place to the description of natural texts and the use of corpora; to encompass discourse 'above the sentence'; to relate language to other semiotic systems; to apply linguistics in fields such as education, language pathology and law; and to explore the areas that lie between linguistics and its neighbouring disciplines such as semiotics, psychology, sociology, philosophy, and cultural and literary studies.

Continuum also publishes a series that offers a forum for primarily functional descriptions of languages or parts of languages – *Functional Descriptions of Language*. Relations between linguistics and computing are covered in the *Communication in Artificial Intelligence* series, two series, *Advances in Applied Linguistics* and *Communication in Public Life*, publish books in applied linguistics and the series *Modern Pragmatics in Theory and Practice* publishes both social and cognitive perspectives on the making of meaning in language use. We also publish a range of introductory textbooks on topics in linguistics, semiotics and deaf studies.

Recent titles in the series:

Relations and Functions within and around Language

Edited by

Peter H. Fries, Michael Cummings,
David Lockwood
and William Spruiell

continuum
LONDON • NEW YORK

Continuum

The Tower Building, 11 York Road, London, SE1 7NX

370 Lexington Avenue, New York, NY 10017-6503

First published 2002

British Library Cataloguing-in-Publication Data
A catalogue record for this book is available from the British Library.

ISBN 0-8264-5368-6 (hardback)
　　　0-8264-5369-4 (paperback)

Library of Congress Cataloging-in-Publication Data
Relations and functions within and around language / edited by Peter H. Fries ... [et al.].
　　　p. cm — (Open linguistics series)
　　　Includes bibliographical references and index.
　　　ISBN 0-8264-5368-6 (hbk.) — ISBN 0-8264-5369-4 (pbk.)
　　　1. Functionalism (Linguistics). 2. Discourse analysis. I. Fries, Peter Howard. II. Series.

P147 .R45 2002
415—dc21   2001037094

Typeset by BookEns, Royston, Herts.
Printed and bound in Great Britain by MPG Books Ltd, Bodmin, Cornwall

Contents

Contributors

Wallace Chafe is Professor Emeritus at the University of California, Santa Barbara. His previous publications include *Meaning and the Structure of Language* (1970) and *Discourse, Consciousness, and Time* (1994).

Peter Fries is Professor of English and Linguistics at Central Michigan University. His previous publications include *On Subject and Theme: A Discourse on Functional Perspective* (edited with Ruqaiya Hasan, 1995), *Discourse in Society: Systemic Functional Perspectives* (edited with Michael Gregory, 1995) and *Functional Approaches to Language, Culture, and Cognition* (edited with David Lockwood and James Copeland, 2000).

Michael Gregory is Professor Emeritus and Senior Scholar at York University, Toronto. His previous publications include *Linguistics and Style* (with Nils Enkvist and John Spencer, 1964), *Language and Situation* (with Susanne Carroll, 1978) and *Discourse in Society* (edited with Peter Fries, 1995).

Sydney Lamb is Professor Emeritus of Linguistics and Cognitive Sciences at Rice University. His previous publications include *Pathways of the Brain: The Neurocognitive Basis of Language* (1999).

Jay Lemke is Professor of Education and Executive Officer, Ph.D. Program in Urban Education, at the City University of New York. His previous publications include *Textual Politics: Discourse and Social Theory* (1995), *Talking Science: Language, Learning, and Values* (1990) and *Using Language in the Classroom* (1989).

David Lockwood is Professor at Michigan State University. His previous publications include *Introduction to Stratificational Linguistics* (1972) and *Functional Approaches to Language, Culture, and Cognition* (edited with Peter Fries and James Copeland, 2000).

Paul Thibault is Associate Professor at the Università degli Studi di Venezia. His previous publications include *Text and Context: A Social Semiotic Approach* (1986), *Social Semiotics as Praxis* (1991) and *Re-reading Saussure: The Dynamics of Signs in Social Life* (1997).

Stephen Tyler is Herbert S. Autrey Professor of Anthropology and Linguistics at Rice University. His previous publications include *The Said and the Unsaid* (1978) and *The Unspeakable* (1987).

Dedicated to friends and mentors

James Copeland and Michael Gregory

Introduction

One of the tasks addressed by any theory of language should be an account of the ways language is used in social interaction: a theory of discourse. Many different sorts of discourse theory abound, and in their present state of development, discourse theories are still weighted towards the written text. Effort is required of the linguistic community both to bring different theoretical approaches together and to advance the understanding of spoken texts. This book is an attempt to further both such causes. It has both a theoretical section and an analytical section. The theoretical section offers a number of different, though complementary approaches to the description of discourse within a theory of language. The analytical section undertakes the study of a single spoken text, from several theoretical points of view.

Each of these two sections of the book is inspired by a historical occasion in the coming together of linguistic scholars. The theoretical section of the book revisits a common theme by a number of different theoreticians who first came together to discuss and compare their approaches on the occasion of a conference at Glendon College, York University, in 1988: a meeting of the *Annual Spring Colloquium* of the Applied Linguistics Research Working Group. The participants in that colloquium were asked to reconsider their approaches ten years later, and to come together again in a volume which takes its name from the theme of that original meeting: 'Relations and Functions within and around Language'. The analytical section of the book was inspired by a meeting of some of the same scholars at Rice University in 1984, on the occasion of the *Second Rice University Symposium in Linguistics and Semiotics*, entitled 'Text Semantics and Discourse Semantics', chaired by Professor James E. Copeland, Department of Linguistics and Semiotics. The work of that symposium was to compare the approaches of different text analysts to the same text, a dialogue interview between pseudonymous Sue and Kay. Again the analysts were asked to revisit and revise their approaches fifteen years later for the purposes of this volume.

The book then falls into two parts. Part One, the theoretical part, presents a variety of functional approaches using concepts motivated by the theoretical description of language to describe discourse. Part Two, the analytical part, compares approaches to a single spoken text. Since all but one of the chapters in Part Two make reference to the same spoken text, a transcription of this text appears in the Appendix, courtesy of Professor Copeland. All of the chapters in Part Two have utilized this transcription except for Wallace Chafe's 'Prosody and Emotion in a Sample of Real Speech'. Chafe's approach to the Sue/Kay interview required a different take on the problem of transcription, and his own transcription with a very different lineation is included at the end of his chapter.

All the chapters in this volume take a functional approach to the description of language. That is, they place a priority on describing the functions which each unit fills, as well as the forms that these units may have. Functional approaches range from those which address issues concerning ways in which language can be used for various practical purposes to those which see an integral relation between the functions which language fills and the internal structure of language (see Ruqaiya Hasan, The conception of context in text, in Peter H. Fries and Michael Gregory (eds.) *Discourse in Society: Systemic Functional Perspectives, Meaning and Choice in Language: Studies for Michael Halliday* (Norwood, NJ: Ablex, 1995:184). Advocates of extreme versions of the first approach typically treat language-internal functions (such as the typical grammatical functions of Subject, Object, etc.) but see little relation between the internal structure of language and its function in interaction. Advocates of the second view of functionalism believe that language is the way it is because it performs the sorts of functions in interaction that it does. Let us call this second view of functionalism 'intrinsic functionalism'.

Several of the chapters (those by Fries, Lemke, Thibault and Gregory) take an 'intrinsic functionalist' approach using variants of 'systemic-functional linguistics' (henceforth SFL); and since some of the basic tools of the analysis are not there expanded on, it will be useful to explore these basic concepts here. In the view of these theorists, language functions to realize social interaction. It is able to do so because there is a predictable relation between certain aspects of the social interaction and specific aspects of the language. Social interactions are seen as a combination of three factors: field, tenor and mode. Field is the socially validated interaction that is taking place at the time. What is taking place through language? Is the interaction one of buying and selling, a lecture on linguistics, a conversation about crying babies? (While topic is one feature of field, other aspects of the interaction are also relevant. Thus, a casual conversation among several parents about crying children does not illustrate the same field as an article in a popular magazine written for parents whose children cry a great deal.)

Tenor concerns the relation which holds among the participants in the interaction. Is the interaction a conversation between peers? Is one participant an expert and the others novices? What long-term social relation holds among the participants? Is the interaction a conversation among family members? Is this a text written for strangers? What attitudes do the participants take up in relation to each other and in relation to what is said?

Mode concerns the role of language in the interaction. Does the language constitute the interaction? For example, a lecture on physics could not take place without the language used by the lecturer. In this case, the language constitutes the lecture, so the mode is 'constitutive'. On the other hand, the language used while playing football does not constitute the interaction but rather makes the interaction more efficient. In such interactions the language facilitates the interaction taking place, so the mode is 'facilitative'. Of course, the situations just mentioned here represent extreme examples. Other texts (e.g. most advertising texts) illustrate complex mixtures of constitutive and facilitative modes of language.

The intrinsic functionalist approach does not stop there, however. Rather it views the internal structure of language as related to its functions. Thus, systemic-functional approaches to language see the internal structure of language as consisting of three major systems of interrelated choices in the lexico-grammar. These three major systems of choices are called 'metafunctions': the ideational metafunction, the interpersonal metafunction and the textual metafunction. The ideational metafunction concerns the representation of the world. What actions or states are described? Who or what takes part in these actions and states? Under what circumstances? The interpersonal metafunction concerns choices which involve ways in which the speaker acts on the listeners and the ways the speaker expresses attitudinal stances toward other participants and toward what is discussed. Through the use of grammatical structures such as command, question or statement the speaker can place the listeners in the potential role of complying with a request, of providing information or of simply accepting information being provided by the speaker. Through the use of negation, of modal verbs and of modal adverbs, the speaker can indicate the degree of certainty invested in what is being claimed. The textual metafunction concerns the ways that the speaker indicates the connection between what is being said and the larger context. The use of the pronouns *he, she, it* and *they* indicate that the listener already knows the referential identity of the entity referred to. Conjunctions indicate relations between portions of the text such as clauses. Other connections may be indicated through structural means such as by indicating which portion of the message is to be interpreted as New, and which is Given, i.e. information structure in SFL. Similarly speakers may indicate information they wish to use as a framework for interpreting the remainder of the message by placing the framework first, i.e. thematic structure in SFL.

In the intrinsic view of functionalism, language communicates because participants in a social interaction can relate it to the three features of social interaction: field, tenor and mode. The ideational metafunction relates most closely to the field of discourse. The interpersonal metafunction relates most closely to the tenor of discourse, and the textual metafunction relates most closely to the mode of discourse.

We can look at the relation between language and social interaction from the standpoint of the interaction that is taking place, and predict what is likely to be said on the basis of what we know is going on. Thus people who are applying for a job are extremely unlikely to use direct command forms to the people who are interviewing them, and when they do, they typically do so only under very circumscribed conditions.

But language works because the opposite sort of inference is also possible. Given the language that is being used, we can infer relevant things about the social interaction that is being encoded in that language. Thus, if we notice that one participant in an interaction generally refrains from making requests of the other participants, or makes requests only very indirectly, we can infer that he is attempting to avoid being seen as placing demands on the other participants. Often such avoidance is seen as 'being polite'.

While systemicists believe texts interpretable in relation to the social interaction that is taking place, Lemke and Thibault point out that more is involved. Both introduce the notion that texts are understood by relating them to other texts. The relations which concern Lemke and Thibault involve similarities of messages which exist within sets of similar texts. Lemke has coined the term 'thematic formations' to describe the basis of these intertextual similarities – a term which is not to be confused with the notion of Theme in SFL lexico-grammar. Thus, in a discussion of a chemistry lesson, Lemke ('Intertextuality and text semantics', in Peter H. Fries and Michael Gregory (eds), 1995:93) suggests that most of the clauses of the text may be related to 'a thematic formation in which a certain [Number] of [Electrons] are [Located] in certain [Types] of [Orbitals], the latter being considered parts of [Shells] in which the [Electrons] [Have] a certain [Amount] of [Energy].' (Square brackets represent variables within the formation.) Few clauses would actually reproduce the entire formation. Rather each clause would verbalize only a small portion of the formation and the formation would be found by looking at a number of clauses in the text. Indeed, it is quite possible that an entire text might not actually encode a complete formation. Thus, in the lesson he analyses, he finds sentences such as

Hydrogen would have one electron somewhere in there, . . .

If I have one electron in the 2p, . . .

Electrons occupy orbitals that differ in size, . . .

How many electrons in the outside shell?

Sodium has all the electrons Neon has, plus 3s, one.

Electron comes to town, wants to go into the cheapest hotel.

None of the sentences encodes the complete formation, but all of them express part of the formation, and are interpretable when participants relate them to that formation.

While the formation predicts that certain vocabulary is likely, the last example illustrates that no particular vocabulary or grammatical constructions are required. Much more important are the relations which hold among the various concepts. Thus, orbitals are conceived as locations for electrons, and are related to the energy which the electrons have, etc.

Each of the chapters in this volume relates to these issues differently, but different chapters often relate to them in complementary ways. In the keynote chapter of Part One, 'Relations and Functions within and around Language: The Systemic-Functional Tradition', Michael Gregory explores the dimension of discourse analysis termed 'gnostology', the underlying realm of culture-specific knowledge and culture-specific assumptions which both enables and limits the language potential of discourse participants. He sketches the evolution of this concept through Louis Hjelmslev, J. R. Firth, Sydney Lamb and M. A. K. Halliday, and relates it to his own development of a 'communication linguistics' within systemic-functional linguistics. On his own terms, gnostology manifests itself as a 'communicating community context', whose scope is limited to what is at risk in particular discourses, and whose content can be explored through the concept of the 'generic situation'-specific configurations of perceived participants and circumstances, which amount to expectations of what discourse will be about.

J. L. Lemke's chapter 'Ideology, Intertextuality and the Communication of Science', examines intertextuality in its social context. It considers what kinds of intertextual ties pertain among texts, their relative significance and how such ties reflect the social culture which occasions texts, particularly with respect to social heteroglossia, evaluative meaning and the role of ideology. These implications of the theory of intertextuality are demonstrated by analyses of two texts in the field of teaching science. Linguistic details in these texts reveal the features of 'technocratic discourse', one of whose functions is to maintain and promote the ideology of scientism.

The Global Modal Program in the title of Paul J. Thibault's chapter, 'Interpersonal Meaning and the Discursive Construction of Action, Attitudes and Values: The Global Modal Program of One Text', represents the interpersonal meaning of the text in terms of its organization on the discourse stratum. This kind of meaning is construed by interrelated selections from systems for mood, modality, modulation, lexis and turn-taking on the lexico-grammatical stratum. The organization of meanings on the discourse stratum reveals a complex of relationships among actional, attitudinal, axiological and dialogic components. The theory is demonstrated by an analysis of the Global Modal Program of one discourse, an exchange of messages between a magazine reader and an 'Agony Aunt' column.

Three interconnected areas of clause analysis are considered in Peter Fries's chapter, 'The Flow of Information in a Written English Text'. These areas are the theme/rheme structure, information structure and participant identification. Theme is the stretch of wording which represents the point of departure of the clause. Focus of information within information structure represents the focal point of 'newsworthiness' in the clause. Participant identification includes the definite/indefinite distinction and lexical/pro-form alternatives. Investigation of these areas of clause grammar is made with reference to the 'Zero Population Growth' letter that has served as the focus of comparison in William C. Mann and Sandra A. Thompson (eds.) *Discourse Description: Diverse Linguistic Analyses of a Fundraising Text* (Amsterdam: John Benjamins, 1992). The investigation reveals the utility to discourse theory of the intersection between rheme and 'new information' (the N-rheme).

David G. Lockwood, in 'Intrastratal and Interstratal Relations in Language and their Functions', undertakes an analysis of the basic premises and notational systems of stratificational linguistics. The relational network diagram as a method of linguistic description offers a representation of both paradigmatic and syntagmatic language resources in terms of the two most fundamental types of logical relations that underlie language encoding and decoding, the AND and the OR relation. Language resources on whatever level, from the phonological to the semantic, can be modelled as the multiple interconnections of just these two primitive relations; the same types of relation account for the multiple interconnections between contiguous language strata as well. Stratificational linguistics has undergone a number of developments in its accounting for the basic relations since its origins in the work of Sydney Lamb in the 1960s. Lockwood traces these developments in his own work and that of his stratificational colleagues to the present day, returning, appropriately, to Lamb's investigations in his most recent work on the neurological basis of language.

Part Two begins with 'Memory and Discourse' in which Stephen A. Tyler undertakes an analysis of the Sue/Kay interview by making connections between modern discourse theory and the ancient discipline of rhetoric. With reference to rhetorical *schemata*, this chapter demonstrates the utility in spoken discourse of idiomatic filler phrases which create a rhythmical underpinning for the discourse structure. Topical organization and coherence in discourse structure are placed in relation to rhetorical *inventio*. Rhetorical *memoria* and modern theories of memory are related to various prosodies in discourse, from larger discourse structures down to stress rhythm. The concept of *schemata* informs all of these approaches to analysis, whether as empty filler phrases or the complex realization on all levels of language of culturally specified *topoi*.

A complement to Fries's discussion of theme in two other chapters in this volume, David G. Lockwood's chapter, 'Highlighting in Stratificational-Cognitive Linguistics', deals with marked theme and other 'highlighting' functions in the clause, which include patient-as subject in passive-voice clauses, cleft and pseudo-cleft constructions, and contrastive accent (i.e. the systemicist's 'marked focus of information'). All of these constructions are examined in light of the Sue/Kay interview. The chapter concentrates on the development of the highlighting concept in stratificational-cognitive linguistics, and how this development relates to parallel work within other approaches, especially the systemic-functional.

Sydney Lamb's treatment of the Sue/Kay text in 'Interpreting Discourse' involves taking a small segment of the interview which represents narrative genre, and demonstrating from this example how a neurocognitive approach will illuminate the structure of the discourse. The discourse is seen to exist not in itself, but only as reconstructed in the mind of the hearer/reader. Cognitive reconstruction is conceived in terms of relational networks, where new perceived data function as new nodal items in a forming network of relations. The network embraces relations within and among all linguistic levels from the phonological to the semological, and involves trial-and-error reinterpretation and self-correction until some final cognitive approximation of the discourse is achieved.

In 'Prosody and Emotion in a Sample of Real Speech', Wallace Chafe uses the Sue/Kay interview as data to illustrate the communication of personal involvement through various acoustic features of spoken utterance in discourse. The principal feature which is examined is change in the fundamental frequency of utterance, but additional features found to be relevant to the communication of attitude and personal emotion include controlled change in the length of syllables, and controlled change in the tempo of utterance. At any point in the discourse, the connection between a particular acoustic configuration and the kind of personal attitude involved is very context-oriented; of themselves, such configurations may signify only changes in the degree of involvement.

In 'Phasal Analysis within Communication Linguistics: Two Contrastive Discourses', Michael Gregory demonstrates the techniques of phasal analysis by using it to examine, illuminate and contrast two separate discourses: Ernest Hemingway's short story 'The Sea Change' and the Sue/Kay interview. In phasal analysis, the underlying tree-like structure of discourse is revealed by the minute examination of coherence features among adjacent stretches of text. The analyses provided in this chapter also serve as instantiation of the principles of communication linguistics introduced in the keynote chapter of Part One of this volume.

The Sue/Kay text is scrutinized to discover the sources of its coherence in Peter Fries's chapter, 'Some Aspects of Coherence in a

Conversation'. The jumping-off point is John Sinclair's definition of coherence as the characteristic of a text whose parts 'fit together so well that it is clear and easy to understand', but for Fries the source of such coherence is the social interaction which the text encodes. The main investigation is in deconstructing this linguistic encoding in terms of narrative structure, thematic progression and Hasan's technique of investigating 'cohesive harmony'. The analysis details and tabulates a rich variety of cohesion ties which help to realize the lexico-grammatical construal of social-interaction schemata.

Acknowledgement

The editors wish to thank the University of Wisconsin Press for permission to reprint 'Memory and Discourse', Chapter 4 in Stephen A. Tyler, *The Unspeakable: Discourse, Dialogue, and Rhetoric in the Postmodern World* (Madison: University of Wisconsin Press, 1987).

PART ONE

THEORY

1

Relations and Functions within and around Language: The Systemic-Functional Tradition

Michael Gregory

To begin with some snippets of text more or less obliquely relevant to this chapter: an anthology as prologue to a monologue. First of all, the character Clea 'speaking' in the novel of that name by Lawrence Durrell:

> an impatience with partial knowledge which is ... well, unfair to knowledge itself. (1963:101)

and a little later:

> Sometimes I try and think of us all as habit-patterns rather than human beings. I mean, wasn't the idea of the individual soul grafted on us by the Greeks in the wild hope that, by its sheer beauty, it would 'take' – as we say of vaccination. (1963:127)

and Pursewarden in the same novel:

> Language is not an accident of poetry but the essence. The lingo is the nub. (1963:249)

And finally, from a publication of 1840, *What Is Property?* by Pierre Joseph Proudhon:

> Convinced at once that, in order to break loose from the beaten paths of opinions and systems, it was necessary to proceed in my study of man and society by scientific methods, and in a rigorous manner, I devoted one year to philology and grammar; linguistics, or the natural history of speech, being, of all the sciences, that which was best suited to the character of my mind, seemed to bear

the closest relation to the researches which I was about to commence. (1970:1)

1

In May 1986, I gave a plenary address to the *Second International Congress on the Catalan Language*. I had been invited to do so because over the previous decade a considerable amount of research on Catalan had been conducted in terms related to the framework for language variety differentiation I proposed in 1967 and developed and expanded with Susanne Carroll in 1978 (Gregory 1967, Gregory and Carroll 1978, see also Benson and Greaves 1973).

The organizers were so kind as to want my current views. I began with these observations:

> Any language event engages the knowledge of both user and receiver: knowledge of the world and knowledge of a language. These are not, of course, two distinct knowledges. Our knowledge of the world is something we largely receive, store and process in terms of language; and the languages we know themselves answer to the worlds in which they are used. (Gregory 1986/1988:301)

I then pointed out that it was in terms of this dialectical socio-cognitive view of language that, together with associates at York University and elsewhere, I have been attempting to develop the *communication linguistics* strand of systemic-functionalism. One of our developments is to recognize that dialect and diatype (or register) theory and description is a way into the establishment of a *gnostological* dimension in the analysis and catalysis of discourse.

There is really no need for linguists, or indeed anyone else, to take fright at the words 'gnostology' or 'gnostological'. For technical terms they have quite a long history, of over 150 years. Even if *The Oxford English Dictionary* does designate the term 'gnostology' as 'rare', that should not, taking into account past form, deter linguists from using it. Those with a classical education will recognize that it is the combination of the Greek form for *known* or *knowable* with *-logy* used in its sense of a science or department of study. So gnostology can be taken as the study of what is known or, more dynamically, of what is knowable. It was reintroduced into modern linguistics by Sydney Lamb and his associates. In 'The crooked path of progress in cognitive linguistics' (1972/1973:31) Lamb wrote as regards what he had previously called the 'hypersememic' stratum:

This stratum has to contain all of the individual's knowledge of his culture, his personal history, his physical environment, in short everything he knows, save the language itself, which is already represented in the lower strata. In other words one is dealing here with information that lies outside the scope of what is traditionally considered language. And one is dealing with a system of far greater complexity than any of the lower stratal systems – indeed probably more complex than all of them put together. Therefore it seems appropriate to give special status to this higher level – to consider it as outside the language proper (which does not mean for a moment that the linguist is prohibited from its premises) and to give it a more fitting name than the awkward term 'hypersememic'. Accordingly I now call it the *conceptual system* or for those who would like another Greek term, the *gnostemic system*.

While applauding Lamb's recognition that statements about the speaker's knowledge are relevant to linguistic inquiry and the description of the texts people produce and understand, I have reservations about some of the implications of his position. I am not sure, for example, what he means by 'This stratum has to contain all of the individual's . . . physical environment, in short everything he knows'. What individual? which individual? one might ask. Is this some sort of an idealized individual (if one were to permit such a paradox) representing all language users as individuals? I hope not, because such a construct must ultimately lack viability. As Robin Fawcett has aptly pointed out 'one characteristic of cultural knowledge is that no single individual, in the typical case, knows it all' (1984:163).

I also have to question the relevance of Lamb's assertion that this stratum has to contain 'everything [the individual] knows'. This seems to ignore matters of pattern and of pertinence. Our concern as social and behavioural scientists is not so much with the unique as with the shared and sharable. We should not be asked to be either biographers or encyclopedists. What we are to be concerned with is the knowledge that a speaking community can exchange; this is what enables it to act, to make meanings which can become 'wordings' and so 'soundings' or signings. Fawcett has said that a culture '. . . is *what a member of that social group knows* – whether or not he is conscious of the knowledge – *that is also known by the other members of the social group*' (Fawcett 1984:153), which is why I find it surprising that he also says that 'a culture is not something that some outsider can observe about the social groups that he is studying'. Rather,

I maintain that it is precisely because members of a social group share their implicit and explicit knowledge by way of their discourses that the *pattern* of their knowledge is observable and so describable, and this caters too for what is *pertinent* about an individual's knowledge. In Jonathan Culler's terms: 'Even the idea of personal identity emerges through the discourse of a culture: The "I" is not something given; it comes to exist, in a mirror stage which starts in infancy, as that which is seen and addressed by others' (Culler 1976:82). We can, in some respects, be seen 'as habit patterns'.

What we have to do in order to help linguistics strive towards what Hjelmslev (1961:127) called its prescribed goal '*humanitas et universitas*' is 'make explicit the implicit knowledge which enables people within a given society to communicate and understand each other's behaviour' (Culler 1976:103).

This is why in my paper 'Generic expectancies and discoursal surprises' (1986/1995) I insisted that *discourse*, not sentence or clause, is the subject and object of linguistic inquiry. I characterized discourse as the linguistic exchange of messages in situation, which is compatible with its etymology as that which runs to and fro between people. It is what we have to study in order to explain language behaviour, and the goal of understanding language behaviour is to explain discourse. Because language is so central to our knowing-and-doing existence this means that we will explain a text as much more than an aggregate of linguistic items, or indeed as a patterned set of linguistic items chosen from a range of linguistic options. From a holistic rather than reductionist point of view, any instance of discourse, like any organic whole, is to be considered as more than the sum of its parts, not only a matter of the linguistic items that occur in it but also the relations they enter into with each other in terms of the systems of the code, and the relations they enter into with the knowledge of users and receivers.

I also pointed out that we do not have to start by trying to account for all of human knowledge at any one time. ('an impatience with partial knowledge which is ... unfair to knowledge itself'). Rather we have to be prepared to account, in a principled way, for the knowledge that is 'at risk' in the discourse(s) we are describing; that is, the knowledge that the parts and their internal relations call into relevance. And the systemic-functional tradition in linguistics can be well suited to this task.

Systems and system networks are models of relevant potential. What is selected in discourse can be seen in terms of what could have been selected in context. The concepts of *stratum* and *rank* within the codal resources, and the concepts of *dialect* configuration and *register* potential in the area of linguistic usage locate and restrict what may be chosen. In the communication linguistics form of the model, the planes of experience *situation* (considered as instantial), *discourse* (as the instantiation of micro-registers) and *manifestation* (the seriality of sound and/or physical sign) further delimit and predict meaningful choice. *Dialect* and *register*, I will be arguing, can help us proceed to take into account the knowledge that is at risk in a discourse without being daunted by the task of characterizing everything that an imaginary individual knows.

But first some remarks about the pertinent matter of *catalysis* and *analysis*. Again I quote from Lamb:

> Of great value is Hjelmslev's notion of catalysis. This notion is quite unrelated to the catalysis of chemistry. In Hjelmslev's use of the term, which is quite close to its etymological meaning, catalysis is similar to but opposite from analysis. It differs in that it involves a building up of that which is not directly observable rather than a breaking down of that which is; the latter is, of course, analysis ... an attempt to understand linguistic structure, in a Hjelmslevian context, requires first the recognition of a structure lying beyond the linguistic data, of which the data are manifestations or outputs ... of course the process of catalysis requires that analysis of linguistic data also be done. (1984:72–73)

Systemic linguistics, capturing as it does the potential for linguistic behaviour as sets of meaningful options, with intrastratal and interstratal realizations, is essentially a catalytic model: what is, is seen in terms of what is not directly observable. We will be more complete insofar as we can model the knowledge that lies behind the meanings that lie behind the linguistic data. And this is where functionalism enters into the matter. From the social semiotic perspective, we can approach knowledge as communicable or viable knowledge, knowledge as cultural function, as social fact. Indeed this has been, at the very least, implicit in the use of the terms *context of culture* and *context of situation*.

2

Context of culture and context of situation are constructs that have a long history in the tradition in which systemic linguistics stands; they stretch back to Malinowski, Firth and Gardiner. The contextual dimensions of registerial description – *field, mode and tenor* –

preceded in Halliday's work the explicit delineation of the ideational, interpersonal and textual metafunctions. The work on language varieties several of us (Catford, Ellis, Gregory, Halliday, Hill, Strevens and Ure) were involved with during the sixties, sprang from and was sustained by the analysis of texts. We were interested in describing the grammatical and lexical similarities and differences amongst texts. The focus was initially on text varieties. However, M. A. K. Halliday from the mid-sixties onward developed the more abstract and powerful metafunctional perspective; and, because he has always been concerned with renewal of connection, he has demonstrated that such a perspective has both intrinsic and extrinsic justifications (see Halliday 1977 and 1978).

I was mostly concerned during the same period with the correlation between recurrent and typical situational dimensions, such as the user's *temporal provenance* and *medium relationship* with typifyingly recurrent sets of linguistic features which index, for example, *temporal dialects* and *modes of discourse* (Gregory 1967, Gregory and Carroll 1978). I used this framework to interpret literary texts by way of their particular selection from the spectra of dialectal and diatypic possibilities (e.g. Gregory 1974, 1978). In other words, although I was not explicit about it, I was concerned with what had to be known to decode a literary text. In recent years I have come to the conclusion that this matter of knowledge cannot be begged in linguistics, and that it can be satisfactorily approached by developing further aspects of the ethnographic tradition.

If one must take a locational view of cognition, it is, in some senses, undeniable that knowledge or culture 'resides in the brains of members of a social group' (Fawcett 1984:156), but it becomes describable and to some measure predictable because it manifests itself in forms of 'doing' of which language 'doing' is a richly complex and examinable type. This means that a theory of knowledge relevant to linguistics as essentially a social science is a dialectical materialist one. My colleague Elissa Asp puts it this way:

> The materialist aspect of the theory recognizes that knowledge is the consequence of conscious and unconscious generalization and abstraction of meaningful patterns from ongoing life activities. The process is dialectic insofar as it is continually renewed in the conduct of daily life. Abstractions are mutable, open to modification in contact with new instantiation. And perception of phenomena is modified by existing abstractions, by what we already know. (Asp 1986/1995)

In order to cope, semiotically and linguistically, with this process of acquisition, use and dynamic variety of knowledge, I have re-articulated and developed the notion of context of culture as *communicating community context* (CCC), and that of context of situation as *generic situation* which is an abstraction from the *instantial situations* of our everyday experience.

Communicating community context is the macro-environment of our knowing and doing, including of course the doing that is meaning and saying. It is initially describable along the intersecting dimensions of *temporal provenance, geographical provenance* and *social provenance*. Furthermore any particular communicating community context is created, maintained and developed in the semiotic behaviour of individuals interacting with each other, so *individual provenance* is a fourth relevant dimension. It is important to note that the social provenance dimension is not concerned only with the more superficial aspects of social class membership but involves description of ideological, economic and political systems, particularly, as we shall see, as regards relationships surrounding the means of production. Individual provenance recognizes that we are individuals insofar as each of us has a 'self'; a more or less clearly defined identity recognizable to ourselves (except in cases of abnormality) and to others with whom we interact. Nevertheless, from the socio-cognitive point of view, it is important to acknowledge that the individual as a known self does not exist except within the communicating community context of which it is a sustaining constituent. In Marx's terms (1939/1973:84):

> The human being is in the most literal sense a *zoon politicon*, not merely a gregarious animal, but an animal which can individuate itself only in the midst of society. Production by an isolated individual outside society ... is as much an absurdity as the development of language without human beings living together and talking to each other.

As regards 'talking to each other', the communicating community context as the macro-environment of our knowing and acting semiotically is usually congruently reflected in the choice of one particular language rather than another, and, within the language chosen, in the particular *configuration* of *temporal, geographical* and *social dialects*. An individual's own response to this environment is reflected in his/her *idiolect*, his or her version of a particular *dialect configuration*. Because the communicating community context as the knowledge macro-environment is the ultimate source of message potential for its members, and messages may be constructed and transmitted by codes other than the linguistic, the distinct, though related categories temporal provenance–temporal dialect, social provenance–social dialect, etc., are necessary, and also make provision for significant, if occasional, non-congruity.

What I have called 'the knowledge at risk' in a discourse is clearly circumscribed by these interrelating parameters of time, place, social system and authorship. It is necessary to recognize that what is knowable is not only a matter of the individual within his/her social relations but also that this dynamic interrelationship is itself peculiar to time and place, and that there is variation in the knowledge potential along these dimensions, and in terms of their intersection. At this point, in the first decade of the twenty-first century those of us who live in Britain, Western Europe, the Soviet Union, the United States, Canada and Australia could well be said, in a shallow way, to be living in the 'computer age', and this is a partial statement of our knowledge potential; but there are still many parts of the world, in Africa, Asia and South America, where such a gnostological statement would have little descriptive pertinence.

The crux of the matter is that the knowledge available in a communicating community context is created and sustained by the ongoing life activities of that particular community. These ongoing life activities, from which members of the community consciously and unconsciously generalize and abstract meaningful patterns as they both create and use knowledge, are made up of *instantial situations*. These activities are regularly renewed in the conduct of our daily lives as social practices and so reflect *generic situations*, the micro-environments of our knowing and doing.

The knowledge that is both activated in, and gained through, instances of the generic situations in which we are communicatively involved is in terms of a relationship to a human experience or experiences, real or imagined, in terms of an interactive relationship to our fellow human beings and/or to ourselves, and in terms of a relationship to a medium of communication/processing. It is this configuration of *experience relationships, interaction relationships* and *medium relationships* which provides a complex and integrated *communicative function* to a generic situation and its instances, and they are the dimensions along which it is describable.

Any particular communicating community context is theoretically characterizable in terms of the generic situations which are potential within it. Communicating community context and generic situation are then in a model to instance relationship in the sense in which

Hudson defines and uses that relationship in his *Word Grammar* (1984:14–31). Asp (1986/1995) has pointed out that there are four basic concepts relevant to understanding, describing and predicting the generic situations which are both potential within and constitutive of a given communicating community context. These are the *division of labour, the relations that surround the means of production,* the *legitimations* made regarding these relations and *instantial situation.*

Generic situations relate to the division of labour so long as people live together in social groups whose productive activity requires differentiated skill levels. The division of labour gives rise to varying patterns of social activity relevant to the cooperative (or, for that matter, coercive) accomplishment of particular tasks. It is the repetition of these activities which allows abstraction of situations as being generic. Such generic situations are, individually, functionally integrated networks of experience, interaction and medium relationships but they need not be logically consistent, or even coherent with each other. Legitimations for inconsistency and incoherence may then have to be provided. Asp points out that 'insofar as such legitimations are effective they confirm the "rightness" (or in some cases the "wrongness") of existing clusters of generic situation' and also 'involve generic situations proper to themselves'. She instances that generic situation which gives rise to discourses about 'social mobility' and 'equality of opportunity'. These legitimize the unequal distribution of wealth that a capitalist organization of production presupposes. The conflict on which these legitimations are based lies between the relations of production (capitalism) on the one hand and its positive legitimation (democracy) on the other. As Asp puts it ibid.: 'the inalienable right (in the American formulation) of individuals to life, liberty, and the pursuit of happiness conflicts with the unequal distribution among classes of the means for achieving these rights'.

The relations that surround the means of production are relevant because they influence how labour is divided within a particular communicating community context and so determine the amount of participation individuals and groups have in the control and ownership of production. This means that they also largely determine 'who one is' within the social provenance; they determine what people do, and in what conditions, as compared to others within the same community. What people know, and can know, is inextricably related to what people do. In communication linguistics' terms, the knowledge available to individuals and groups within a particular communicating community context is constrained by what generic situations they regularly enter into, and what roles they regularly play in these generic situations.

Communication linguistics stresses, then, the importance of the relations surrounding the means of production as descriptive not only of the socio-economic character of a communicating community context but also of the availability and distribution of knowledge within that community. However, Asp points out, the model does not presuppose a monolithic cultural stasis. Communicating community contexts are dynamic rather than static and have relations along the temporal dimension to past, present and indeed to future and, diatopically, they relate to accompanying alternative communicating community contexts. Generic situations from past communities may be maintained even though the contemporary relations surrounding the means of production conflict with those which produced them. The provision of dowries for brides and the discourses surrounding them, which continue in a limited way in New China, are instanced by Asp (1986/1995).

Furthermore, the importing of alternative generic expectancies into otherwise homogenous communicating community contexts happens in most cultures to a greater or lesser extent. Contiguities of various kinds – neighbourliness, trade, tourism and colonialism – are all factors; in the mid-1980s China imported several quite incongruent generic situations as a side-product of its 'open door' policy.

The importance of instantial situation in understanding these processes is stressed by Asp (1986/1995):

> Generic expectancies are part of the lived and living experience of members of the community because the knowledges of individuals and groups within the community are connected moment by moment through instantial situations to past and present alternative ways of seeing and doing in the world ... the importance of instantial situations must not be underestimated for it is in them that generic expectancies are manifested and from them that such expectancies are abstracted [and modified]. The recognition of them ensures that the model has renewal of connection and renders impracticable the sort of narrow determinism that mars some Marxist social thought.

Renewal of connection leads us back to language and discourse. Our knowledge includes a knowledge of the meaning and realizatory potential of the medium/media of communication open to us. In the case of language as a semiotic activity, the potential associated with a particular generic situation is what I understand by *register* (see Halliday 1978:31–35; Gregory 1986/1988:301–330).

Now, in the *same* way as a communicating community context is characterizable in terms of the generic situations potential within it, so too any configuration of temporal, geographical, social and individual dialect is characterizable by way of its available registers. A register itself is characterizable in terms of those ideational (field), interpersonal (tenor) and textual (mode) choices from the language's resources favoured by users in a particular generic situation; it is the linguistic reflection of a knowledge potential. This is why I have maintained that the key category in the description of discourse as activity and process is that of *phase* (see Gregory and Malcolm 1981, Gregory 1981/1982, 1984, 1984/2000, 1985a, 1985b, 1986/1995). It links the analysis of the linguistic data of a discourse, by way of register and dialect configuration, to the knowledge 'at risk' (i.e. relevant) to that discourse.

How does it do this? By distinguishing, at varying degrees of delicacy, continuous or discontinuous stretches of discourse which share ideational, interpersonal and textual consistency and congruity, phasal analysis reflects not only what at the *Rice University Symposium on Text and Discourse Semantics* I called the dynamic instantiation of micro-registers, but in so doing it reflects also the micro-instantial situations of the discourse, the active knowledge of the particular experiences, interactions and medium organizational possibilities that the language is representing and/or creating.

As a major component in the analysis of several discourses – a Hemingway short story and part of a videotaped conversation between two women in 'Phasal analysis within communication linguistics: two contrastive discourses' (1984/2000); a spontaneous monologue in 'Discourse as the instantiation of message exchange' (1985a); and a John Donne poem in 'Generic expectancies and discoursal surprises' (1986/1995) – I have charted the movement of the phases of the discourses. Such *discourse plots* draw attention to the micro-registerial instances as process, as dynamism, as succession, and, in some cases, as partial or complete return. The particulars of the phasal analysis (including the transitions from phase to phase) provide the way for a consistent catalysis, an awareness of the socio-cognitive structure that lies behind the linguistic data. It will be apparent that, from this point of view, what is called pragmatics in other models is neither more nor less than instantial semantics (instantial gnostology and semology). Nor do I see any great need to make use of any distinction between short-term and long-term

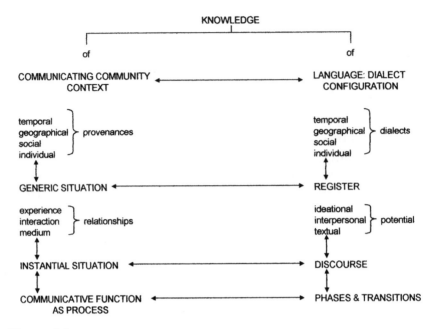

Figure 1.1

knowledge (contrast Fawcett 1984:154–155). Actuation of knowledge, the capacity of discourse to make knowledge pertinent, is, from my perspective, more to the point.

Figure 1.1 (from Gregory 1986/1995) schematizes the relationships I have been discussing. As the philosopher David L. Miller (1982:26) put it, discussing the work of George Herbert Mead, 'the locus of universality and generality is in the process'.

I am not, in this chapter, going to give another example of phasal description. As well as my own exemplification of it in the papers and articles I have already referenced, there exists the considerable body of exemplification in the heavily data-based doctoral dissertations of Karen Malcolm (1985) and Lynne Young (1987/1988) as well as contributions by Elissa Asp (1983), Janet Dill (1985) and Glenn Stillar (1989, 1990). In practice there seem to be no great problems of descriptive replicability in the application of the categories of phase and transition conducted in terms of the schema presented in Figure 1.2. The tri-functional system/structure analysis shows movement and change even in the field, mode and tenor of a particular discourse, and such analysis and catalysis can contribute significantly to the detailed characterization of registerial potential as *synopsis* as well as demonstrating the dynamism of registerial realization.

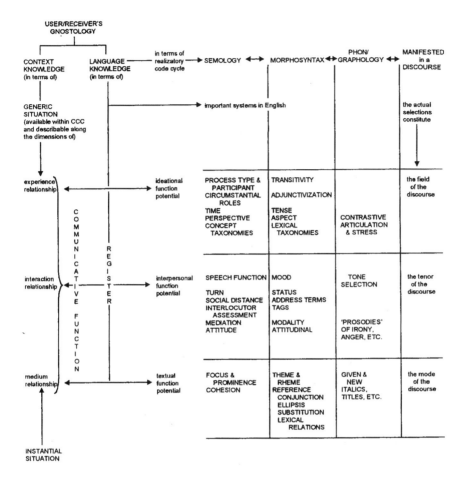

Figure 1.2

3

I have in the past (e.g. Gregory 1974) often quoted approvingly the following passage from J. R. Firth's 'Modes of meaning' (1951/ 1957:190):

> The constructs or schemata of linguistics enable us to handle isolates that may be called language events ... [*As will already be apparent that is a position with which I still completely agree.*] These systematic constructs are neither immanent nor transcendent but just language turned back on itself ... [*I now consider that, in a way, Firth was here begging the question: our constructs have to* **reflect** *both immanence and transcendence on the basis of immanence;*

in philosophical terms Firth was taking an exaggeratedly nominalist position in reaction against an untenable realist position; I prefer what might be called the Abelardian or conceptualist position, particularly in the light of the end of Firth's passage with which I still totally agree and which is somewhat contradictory to his statements on immanence and transcendence.] The disciplines and techniques of linguistics are directed to assist us in making statements of meaning. Indeed the main concern of descriptive linguistics is to make statements of meaning. [*To which I would add that statements of meaning necessarily involve statements of knowing.*]

What I would now quote with virtually unqualified approval is the following passage from Hjelmslev's *Prolegomena to a Theory of Language* (1961:127):

In its point of departure linguistic theory was established as immanent, with consistency, system and internal function as its sole aims, to the apparent cost of fluctuation and nuance, life and concrete physical phenomenological reality. A temporary restriction of the field of vision was the price that had to be paid to elicit from language itself its secret. But precisely through that immanent point of view and by virtue of it, language itself returns the price that it demanded. In a higher sense than in linguistics till now, language has again become a key position in knowledge. Instead of hindering transcendence, immanence has given it a new and better basis; immanence and transcendence are joined together in a higher unity on the basis of immanence. Linguistic theory is led by an inner necessity to recognize not merely the linguistic system, in its totality and its individuality but also man and human society behind language, and all man's sphere of knowledge through language.

It will be clear that I consider that the systemic-functional view of language that M. A. K. Halliday has done so much to develop is both extrinsically and intrinsically justifiable and can provide the immanent basis for viable transcendent statement. It enables us to predict not only that a minimum discourse such as an independent clause will simultaneously configure ideational, interpersonal and textual meaning, but also, if we continue to develop a gnostological dimension, it can predict, in a rule-referencing rather than a rule-governed way, what particular ideations, interactional intents and attitudes, what organization a discourse of a particular kind will have in a particular culture. In saying 'continue to develop' I am, of course, not only referring to my own work and that of my immediate associates but also to the work on context, text structure, social cognition, genre and intertextuality by Kress and Hodge (1979), Fawcett (1980), Ventola (1983), Halliday and Hasan (1985), Lemke (1985) and Martin (1985).

As I have said and written elsewhere (Gregory 1986/1988) I am now interested in the study of discourses which are ideologically central to our culture, which represent our dominant hegemony with its incipient discrimination on the bases of age, class, gender, race, sexual orientation and notions of mental and physical 'normality'. It is crucial that we are able to make explicit what the discourses of our society implicitly demonstrate as the knowledge that our society lives by, the knowledge taken for granted in the 'noises we make with our faces in order to live'. If we are to be responsible as social and human scientists, we have to be prepared, as Freud, Darwin and Marx were, to turn over some stones, and expose what lies underneath them. Common sense has to be met with genuine scientific sense. It should not be that linguists neglect the 'content' or knowledge side of discourse, that people '*know* what they're talking about' (i.e. talk about what they know) because this might bring them into the political or cultural firing line.

Some extraordinary claims have been made for linguistics. In 1945 the philosopher Ernst Cassirer wrote in the first volume of *Word*:

> In the whole history of science there is perhaps no more fascinating chapter than the rise of the new science of linguistics. In its importance it may very well be compared to the new science of Galileo, which in the seventeenth century changed our whole concept of the physical world.

Central to what he had in mind was European linguistics' insistence on the primacy of relations, that relationships create and define objects and not *vice versa*. Since he wrote there has been much development as regards relations (and functions) *within* language: system networks, the tagmeme as unit-in-context, -emes and tactics and interstratal realization, transformational rules, and the principles and parameters of U. G. and G. B. theory; every major post-war model has been strongly relational. However, in order to study language and/or humanity it is also essential to study the various systems by which men and women and their cultures organize and *give meaning* to their world. This means that our concern has to be not only with relations and functions within language but also with relations and functions around language.

If linguistics, reputedly the most advanced of the social, behavioural, human sciences, is to justify the claims that have been made for it, then surely in addressing its object, human discourse, it must have a goal which includes being of use in helping humankind to understand itself, become so self-aware, that it improves its ability to avoid disaster and to recognize its universality. In Gregory Bateson's idiom, we need to replace that purposive but partial consciousness which so often leads us to life-destroying mistakes with a genuine systemic wisdom (Bateson 1972).

I am not, to borrow a wicked phrase from an unpublished parody by Michael O'Toole, suggesting that the linguist be the 'semiotic redeemer' for all our social and global ills; but I am suggesting that we are called upon to deliver some of the goods, to make the contribution we can make to humankind's understanding of itself and its world. Otherwise we really will be, ultimately, trivial and uninteresting, except perhaps to ourselves and our own self-esteem.

References

Asp, Elissa (1983) The dynamics of discourse: an analysis of Dylan Thomas' 'Memories of Christmas'. Unpublished honours thesis, English Department, Glendon College, York University, Toronto.

Asp, Elissa (1985) The communicative functions of metaphor: a cognitive, cultural and linguistic catalysis. Unpublished M.A. thesis, York University, Toronto.

Asp, Elissa (1986/1995) Knowledge and laughter: an approach to a socio-cognitive linguistics. Paper presented to the *XIIIth International Systemics Workshop*, University of Kent at Canterbury, 1986, and in *Discourse in Society*, ed. by P. Fries and M. Gregory. Norwood, NJ: Ablex, 1995, 141–157.

Bateson, Gregory (1972) *Steps to an Ecology of Mind*. New York: Ballantine.

Benson, J. and Greaves, W. S. (1973) *The Language People Really Use*. Agincourt: The Book Society of Canada.

Cassirer, E. (1945) Structuralism in modern linguistics. *Word*, 1:99–120.

Culler, Jonathan (1976) *Ferdinand de Saussure*. New York: Penguin Books.

Dill, Janet (1985) The space-time novel as a message event: Pursewarden's Suicide. Unpublished M.A. thesis, York University, Toronto.

Durrell, Lawrence (1963) *Clea*. London: Faber & Faber.

Fawcett, R. P. (1980) *Cognitive Linguistics and Social Interaction*. Heidelberg: Julius Groos Verlag.

Fawcett, R. P. (1984) System networks, codes, and knowledge of the universe: a cognitive-systemic approach to the relationships between language and culture. In Fawcett *et al.* (eds.), *The Semiotics of Culture and Language, Vol. 2: Language and Other Semiotic Systems of Culture.* London: Pinter, 135–179.

Firth, J. R. (1951/1957) Modes of meaning. In *Essays and Studies,* The English Association 1951, reprinted in J. R. Firth, *Papers in Linguistics 1934–1951.* London: Oxford University Press, 1957, 190–215.

Gregory, Michael (1967) Aspects of varieties differentiation. *Journal of Linguistics,* 3:177–198.

Gregory, Michael (1974) A theory for stylistics exemplified: Donne's 'Holy Sonnet XIV'. *Language and Style,* 8(2):108–118.

Gregory, Michael (1978) Marvell's 'To His Coy Mistress': the poem as a linguistic and social event. *Poetics,* 7(4):351–362.

Gregory, Michael (1981/1982) Linguistics and theatre – Hamlet's voice: aspects of text formation and cohesion in a soliloquy. *Linguistics and the Humanities Conference,* University of Texas, Arlington, and *Forum Linguisticum,* 7(2):107–122.

Gregory, Michael (1984) Propositional and predicational analysis in discourse description. *Tenth LACUS Forum 1983.* Columbia, SC: Hornbeam Press, 315–321.

Gregory, Michael (1984/2000) Phasal analysis within communication linguistics: two contrastive discourses. Paper presented to the *Second Rice Symposium on Linguistics and Semiotics: Text Semantics and Discourse Semantics,* 1984, and this volume, Chapter 10.

Gregory, Michael (1985a) Discourse as the instantiation of message exchange. *Eleventh LACUS Forum 1984,* Columbia, SC: Hornbeam Press, 243–254.

Gregory, Michael (1985b) Towards communication linguistics: a framework. In *Systemic Perspectives on Discourse, Vol. 1: Selected Theoretical Papers from the 9th International Systemic Workshop,* ed. by J. Benson and W. Greaves, Norwood, NJ: Ablex, 119–134.

Gregory, Michael (1986/1988) Generic situation and register: a functional view of communication. Paper presented to the *Second International Congress of the Catalan Language,* Palma di Mallorca, 1986. In *Linguistics in a Systemic Perspective,* ed. by J. Benson, M. Cummings and W. Greaves. Amsterdam: Benjamins, 1988, 301–329.

Gregory, Michael (1986/1995) Generic expectancies and discoursal surprises: John Donne's 'The Good Morrow'. Paper presented to the *XIIIth International Systemics Workshop,* University of Kent at Canterbury, 1986, in *Discourse and Meaning in Society,* ed. by Peter Fries and Michael Gregory, Norwood, NJ: Ablex, 1995, 67–84.

Gregory, Michael and Carroll, Susanne (1978) *Language and Situation: Language Varieties and Their Social Contexts.* London: Routledge & Kegan Paul.

Gregory, Michael and Malcolm, Karen (1981) Generic situation and discourse phase: an approach to the analysis of children's talk. Mimeo. Toronto: Applied Linguistics Research Working Group, Glendon College, York University.

Halliday, M. A. K. (1977) Text as semantic choice in social contexts. In *Grammars and Descriptions*, ed. by Teun A. van Dijk and Janis Petofi, Berlin: De Gruyter, 176–225.

Halliday, M. A. K. (1978) *Language as Social Semiotic: The Social Interpretation of Language and Meaning*. London: Edward Arnold.

Halliday, M. A. K. and Hasan, R. (1985) *Language, Context and Text*. Geelong: Deakin University Press.

Hjelmslev, L. (1961) *Prolegomena to a Theory of Language*, trans. by F. J. Whitfield. Madison: University of Wisconsin Press.

Hudson, R. (1984) *Word Grammar*. Oxford: Basil Blackwell.

Kress, G. and Hodge, R. (1979) *Language as Ideology*. London: Routledge & Kegan Paul.

Lamb, S. M. (1972/1973) The crooked path of progress in cognitive linguistics, *Monograph Series in Languages and Linguistics*, 24:94–123. Reprinted in *Readings in Stratificational Linguistics*, ed. by A. Makkai and D. Lockwood. University, AL: University of Alabama Press, 1973.

Lamb, S. M. (1984) Semiotics of language and culture: a relational approach. In Fawcett *et al.*, (eds.), *The Semiotics of Culture and Language, Vol. 2: Language and Other Semiotic Systems of Culture*. London: Pinter, 71–100.

Lemke, J. L. (1985) Ideology, intertextuality and the notion of register. In *Systemic Perspectives on Discourse, Vol. 1: Selected Theoretical Papers from the 9th International Systemic Workshop*, ed. by J. Benson and W. Greaves, Norwood, NJ: Ablex, 275–294.

Malcolm, Karen (1985) The dynamics of casual conversation: from the perspective of communication linguistics. Unpublished Ph.D. dissertation. York University, Toronto.

Martin, J. R. (1985) *Factual Writing: Explaining and Challenging Social Reality*. Geelong: Deakin University Press.

Marx, K. (1939/1973) *Grundrisse: Foundations of the Critique of Political Economy: Rough Draft*, trans. by M. Nicolaus, 1973. London: Pelican Books.

Miller, David L. (ed.) (1982) *The Individual and the Social Self: Unpublished Work of George Herbert Mead*. Chicago: University of Chicago Press.

Proudhon, P. J. (1970) *What Is Property? An Inquiry into the Principle of Right and of Government*, trans. by Benj. R. Tucker. New York: Dover.

Stillar, Glenn (1989) Chapter I: 'The Port' in The power and the glory: a communication linguistics explication de texte. Unpublished M.A. thesis. York University, Toronto.

Stillar, Glenn (1990) Emerging discoursal patterns: a phasal analysis and catalysis of Leonard Cohen's 'Alexander Trocchi, Public Junkie, Priez Pour Nous'. Paper presented to the *XVII International Systemics Congress*, University of Stirling.

Ventola, Eija (1983) Contrasting schematic structures in service encounters. *Applied Linguistics*, 4(3):242–258.

Young, Lynne (1987/1988) Language as behaviour, language as code: a study of academic English. Unpublished Ph.D. dissertation, Katholieke Universiteit, Leuven.

2

Ideology, Intertextuality and the Communication of Science

J. L. Lemke

Intertextuality revised

Our understanding of how meanings are made with language must include an analysis of the social systems of intertextuality in a community (Lemke 1985a). The meanings made in any text, or on any occasion of discourse, depend on *how* the members of a community construe semantic relations between it and other texts or occasions of discourse. The social system of intertextuality in a community is defined by *what kinds* of relations are construed between texts, *which* texts are so connected and *how strong* the ties are. We make sense of any text only by relating it to other texts, or to textual patterns (see Lemke 1983a, 1995a and below) abstracted from many texts. Readers and listeners must bring to a text a large proportion of what is needed to make sense of it; speakers and writers create only suggestive traces of the meanings they would communicate, leaving out vastly more than what they say or write. The social system of intertextuality is an essential part of how we make meanings with language.

In a sense modern linguistics has always recognized that the meanings of words and the semantic relations underlying grammatical constructions are necessarily abstractions from some large body of texts encountered in their extralinguistic contexts. But linguistics has mainly concentrated on identifying the universal meaning-making *resources* of a language, those which are in principle available in every text and on every occasion of discourse. Language in this sense is a *semiotic resource system*. But we know that not all these resources are in fact deployed in every text, and register theory tells us that each human social activity type in which language is used (defined by its field, tenor and mode; see Gregory 1967; Halliday 1978:31–35) tends to give rise to texts in which different semantic and lexicogrammatical sets of options are 'at stake' or 'at risk', i.e. particularly relevant to the kinds of meanings that typically get made in such an activity.

In fact, because a speech community is an organized social system, not all possible combinations of fields, tenors and modes are equally likely to occur, and therefore choices in different linguistic systems in the texts of any register co-pattern; i.e. they are not statistically independent. (This is a special case of semiotic metaredundancy, the necessary basis of all contextual meaning, see Lemke 1984:35–39.) But register theory is basically a theory of semantic variation: a correlation between differences in social uses of language and differences in the ways in which the resources of language are deployed in them. It still looks at language as a semiotic resource system, and tries to look at the system of human social deployments of language in the same way.

While it is certainly useful to look at human social life as a semiotic resource system, i.e. as an *actional semiotic system*, and to identify which combinations of choices in that system tend to occur and which do not, the apparatus of theoretical analysis becomes over-burdened with the richness of choices deriving from the language (and more generally from the actional system as a whole) as it seeks to analyse the semantic strategies of a given text or the semiotic strategies of a given action sequence. Between semiotic resource systems and actual semiotic productions, between language-as-resource and an individual text, we need an intermediate level of theoretical constructs. Register analysis can in principle be made delicate enough to define each text as a unique microregister, or to characterize a class of texts that have some socially recognized features in common. But for it also to handle the complex, socially imposed co-patternings of selections (or selectional probabilities) in all systems at that level of delicacy is expecting far too much.

In the analysis of a text we need to supplement register theory with a direct analysis in terms of the socially repeated co-patternings, not just of lexicogrammatical choices, but of genre-rhetorical ones as well. We need, in short, to analyse language *use* not only in terms of the semiotic resource system of language, but also in terms of the socially repeated *semiotic formations* in which those resources are habitually deployed in a community. I use the term 'formation' here to mean a co-patterning of semantic (or more generally, including meaning resources other than language, semiotic) features (a.k.a. options, selections) which is repeated across a number of different texts (or more generally, meaningful actions and their products).

There are *weak* intertextual ties made in a community between texts that merely share some lexis or some grammatical constructions; that is, people regard them as at least possibly relevant for interpreting each other's meanings. But there are *strong* intertextual ties made between texts that employ or participate in the same semiotic formations. From the viewpoint of social semiotics, language use is just one more way of making social meaning, a semiotic practice that makes use of the semiotic resource system of language. But it makes use of that resource not just in any way, but preponderantly by reconstructing with it certain (co-patterned) sets of semantic relationships, organized according to particular rhetorical and genre patterns, and sometimes even realized by the same lexicogrammatical means, from one text to the next, from one occasion of discourse to another.

The shared and repeated patterns of semantic relationships, mainly ideational ones, usually characteristic of a register's Field, I have called *thematic formations* (Lemke 1983a). They consist of context-specific thematic items (ideational semantemes, but with meanings limited to those typical of the field) and semantic relations among these items (less-to-more-delicately described as needed). They are in general neither syntagms nor paradigms, neither structures nor systems, but co-patternings of each with the other. Every text partially reconstructs and interconnects one or more, smaller or larger, thematic formations. Thematic items and their thematic-semantic relations are realized most often by lexicogrammatical structures, but also by the larger-scale semantic structures of rhetorical and genre patterns (see below). Every text can be analysed as weaving patterns within and between thematic formations across its length (Lemke 1995a). Every text explicitly realizes parts of formations, but also makes its meanings *intertextually* by relying implicitly on semantic relations in the unexpressed remainder of the formation (to be supplied by the hearer or reader on the basis of having read other texts that share the same thematic patterns). This is the component of the system of intertextuality in a community that I have called thematic intertextuality (Lemke 1985a, 1988, 1995a).

The notion of a thematic formation may feel more familiar if we recognize its shared roots with the notions of collocation and cohesion. If I see 'smoke' and 'pipe' in the same clause, then my experience of other texts leads me to expect not only that I might also see 'tobacco' or 'match' nearby, but that if I do, I can be reasonably sure that the semantic relationships among them (however they are expressed in the grammar of this particular text) will be those typically realized by such expressions as 'smoke a pipe', 'smoke from a pipe', 'tobacco in a pipe', etc., which are the basis on which we interpret less semantically explicit expressions such as 'pipe smoke', 'pipe tobacco', 'tobacco smoke', etc. Moreover, while one could analyse each separate relationship as a binary one between just two semantemes, it is clear that in text after text there is a larger interlocking pattern of semantic relationships that encompasses all of these terms and a few more (e.g. 'burn', 'light', 'smell', plus some thematic participant roles for human actors and sensors). The whole typical pattern, which is rarely closed but rather has open links to more extended patterns, is an instance of a thematic formation. The semantic continuity of a text, represented by its lexical cohesion (Halliday and Hasan 1985), and especially by the 'cohesive harmony' (Hasan 1984a) among the text's 'cohesion chains', is construed by readers as much by the continuity of whole thematic patterns as by means of the more elemental relationships of individual cohesive ties. Cohesive harmony is based on semantic relations typically realized by process-participant and modifier-head grammar; these are the same semantic relations that pattern a thematic formation. The cohesion chains themselves, especially reference and identity chains, are akin to thematic items, i.e. to the semantemes-in-a-thematic-formation which are the nodes in the web of thematic relationships that defines the total pattern.

The shared and repeated patterns of organization for the exposition of thematic formations in a text in terms of sequences of functionally defined parts ('stages' or 'macro-phases') I call the *rhetorical-generic formations* of a community. They derive from the more general semiotic formations I refer to as *activity structures*. A *genre* organizes the use of language in a manner specific to a particular social activity (definable with greater or lesser delicacy), even if that activity is simply 'writing a haiku'. The abstract representation of a genre includes paradigmatic options as well as syntagmatic orderings (see Martin 1985, Ventola 1987 on flowcharts, Hasan's 1984b generic structure potential (GSP) notation; see also Halliday and Hasan 1985:52–69), with some co-patterning between them (and with the context of situation, i.e. the encompassing activity structure).

A genre element is always specific to some activity structure, but its realization is usually in terms of a *rhetorical formation* (RF), which is formally like a mini-genre, but which is not specific to a particular activity structure and occurs in essentially the same form in many different such structures (e.g. Question–Answer; Problem–Solution; Cause–Effects). RFs are then in turn realized by lexicogrammatical constructions. Clause-complexes, for instance, lie on the boundary between lexicogrammar and RFs. In this way, as with thematic formations, contact is made between an approach to the description of textual meaning-making based on semiotic formations (genres, RFs) and one based on the semiotic resource systems (register, lexicogrammar), and so between an analysis in terms of what typically *is* said in a community (the formations) and an analysis in terms of what *can* be said in the language of that community (the resources).

Two texts which just share the same RFs are only weakly tied intertextually; i.e. members of the speech community consider the texts to be at best only distantly relevant to one another's interpretation. Two texts which are of the same genre (to some degree of delicacy) are considered to be more strongly tied. Two texts which occupy functionally related roles in the same 'macro-genre' or activity structure are very strongly tied in that each is regarded as highly relevant to interpreting the other, even if they do not happen to share much in the way of purely thematic verbal patterns. This last case illustrates the aspect of the system of intertextuality that I have called *actional intertextuality* (Lemke 1985a). Because of the multi-dimensional complexity of the ways in which two patterns of activity can be alike and different, there exists in principle a 'topology' of rhetorical-generic formations, within which any two may be said to be closer together and further apart in some multi-dimensional space of meaning-relevant features (i.e. more or less alike in specific respects).

Texts which share the same thematic formation, but are of very different genres are still strongly tied intertextually, more so than those which share genre forms and RFs but not thematic formations. Sets of texts which share both thematics and genre organization constitute the distinctive *text-types* of a community. Because of social habits and conventions of co-patterning, texts of the same 'type' will also tend to share the same RFs and lexicogrammatical choices in their realizations. Just sharing the same RFs and probabilities for specific lexicogrammatical realizations, even when genre and thematics are not shared, is what some analysts mean by *stylistic* similarity. This is the basis for another sort of weak intertextual tie. Weak ties become stronger when they are supplemented by other bases for making an intertextual connection; i.e. the more kinds of intertextual ties between two texts the more likely we are to regard each as highly relevant for interpreting the meaning of the other.

The web of intertextual ties in a community tells us more about its social practices than it does about its language as such (though it does tell us some of what language has to provide resources to do). It is needed to describe language *use* rather than a language purely as a resource for meaning in general. It tells us how the resources of language are deployed and provides the interface between linguistics on one side and stylistics, rhetoric, thematics and social semiotics generally on the other. The link is through *semantics*. In the narrow sense, semantics is a stratum in the linguistic resource system; it tells us what kinds of meanings *can be* made with the language. But in social semiotics we are interested also in what kinds of meanings *are* made with the language and how these co-pattern with meanings made with other, non-linguistic semiotic practices (drawing, dressing, gesturing, touching, etc.). The total semiotic meaning system includes meanings that can be made with language, meanings that can be glossed (but not *made* in the social sense) with language, and meanings that have no counterpart in linguistic semantics.

I should note that in this chapter and elsewhere I use the term 'system' most often to mean a coherent set of (second-order) relations among (first-order) relations of some entities. So the 'system of intertextuality' is a system of relations (constituting the coherent logic among the principles by which intertextual connections are made in a community) among the relations (i.e. the intertextual ties themselves) among texts. A 'semiotic system' is a system of relations among the relations between possible meaningful acts or events. The bare term 'system' in systemic-functional linguistics normally means a set of (first-order, mutually exclusive) paradigmatic meaning-contrast relations among grammatical choices (also known as 'features' or 'options'), while the term 'system network' refers to a true semiotic *system* in my terms: the second-order, logical relations among the individual grammatical 'systems' in the common SFL sense.

Since the system of intertextuality provides an interface between language and social semiotics generally, we should not be surprised to learn that it is not satisfactorily described solely by its relations to text semantics and text structure. We must also describe how practices of constructing intertextual relations in a community are used for wider social purposes than just making texts. We need to describe their relations to social structure and social dynamics.

Heteroglossia and the ideological uses of language

The focus of register theory is on the relations of texts, and the semantic options they realize, to the immediate contexts of situation of their production and use. The focus of semiotic formation analysis is on the relations of texts and webs of connected intertexts to their wider contexts of culture (see Malinowski 1923). Social semiotics as a whole seeks to connect the meaning-making practices deployed in particular situations to the processes by which social and cultural systems are made and changed.

We make sense with a text in part by construing relations between it and other texts, according to the intertextual practices of our community. But social communities, as complex articulated systems of all the social practices that constitute them, are internally heterogeneous and can be analysed into subcommunities which have many specific kinds of formal relation to, and functional modes of interaction with, one another, as well as with what we choose to call 'other' communities. An important component of the identity and interactions of a community or subcommunity is how it uses language, and how it constructs the relations of its texts and ways of talking to those of other communities and subcommuinities. This macro-social dimension of intertextuality has been called the system of social *heteroglossia* of a community's language use (Bakhtin 1981).

Each social subcommunity, defined by its ways of using language thematically, rhetorically, generically (i.e. in terms of genres) and axiologically (see below), is said to have a distinct social 'voice', and these social voices define themselves as much by how they (or the analyst) construe their relations to one another as by any positive feature in their texts. Social voices can be defined with varying degrees of delicacy. It is essential to see that these voices have relations to one another in the system of social heteroglossia that mirror and help constitute social relations among the sub-communities that speak them. These relations are mainly those of Alliance and Opposition. There are social class voices, voices of distinct generations, gendered voices, hegemonic and dominated voices, and voices of distinct social segments (professions, house-wives, technocrats, Catholics, etc.).

We make sense with every text in part by construing its meanings against the background of social heteroglossia. We situate a text in relation to ourselves and our model of social relations. We situate the uses a text makes of thematic and rhetorical-generic formations in relation to the same or alternative views and ways of speaking of our own and other social groups, segments of opinion, etc. Every text can be read as carrying on an implicit dialogue with other social voices that may stand in alliance with or opposition to it. Every text, in some sense, does the social work of reconstituting the social relations of the community.

One of the most important kinds of meaning that we make with language is *evaluative* meaning. No text is free of value-laden language, of implicit or explicit value-judgments regarding its own content and views in relation to other possible ones. We construe a text as representing the value-judgments regarding its own content and views in relation to other possible views. We construe a text as representing the value system of its source, and we evaluate its value-judgments in turn in relation to our own. Every social voice within the heteroglossic whole is positioned in relation to every other not solely in terms of its thematic and rhetorical-generic uses of language, but also in terms of its *axiological* (i.e. value-construing) use of language. The axiological function of language extends to the social and intertextual domain the *interpersonal* function of the linguistic resource system (cf. 'attitudinal' meaning). In its broadest sense, the axiological position of a discourse voice is determined by its stance toward itself and other voices, and its dialogic paradigm is 'I am right; you are wrong'. I believe that together thematic analysis, rhetorical-generic analysis and axiological analysis provide a fairly complete account of the social positioning of a text. If we add to these a fourth analysis: how that text is used in a social activity structure, then the account is essentially complete for social semiotic purposes.

It may perhaps be too neat, but it is worth pointing out the not unexpected correspondence:

Semantic Resources	IDEATIONAL/INTERPERSONAL/ TEXTUAL
Registral Variation	FIELD/TENOR/MODE
Semiotic Formations	THEMATIC/AXIOLOGICAL/ RHETORICAL-GENERIC

It is important to note, however, that especially in the case of the intertextual semiotic formations, the co-patternings (metaredundancies) among the different formations are critical to the social work done by texts in each of these respects.

What then of ideology? I do not believe that any thematic formation, even combined with an axiological stance and a rhetorical-generic pattern of organization, is *intrinsically* ideological. A discourse formation (in the sense of a regular co-patterning of these formations with one another) is ideological or not depending on its use within a social activity structure. It is ideological exactly to the extent that its use serves to maintain the social power of one community or subcommunity over another. Of course there may be many discourse formations which tend to do this in all or nearly all their typical social uses, but there are others which do so only in some of their uses (though all use of such formations helps maintain and legitimate them for their more directly ideological uses).

Thematic formations tend to be most closely associated with the social groups that endorse them, but they can often be turned to use by opponents. Axiological stance is probably the formation feature that in fact most reliably distinguishes social groups of opposing interests, though a particular stance may be disingenuously or ironically adopted by opponents. Rhetorical-generic formations seem to be least socially polarized, but this perception may itself be the result of ideologically functional metadiscourse in our own community. Thematic formations are relatively flexible and can change rapidly; rhetorical-generic formations are much more deeply in-grained and change only very slowly. They index the deepest cultural and institutional commitments of a community. Even axiological stances, dependent as they are on thematics for their articulation, are more fluid. Of course the cryptotypical semantics of the linguistic resource system itself is even slower to change than any semiotic formation built with it.

Language functions ideologically not only by enabling us to make meanings that maintain the dominance of one group over another, but also by *not* providing ready-made ways of challenging that dominance. Here it is not, of course, the resource system which is at fault (resources which can build ideologically functional discourses can also challenge or subvert them). Rather, it is the system of discourse formations whose co-patternings of thematic, axiological and rhetorical-generic meanings systematically omit certain com-binations. There are certain combinations of things that might be said, attitudes toward saying them, and legitimate ways of expressing them that simply do not exist. To the extent that these missing elements 'outline' the frontiers of vulnerability of the social formation, defended as it is by its ideologically functional discourses, they form a negative, or perhaps a 'virtual', subsystem of their own, which I originally called the 'system of disjunctions' (Lemke 1985b:132–142; 1995b:176–184).

Social contestation is discursively effective only to the extent that it crosses this frontier, not simply reversing the axiological stance of an existing discourse, or posing a counterthematics, but providing a mode of articulation that undermines the deepest grounds of an ideological claim for the 'necessity' of some formation. In essence it must say something in a way that, once said, makes old truths and old rights transparently matters of special interest rather than common-sensical and necessary. Such counterdiscourses are, of course, highly specific to particular historical moments of particular communities.

Scientific discourse and technocratic ideology

To illustrate some of these points, I want to consider two texts. Each is a dialogue between a teacher and his students. Each illustrates the form of discourse about science which has the widest impact in our society: science as taught in school. For most members of our society, this is the only form of scientific discourse with which they have any direct encounter in their lives. Certainly for most people it is the most sustained encounter and the only one in which they are likely to find themselves actually using scientific discourse. I want to illustrate some of the thematic, axiological and rhetorical-generic formations being reconstructed in these texts, and to focus on two discursive elements of *technocratic ideology* which, in their small way, these texts work to sustain.

Technocratic ideology comprises discourse formations that are used to sustain and increase the dominance of a technocratic elite over other groups in our society. That elite is defined by its effort to monopolize the management of complex social institutions through a claim to expertise in making use of the results of technical practices. The technocratic elite does not include the technical practitioners themselves, except insofar as they also control the use of the results of their technical practices. The technocratic elite is also sometimes called the 'scientific management' elite, or the practitioners of 'management science'. More generally it consists of those who claim to set policy for the good of all on the basis of objective technical knowledge, their own or others'.

Technocratic discourse is always about policy and action, manage-ment and decisions, but never about values and interests except where these are represented as an already given consensus. Technocratic discourse maintains that particular decisions must be made, policies be set and actions be taken because the facts require them, irrespective of any consideration of conflicting value-claims or particular interests. Technocrats, I believe, have been so successful in supporting their own interests and power with this ideological discourse that they are wresting control of many societies, including our own, away from the previously dominant group, the owners of capital. Today the two groups overlap substantially and coexist and share power somewhat uneasily, but the momentum of social change seems to favor the accumulation of power by those whose claim to rule is that they know best what to do, rather than by those whose claim is that they have (own) the means to do it.

Technocratic ideology is predicated on two fundamental premises borrowed from technical and, more broadly, from scientific discourse: (1) that scientific-technical truth is 'objective' (i.e. free from the biases of particular interests), and (2) that it is a 'special' truth, available only to those who have mastered the intricacies of scientific-technical discourse and practices that are often divergent from commonsense beliefs. The technocrats function as 'middlemen', appropriating the 'objective, special truths' of scientific and technical practice as the means of imposing their own policy preferences on a public which does not consider itself in a position to dispute the objectivity of their claims or to examine their 'special' grounds (see Lemke 1990a).

And how is the public convinced of all this? In large part, I believe, by the discourse of science as presented in school (Lemke 1983b, 1987, 1990b). Let's have a look at the thematic, axiological and rhetorical-generic formations of these two texts of science dialogue in the classroom, focusing particularly on their reinforcement of the twin ideological claims of the 'objective truth' and the 'special truth' of science.

Discussions of the thematics of the first text, and of the ideological stances of both texts can be found in Lemke (1983a) and (1987), respectively.

Thematic formations

Text 1: 'Crustal uplift debate'
   1 *Teacher*: Now let's try and understand this Answer
   2 that I gave you here. It says 'Marine fossils are
   3 found in mountains of high elevation; this suggests
   4 that the crust has been *uplifted*.' It means the earth
   5 is pushed up, OK? the earth is pushed up. That's what
   6 we mean by uplifting.
   7 *Charley*: Couldn't the water go down?

8 *Vito*: Yeah!

9 *T*: It's *possible* that the water level has gone down,

10 but we believe, OK? we believe that the earth has

11 been uplifted.

12 *Scott*: It's just a theory though.

13 *Vito*: It's always a theory.

14 *T*: This, this is *fact*. This is *fact*, OK? This is not

15 a theory.

16 *Vito*: It's *fact*?

17 *Scott*: Wait a minute, it can't be a *fact*, there's no

18 *proof* that the earth was raised up, unless they took

19 *measurements*.

20 *T*: They – measurements have been taken

21 *Scott*: Measurements have been taken?

22 *T*: Right now, OK? I'm gonna try 'n explain you

23 something else

24 *Robert*: How can you prove that that's a fact?

25 *T*: I'm gonna try and tell you what happens. Just a second,

26 Scott. Just listen carefully. Somebody by the name of

27 James Hutton came out with a theory of *Uniformitarianism*.

28 Does anyone know what that means?

29 (. . .) [In the omitted lines teacher rejects three answers.]

30 OK. What Monica is trying to say, in one

31 sentence is, what James Hutton tried to prove was: The

32 *present* is the key to the past. OK? We look at things,

33 things that are happening today, happened exactly the

34 same in the past. (. . .) [He repeats this.] So the present

35 is the key to the past. So by looking, by looking at

36 geologic formations, we can tell, if things were uplifted,

37 *uplifted*, or things subsided. OK, just by *looking* at

38 them. And that's how, that's how there's ways, in which

39 they prove, that things were uplifted, how can they tell

40 they were uplifted. All right, let's go on to our Question.

What does this text say that reproduces semantic relationships, specific to a particular field, which we could find in many other texts? One segment is actually quoted (lines 2–4) and so must occur elsewhere. In fact the teacher is reading it from the chalkboard. He has copied it there from his own notes; the students are busy copying it into their notebooks. These copies may or may not count as separate productions of the semantic text, depending on how fussy we wish to be about type/token relationships, but certainly the statement quoted could be found in some *thematically* equivalent form (Lemke 1983a) in many textbooks of geology (and probably in many research papers of an earlier period in the history of geology) and it is probably implicit in the thematic meaning of many current written texts in geology. To give some idea of the thematic variants on this same statement that have already been constructed in this class alone, the day before the teacher had said, at two different points:

(1) What happened was, more than likely is, the crust was pushed up. OK, and when we say the crust was pushed up, we say that it's *uplifted*. And that's why we find these marine fossils up on high mountaintops.

(2) The other marine fossils helped us, showing that we found – that there was a regional uplift.

Comparing the example in Text 1 (lines 2–4) with these two other examples you will find changes in lexicogrammatical construction of the common thematic-semantic relations. What remains invariant across the three texts is the basic thematic formation: a set of semantic relationships between thematic items such as FOSSILS AND HEIGHTS, CRUST and MOVED-UP. (Note that items in CAPS are thematic items, which can be realized not just by the word given but equally well by other wordings that are functionally synonymous in the relevant register.) In the third example mentioned above ('The other marine fossils ... regional uplift'), HEIGHTS is missing, so the reader must bring it, and its semantic relation to FOSSILS, to the text to make full sense of what is being said. In all three examples, there is also a semantic relation between two thematic clusters,

[MARINE–cl/th–FOSSILS]–loc–HEIGHTS

and

CRUST–m/pr–MOVED

which we could call Cause/Consequence, or perhaps in this case,

Evidence/Conclusion. This relation is constructed through a clause-complex relation or through the relations between functional elements in a common rhetorical formation. (Note that I tend to label semantic relations by their most congruent grammatical realization in Halliday's terminology; e.g. Classifier/Thing, Circumstance: Location, Medium/Process.)

This is a thematic formation which runs through the larger text of a lesson from which this portion is excerpted. There it is both expanded (to include the contrasted alternative CRUST–m/pr–MOVED-DOWN) and linked to another formation, only portions of which are present in the lesson text, that connects FACT, THEORY, OBSERVATIONS, MEASUREMENTS and PROVE. The link between the two is metadiscursive. Finally, still another formation, one that is quite common in the lore of geology, is introduced and linked to the others (the Principle of Uniformitarianism).

Text 2: 'Longitudinal waves'

1   *Teacher*: *Now*. If you compress a spring, as you saw in

2   here, what we did, last week, what we did, before yesterday.

3   If you compress a spring, a pulse goes down that spring.

4   Now notice that the *spring* does not move, from me to the

5   door, say, if I have it attached to the door. The spring

6   *is* between me and the door. But something *does* move,

7   if I push that spring, something *does* move between me

8   and the door. What moves, William?

9   *William*: A wave

10   *T*: All right, a pulse *does* move. Now notice that the

11   wave motion *goes* to the right, from me to the door if

12   I push it in that direction. So the wave *motion*, is

13   toward the door. [Pause] Which way does the *spring*

14   move? Paul?

15   *Paul*: The opposite.

16   *Student*: It's not moving.

17   *T*: But it *is*! If you recall that spring, it *did* wiggle.

18   Which way does the spring move?

19   *Student*: The same way.

20   *T*: If it didn't *move*, there would be no wave *traveling*.

Without going into as much detail, it should be apparent that in the second text the discussion is being conducted, by the teacher at least, in terms of a thematic formation that links SPRING, MOVE, WAVE, WIGGLE, DIRECTION and TRAVEL in ways which are certainly 'special' to this formation. Here is another example of the same formation from elsewhere in this lesson:

> That compression wave travels *through* the medium in a direction I have drawn here, to the right, and the medium must move *both ways*. (...) The medium's motion moves in the *same* direction, parallel and *anti*-parallel, same and opposite direction, parallel to the direction of the wave.

Here SPRING has been generalized (hypernymy, or Token-to-Type) to MEDIUM, and WIGGLE is expressed as *move*, elaborated by the doubled expression of DIRECTION (the more usual representative of WIGGLE would be *oscillate*).

Axiological stance

Text 1

Axiological analysis is just as complex as either thematic-semantic or rhetorical-generic analysis is, and I do not want to attempt a very detailed treatment here (see Lemke 1989, 1998). Let me just indicate a few features.

In the opening metadiscursive comment (lines 1–2) the hortatory 'let's try and understand' carries positive valuation as an exhortation, viz. to do what the speaker *wants*, and the lexical choices *try* and *understand* are both positively valued within the value system of teachers generally (i.e. it is GOOD that students try, and it is GOOD that they understand). The 'Answer' is a GOOD in relation to a Question (the ones written on the board) within an axiological stance that says that it is GOOD to know Answers (*pace* Oedipus). 'I gave you' is also generally GOOD in the community, when what one gives another is, as in the case of the Answer, an accepted GOOD.

There is of course an undercurrent, perhaps one might say a dialogic countercurrent here also. *Try* as a thematic item, and even as a semantic one, may suggest its opposites 'not try' and even 'fail' from an axiological stance that either denies some of these GOODS or the GOOD expectation of the hortatory that they will be attained. This is all the more likely if 'Answer' is not counted as a GOOD in the opposing stance, and indeed we know that some students do not want to learn, resent a forced curriculum, feel burdened by more and more Answers from others that they are expected to memorize for tests. There would be less reason to say what the teacher does say here if there were no conceivable alternative motivation.

The foregoing analysis is a very microscopic one, greatly magnifying what is in the moment of its use in the activity structure an almost *pro forma* utterance. But it is possible to make the analysis at least somewhat cogent because we do recognize that the teacher's words index the persuasive uses of language, that those uses presume a GOOD and a possible opposition, and that the community of this classroom could very well be polarized in its attitudes toward whether trying to understand another Teacher Answer is indeed an unalloyed GOOD or not.

The answer itself is also hortatory and persuasive through *suggests* which here realizes what is elsewhere a strong form of the Evidence/ Conclusion relation in the thematics. *Suggests* is weakened in degree (cf. degrees of modalization in Halliday 1985:334–341), compared to the possible 'proves' or even the 'that's why' or 'showing that' of the other examples. Elsewhere in this class we find 'help us know that' and 'evidence that' as well as the weaker 'what happened ... more than likely is that ...' above. The 'official' formulation of the Answer employs the CAUTION characteristic of scientific discourse's stance toward its own truth. It also, by modalizing the *relation* of Evidence to Conclusion, implies that there are degrees of trustworthiness of evidence, and maintains the semantic potential for FACT, i.e. for the unmodalized Positive choice (e.g. the self-corrected, 'What happened was –' above).

Note that otherwise the Answer is almost free of value-laden expression. In our community it is neither GOOD nor BAD that the crust rises rather than falls, or that fossils are found there rather than here. For paleontologists it is perhaps GOOD that the fossils are found at all, rather than not found. Maybe some will take it as GOOD that there is a surprise here. At one time historically there were of course those who took it as BAD that the Earth should be other than timeless and stable; I assume that that axiological stance is no longer widely shared among us or the participants in this classroom.

In line 7 Charley offers a Challenge to the Answer, or more exactly to the teacher's Assertion of it. This is a regular move in an activity structure of the classroom, the Teacher–Student Debate (see below), and in its transcribed, purely linguistic form it certainly begins to construct the elements of a genre. Many genres co-pattern axiological stances or at least relations with their functional elements. In a Debate, there are at least two Opposed stances. Charley offers a counter-thematics, and the GOOD at stake is the GOOD of being right, or at least of winning the argument in some sense.

Modality is now foregrounded. *Couldn't, possible, believe* and later *prove* carry the opposed stances (along with thematically equivalent realizations). Within the thematics employed in this text, however, a shift takes places from the modalized forms to absolute (positive and negative) forms (lines 12–15). Both sides in the Debate accept a thematic system that distinguishes FACT from THEORY (Absolute vs. Middle-to-Low modalized assertion). This thematic system, for them, is co-patterned with an axiological stance: FACT is a greater GOOD than THEORY; MEASUREMENTS are a contributing GOOD to this.

Lines 22–23 have a similar character to lines 1–2 (see also lines 25–26), where issues of power and control in the activity structure are also at stake.

In lines 26–27, there is an Appeal to Scientific Authority, taken by the teacher as a GOOD (i.e. knowledge of applicable principles). The high value of PROVE returns and is linked again with that of MEASUREMENTS (or more generally in the thematics to OBSERVATIONS), realized (lines 36–37) by *looking*. The strict logic of the argument (a matter of rhetorical-generic standards) may be poor, but axiological valuations, insofar as they (if not the thematics) are shared by both sides, carries the argument along. Ultimately, we might want to say that it is the teacher's power, exercised through the activity structure, that wins him the argument in any sense, or at least gives him the dominant voice and the last word.

Text 2

The axiological stances are rarely explicit in this text, though there is clearly some resistance on the part of the students to the teacher's relentless inquiry/interrogation (even more evident in the surrounding dialogue). For the teacher, what is at stake here thematically is partly a review of prior work (see lines 1–2), and so it is a GOOD that students REMEMBER (see also line 17). He is recreating that demonstration now so it is also a GOOD that students OBSERVE (see 'notice' in lines 4, 10; and implicitly in the questioning). Mostly it is a GOOD for him that the students Answer correctly, i.e. using the same thematics he does. But there is an alternative, commonsense thematics (see line 16) that is in some respects Opposed to the teacher's, and maintaining it can be a GOOD for the students.

Rhetorical-Generic Formations

Text 1

The genre of this text derives from that of the classroom Activity Structure of a Student–Teacher Debate (Lemke 1983b, 1987, 1990b). Its elements consist of a Teacher Assertion (lines 2–4), a Student Challenge (lines 7–8), a Teacher Response (lines 9–12), a series of Arguments and Counter-Arguments (lines 12–21), and a Teacher Closure, usually in the form of an Appeal to Authority that ends with a Teacher Re-Assertion of the initially Challenged statement (lines 22–27, 30–40). This is a regular and repeated discourse pattern in science classrooms.

Lines 1–6 also belong to another genre, deriving from another Activity Structure of the classroom, the Teacher Summary. They contain first an optional, but highly likely, Introductory Meta-statement, that announces that what follows is in fact a Summary. Then there is the Summary Statement itself. Finally there is an optional Restatement of a portion of the Summary in an alternative wording. The Teacher Summary is itself part of a larger structure, preceded by Developmental Question-and-Answer, followed by an optional Request for Questions and Student-Questioning Dialogue sequence (here replaced by the Student–Teacher Debate), and followed by a Boundary Metastatement (line 40) that closes off the thematic unit that has been Summarized and prepares for the Introduction of a new thematic subtopic and the repeat of Developmental Question-and-Answer Dialogue (also known as triadic, IRE or IRF dialogue).

The elements of genre structures that are specific to this Activity Structure may be realized by Rhetorical Formations that are used in essentially the same form in many other genres. For example, it is quite common, as done here in lines 9–11, that a Teacher Response to a Student Challenge will be constructed using the Rhetorical Formation I call Concessive-Adversative. This is the familiar 'Yes, but ...' of many Argument genres. The first element concedes a partial agreement with the previous move, the second element then offers a more important disagreement. Thematically, a link is created between the heteroglossically Opposed thematic formations, showing that they contain some thematic propositions in common (the Concessive). But then a difference is highlighted, with the axiological stance favoring the speaker's formation as RIGHT (the Adversative).

Lines 30–40 have the form of an RF we may call Generalization-Application. First the teacher introduces a General Principle (Hutton's geological principle of Uniformitarianism) and states it. He then adds optional Glosses and Repeats. Then in line 35 we get the rhetorical structure marker 'so' that indicates the onset of the Application. Thematically, there is a logical link made here (at least formally) from the Uniformitarianism thematics to that of the lesson subtopics UPLIFT vs. SUBSIDENCE. If the argument seems incomplete, it is because there is no other thematic-semantic tie that involves the critical items. The only available linking item GEOLOGIC FORMATIONS is not sufficient to produce a 'Minor Premise' to lend the conviction of a syllogistic RF to the argument.

Finally, we get (lines 38–40) a 'QED' move (i.e. 'quod erat demonstrandum', the formal conclusion of a classical proof or argument stating that that which was to be proven has been proven) which embeds the Generalization-Application RF in a larger Argument in the Debate. Line 24 functions as a skeptical demand/ request for proof. The Proof takes the form of the Generalization-Application RF, and the QED move is metadiscursive, linking back to the Demand. It also functions as a closing Re-Assertion of the Challenged Statement.

A full Rhetorical-Generic analysis here would be very complex, since there are multiple, overlapping RFs here as well as both a compositional and a realizational hierarchy. Many utterances are plurifunctional, playing roles in several formations at once.

Text 2

The genre here is that of Developmental Question-and-Answer Dialogue (which I call Triadic Dialogue elsewhere, e.g. Lemke 1983b, 1985b, 1990b). It again derives from an Activity Structure of the classroom. Its usual pattern is: Teacher Preparation, Teacher Question, Student Bid to Answer, Teacher Nomination, Student Answer, Teacher Evaluation, Teacher Elaboration. Only the second, fifth and sixth moves are obligatory; they form the irreducible Triad of a dialogic Exchange in this Activity Structure.

For example, the Preparation here is extended (lines 1–8) because it is also functioning as a Teacher Inform move which is optional in the Activity Structure but not formally part of the Triadic Dialogue genre. The Question is found in line 8, elliptical and thematically dependent on the formation constructed in the Preparation/Inform move. There is no Bid. The Nomination is also in line 8. The Answer is line 9. Line 10 begins with the Positive Evaluation ('Alright'), and then Elaborates on the answer (introducing a local synonym 'pulse' that is also here a hyponym of 'wave'). Lines 10–13 are the Preparation for the next Question. The pattern is broken with line 16, a Student Objection. We do not get a Debate genre here, so it is not (synoptically and retrospectively) a Challenge (though dynamically, at the moment it happens, it *could* be interpreted as a challenge and the start of a Debate). Line 17 is a Teacher Response. In line 18 the Question is repeated and, retroactively, the Response becomes a Preparation for it. Line 19 is the Answer. Line 20 can be construed both as a conflation of Evaluation and Elaboration, and as an extension of the Response to the Objection.

Rhetorically, we might look briefly at the Objection/Response mini-genre. One could perhaps consider it to be itself a rhetorical formation, though the nature of these elements, as defined by the probabilities for various kinds of realizations and thematic and axiological co-patternings, is I think still quite specific to the teacher–student interaction patterns of the classroom. What is more general is the RF used to implement the Response here (line 17). It begins with a Contradiction of the Objection statement (itself a Contradiction of a Premise of the Question, and of a feature of the teacher's thematic system in use). It then supports the positive Assertion thematically implied by the Contradiction by adducing Evidence. The pattern below is a common RF of Argument:

[Contradiction: Counter-Assertion] – Evidence.

Interpreting the words spoken here as in fact Evidence relevant to the Assertion requires reference to the thematic formation, which classes WIGGLE as a hyponym of MOVE. We will see shortly that dictionary meanings and the lexical semantic potential of *wiggle* and *move* are not sufficient for this; a particular, specialized thematic formation is needed. Finally, the Elaboration/Response in line 20, as a response, uses a different RF to argue for the Assertion, namely Reductio (Counterfactual Argument). The completion of the Argument requires the Evidence that there is a 'wave traveling' and this is recoverable from the thematics of the dialogue so far (as well as from a previous class demonstration).

The 'Objective Truth' of Science and the 'Special Truth' of Science

Close study of these texts should have begun to make clear how they illustrate the twin ideologies of scientism that help make technocratic discourse convincing.

In Text 1 we see quite clearly that the Debate is over the epistemological status of an assertion. What matters however is not its particular status, but rather the system of statuses available for it and the criteria by which a status claim is judged. The status is either that of a FACT or a THEORY (by which is meant what in the wider thematics would be labeled a HYPOTHESIS). The criterion is whether or not MEASUREMENTS/OBSERVATIONS *prove* or CONFIRM 'facthood'. In the end, the teacher uses a THEORY (Uniformitarianism) to argue that his assertion is a FACT. The students, however, have clearly already accepted the ideology that 'objective truth' is a status of many scientific assertions. Indeed, there would be no Debate otherwise. Teacher and students share the same axiological stance toward this ideological thematics: FACT is a greater GOOD than mere THEORY.

In Text 2 something much subtler is happening. Two thematic formations are competing here, one derived from Common sense, the other a 'special truth' of Science. In Common sense, either the spring moves or it does not. In line 4 the teacher has said it does not move; reinforced by the apparent thematic contrast that something else (the wave) does move (lines 6–10). So when the teacher asks (lines 13–14), *which way* the spring moves, a student objects that it doesn't move at all.

In the special thematics of this field of science, the spring can both move and not move. Movement is relevantly either TRANSLA-TIONAL or OSCILLATORY; either the whole object undergoes a net movement, changing the position of its center of mass, or it undergoes a kind of internal movement, back and forth, with no net change in position of the spring as a whole. TRAVEL is a Process assigned only the to WAVE; it is TRANSLATIONAL–cl/th–MOTION. WIGGLE is a process assigned only to the spring: it is OSCILLATORY–cl/th–MOTION. But the lexical item *move* is used for both, and in senses that are inconsistent unless assigned to the correct thematic item in the Science formation.

None of this is explained to the students. Instead of pointing out that science has its own special ways of talking about motion, ways that highlight certain distinctions and background others, something else is done here, something which is quite usual in science teaching. The students are asked to answer questions, and participate in a discourse, based on what they *observe*. They are told to 'notice' and to 'recall' what they observed previously. The message is that the *phenomena* are 'objective'; they are there for all to see. They are FACTS of observation (and measurement). But in this episode, and throughout much of this lesson, many students do *not* see things as the teacher does, because they do not observe them in relation to the same expectations. They do not highlight the same features and background the same features. They do not attach importance to some relationships rather than to others. They do not describe what they see to themselves in the same terms as the teacher while they are seeing it, or after. The terms of description, which are normally also the terms of perception, must be the items and semantic relations of some thematic formation. The formations of the teacher and the students differ. They see, or at least make sense of what they see, differently.

But this is not how the situation is presented to them. They are told that they ought to be able to see these things for themselves, and be able to figure out other things for themselves, using their 'intelligence' and 'powers of observation'. If they cannot, they are left to conclude (and often encouraged to conclude) that the fault is with their own abilities, not with the formations they have or have not been taught. This is true not just of thematic formations. What we call students' abilities at logical reasoning are in fact their rhetorical-generic practices, judged by the extent to which they do, or do not agree with our own. Even 'taste' or aesthetic judgment, and more critically perhaps our view of others' moral and ethical judgment, depends on the match or mismatch of our axiological stances and theirs. Social heteroglossia ensures that members of social groups with opposed interests will rarely agree in any of these respects.

Of course the axiological stance toward scientific vs. commonsense thematic formations is crucial to establishing the superiority of the 'special truth' of science. It is 'special' because only those with superior intelligence and powers of observation can 'see' it. It is 'special' because it is divergent from and contradictory to common sense. And it is superior because it agrees with, or explains, the 'objective' FACTS that only it can see. 'Facts' that only its thematics lead it to look for, that only its axiological stance leads it to regard as important.

I have discussed elsewhere the pervasive construction of the ideology of the 'objective' truth of science and its 'special' truth opposed to and superior to that of common sense or any other thematic formation or value-system, any other discourse of any other community, throughout the day-to-day teaching of science in the schools (Lemke 1983b, 1987, 1990b). It can also be found in popular science writing and journalism. And it is taken for granted in technocratic discourse (see Lemke 1990a).

I hope that this chapter has shown how the approach of social semiotics, with its analysis of how social meanings and social relationships are constructed by the deployment of semiotic resources, can expose the ideological uses of language which maintain patterns of social domination and control. That analysis critically requires that we show how meaning-choices in a text tend to use and reconstruct the intertextual semiotic formations of a community – thematic, axiological, and rhetorical-generic – and their heteroglossic social relations to one another. In this way we can use the power of linguistic-semantic analysis to link the situated use of language to wider contexts of social conflict and change.

References

Bakhtin, Mikhail (1981) Discourse in the novel. In *The Dialogic Imagination*, ed. by M. Holquist, Austin: University of Texas Press, 259–422.

Gregory, Michael (1967) Aspects of varieties differentiation. *Journal of Linguistics*, 3:177–198.

Halliday, M. A. K. (1978) *Language as Social Semiotic*. London: Edward Arnold.

Halliday, M. A. K. (1985) *An Introduction to Functional Grammar*. London: Edward Arnold.

Halliday, M. A. K. and Hasan, Ruqaiya (1985) *Language, Context, and Text*. Geelong: Deakin University Press. (Republished by Oxford University Press, 1989.)

Hasan, Ruqaiya (1984a) Coherence and cohesive harmony. In *Understanding Reading Comprehension*, ed. by J. Flood, Newark, DE: International Reading Association.

Hasan, Ruqaiya (1984b) The structure of the nursery tale. In *Linguistica Testuale*, ed. by L. Coveri, Rome: Bulzoni.

Lemke, J. L. (1983a) Thematic analysis: systems, structures, and strategies. *Recherches semiotiques/Semiotic Inquiry*, 3:159–187.

Lemke, J. L. (1983b) *Classroom Communication of Science*, Final Report to the US National Science Foundation, Arlington, VA: ERIC Documents Service (ED 222 346).

Lemke, J. L. (1984) *Semiotics and Education*. Monograph in Toronto Semiotic Circle Monographs Series. Toronto: Victoria University.

Lemke, J. L. (1985a) Ideology, intertextuality, and the notion of register. In *Systemic Perspectives on Discourse, Vol. 1: Selected Theoretical Papers from the 9th International Systemic Workshop*, ed. by J. Benson and W. Greaves, Norwood, NJ: Ablex, 275–294.

Lemke, J. L. (1985b) *Using Language in the Classroom*. Geelong: Deakin University Press.

Lemke, J. L. (1987) Social semiotics and science education. *American Journal of Semiotics*, 5:217–232.

Lemke, J. L. (1988) Discourses in conflict: heteroglossia and text semantics. In *Systemic Functional Approaches to Discourse, Vol. 1*, ed. by J. Benson and W. Greaves, Norwood, NJ: Ablex 29–50.

Lemke, J. L. (1989) Semantics and social values. *Word*, 40(1–2):37–50.

Lemke, J. L. (1990a) Technical discourse and technocratic ideology. In *Learning, Keeping, and Using Language: Selected Papers from the 8th AILA World Congress of Applied Linguistics, Sydney 1987, Vol. 2*, ed. by M. A. K. Halliday, John Gibbons and Howard Nicholas, Amsterdam: John Benjamins, 435–460.

Lemke, J. L. (1990b) *Talking Science: Language, Learning, and Values*. Norwood, NJ: Ablex.

Lemke, J. L. (1995a) Intertextuality and text semantics. In *Discourse in Society: Functional Perspectives*, ed. by M. Gregory and P. Fries, Norwood, NJ: Ablex.

Lemke, J. L. (1995b) *Textual Politics: Discourse and Social Dynamics*. London: Taylor & Francis.

Lemke, J. L. (1998) Resources for attitudinal meaning: evaluative orientations in text semantics. *Functions of Language*, 5(1):33–56.

Malinowski, Bronislav (1923) The problem of meaning in primitive languages. Supplement I to C. K. Ogden and I. A. Richards, *The Meaning of Meaning*. New York: Harcourt Brace.

Martin, James R. (1985) Process and text. In *Systemic Perspectives on Discourse, Vol. 1*, ed. by J. Benson and W. Greaves, Norwood, NJ: Ablex.

Ventola, Eija (1987) *The Structure of Social Interaction: A Systemic Approach to the Semiotics of Service Encounters*. London: Frances Pinter.

3

Interpersonal Meaning and the Discursive Construction of Action, Attitudes and Values: The Global Modal Program of One Text[1]

Paul J. Thibault

Defining the notion of the Global Modal Program

On one level of organization, linguistic texts – spoken, written, performed – exhibit global patterns of thematic meaning relations[2] and their development (see Lemke 1983; Thibault 1989). In this perspective, the text is seen from the point of view of the ways in which experiential selections in clause, group, word and other units contribute to the development of the text as being 'about' particular textual participants and the actions, events, sayings, cognitions, and so on, of these participants and processes in relation to specific temporal, locational, and other circumstances in some referent situation – real, imaginary, hypothetical – that is indexed by the text. In this perspective, we can also include the various cohesive resources for anchoring the thematic development of the text to particular patterns of Theme–Rheme development, as well as for indicating, among other things, continuity of reference, temporal, causal and other sequencing, and so on.

On another level, the text is characterizable in terms of its global (inter)actional organization and coherence. It is the level of 'what is being done or performed' through the text. In this view, the text is a structured sequence of recognizable interactional units or dialogic moves which function to position the participants in the interactive event in dialogically organized interpersonal role relations in the ongoing taking up, responding to and negotiating of the meaning of the other, construed either (1) interpersonally as categories of 'I' and 'you' located in an intersubjective space of dialogic interaction whereby the mutual assignment of modalized responsibilities through the interpersonal grammar and semantics of mood and speech function takes place, or (2) ideationally as 'other' third person participants and their associated (inter)texts with which the interaction to hand negotiates and orients to.

In this text-as-interaction perspective, interactants enact a dialogically coordinated and jointly created instance of social action which conforms to varying degrees to some generic model or text-type. In so doing, they also invoke specific axiological orientations, social viewpoints and social values in relation to: (1) the text's thematic meaning or some local part of this; (2) each other as the occupants of discursively constituted though generically constrained participant roles; and (3) the wider system of social heteroglossia (Bakhtin 1981) whereby all texts participate in, respond to and are organized in relation to the diversity of discursively construed values, viewpoints and domains of validity in a given discourse community. In this perspective, the analyst is concerned to show how the specifically interpersonal resources of the lexicogrammar are globally deployed to enact what I shall call the Global Modal Program of the text. The further question concerns how the Global Modal Program maps onto the other kind of text-level ideational patterning referred to above as the global patterns of thematic meaning relations such that the text is seen as being 'about' something.[3]

Presenting the texts to be analysed

The two texts to be analysed were published in the problem pages of *Cleo* (Australia) magazine (September 1985, p. 155). They have been segmented below in terms of clauses and clause-complexes. Arabic numerals refer to the clause-complex and lower case Roman letters designate the constituent clauses in each complex. The two texts, referred to as A and B, are assumed to be components of a single entextualized[4] social activity, comprising a young female writer's Letter to Agony Aunt and the Agony Aunt's Reply. Thus, A1a–b refers to the clause-complex comprising clauses 1a and 1b in Text A. This notation will be used throughout this chapter in order to identify the clauses and clause-complexes in the two texts.

Text A

Q. 1a. I am a 17-year-old virgin
    1b. and am very scared.
    2a. I have never been brave enough
    2b. to try sexual intercourse.
    3a. Could you please give me some idea
    3b. as to how I will feel,
    3c. what will happen
    3d. and what to expect
    3e. when I finally share my body with another?
    4. Reader, Vic.

Text B

R. 1a. I can't tell you
    1b. how you'll feel about your first experience of intercourse.
    2. So much depends on how ready you are emotionally for the experience, and the type of relationship you have with your partner.
    3a. From the sound of things you have not been in a situation
    3b. where you are ready
    3c. to proceed to a more intense sexual relationship.
    4a. There is nothing brave
    4b. about trying sex –
    5a. it often takes more courage
    5b. to wait
    5c. until you know
    5d. the time is right for you.
    6a. In the right relationship, a loving sensitive male will take things gradually,
    6b. and you will progress naturally.
    7a. You may care
    7b. to take a look at the excellent book *Will I Like It?* by Peter Mayle (Hutchinson, 1978).

Some analytical preliminaries

We may now consider how the metafunctional hypothesis (Halliday 1979), with its emphasis on the simultaneous, configured nature of meaning selections from the experiential, interpersonal, textual and logical metafunctions in a given lexicogrammatical form at, say, clause rank, demonstrates that linguistic forms consist of co-varying selections from all four semantic metafunctions, each with their distinctive structural realizations. The four metafunctions simultaneously enact a plurality of indexically presupposing and/or creative relations with relevant features of their contexts. In order to explain the metafunctional relation between clause and text, Halliday (1980) proposes a two-way relationship – in both size and abstraction – along what he calls the metonymic and the metaphoric dimensions of this relationship. These are summarized in Table 3.1 in relation to all four metafunctions.[5] Table 3.1 shows that on both the micro-level of lexicogrammatical selections as well as on the macro-level of overall text organization, each of the four kinds of meanings shown here has its distinctive type of formal realization. In this chapter, I shall be concerned with the ways in which selections in interpersonal meaning enact the Global Modal Program of a particular text.

Table 3.1 Clause–text analogy: all four metafunctions

Metafunction	Type of clause–text relation	Clause	Text	Typical realization
experiential	metonymic	process-participant configurations	staged schematic structure elements	constituency; particulate, segmental
	metaphoric	as above	lexico-semantic participant chains; thematic development	chain identity and harmony
interpersonal	metonymic	mood; exchange structure	interactional structure	prosodic, scopal
	metaphoric	modality, modulation, person deixis, interpersonal lexis	value chains; metadiscursive construal of axiological stances	
textual	metonymic	Theme–Rheme	beginning-middle-end	periodic, culminative, wave-like
	metaphoric	information	interclausal cohesive linkages	
logical	metonymic	taxis	transition pathways	recursion
	metaphoric	conjunction	interdependency	

It is important to point out that there is no necessary hierarchy of dominant and less dominant functional components in the way

Jakobson (1985 [1956]:113–114) suggests, unless, of course, such a hierarchy is construed on the basis of some metarule of contextualization which selectively foregrounds one or the other functions in a given textual instance or discourse genre. The analytical task is, rather, to specify which units and structures on the lexicogrammatical and discourse strata realize which kinds of meanings, and how foregrounded co-patternings of these meanings indexically create or presuppose specific contextual relations and effects in different phases[6] of the ongoing discourse. Thus, we have the basis for showing, in the present analysis, how foregrounded text-internal relations and patterns among units and structures in the *interpersonal* metafunction both contribute to the formation of interactional coherence as well as instantiate a metasemantic framework 'which gives to the different phases distinct kinds and degrees of negotiability of the indexical functions$_2$ in play at any given time' (Silverstein 1987:35).[7] The ways in which readers and writers achieve this are dependent on the particular, historically contingent, social meaning-making practices which are in operation. This entails an ongoing synchronic and diachronic dialectic between linguistic forms, text and the social semiotic. In order to explore how the resources of interpersonal meaning contribute to this dialectic, I shall develop a multifaceted approach to interpersonal meaning by drawing on some highly relevant proposals made by Kenneth Burke.

In his essay 'Four master tropes' Burke (1969 [1945]:503–517) argues that metaphor, metonymy, synecdoche and irony are more than just figurative usages: that they play a 'rôle in the discovery and description of "the truth"'. Burke points out that each of the four terms can be substituted by a different set of names, as follows:

metonymy → reduction
metaphor → perspective
synecdoche → representation
irony → perspective.

It is with these four perspectives in mind that I propose to explore and develop the notion of the Global Modal Program of the text as defined in the first section of this chapter. In so doing, I shall have occasion to refract Halliday's arguments concerning the metonymic and metaphoric dimensions of the clause–text relation through the tools of thought provided by Burke's four perspectives.

The clause–text homology: the metonymic dimension

In the first instance, the global interpersonal organization of the text can be interpreted, by metonymic reduction (Burke 1969 [1945]:506), in terms of the mood system in the grammar. In English, mood is a grammatical category which is realized at clause rank in the independent clause. In clause-complexes comprising an independent clause and one or more dependent clauses, the mood operator holds in its scope the entire complex and modifies it interpersonally in order to indicate how the complex as a whole is to be defined interactionally. In this way, entire complexes can function as extended moves in discourse with a specific interpersonal force.

According to McGregor (1997:216–217), it is the mood operator which specifies whether a clause is a proposition or a proposal. Declarative and interrogative clauses express propositions. The mood element is an operator which holds the proposition expressed by the clause in its scope and indicates whether the proposition is being asserted (declarative) or questioned (interrogative). A proposition is something which can be argued about as to its truth or falsity, its believability, and so on. Oblative and imperative mood clauses, on the other hand, express proposals, rather than propositions. Again, the mood operator holds the proposal in its scope and modifies it interpersonally as either oblative or imperative. A proposal is either a proposal to act on the part of the addresser (oblative) or a demand by the addresser for the addressee to act (imperative).

In declarative clauses, the addresser, who is the agentive source of the proposition and associated modalizations, posits a specific modal investment in a proposition about some clausal Subject (Thibault 1995), as illustrated in Figure 3.1. This modal investment therefore positions the addresser as having a particular modal status in relation to the proposition. It may, for example, be a modalized relation of knowledge, belief, doubt, certainty, and so on, with respect to the proposition. By the same token, the uttering of a declarative proposition has the potential to transform the modal status of the addressee by, for example, changing his or her knowledge about the proposition, or by persuading him or her to adopt a different attitude or belief with respect to the proposition. This potential for transforming the modal status of the addressee means that the uttering of a proposition is an *act of modalization* in which modal competencies may be transferred from one agent to another in the course of the interaction between them. In uttering the proposition, the addresser seeks to conjoin the addressee to the former's modal

ADDRESSER	friendship	takes		time	ADDRESSEE
Source of Proposition	Subject	Finite: Present	Predicator	Complement	Target of Proposition
	Mood Operator		Residue		
	DECL [Proposition]				
+ MODAL INVESTMENT	Trajectory of Modalization ⟶				− MODAL INVESTMENT

Figure 3.1 Modal status of addresser and addressee relative to declarative proposition

investment in the grammaticalized Subject of the Proposition. The Mood structure positions the addressee as being in a (potentially) different modal position – see Bakhtin's 'alien word' – which can be negotiated, as initially seen from the point of view of the addresser. The further negotiation in the discourse of this modalized 'friction' or difference depends on the addressee's willingness to take up and accept, or not, the modal position posited by the addresser. If a given addresser is trying to persuade his or her addressee to another point of view, to adopt a different evaluation, or to acquire some knowledge or belief, then semiotic friction in the form of the differing modal positions of the two is necessary in order that appropriate interpersonal (and other) semiotic choices are made. In this way, a particular modalizing strategy can be related to the addresser's purpose in the interaction. Thus, the use of a given mood choice presupposes some kind of semiotic and/or material 'friction' or difference between addresser and addressee as the starting point of the interaction (Thibault 1995).

From the addresser's point of view, the modal status of the addressee constitutes a modal lack or difference which can be glossed as follows: 'This is my modal investment in the Subject of the Proposition; do you agree, or not?' or 'I'm going to tell you something you don't know'. Whether the addressee accepts or not this transformation of his or her modal status depends on the way in which the act of modalization is resolved or finalized in the ensuing discourse negotiation of the clausally realized propositional meaning (Thibault 1999). This may entail, for instance, the transformation of the addressee from an initial state of modal disjunction (e.g. ignorance, uncertainty) with respect to the proposition to a final state of modal conjunction with it as the addressee is persuaded,

ADDRESSER	Can	she	come?	ADDRESSEE
Source of Proposition	Finite: Modality	Subject	Predicator	Target of Proposition
	Mood Operator		Residue	
	INTER [Proposition]			
– MODAL INVESTMENT	Trajectory of Modalization			+ MODAL INVESTMENT

Figure 3.2 Modal status of addresser and addressee relative to interrogative proposition

convinced or otherwise induced or manipulated to adopt a specific modal investment in the proposition (e.g. knowledge, certainty, agreement). In this way, an act of modalization constitutes a transformation from some discursively prior modal state to a new one. Mood is, then, a central system in the interpersonal grammar for organizing the modal programs whereby agents, in taking up specific modal investments in propositions, seek to act on, influence and transform the modal investments of others in the processes of discourse negotiation.

In interrogatives, the addresser seeks the addressee's modal investment in the Subject of the Proposition in order that the *addresser's* initial lack of a specific modal investment in the proposition can be transformed into a specific modal position with respect to it, as shown in Figure 3.2. In other words, the addresser asks the addressee to take up a modal position with respect to the Subject of the Proposition in his or her response. In so responding, the addressee, in turn, becomes the Source of the Proposition. Depending on how the addressee negotiates the interrogative in his or her reply, the addresser of the interrogative proposition, in turn, undergoes a process of modalization whereby his or her modal status is transformed from, for example, [-KNOWLEDGE] to [+KNOWLEDGE]. That is, the addressee of the initial interrogative, in responding in his or her turn, transforms the original addresser's lack of knowledge into a modal competence, i.e. [+KNOWLEDGE], along with whatever social values may be associated with this. In interrogatives, the 'friction' or modalized difference between the addresser and addressee is based on an initial modal lack on the part of the addresser. The successful negotiation of this difference depends on whether the addressee knows the answer and/or is willing to provide it, and so on. From the point of view of the addresser of the interrogative, the relevant gloss is: 'I don't have a specific modal investment in the Subject of the Proposition; can you tell me yours so that I may have one?' In the case of polar interrogatives, the negotiation of this modal position can be represented as a modal cline between the polar values of 'yes' and 'no'. In the case of wh-interrogatives, the element to be negotiated is realized by the Wh-Complement, which may be more delicately specified with reference to choices in transitivity. For example, the wh-element *where* seeks a response in the experiential semantic area of [Circumstance:Location] from the addressee. Thus the resolution or finalization of the initial disjunction between the modal status of addresser and addressee depends on a subsequent process of modalization which conjoins the addresser with the desired, though previously lacking, modalization of the proposition. In this case, the result is a transformation in the modal status of the addresser.

In defining propositions and proposals in this way, I am taking up a position which follows to some extent the definition put forward by McGregor (1997:216–217), rather than Halliday's (1994 [1985]:68–71) distinction between propositions and proposals, which is defined with reference to the semantic stratum. In Halliday's account, propositions are concerned with the semantics of information exchange, as realized by the speech functions Statement and Question; proposals are concerned with the semantics of goods-&-services exchange, as realized by the speech function categories Offer and Command.

In attempting to negotiate between the differing positions of McGregor and Halliday, I would say that the question of whether the clause expresses a proposition or a proposal is a matter of the mood selection rather than Speech Function. There can only be one mood selection in any given finite clause. However, the further question as to whether the clause is oriented to information or to goods-&-services exchange, or to both of these simultaneously, is a question of the ways in which the semantics of Speech Function is construed not on the basis of mood *per se*, but on the basis of the more delicate co-patternings of mood with other interpersonal and experiential selections (Thibault and Van Leeuwen 1996). The discussion in the following paragraph serves to illustrate this with reference to an example in our text.

According to Halliday's view, the clause-complex B7a–b, *You may care to take a look at the excellent book 'Will I like it?'* by Peter Mayle (Hutchinson, 1978) would be a case of mood metaphor. That is, it can be construed as either a proposition or a proposal. In the present view, this clause-complex expresses a proposition as defined by the declarative mood operator which holds the proposition in its scope. It is a declarative proposition which can be believed or disbelieved, agreed with or denied, treated as true or false, and so on, in accordance with either the way the addressee takes up and negotiates the mood element or the future actions of the Subject 'you'. The further question as to how the clause can also be construed as a 'suggestion to act' lies in the way that a number of more delicate selections from diverse interpersonal and other systems co-pattern in specific ways. In my view, it is the delicate co-patterning of features across different metafunctional systems that can best resolve this question. Mood and the related question of whether the clause expresses a proposition or a proposal is a fact about the interpersonal *grammar* of the clause. Mood is just one of a number of lexicogrammatical systems that may interact to produce a subtle tension between information and goods-&-services exchange in discourse (see also Hasan 1988; Thibault and Van Leeuwen 1996).

Thus, the assigning of modal responsibility to the second person Subject 'you', the selection of the modality of possibility 'may', and the mental process of affection:inclination 'care', constitute a projecting clause which hypotactically projects the non-finite clause *to take a look at the excellent book* Will I Like It? by Peter Mayle (Hutchinson, 1978) as being held within the mood scope of the projecting clause A7a. That is, the projecting clause holds the projected clause within its scope so as to modify it interpersonally by positing a particular modalized stance on it. In this case, the agony aunt's – i.e. the addresser's – modal position in the projecting declarative clause constitutes an evaluation of the possibility of the 'you's adopting the course of action referred to in the projected clause. In doing so, the agony aunt also positions the 'you' as an agent who has the possibility to undergo the modal transformation which the eventual carrying out of the projected action would entail. The selection of the modal verb 'may' is, therefore, crucial not only because it grounds the clause as an arguable proposition relative to the here-now of the addresser, but also because it sets a particular modal value on the discursive negotiation of the transfer of modal responsibility from addresser to addressee. This means that the 'you' could become the agent who is modally responsible for carrying out the hypotactically projected action as the result of the transferring of the given modal competence from addresser to addressee in the (hypothetical) further development of the interaction, i.e. beyond the text itself as analysed here.

The hypotactically projected status of the non-finite clause A7b also means that the deictic and mood centre of the complex as a whole is shifted to that of the projecting clause. Therefore, the designated course of action in the projected clause does not realize a proposition. It is for this reason non-negotiable in the exchange structure of the complex as a whole. As a non-finite clause, it also expresses a modality of *irrealis* on account of its future-projected and yet-to-be-realized or non-actual status. The non-finite clause A7b has a Predicator, viz. *to take a look at*. This non-finite Predicator specifies a type-specification of a verbal process rather than a fully grounded instance (Davidse 1991:195n). The systems of primary tense, modality and polarity have the function of instantiating the verbal process which is specified in the Predicator in relation to some specific act of meaning exchange between an addresser and an addressee. The point is that, in our example, the given course of action in the projected clause is evaluated by the agony aunt as having the *possibility* of being brought about by the addressee at some future moment. Interactionally, the addressee can either negotiate the mood of the projecting clause and its modalization, viz. 'you may'/'I may/may not', or agree with or disagree with the modal stance towards the future course of action in the non-finite projected clause. In both cases, the addressee can adopt a *propositional attitude* to these two dimensions of the overall meaning of the clause-complex. This is so because Propositions can be made in relation to past, present and future states of affairs. In the present example it is, therefore, possible for addresser and addressee to adopt a propositional attitude towards both the here-now interactional status of the clause-complex (see the modal value in the projecting declarative clause) and to the *irrealis* status of the non-finite future-oriented Predicator in the projected clause. Overall, the interpersonal semantics of the clause-complex in question enacts an arguable – a modally grounded – claim as to a possible future state of affairs. By contrast, the (invented) clause *Take a look at the excellent book by Peter Mayle!* is a proposal that does not assert or deny any arguable or knowable fact or belief about the world (McGregor 1997:211). Instead, it expresses a desired future course of action that the addresser would like the addressee to carry out.

In the present example, the choice of declarative mood in the projecting clause allow the addresser, in selecting 'you' as the modally responsible element, to shift the responsibility to the addressee for the actual carrying out or otherwise of the designated action at the same time that the modality of possibility ('may') allows the addresser to distance herself from the attribution of the mental process of affection:inclination to the addressee. The choice of declarative mood indicates that the addresser views the proposition expressed in the clause as a *possible* desire on the part of the addressee, which can, however, be argued about (see above). The further question as to the Speech Function status of the proposition depends on how the various dimensions of its localized meaning potential are negotiated on the discourse stratum. Typically, this would be described in terms of semantic glosses such as 'evaluation of possibility' (see information exchange) in contrast to 'advice/suggestion/invitation' (see goods-&-services exchange). These glosses themselves have some affinities with the distinction between epistemic and deontic modalities in other accounts (Foley and Van Valin 1984:229–30; Siewierska 1991:125), or between 'knowledge' and 'influence' modalities (Rodríguez-Navarro 1993:Chapters 8–9).

A number of linguists point out that 'may', when used to give permission, has a performative value, which 'indicates authority in the speaker' (Rodríguez-Navarro 1993:227), or that 'may' is one of the modal resources for giving advice, making suggestions and issuing invitations (Leech and Svartik 1975:143, 147–149). Such uses are contrasted with the 'may' of 'possibility' (e.g. Leech and Svartik 1975:128–129). Explanations such as these are useful as notional glosses on the situation-specific semantics of these modals. For this reason, they often occur in pedagogic grammars of the language. In systemic-functional theory, such interpretations are seen as deriving from the ways in which specific co-patternings of lexicogrammatical forms are semantically taken up and negotiated on the discourse stratum (Thibault and Van Leeuwen 1996). However, I remain unconvinced that interpretations such as those referred to above provide a satisfactory account of the ways in which the interpersonal grammar of mood and modality contributes to the enactment and negotiation of speech function moves on the discourse semantic stratum. In my view, the use of 'may' in order to modally evaluate possibility, to give advice and permission and to make suggestions can be explained in a more unified way. Arguments in support of this view can be adduced on both formal and semantic grounds. The fact that the 'may' of possibility and the 'may' of 'permission/advice/suggestion' are both realized in the same locally segmentable linguistic form which is coded in the finite element of declarative and interrogative propositions suggests also that we are dealing with the same interpersonal-*grammatical* category. That is, there is a deeper semantic connection which unifies the glosses mentioned above. I shall now explore the further implications of this argument.

I shall start by proposing that what particular social agents and agencies permit, advise and suggest others to do when they use 'may' is just another way of specifying or evaluating, from the perspective of the agentive source of the modality, what is *possible* (or otherwise) for some category of social participant to do (or be) in relation to specific social practices, social activity-structures, discourse genres and their associated conventions, particular cross-couplings of the material-semiotic, particular social viewpoints and values, and so on. That is, the possibilities for 'doing' of various categories of social agents and potential agents in the social and material world are semiotically organized and constrained in ways that the interpersonal grammar of modality and mood helps to enact and index (see Thibault forthcoming). In the above example, the modal 'may' is the means whereby the agentive source of the modality in the discourse context – i.e. the agony aunt – selects the grammatical Subject of the clause, i.e. 'you', as the entity in which the modal responsibility for a possible course of action is invested. Thus, the choice of declarative mood is a strategy whereby the agentive source of the modality seeks to conjoin the addressee to her modal investment such that the latter is oriented towards the possibility of her 'taking a look at the excellent book *Will I Like It?* by Peter Mayle'. In so doing, the agony aunt seeks to bring about, through interpersonal negotiation, a modal transformation of the girl as a modally competent agent who is endowed with certain possibilities for action in the social world. The declarative proposition therefore functions interpersonally to frame the Subject's orientation to the ungrounded (non-finite) Predicator in the projected clause as a modalized assessment of a possible course of action. This contrasts with, for example, the imposing of an obligation to undertake the proposed action, as in the case of imperative mood. Figure 3.3 presents an analysis of the interpersonal grammar of clause B7a–b.

The agony aunt's modal investment in the 'you' is socially grounded in some form of institutional authority which has the power and/or the knowledge to determine both what is possible or otherwise for determinate categories of subjects and agents, and when – i.e. under what conditions – these possibilities may be enacted as an effective course of action. The modality also expresses the degree to which the agentive source of the modality – the agony aunt – modally invests in the proposition. It is not, then, a question of an epistemic

ADDRESSER	you	may	care	to take a look at	the excellent book *Will I Like It?* by Peter Mayle (Hutchinson, 1978)	ADDRESSEE
Source of Proposition	Subject	Finite: modality	Predicator$_1$ modally grounded	Predicator$_2$ ungrounded	Complement	Target of Proposition
	Mood Operator		Residue$_1$	Residue$_2$		
	Projecting clause			Projected clause		
			DECL [Proposition]			
			Trajectory of Modalization			
+ MODAL INVESTMENT						− MODAL INVESTMENT

Figure 3.3 Analysis of interpersonal grammar in clause B7a–b

scale of truth-values standing in a to-degrees relation of correspondence to some objective state of affairs in the real world 'out there'.
Instead, it is an expression of the extent to which the agentive source
of the modality – the agony aunt as addresser – seeks to conjoin the
'you' to the proposition at the same time that she delegates the
responsibility for the proposition's success or failure to the second
person Subject 'you' of this clause-complex. In this particular
example, the agony aunt, in modally investing certain conditions of
possibility in the addressee, seeks to impose context-sensitive
semantic constraints on the girl's future possibilities for action. In
so doing, the interpersonal grammar and semantics orient and entrain
discursively constituted and negotiable subjects and objects and their
associated values along specific time-bound trajectories in the course
of the further negotiation and development of the discourse. The
choice of mood, modality and so on, in the interpersonal grammar of
the clause-complex is a local attractor space whereby a specific
trajectory is posited and forged in and through the particular cross-
couplings of material and semiotic resources that are harnessed in
order to ensure the success of the specific trajectory. In the final
analysis, such modal investments are always relatable to socially
sanctioned Grounds (Hasan 1992:284–285) which legitimate the
specific allocation of agentive responsibilities with reference to the
practices and values of a particular interpersonal moral order. The
Ground may or may not be lexicogrammatically specified in a given
text. In the event that it is not explicitly realized, it is, nevertheless,
indexable and, hence, recoverable as a relevant intertext.

The metonymic reduction of the global interpersonal meaning of
the text can be summarized as a series of macro-propositions. As
shown in Figure 3.4, these are, at this stage, derived from the
clausally realized mood selections only and do not take into account
other domains of meaning choice with which mood co-patterns. The
full analysis of the mood selections in each clause or the clause-
complexes from which the above schematization is derived is
presented in Appendix I (see the end of this chapter).

The locus of the mood system in the grammar of English is the
independent clause. However, the macro-level exchange units
proposed here derive from stretches of text which include complexes
of independent and dependent clauses, all subsumed by the one
discourse level phase. It is the independent clause in a given clause-
complex which holds the entire complex in its scope and thus defines
the interpersonal orientation of that complex. The clause-complex
functions in discourse to relate clauses and the other units they

Text A

| 1a–b/2a–b: | Macro-proposition: declarative |
| 3a–e: | Macro-proposition: polar interrogative |

Text B

1a–b:	Macro-proposition: declarative
2:	Macro-proposition: declarative
3a–c:	Macro-proposition: declarative
4a–b/5a–d:	Macro-proposition: declarative
6a–b:	Macro-proposition: declarative
7a–b:	Macro-proposition: declarative

Figure 3.4 Clausally derived macro-propositions in Texts A and B

contain to their wider discourse implications. The clause-complex is a necessary level of analysis if we are to specify the kinds of dependency relations which operate between interpersonal units and structures on the discourse stratum. It should also be emphasized that the interpretation of the macro-level units defined in Figure 3.4 does not derive from any one system in the lexicogrammar. This will be shown more clearly in the section below.

The clause–text homology: the metaphoric dimension

If the metonymic dimension of the clause–text relation can be seen as a case of the reduction of some aspect of textual organization to some feature in the clause, then the metaphoric dimension has to do with seeing some feature of the clause from the perspective of its function in text (see Burke 1969 [1945]:503). In Halliday's account, the metaphoric aspect of the clause–text relationship shows how the interpersonal feature in the clause is also the realization of some feature of the text. In the same way that the particulate experiential organization of the clause is punctuated by the field-like prosodic realization of interpersonal selections, the enchainment of interpersonal selections across an entire text enacts the cumulative punctuation of the text's thematic development (see first section of this chapter) by ongoing interpersonal motifs, along with their global interactional coherence. The cumulative effect of interpersonal selections in, say, modality, modulation and attitudinal and evaluative lexis also constitutes the development of a particular global attitudinal or axiological orientation in texts. Thus, the deployment of a particular interpersonal selection at clause-complex, clause, group or word levels is a local contribution to a more global modal orientation on the discourse stratum.

For example, Halliday's (1982) discussion of an excerpt from J. B. Priestley's play *An Inspector Calls* has shown how foregrounded co-patternings of selections in modality, modulation and tense realize the more global interpersonal themes of conflicting obligations, duties and responsibilities, which is the central drama of this play. The realization of attitudinal and axiological meanings in our text shows that selections in modality, modulation, and attitudinal lexis demonstrate a congruity of co-patterning with respect to the distinct textual phases already identified in relation to mood (Figure 3.4). The following analysis relates selections from mood, modality, modulation and interpersonal lexis on the lexicogrammatical stratum to the attitudinal/axiological semantic orientation of each phase on the discourse stratum. This is done by interpreting the global attitudinal/axiological orientation of each phase in relation to the text as a whole.

The detailed analysis of interpersonal selections as seen from the perspective of their contribution to each textual phase on the discourse stratum now follows:

TEXT A: THE 17-YEAR-OLD FEMALE WRITES TO THE AGONY AUNT

Phase 1: clauses A1a–b/2a–b
Phase 1 is a macro-proposition comprising three declarative clauses in which the first person deictic 'I' is Subject. This means that in this phase the Subject 'I' is most at risk in terms of the meanings that are negotiated about the Subject in the intersubjective space between 'I' and 'you'. Experientially, these three declarative clauses are all attributive predications in which the 'I' as Carrier/Subject is experientially construed as (1) an instance of the type-category '17-year-old virgin' in 1a and (2) as an instantiation of the type-qualities 'very scared' and 'brave enough to try sexual intercourse' in 1b and 1c. Thus, specific social categories and qualities, along with the possible values that may be assigned to these in the wider system of social viewpoints and evaluations, are assimilated to the discourse perspective of the 'I'. These particular choices of semantic Attribute contribute to the development of a particular text-specific thematic formation, along with the possible evaluative/axiological orientations and stances that such thematics may participate in (Lemke 1988, 1990b; Thibault 1989, 1991). In other words, the Attributes constitute fragments of a still wider intertextual thematic formation which the specific choices instantiate. Therefore, in this particular textual phase, the lexico-

grammatical resources of the relational processes function to connect, through the attributive process *be*, the deictic perspective of the 'I' to non-sourced heteroglossic variation by means of the modalized attributes which are predicated of the 'I'.

The clause-complex A2a–2b reflects a slightly different interpersonal orientation with respect to the previous complex. Like the prior complex, the second complex situates the 'I' in a specific interdiscursive field of heteroglossic viewpoints by means of the predication of an Attribute of its Carrier/Subject. The difference lies in the use of the modal operator *never* whereby the meaning of this clausal proposition is negotiated. Here, the modal operator focuses the negotiation on the propositional meaning of the clause as located in an intersubject-ive space centred on 'I' and 'you'. In evaluating the proposition in terms of the modal scale of 'usuality' (Halliday 1994 [1985]:357–358), the modality invokes a potential plurality of other evaluations – e.g. never, usually, always – around which interpersonal negotiation can take place. Thus, 'never being brave enough', as implicitly contrasted with 'always brave enough', and so on, thereby implying other possible negotiations, along with their potential for the proposal to be taken up, located and relocated in relation to diverse social viewpoints and evaluative orientations in the overall system of social hetero-glossia, to touch base once again with Bakhtin's term.

We see, in other words, how the clause-complex A2a–2b straddles two distinct regions of interpersonal negotiation. The first is a subspace which is organized in relation to a zero-point constituted by the addresser as indexed by the personal deictic 'I' (see Hanks 1996:180). In this space, the addresser and, by metaphorical implication, her body, constitute the deictic zero-point in relation to which specific thematic items and their associated evaluative orientations are located and assimilated. In the present text, the *be*-processes in the attributive clauses function like relational vectors which radiate out from the 'I' in any direction and to any distance in the (metaphorical) space of social heteroglossic relations to, as here, specific social categories and/or qualities that are connected to the 'I'. The second space, on the other hand, is grid-like. In this space, the 'I' can be located without reference to deictic terms – e.g. near/far, this/ that, now/then – that presuppose a zero-point. Here, there is no privileging centre point. Rather, the scale of modal values spanning, say, the 'usuality' range presupposes and defines a semantic region beyond which a given point, belonging to some other region of modality, falls outside the scale of values that are negotiated by this particular region.

Phase 2: clauses 3a–e

The clause-complex comprising this phase selects for polar inter-rogative mood in clause 3a. It is this clause which frames and defines the scope of the mood selection for the entire complex. In switching to interrogative mood, the writer shifts the deictic centre to the 'you' as Subject in 3a. The interrogative selection functions to engage the addressee – the agony aunt – by construing her as the source of the meanings that the writer – the girl – wants to know. In other words, the choice of this strategy for engaging with the agony aunt both invokes and presupposes the assumed ideational knowledge and expertise of the agony aunt at the same time that it holds her modally responsible as the interpersonal source of such knowledge.

Interpersonally, this clause-complex is an instance of mood metaphor (Halliday 1994 [1985]:363–367). Given that mood is centred on the independent clause A3a, I shall confine my analysis to this clause in order to develop this point. In clause 3a, the polar interrogative mood choice enacts both a demand for information (proposition) and a demand for goods-&-services (proposal). It can potentially be taken up and negotiated as both a yes/no question and as a request. A more detailed consideration of the specific lexicogrammatical selections in both the interpersonal and the experiential metafunctions will show why.

From the interpersonal point of view, clause A3a co-patterns the following selections: [MOOD: INTERROGATIVE: POLAR], [SUBJECT: SECOND PERSON DEIXIS], [FINITE: MODAL: UNACTUALIZED POTEN-TIAL: COULD], and [MODAL ADJUNCT: PLEASE] (see also Appendix I to this chapter).

Experientially, clause 3a is also construable metaphorically as either a material action process or a verbal process. The two interpretations are presented in Figure 3.5. In this case, a material process metaphorically construes the verbal transaction between the two

	you	give	me	some idea
Material Process	Actor	Process: Material Action	Beneficiary: Recipient	Goal
Verbal Process	Sayer	Process: Verbal	Receiver: Addressee	Verbiage/ Range

Figure 3.5 Two experiential construals of clause 3a

interactants as the transfer of a commodity – *some idea* – from the Actor to the Beneficiary. Significantly, the commodity thus transferred is not a material good, but an abstract *mental* one. Thus, the verbal act of saying or telling is metaphorically construed as the material process of transferring the mental – not material – commodity to the Beneficiary. Furthermore, it is a mental commodity which has to do with knowledge, i.e. something which the agony aunt knows, but which the girl does not, and which the girl desires the agony aunt to tell her. This entails a much more complex chain of modal relations and their transformations than might first appear to be the case. In order to unravel these complexities, it is once again necessary to take into account the synergy – the interfunctional solidarity (Martin 1991:128) – between the interpersonal and the experiential selections in this clause.

The experiential grammar of A3a better lends itself to the transitive rather than to the ergative interpretation. That is, it is concerned with the Actor/Subject's intentionally directing an action/saying to the Goal/Recipient in the clause. The writer of A3a requires her addressee to *do* something, i.e. to *tell* the writer something that her addressee knows. In order to explain the further implications of this, I shall draw on and develop a distinction made by Greimas (1983a:121) between the modal status of propositions and the act of modalization. This in turn takes us back to my earlier point that A3a functions to engage the agony aunt as both ideational and interpersonal source of a certain type of knowledge and expertise. Implicitly, this means that the girl engages the agony aunt on the basis of her socially authorized modal status as the source of this knowledge and expertise. The polar interrogative mood selection indicates that the addresser of this clause (the girl) requires the agony aunt, as the Subject in whom the modal responsibility of the clause is invested, to act in a certain way so as to transform the modal status of the girl through a discursively negotiable process of modalization. That is, to transform the girl's doubt and lack of knowledge into certitude and knowledge. In the Greimasian parlance, this presupposes that the agony aunt is in possession of a certain modal competence which enables her to carry out this operation:

> L'opération qui s'effectue sur la dimension cognitive du discours est de l'ordre du *faire* et présuppose, comme condition préalable de tout passage à l'acte, une certaine compétence modale du sujet. (Greimas 1983a:121)

(The operation which is carried out on the cognitive dimension of discourse is in the area of *doing* [*faire*] and presupposes, as a prior condition for the complete transition to the act, a certain modal competence on the part of the subject.)

In systemic-functional terms, this means that the addresser (the girl) of A3a invests in the *you* as a Subject who is both: (1) in possession of the relevant modal competence, i.e. her knowledge and expertise; and (2) has the power and authority to act so as to bring about a modal transformation of the girl in the process of 'giving her some idea as to how [she] will feel, etc.'.

The entire process of modalization which is semantically condensed in A3a may be unpacked and schematized as follows:

YOU KNOW→YOU DO (TELL)→YOU MAKE ME KNOW HOW I WILL FEEL→I KNOW

As the above schema suggests, the agony aunt's capacity to carry out – to effect – the relevant modalizing operation is based on the logically prior presupposition that she *knows*, i.e. she is in possession of the relevant modal competence, along with the socially recognized authority to exercise it.

In the light of these considerations, we can return to some further experiential implications of the choice of the nominal group *some idea* in the clause (A3a) under consideration. The experiential type-category denoted by the Head noun 'idea' lies, of course, within the class of mental rather than material things (see above). Moreover, the verbal action of telling someone something that they did not previously know implicates a cognitive transformation – an act of modalization – of the semantic Receiver of the verbal process. Thus, verbal processes of, for instance, telling, persuading, convincing, explaining and so on, implicate the potential for the manipulation and transformation of the addressee's modalized cognitive competence (Greimas 1983a:123). This observation now allows us to recast the experiential predication 'you give me some idea ...' as a metaphorical construal of a *mental* process of cognition. More precisely, it is a mental process which potentially transforms the modal status of the Recipient from an initial modal status of [–KNOWLEDGE] to [+KNOWLEDGE]. This may be glossed as shown in Figure 3.6.

The initial interpersonal engagement with the agony aunt as source – both ideational and interpersonal – of meaning and knowledge is, then, the first stage in a Global Modal Program of 'manipulation selon le savoir' (Greimas 1983a:123). In this way, the act of telling functions

you	make ('tell')	me	know	how I will feel ...
Instigator/ Agent	Process: Causative	Senser	Process: Mental: Cognition	Phenomenon: Result

Figure 3.6 Metaphorical reconstrual of verbal process as mental process of cognition

as a metaphor of the negotiation of a given modal competence (knowledge) as invested in the Subject (*you*, i.e. the agony aunt) of this clause by the addresser (the girl) in order that doubt and ignorance may be replaced by certitude and knowledge.

Finally, the logico-semantic relation of elaboration, viz. 'particularization', which is construed by the conjunction *as to* links the nominal group *some idea* to the remaining clauses in this complex by further specifying the nominal group in terms of a different semantic register, one which is concerned with the feelings, happenings and expectations that the girl has in relationship to her future-projected first experience of sexual intercourse.

TEXT B: THE AGONY AUNT'S REPLY

Phase 1: Renegotiate Previous Text (clauses B1a–b)
Initially, the agony aunt responds to the girl in the clause-complex B1a–b by taking up and negotiating the Finite element *could* in the girl's question. That is, the agony aunt responds by taking up and negotiating the first writer's dialogic move as a yes/no question in which the polarity of the Finite element is most at risk, rather than as a request for goods-&-services. She does so both by negating the Finite element and by shifting it from the past tense form used by the young female writer to the present tense form *can't*. However, the real significance of this shift is modal rather than temporal. That is, the shift from the past to the present tense form signifies a shift from the non-actual to the actual (Kress 1977). The use of *Could* by the previous writer in A2a indicates that the writer evaluates the addressee's ability to be able to respond to the proposition in her interrogative clause-complex as an unactualized potential, i.e. 'you might be able to tell me, but haven't yet'. This explains the use of the past tense form.

In the agony aunt's reply, the shift to the present tense form *can't* signifies, by contrast, *actual* inability. Moreover, the use of hypotactic projection ('indirect report') means that the deictic center lies within the frame established by the projecting (reporting) clause *I can't tell you* rather than the projected clause. This means that the girl's text is negotiated as 'other' text – i.e. your text, not mine – along the intersubjective axis of the I–you relationship. It is along this axis that modal responsibilities are sourced at the participants – addressers and addressees – in the interaction rather than at some ideationalized (third person) source that lies outside or beyond the I–you relationship. In the present example, the modal shift to 'actual' and the deictic centering on the projecting context of the agony aunt denote the socially validated and recognized power and authority to make certain kinds of claims with respect to the girl's text.

Phase 2: clause B2
Clause B2 is an identifying process by means of which the verb *depends on* construes a logico-semantic relationship of 'condition' or 'contingency' between the Token *So much* and the nominal group complex *how ready*.... Moreover, the projected text of the girl in the prior complex – i.e. clause B1b – has been textually substituted for by *So much* and is, therefore, fully assimilated into the ideational context of the agony aunt, rather than being allowed to speak with its own textual voice. In this way, the girl's text is reconstrued as a Token to which the agony aunt assigns the Value[8] realized by the nominal group complex mentioned above. The latter is very much an expert discourse deriving from an unspecified ideational source pertaining to some therapeutic intertext.

Importantly, the dependency relation ('condition') which is realized by the identifying process also implicates an interpersonal semantic relation which can be dually construed here as both modulation and modalization. As a modulation of obligation/inclination, the Value in clause B2 specifies the condition on which the girl's first experience of sexual intercourse is dependent. It is also construable as a modalization in the sense that the condition specified by the Value entails a prediction as to the possibility that the desired effect will be brought about by the cause. In both cases, the modulation/modalization is future-projected and is for this reason *irrealis*. The agony aunt thus positions herself as an agent who is able to direct and control expectations concerning future events and their likely outcomes. This shows that much more than cause *per se* is involved in the logico-semantic relation of condition which links the two nominal groups in question. The interaction of the logico-semantics of condition with the interpersonal semantics of modulation and modalization draws attention to the ways in which the allocation of one kind of condition or contingency rather than other possible ones is always an interpersonal question of how moral responsibility and, hence, control of actions and the participants in these is assigned and distributed in a given community through its meaning-making practices.

Phase 3: Interpretation of Textual Evidence (clauses B3a–b)
Clause-complex B3a–b begins with an abstract circumstance of location *From the sound of things.* In this way, the viewpoint of the agony aunt is construed as a particular interpretative stance or angle on the girl's text. Interpersonally, the circumstance has modal scope over the rest of the complex and modifies the way in which the proposition in the rest of the complex is to be interpreted. Here, modal criteria of *evidentiality* are invoked in a circumstance which functions to project the agony aunt's interpretation in the remainder of this complex. In other words, criteria of textual evidence – the girl's text – form the basis for the propositions made in the remainder of this clause-complex. In the present case, the previous gnomic claim concerning 'how ready' one is for a sexual relationship is here negotiated in terms of the 'you' as Subject of the independent declarative clause *you have not been in a situation.* That is, in terms of direct interpersonal engagement between 'I' and 'you'. This contrasts with the non-negotiable status of 'you' in the clause-complex B2a in the preceding phase. In the earlier case, the pronoun *you* occurs in a rankshifted clause in the nominal group and is not, therefore, accessible to discourse negotiation as a potential Subject to which modal responsibility can be assigned.

Phase 4: Gnomic Pronouncement (clauses B4a–b/5a–d)
The presentative clause-complex B4a–b serves to introduce a new discourse entity into the discourse, i.e. the nominal group *nothing brave about trying sex.* Interpersonally, this complex takes up an element in the girl's prior text – see in particular A2a–b – and negates it. Moreover, the interpersonal sourcing of the girl's *I have never been brave enough* . . . is now ideationalized in the form of the generic nominalization *nothing brave about trying sex.* In negating the girl's discourse, the agony aunt abstracts it from the interpersonal and re-locates it in an ideational domain of unsourced gnomic pronouncements.

The clause-complex B5a–d reformulates the gnomic pronouncement of the preceding presentative clause by restating its meaning in terms of another semantic register. This clause-complex shifts the interpersonal orientation back to modalization, which is here realized in the mood structure of the clause. Thus, *often* serves to individuate the knowledge claim here by centering it on the 'usualization' of propositional meaning. As in B1a, it opens up and negotiates an intersubjective space of possible modal stances on the propositional meaning of the clause. Again, the tense is gnomic, in conformity with the generic nature of the advice which is given.

Phase 5: clauses B6a–b
The abstract circumstance of location *In the right relationship* in B6a highlights a different modal orientation to the propositional meaning of its clause-complex. Again, this is an instance of a circumstance having interpersonal scope over the propositional meaning of the entire complex and modifying the way this is to be interpreted. In this case, the circumstance indexes the domain of validity relative to which the propositional meaning is grounded. Thus, the clausal propositions *a loving sensitive male will take things gradually and you will progress naturally* derive their value from a specific contextual domain concerned with moral judgments of 'rightness' and 'wrongness'. For this reason, it may be said to be norm conformative.

In this clause-complex, the agony aunt constitutes two nominalized categories of persons, viz. 'a loving sensitive male' and the 'you' of the young female addressee who 'will progress naturally'. In making this distinction, the agony aunt is doing much more than simply naming the two categories. Rather, she is involved in a complex social act of allocating and distributing power, authority and legitimacy in relation to the two social categories that she invokes. This is also evident in the clause-complex relations involved here. Again, this is more than a simple matter of temporal or causal sequence *per se*.

The paratactic additive relation as construed by the conjunction *and* also implicates the interpersonal resources of modulation and modalization. These may be said to lie within the range specified by the meanings 'obligation/inclination' and 'prediction', as also indicated by the modal verb *will* in clauses B6a–b. The complex of meanings which results from the combined effect of these logico-semantic and interpersonal selections may be glossed as follows: The category 'a loving sensitive male who will take things gradually' presupposes socially constituted norms concerning who, in heterosexual relations, is responsible for leadership and initiative.

It may also be noted here that the embedded clause 'who will take things gradually', in its experiential role as a post classifier of the Head noun, presupposes a quality which is not admitted as negotiable in the exchange structure of the discourse. On the other hand, the young female is constituted as one who will follow this order of things as a

natural process of development without having any active responsibility in the incipient sexual relationship. Furthermore, the paratactic
conjunction *and* construes the relation between the two clauses in the
complex as one in which the young female's actions are consequent
on, rather than merely temporally sequential to, the actions of the
male.

This is also reflected in the two adverbial realizations of comment
adjuncts that are used to qualify the actions of the two participants.
The point here has to do with the differential ascription of
intentionality to the two categories of agent and, hence, the
differential allocation of responsibility. In both cases, the comment
adjuncts index a delimited domain of interpersonal validity relative to
which the clausally realized proposition is to be interpreted. Such a
validity domain is said to be indexically presupposed by the comment
adjunct. In the case of 'gradually', this functions to ascribe features of
intentionality and control to the male participant. This is also
supported by the experiential semantics of this clause, which realizes
the intentionally directed Actor-Process or transitive model. On the
other hand, the clause 'you will progress' realizes the Medium-Process
or ergative model of process instigation (Davidse 1991:65–71). The
comment adjunct 'naturally' presupposes a different domain of
validity in terms of which the (consequential) actions of the young
female are to be understood more in terms of liability rather than full
responsibility. The point is that the future-projected actions of the two
participant categories are explainable and interpretable with reference
to two different sets of intertextually retrievable norms, which are
themselves founded on social norms that regulate sexual relations.

It should be clear that the two comment adjuncts 'gradually' and
'naturally' are not value-neutral; rather, they have strong interpersonal force insofar as they serve to evaluate the actions of the
two participants in specific ways. Thus, we have in these two clauses
two different evaluations pertaining to the appropriate sexual
behaviour of male and female participants. It is as if the two clauses
realize or give voice to two distinct evaluations which are derivable
from two distinct intertextual thematic formations (ITFs) (Lemke
1983). What, then, is the relationship between the two ITFs? This is
where the relevance of the thematized circumstance of location
comes to the fore.

Experientially, the circumstance *In the right relationship* construes
a metaphorical location from which the two clauses are projected.
Importantly, it construes the relationship between the two ITFs from
a particular social viewpoint. In this sense, the projecting function of

the circumstance is metadiscursive and, hence, interpersonal. The lexical distinction between *gradually* and *naturally* may likewise suggest in this context a relationship of semantic contrast between [+INTENTIONAL] and [−INTENTIONAL]. As lexical items, abstracted from use, there is no fixed or necessary semantic relationship of this kind between them. Rather, there is no more than an abstract lexical taxonomic relationship between them (Lemke 1983:160–161). However, the differential ascription of agency to the two participants in their respective clauses, along with the consequential clause-complexing relation, suggest that it is reasonable to postulate a wider contrast between two distinct ITFs through which male and female sex roles are normatively construed. From the point of view of the text, the metadiscursive circumstance here serves to construe a relationship of complementarity between these two different construals of male and female sex roles. The point is that the metadiscourse actively construes this particular relationship between the two thematically distinct systems. There is nothing given about this relation. A different discourse, speaking from a different social viewpoint (e.g. feminist, poststructuralist) may construe the relationship between the two from a quite different axiological standpoint. Values are neither fixed nor given in linguistic forms but are constituted and reconstituted in the processes of discourse negotiation between agents.

Phase 6: clauses B7a–b

In the clause-complex B7a–b, the negotiation is very much centered on the intersubjective I–you axis where modal responsibilities are assigned to the participants in the interaction. In this case, the young female addressee is directly interpersonally engaged and directed to read the book *Will I Like It?* by Peter Mayle. This clause both constructs an implicit dialogical co-actional tie to Peter Mayle's book by suggesting that the reader respond to the proposition by performing the suggested course of action, and, implicitly, it also construes a co-thematic tie between the text of the agony aunt and that of the book on the basis of a presumed high degree of thematic alliance or complementarity between the two texts. This in turn suggests that the two texts can be read in terms of a common metadiscursive perspective which proposes a reading of their shared thematics from the perspective of a specific social viewpoint and its attendant values and norms. Thus, the young female writer of Text A is now seen as being projected beyond the text itself into the wider field of socio-sexual relations. This occurs on the basis of a specific heteroglossic alliance between the entextualized product of this particular encounter between young female writer and agony aunt and the still wider field of indexically presupposing and entailing links to other (co(en)textualizations – actional, thematic and axiological – that are invoked.

The clause–text homology: the synecdochic dimension

I have already noted that the clause is an interactive unit in an ongoing exchange of meaning (Halliday 1994 [1985]:Chapter 4). Thus, the enactment of a given speech function on the discourse stratum is always organized in terms of this dialogical negotiation of meanings. Synecdoche, as Burke (1969 [1945]:503) points out, represents one term in terms of another. These include part–whole, species–genus, signifier–signified, container–contained and effect–cause whereby the one term may be 'converted' or 'represented' in terms of the other. As Burke (1969 [1945]:508) puts it: 'All such conversions imply an integral relationship, a relationship of convertibility, between the two terms.' Along this additional dimension of the clause–text relationship, the mood selections identified above on the discourse stratum by metonymic reduction imply – or are convertible in terms of – a potential and hence anticipated dialogic response in relation to which their exchange structure is organized or 'represented'. Just as the independent clause enters into a dialogically coordinated exchange unit, minimally defined in terms of an adjacency pair comprising an INITIATING ACT and a RE-SPONDING ACT (Martin 1981:69), so, too, does it 'represent' the text or some phase of it as an exchange unit, in the sense that the two are internally synecdochic. The dialogic dimension of textual schematic structure elements has been explored, for example, in Adam (1982). Adam discusses the 'argumentative orientation' of narrative macro-propositions, utilizing the schematic structure discussed in Labov and Waletzky (1967). Adam argues that: 'A discourse is argumentative when it is oriented towards another person (individualised or not, actualised or not in the utterance).' However, his theoretical proposals are vitiated both by his use of a reductionist view of schematic structure as well as by the absence of any clear motivational criteria based on mood and other interpersonal systems. (See the preceding two sections of this chapter 'Concerning the metonymic' and 'Metaphoric dimensions.') The purpose of the present stage of the analysis is to specify the dialogic basis of each textual phase on the discourse stratum in terms of its speech function.

This entails its reciprocal relations with some explicit or implicit dialogical response. The analysis will proceed on the basis of the interrelated variables of mood, speech function, exchange unit and adjacency pair structure.

Along this dimension of the analysis, the sequence of speech function moves on the discourse stratum can be related to the exchange potential of a given speech function. This exchange potential can be expressed, by analogy, in terms of the notion of adjacency pair in conversation structure. Now, the text I am analysing is written rather than spoken and yet the question as to the nature of the explicit and implicit points of dialogic response which each macro-level dialogic move entails remains fundamental. This exchange potential has to do with both the indexically created and/or presupposed role relations between addresser and addressee and the power of linguistically mediated social acts to coordinate, order and define the scope of social actions and sequences of interaction (see Habermas 1984 [1981]:296). The coordinating power of linguistically mediated social acts and their potential for directing the actions of participants according to what Habermas (1984 [1981]:297) calls 'conventionally fixed obligations' is suggested in the following observation by Martin:

> From a discourse perspective, this allows us to interpret Questions as demands for modality and Statements as opportunities to modalise ... [...] ... As far as modulation is concerned, Offers express inclination (inviting obligation) whereas Commands assert obligations (inviting inclination) ... (Martin 1992:363)

Martin's proposals here suggest a framework for accounting for the ways in which addressers and addressees articulate and reciprocally accept or reject the validity claim of a speech act (Habermas 1984 [1981]:301) and direct their actions accordingly. Validity claims are articulated by both propositions and proposals and are, in the words of Habermas (1984 [1981]:301), 'internally connected with reasons and grounds' insofar as their 'conditions of acceptability' constitute part of the meaning of the speech function move (see also Hasan 1992).

The exchange potential of speech function moves on the discourse stratum and the dialogic processes which they define and coordinate can be characterized as follows for each discourse phase. The notational symbol ^ under the heading Dialogic Orientation in the analysis below designates the dependency relation between the two parts of the presupposed adjacency pair.[9]

DIALOGIC STRUCTURE OF TEXT AND RELATED SYSTEMS; STRATUM: DISCOURSE;
LOCI: SPEECH FUNCTION AND ADJACENCY PAIR

A/1a–2b
Speech Function: Statement = opportunity to modalize;
Type of Action: Confession/Dramaturgical;
Orientation to World: Subjective; express self; truthful revelation of
personal problems and inner 'self';
Dialogic Orientation: Make modalized claim about self ˆ Addressee
accepts (or not) the addresser's claim to tell truth;
Validity Claim: Truthfulness about 'inner' self; sincerity.

A/3a–e
Speech Function: Directive = assert obligation/invite inclination;
Question = demand for modality;
Type of Action: Seek addressee's modalization;
Orientation to World: Understanding self; social knowledge;
Dialogic Orientation: Seek addressee's modalization;
Validity Claim: Truthfulness; rightness.

B/1a–b
Speech Function: Statement = opportunity to modalize;
Type of Action: Norm conformative refusal to respond to A/2ii in
terms specified by first addresser;
Orientation to World: Moral-practical; addresser acknowledges the
addressee's exchange; Regulation and establishment of appropriate
expectations concerning interpersonal role relations and consequent
distribution of responsibilities;
Dialogic Orientation: Respond to and renegotiate client's request for
modalization; Incline addressee to accept and understand redefinition
of role relations and obligations these entail;
Validity Claim: Norm conformative; rightness of Agony Aunt's
definition of social roles of addresser and addressee, which are
brought into focus here;

B/2
Speech Function: Statement = opportunity to modalize;
Type of Action: Reason/Justification for refusal in B1a–b;
Orientation to World: Universalizing, gnomic truth;
Dialogic Orientation: Validation of prior refusal;
Validity Claim: Truth; rightness.

B/3a–b
Speech Function: Statement = opportunity to modalize;

Type of Action: Interpretation based on textual evidence;
Orientation to World: Evidential;
Dialogic Orientation: Take up and negotiation of A/1a–2b;
Validity Claim: Understanding.

B/4a–5d
Speech Function: Statement = opportunity to modalize;
Type of Action: Response to and negotiation of A/2a–b;
Orientation to World: Universalizing, gnomic truth; social norms;
Dialogic Orientation: Response to and negotiation of A/2a–b;
Validity Claim: Truthfulness; rightness.

B/6a–b
Speech Function: Statement = opportunity to modalize;
Type of Action: Prediction;
Orientation to World: Social; Universalizing;
Dialogic Orientation: Claim;
Validity Claim: Norm conformative.

B/7a–b
Speech Function: Directive = assert obligation/invite inclination;
Type of Action: Suggestion to Act;
Orientation to World: Strategic/instrumental; social;
Dialogic Orientation: Suggestion to Act ˆ Addressee can undertake (or not) prescribed course of action in social world;
Validity Claim: Effectiveness; rightness.

Notions like 'truth' and 'sincerity' as used in the above analysis are neither psychological nor linguistic notions. There are no lexico-grammatical realizations corresponding to these notions. Never-theless, the lexicogrammatical resources of transitivity are used to construe referent situations in ways that language users may deem to be truthful, sincere or otherwise (Hasan 1992:274–279). Nor are such notions descriptors of psychological states whereby a speaker commits him- or herself to the 'truthfulness' or 'sincerity' of a given assertion (Holiday 1988:89). That is, truth, sincerity, trust and so on, are not a matter of a proper matching of internal intentional state to speech act. In my view, following Holiday, the best solution to showing the relevance of these notions to interpersonal meaning lies in the notion of a semantics of moral necessity which regulates such exchanges between social actors. The genre conventions and practices that regulate the kinds of entextualized products that I have analysed in this chapter cannot therefore be reduced to the kinds of schematic structure analysis that have prevailed (Labov and

Waletzky 1967; Van Dijk 1979). The individual-centered and largely instrumental[10] models of action that such models underwrite are unable to account for the ways in which discoursing 'truthfully' and 'sincerely' depends on a principle of moral necessity which regulates linguistic exchanges between social agents (Holiday 1988:88–89). This means that there are socially shared and maintained moral norms which establish the conditions whereby utterances are construed as truthful, sincere, and so on. Furthermore, the very fact that interactants in discourse make judgments – both positive and negative – as to the truthfulness, sincerity, trustworthiness and so on, of their interlocutors constitutes an integral if largely tacit component of the meaning-making practices that regulate interpersonal exchange. The point is not simply whether a particular local referent situation is being referred to truthfully or not, but that the use of a particular language, along with its genre conventions, necessarily entails interpersonal judgments concerning the nature of the social and moral commitments that interactants implicitly enter into when they exchange linguistic meanings (Thibault 1992). That is, truth, sincerity, trust and so on, constitute the ethical grounds in relation to which the validity of specific exchanges may be referenced or grounded.

Thus, the contractual relation which frames the text and which is inherent in its interpersonal semantics means that the expectation on the part of the client that her fears and doubts can be allayed by the agony aunt leads to a relation of trust or confidence between the two. This relationship is also based on the satisfaction of the condition that the young female, in writing to the agony aunt, is speaking truthfully and sincerely about herself. This relation of 'fiduciary expectation' (Greimas 1983b:229–230) is, in this case, derived from the ritual constraints of the generic schema Letter to Agony Aunt^Reply to Letter, as well as from a whole cluster of associated meaning-making practices in other social domains. In this way, both interactants harbour expectations regulated by interpersonally binding principles of moral and semantic necessity as to the 'forms of life', in the Wittgensteinian parlance, which they share in a given 'language-game' and on which the social fabric – the de-linguistified lifeworld in the Habermassian terminology – that forms the taken-for-granted backdrop to interpersonal exchange is constituted (Holiday 1988:93).

Rosalind Coward discusses this injunction to speak out and confess through the personal columns in the following terms: 'This injunction to confide and tell all, to talk it through calmly, is, after all, only an extension of the activity of the problem pages themselves'

(1984:135). The problem pages thus constitute the optimum generic environment for the facilitation of this public act of confession, which is also seen as an expression of one's personal freedom. The implicit contractual nature of the exchange is regulated by a set of generic conventions and expectations concerning the interpersonal relations between agony aunts, their clients and readers. It is implicit in the sense that it occurs at a higher order of logical typing (Bateson 1973:153) than the textual instance which it frames. In Bateson's terms, it is a metacommunicative frame which enables the Global Modal Program of the text to be enacted according to the generic conventions (cf. socio-discursive practices) associated with the writing to and receiving advice from the Agony Aunts.[11] The fiduciary contract which frames the text has a quasi-juridical status insofar as it fixes norms and meanings as organized interactional networks within which subjects are positioned as embodied participants whose modalized values, passions and knowledges and their negotiation are the causes and not simply the consequences of entextualized social work.

The ironic dimension: the Global Modal Program

Burke's fourth 'master trope' is that of irony, which is characterized by dialectic. 'Irony', Burke (1969 [1945]:512) writes,

> arises when one tries, by the interaction of terms upon one another to produce a development which uses all the terms. Hence, from the standpoint of this total form (this 'perspective of perspectives'), none of the participating 'sub-perspectives' can be treated as precisely right or wrong.

The interaction of the metonymic, metaphoric, and synecdochic dimensions of our analysis produces a further dialectical development which yields the concept of the Global Modal Program of the text. The interpersonal meaning of the text, as seen from the point of view of its organization on the discourse stratum, is generated by interrelated selections in mood, modality, modulation, interpersonal lexis and turn-taking on the lexicogrammatical stratum (see the three preceding sections of this chapter). The organization of these meaning selections on the discourse stratum shows that there is a systematic relationship between the actional, attitudinal, axiological and dialogic components which realize the Global Modal Program of texts.

The notion of the Global Modal Program also entails a further development of the prevailing definitions of interpersonal meaning in the systemic-functional framework. Typically, interpersonal meaning is defined in terms such as the 'interaction between speaker and listener', or 'the resources for interacting with the listener by establishing and maintaining an ongoing exchange with him'. In my view, the further development that I have mentioned above means that we need to give more centrality in our definition of interpersonal meanings to the organization of actions, passions and agents in occasions of discourse and the processes of entextualization associated with these. The (inter)actional dimension of the text and attitudinal/axiological/affective meanings are necessarily interrelated for, as Kenneth Burke (1969 [1945]:459) points out, an attitude is an 'incipient act', thereby providing the motivation for an act. The prosodic, field-like character of interpersonal meanings and the global enchaining and interweaving of these across texts raises some fundamental questions that suggest the possibility of a fruitful meeting between the semiotics of the passions proposed by Greimas and Fontanille (1991; see also Fabbri 1998:39–48) and systemic-functional theory:

> Les passions apparaissent dans le discours comme porteuses d'effets de sens très particuliers; il se dégage comme une senteur équivoque, difficile à déterminer. L'interprétation qu'en a retenue la sémiotique est que ce parfum spécifique émane de l'organisation discursive des structures modales. En passant d'une métaphore à une autre, on pourrait dire que cet effet de sens provient d'un certain arrangement moléculaire: n'étant la propriété d'aucune molécule en particulier, il résulte de leur disposition d'ensemble. Une première constatation s'impose: la sensibilisation passionnelle du discours et sa modalisation narrative sont co-occurrentes, ne se comprennent pas l'une sans l'autre, et sont pourtant autonomes, soumises probablement, en partie du moins, à des logiques différentes. (Greimas and Fontanille 1991:21)

> (The passions appear in discourse as bearers of very particular effects of meaning; it emanates like an equivocal scent, difficult to determine. The interpretation maintained by semiotics is that this particular perfume emanates from the discursive organization of the modal structures. To pass from one metaphor to another, it could be said that this meaning effect is due to a certain molecular arrangement: not being the property of any one molecule in particular, it results from their arrangement as a whole. A first observation is necessary: the passional sensibilization of discourse

and its narrative modalization are concurrent, one cannot be understood without the other, and yet they are autonomous, probably subjected, at least in part, to different logics.)

The conjoint text comprised of the Letter to Agony Aunt^Agony Aunt's Reply is a semiotic artifact in which is implicated a contract that may be glossed as follows: 'Speak out sincerely and truthfully about your sexual problems and in exchange I will insert you into the prevailing heterosexual norms.' The textual artifact is an extra-somatic resource (Latour 1986:278) embedded in still wider networks of agents and actions and whose performance or entextualized uptake constitutes the means whereby entire systems of social actors, their artifacts and associated technologies come into play to create the social. In the first instance, the text under analysis is concerned with an entextualized interactional structure between the two agents – young female and agony aunt – which is situated on the cognitive dimension. That is, the text is concerned with the manipulation and transformation of KNOWLEDGE rather than with the performance of ACTION.

Thus, the girl calls on the agony aunt to modalize her; the agony aunt responds by modalizing her as a Knowing Subject rather than, for example, as a Doing Subject. This rests on the further premise that modal competences concerned with KNOWLEDGE are logically prior to the realization of a given social action or performance. The textual encounter between the two agents can be described as the manifestation of what Greimas and Fontanille (1991:57) call an 'actualised competence' prior to its realization as social action or performance. That is, the end result of the entextualized modal transformation that takes place is that the girl is provided with the appropriate knowledge on which is premised the potentiality for appropriate courses of action in the social world. The acceptance of the contract and the ensuing modality of 'knowing what/how to do' is integrated into a prior modal program of 'wanting to know' which, on the part of the girl, can be said to be the initial motivation for writing her letter and which is both prior to and implicit in the textual artifact that appears in *Cleo* magazine.

The personal deictics such as English 'I' and 'you' are more than elementary shifters that refer to a given individual as occupying the addresser or addressee roles on some contingent occasion of discourse (Silverstein and Urban 1996:16). Thus, the personal deictics are referents which instantiate the experiential class that is established by the particular personal pronoun – e.g. 'I', 'you', and so on – in the

Head of the nominal group. It is in this sense that the personal deictics have a 'metapragmatic deictic backing', as Silverstein and Urban put it. However, this still leaves open the question as to how a given individual comes to 'occupy' a particular interactional role and whether such roles are always the same for different classes of individuals both in relation to historical-biographical time as well as in relation to the specific field of interdiscursive relations in which the I–you relation is situated. It is the metapragmatic backing provided by the experiential class category denoted as 'first' and 'second person' which leads to the 'essential categories denoted as "first" and "second person"' (Silverstein and Urban 1996:16). By the same token, these same personal deictics are, again in the words of Silverstein and Urban, 'metapragmatic labels ... that denote the achievement of such role-category inhabitance as a result of entextualizing processes themselves' (1996:6).

In terms of personal deixis, the emphasis in the above analysis on the complex negotiations that take place between interpersonalized and ideationalized discursive sources shows that a simple distinction between addresser ('I') and addressee ('you') is not adequate. The constant dialectic between metadiscursive role category and entextualization processes highlights the need for an analytically more complex picture. Following a suggestion in Irvine (1996:138–139), we can as a first approximation distinguish between the following classification of speech roles as a means of showing the ways in which responsibility is distributed over a variety of discursively implicated voices and sources: the actual writer of the letter(s), or the Transmitter; the Sponsor who makes the publication of the overall entextualized event possible (i.e. *Cleo* magazine); the Formulator (e.g. an editor), who is responsible for the final wording of the text; and the Source in the form of usually implicit ideationalized expert discourses and their intertexts. On the reception end, there is the Recipient, i.e. the second person participant ('you'), to whom the text is, in the first instance, directed; secondly, there is also the wider Audience in the form of the readership of *Cleo* magazine; and thirdly we can also distinguish the Target, e.g. 'a loving sensitive male', as a further category of ideationalized participant, in the form of some kind of 'off-stage' overhearer, to whom the text or some part of it is indirectly addressed.

At the level of the Global Modal Program, there are, initially, two modalized subjects: (1) the girl, corresponding to the subject-of-being and Transmitter of Text A; and (2) the agony aunt, corresponding to the subject-of-doing and Transmitter of Text B. These two terms are borrowed from Greimas (1983b:228) and will be reconstituted within the present perspective in the discussion which follows. The basic modal program consists in the attribution by the Subject of Doing, S_1 of the object of value – initially defined by the girl in Text A in the complex *some idea* ... (clauses A3b–e) – to the Subject of Being, S_2. In the clause-complex A3a–e, the girl delegates to the agony aunt the modal responsibility for bringing about the desired modal transformation. She does so by seeking to mobilize the agony aunt's knowledge and expertise concerning sexual relations. Importantly, the girl's 'wanting to know' presupposes a prior 'wanting to be' in the sense that she positively identifies with the future-projected object of value as realized in clauses A3b–e. That is, she 'wants to be brave enough to try sexual intercourse', though this is not *explicitly* asserted in the text.

In particular, the locution 'when I finally share my body with another' entails a positive re-evaluation of the previously mentioned 'sexual intercourse' which had occurred in the axiological environment of 'scared' and 'never brave enough'. In other words, the previously dysphoric conception is here re-evaluated in terms of a euphoric conception in which the Subject of Being modally invests. The subsequent attainment of this by the Subject of Being defines the further modal development of the text as a trajectory which is oriented towards the definition and valorization of a cognitive competence with which the girl is modally conjoined. Overall, this means that the girl's initial, negatively evaluated modal status is transformed into a qualitatively different and positively evaluated status at the conclusion of this entextualized transaction between her and the agony aunt.

The female addresser in Text A – the subject-of-being – is thus initially positioned in terms of the following sets of modalized oppositions:

(1) /disjunction/ vs. /conjunction/: the subject-of-being is not conjoined to the desired object of value, and yet she desires that the agony aunt – the subject-of-doing – bring about this conjunction (Greimas 1983c);

(2) /disequilibrium/ vs. /equilibrium/: the initial emotional conflict of the subject-of-being is articulated in terms of feelings ('scared', 'never brave') as attributes of the individual which are 'discovered' and identified during the confessional process in A1a–2b. The latter is itself a necessary stage prior to the subsequent adjustment of the subject to the prevailing male order in relation to which this conflict is articulated;

3. /doubt/ vs. /belief/: the subject-of-state exists in a state of doubt or incertitude which motivates the interrogative proposition in A3a–e.

We can now see how the Global Modal Program as so far defined can be subclassified into the following modal relations between subjects. Following Greimas, S_1 designates the subject-of-being; S_2 the subject-of-doing, as in the following act of modalization: S_1 DESIRE $[S_2 \rightarrow (S_1 \cap O]$, where S_1 desires S_2 to conjoin S_1 with the object-of-value, O. Here, the object of value is understood to correspond in the first instance to the knowledge sought in A3a–e, the restoration of a state of belief or certitude, and the resolution of emotional conflict.

A further modalized relation expresses S_1's trust in the expectation that she imposes on S_2: S_1 EXPECT $[S_2$ OBLIGE $(S_1 \cap O]$, where S_1 expects S_2 is obliged to act in order to bring about the desired state of affairs.

The basic program calls, then, for the entextualization of a production program whereby the object of value is produced and modally conjoined to the girl in her role as the Subject of Being, S_1. In the present case, the desired object of value corresponds to an increase in knowledge concerning sexual relationships, accompanied by a euphoric sensation of diminished fear and anxiety about her first sexual experience. Thus, the Subject of Being modally invests value in a complex discursive object, the construction of which requires the execution of a set of entextualized subprograms of interpretation and explanation, which culminate in the production of the desired object of value (see below). The conjoining of S_1 to this discursive object re-modalizes her as being in possession of knowledge which she previously lacked.

Whereas, on the one hand, these roles – viz. Subject of Being/Transmitter and Subject of Doing/Transmitter – are constrained by specific genre conventions, the emergent and creative possibilities of specific textual instantiations additionally mean that interpersonal roles and their associated norms are not fixed and static (Silverstein and Urban 1996:8). Rather, their negotiation in discourse means that the roles themselves can be reconstituted in and through the ways in which texts are taken up and recontextualized in the system of social heteroglossia of a given discourse community, itself arising from particular historically contingent conjunctions of resources and practices. Inasmuch as social heteroglossia always involves questions concerning the diversity of social values, viewpoints and interests that are variably aligned and/or in conflict in a given society, it is fundamentally a question of the politics of discursive practice. To the extent that the generic conventions of writing to and receiving advice from the problem pages involve an understanding of male and female sexual relations in terms of individual psychology and the emotional life of the couple, the locus of modalized control and responsibility will be either individual or therapeutic. If, on the other hand, these same concepts are heteroglossically realigned as part of a wider process of political understanding, then the locus of control and responsibility also shifts in relation to broader questions of political control and social struggle.

The production program and its entextualization also entails a temporal perspective. The acquisition of the desired modal competence is a temporal process of narrativization in which S_1 is modally transformed from one modal state to another. The entextualizing procedures at work produce an effect of narrativization insofar as different temporal scales in the biography of the girl are condensed and the various stages in the modal transformation of the Subject of Being are represented as successive textual differences. That is, the text indexes the differences between successive modal states – agents and their associated passions – as occurring within a specific temporal perspective. This effect of temporal condensation and its relationship to the modal transformations which are enacted may be schematized with reference to Text A as in Figure 3.7. The text is a program for the modalized construction of both discursive subjects *and* objects. The production program that is transacted in the conjoint A–B text may be schematized as follows:

Text A
(1) The girl's situating of herself in a dysphoric space (anxiety, displeasure) which links past to present in clauses A1a to 2b;

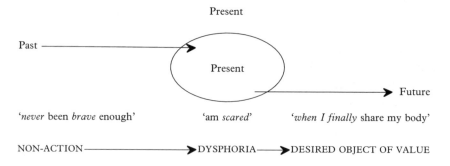

Figure 3.7 Temporal condensation and its modalization in Text A

(2) The delegating of the agony aunt as the agent who will be responsible for instigating the desired modal transformation in clause A3a;

(3) The opposing of the initial state of dysphoria to a future-projected state of euphoria in the form of the desired object of value in clauses A3b–e;

Text B

(4) The agony aunt's refusal to meet the girl's request in the terms specified and her renegotiation of and redefinition of the object of value in clauses B1a–b;

(5) The agony aunt provides a reason in the form of a general principle for her refusal (clause B2);

(6) The agony aunt's evidential interpretation of the girl's lack of readiness to enter into a sexual relationship (clauses B3a–c);

(7) The agony aunt's reevaluation of the girl's modal stance ('never been brave' → 'nothing brave') and the installation of a tensive orientation to a new object of value ('trying sexual intercourse' → 'more courage to wait') in clauses B4a–b/5a–d;

(8) The installation and definition of the newly appraised object of value and the modal conjunction of the girl with this in clauses B6a–b so as to define a future-projected euphoric state;

(9) The qualifying of the girl as being in possession of an actualized modal competence in the form of her increased knowledge along with her ability to further increase this through the undertaking of a particular recommended course of action (clauses A7a–b).

Earlier systemic-functional analysis of interpersonal meaning in discourse (Lemke 1988, 1990b:446–450; Thibault 1989, 1991:288–294) has shown that axiological orientations towards thematic items are constructed by specific alignments of chains of positively and negatively valued elements in texts. These entail complex structurations of axiological and affective meanings in texts. In the present text, we see how agents are modalized according to their mode of being (Greimas and Fontanille 1991:58). In this text, this value chain and its axiological transformation (re-evaluation) can be seen in the following progression of molecular elements:

MODAL DISPOSITION	+ ACTION
very *scared* (A1b)	–
never been *brave* enough	to try sexual intercourse (A2a–b)
when I *finally*	share my body with another (A3e)

I *can't* tell you	how you'll feel about your first experience of intercourse (B1a–b)
how *ready*	you are emotionally for the experience, etc. (B2a–b)
you are (*not* yet) *ready*	to proceed to a more intense sexual relationship (B3a–c)
nothing brave	about trying sex (B4a–b)
often more *courage*	to wait until you know the time is right for you (B5a–d)
a loving sensitive male *will*	take things gradually (B6a)
you *will*	progress naturally (B6b)
you *may care*	to take a look at the book *Will I Like It?* ... (B7a–b)

In each case, the items in italic type illustrate the progression of a value chain whereby the first component of the two-part DISPOSITION + ACTION structure indicates a specific dispositional and axiological stance on the action denoted by the mainly non-finite clauses in the second part of the overall structure. For this reason, these can be said to have a modality of *irrealis* by virtue of their non-actual (non-finite) status. The non-finite clauses are inherently without tense and modality and are not for this reason grounded in the exchange structure of the clauses or clause-complexes in which they occur. The modalized adjective or noun in the first part of the structure holds these ungrounded actions in its scope and inter-personally modifies them in the way shown.

The attributive clauses A1a–b to A2a–b function to conjoin the girl to a series of modalized attributes which have more to do with 'states of the soul' (Greimas and Fontanille 1991:59) than with states of affairs in the external world. In so conjoining herself to a series of relational predications such as 'very scared' 'not brave', and so on, the girl modally constitutes herself as being in a complex modal state of 'wanting not to be' with respect to the hypothetical conjunction with the initially negatively valued and feared anti-object 'sexual inter-course'. Modalized Attributes such as 'scared' and 'brave' designate, in a lexically highly condensed way, complex modal dispositions or tendencies to act. Thus, the Attribute 'scared' has to do with a passive disposition or a liability whereby the girl, in this case, fails to acquire the modalized status of an agent. She is blocked or inhibited in a state of being not conducive to action or change. On the other hand, the modalized Attribute 'brave' semantically entails not only an active tendency to act, but also a certain generosity and willingness to do so.

This modal stance on the part of the girl also implies a complex modal stance of 'wanting not to be' with respect to the non-finite clause that realizes the action 'try sexual intercourse' in A2a–b. This modal stance implies, in its turn, an imaginary – i.e. future projected and modally ungrounded – though feared ('scared') conjunction with the negatively valued object 'sexual intercourse', as evidenced by the *irrealis* modality of the non-finite clause. That is, there is implied here a dysphoric, though merely hypothetical, rather than euphoric image of the subject who 'tries sexual intercourse'.

Moreover, the initial 'wanting not to do' presupposes a realized state which has been overdetermined by a prospective conviction which the girl projects from her initial state of dysphoria into an imagined future state of being. Thus, this first phase defines the modalized *being* of the girl rather than any specific modal competence concerned with knowing, doing and so on. The subsequent transformation of this modalized state of being can only take place through the intermediary role of 'wanting to be' as enabled by the desired object of value – the attainment of the desired knowledge – and/or by the mediation of a second agent – in this case, the agony aunt. The remaining items in the above value chain demonstrate the re-evaluation which the agony aunt in her role as Subject of Doing undertakes. The modal adjunct *finally* in clause A3e, on the other hand, expresses a semantically highly condensed modal structure (disposition) which I shall gloss as WANT TO DO + CAN'T DO with respect to the action referred to on the left. This modal disposition is a consequence of the passive disposition that is expressed by 'scared' and 'not brave'. That is, the girl lacks the necessary dispositional structure for acting as a true agent.

The agony aunt's reply in Text B puts into operation a process of what Greimas and Fontanille (1991:155) refer to as 'sensibilisation'. On the basis of presupposed dispositions, 'sensibilisation' is 'the operation by which the discursive subject is transformed into a suffering, feeling, reacting, moved subject' (1991:170). This definition helps us to clarify the sense of the agony aunt's refusal, so to speak, to answer the girl's question in the terms initially sought. Thus, the modality *can't* in B2a can be semantically unpacked to mean as follows: 'you have to be animated by your own passions; I can only sensibilise you as the first phase in the eventual realising of your own passions'. The further development of the value chain illustrated above demonstrates precisely this modal transformation, as I shall show in the following paragraphs.

The two succeeding elements in the chain are concerned with the modal region of 'readiness'. 'Readiness' lies on the low end of the INCLINATION scale. Semantically, the notion of readiness means that an agent is in possession of the requisite tendencies, powers or competences for the realization of different categories of social action or performance. The agony aunt infers in B3a–b/4a–b that the girl lacks the requisite 'emotional readiness', which is a necessary prerequisite to the removal of the dispositional liabilities which thus far have prevented her from participating in a sexual relationship.

The further development of this process of modal sensibilization occurs by reversing the girl's evaluation of the non-finite clause, as shown by the shift to 'nothing brave' in the agony aunt's discourse. A second step in this overall process is shown by the substitution of 'brave' with 'courage' and the replacement of the previous non-finite elements with a new thematic item whereby the desired object of value is shifted from 'trying sex' to 'waiting until the time is right for you'. In so doing, the agony aunt introduces both a new, positive affective/axiological stance (*courage*), a new thematics whereby the object of value is defined, as well as a new temporal aspectualization of the modalized relationship between passion (*courage*) and act (*waiting* . . .). In this way, the agony aunt makes the girl aware of the fact that the 'courage to wait' is an acquired and positively valued dispositional tendency which will, at the appropriate time, enable her to release the restraint and exercise her own modalized powers to act.

The agony aunt deploys her powers of transformation by installing structures of manipulation whereby the Subject of Being is re-modalized as to her 'readiness' for a sexual relationship. This entails a correspondence between: (1) the entextualized temporal processes and the modal transformation from 'not ready' to 'ready' and (2) the remodalizing of 'never been brave enough' to 'more courage to wait until you know the time is right for you'.

In B6a–b, the two uses of *will* in relation to 'a loving sensitive male' and 'you' in these two clauses position these participants as having the actualized (not realized) competences or tendencies specified in the Action component of the two-part DISPOSITION + ACTION structure. In this case, these correspond to the Residues of these two clauses. For the first time in the modal transformation under examination here, the ACTION component is realized in a sequence of finite clauses. Here we see that the overall modal prosody that this chain exemplifies in the DISPOSITION + ACTION structure reaches a peak with a clustering of finite clauses which realize the modal region INCLINATION in the form of the modal *will* (B6a–b) and the modalized projecting mental process of affection *may care*

(B7a). That is, the text reaches its interpersonal peak when the girl is modally grounded in a semantic environment of active tendencies, as a prerequisite to the release of these in the social world as agentive acts beyond this entextualized encounter. Significantly, all three expressions of INCLINATION fall within the median, as distinct from the high or low, range. This is coherent with the overall process of sensibilization that this value prosody exemplifies. Rather than being, for example, compelled to act, the modal drift of sensibilization here works to transform the girl from a non-agent who was initially blocked by passive dispositions to an agent in possession of the positively defined emotional dispositions that will incline her to act in 'the right moment'.

The Global Modal Program is, then, a way of talking about the dynamic modal operations whereby social agents and agencies, through their entextualizing operations, act on, mediate and delegate powers, passions and knowledges to the indexically presupposed and/ or created participants in discourse practices. It shows that propositions and proposals, derived from the mood component in the grammar, necessarily implicate attitudes, values, beliefs and passions, as well as socially coordinated actions and dialogic orientations. The integration of these diverse regions of interpersonal meaning in the notion of the Global Modal Program thus draws attention to the metacommunicative dimension of interpersonal meaning. This can help us to understand the constantly shifting boundaries between propositions and proposals and values, which Bateson (1987 [1951]:176–183) has discussed in terms of the 'report' and 'command' dimensions of every act of communication. This dual aspect of communication can never be resolved at the formal syntactic level but only at some higher-order or metacommunicative level. To quote Bateson:

> We shall describe as 'metacommunication' all exchanged cues and propositions about (a) codification and (b) relationship between the communicators. We shall assume that a majority of propositions about codification are also implicit or explicit propositions about relationship and vice versa, so that no sharp line can be drawn between these two sorts of metacommunication. Moreover, we shall expect to find that the qualities and characteristics of metacommunication between persons will depend upon the qualities and degree of their mutual awareness of each other's perception. (Bateson 1987 [1951]:209–210)

Interpersonal meanings are, then, metacommunicative along both of the dimensions discussed by Bateson. They talk about both the propositional meaning of the utterance and the interpersonal relations between the interactants in ways which frequently leave ambiguous the boundary between propositions and proposals and the implicit validity claims which these entail. This functional ambiguity is systematic in the metafunctional organization of language in the sense that a given linguistic form realizes a functional plurality of interacting subcomponents, any aspect of which may be selectively foregrounded and negotiated on a given occasion of discourse. This selective awareness of linguistic form and function is dependent on which metadiscursive resources and strategies are deployed, how, when and by whom. In other words, it shows that the writing, reading and analysing of texts is about the possibilities of textual meanings and readerships rather than the recuperation of a positive textual meaning (see also Threadgold 1997:376).

The injunction to speak out about one's own sexuality and feelings effectively binds both agony aunt and client to a dynamic interplay of social and linguistic practices whose function is to produce 'self-regulated, rational and autonomous subjects' (Walkerdine 1985:212). The generic structure of the text is the social site where the injunction to speak out acts as the facilitator of one's 'natural' impulse to use language as an expression of one's personal experience, rather than as a site of social and political intervention (Walkerdine 1985:212). Thus, the generic structure here fulfils a covert regulatory function. The exhortation to speak out accordingly prescribes limits within which the subjects involved can act and speak. These limits, as prescribed by the institutionalized genre, take the 'spontaneous', natural confessional mode as the norm against which 'an absence of language and of reason can be nothing but a pathology' (Walkerdine 1985:212). Thus, the generic schema Letter to Agony Aunt^Reply to Letter is a socially symbolic act which works to recontain any expression of power and conflict within the confines of one's individual needs or feelings, i.e. to shift it away from the domain of the social and the political 'back to the couple with all the misunderstandings and irrationality filtered out' (Coward 1984:142).

Conclusion

Halliday's proposals concerning the clause–text relationship show that texts, like clauses, are metafunctionally organized. (See the section entitled 'Some analytical preliminaries' pp. 58–60.) There are regularities in the co-patterning, structuring and distribution of selections in all four metafunctions which provide a basis for the metafunctional analysis of texts on both the lexicogrammatical and discourse strata. The above analysis shows that on the discourse stratum and the distinct phases which enact it there are regularities and systematicities in the realization, distribution and co-patterning of interpersonal meaning selections that cannot simply be marginalized as epiphenomenal additions to clausally realized grammatical forms, conceived entirely in constituency terms, along with their analogous notions of text-structure. Textuality thus encompasses interclausal and intersentential interactions of selections in the interpersonal systems of mood, modality and modulation, person deixis, interpersonal lexis and so on, which contribute to the construction of more global interpersonal discourse formations. My attempt to project these regularities on to the discourse stratum is intended to show that these co-patternings and distributions of interpersonal selections provide important insights into the functional organization of texts as modes of social interaction and axiological/affective orientation. This is, after all, the central task of a truly semiotically informed account of the multifunctional relations between linguistic forms and their contexts of use.

Furthermore, these co-patterned interpersonal selections are not organized at either the clausal or the textual levels on the basis of a constituent structure hierarchy. Interpersonal meaning selections are realized as grammatical and semantic prosodies which are interwoven throughout selections from the other metafunctions in cumulative, field-like structures whose semantic scope often extends beyond the particular segment in which they occur (see also Poynton 1988). Halliday's (1979) adaptation of Pike's (1971:510–513) trimodal perspective on language as particle, wave and field shows that the prosodic, field-like interweaving of interpersonal selections can be viewed in terms similar to Pike's (1971:511) manifestation mode. This emphasizes the dynamic, processual and transformative dimensions of interpersonal prosodies, which calibrate with the thematic development of the text, or 'what is said' (see the first section of this chapter). The trimodal perspective on language as particle, wave and field recognizes that there is no hierarchically privileged functional organization or *a priori* essence to which linguistic and textual forms are reducible. Rather, both clause and text are the simultaneous products and processes of the ways in which selections from all four metafunctions are systematically and simultaneously configured as distinctive structural realizations within the same linguistic or other semiotic form.

The four dimensions of the present analysis that I have adapted from Kenneth Burke provide a tool kit for further developing Halliday's insights concerning the metonymic and metaphoric nature of the links between clause and text. These help to show how the analysis of co-patterned lexicogrammatical selections from the interpersonal metafunction and their instantiations in discourse can provide us with rich insights into the social presuppositions and entailments of linguistic forms in their contexts of situation and contexts of culture. The metonymic dimension illustrates the way in which interclausal and intraclausal relations are reducible to and hence constrained by a given reductionist account. The metaphoric dimension points to the internally cohesive nature of discourse, whereby foregrounded selections and co-patternings from all four metafunctions demonstrate that language is, in part, constitutive of its own context. This does not mean that context is automatically read off from textual co-patternings of linguistic forms. Rather, the forms provide differentially positioned agents with variably inter-pretable, if contextually constrained, cues as to which contextualizing relations are relevant, how, and why (Gumperz 1992). This is so in the sense that lexicogrammatical forms co-vary with other discourse level and (con)textual features. The semantics of the text is not simply another plane or level of realization, 'above' the lexicogram-matical stratum. Rather, the selective attending to 'automatized' or 'de-automatized' textual patterns of use of the lexicogrammatical resources functionally constrains lexicogrammatical forms by pro-jecting on to them a discourse level semantic substrate, itself a metaphor of the particular textual patterns which are foregrounded and whose semantics these foregrounded patterns serve to frame. This suggests the need for both a clause-level semantics of lexicogrammatical forms, functionally defined in local terms as a 'meaning potential', and a discourse-level semantics of the thematic and interpersonal formations (see the Global Modal Program) which are globally assembled, co-patterned and instantiated within texts as well as in and through entire intertextual systems.

Those theories of text which are based entirely on the metonymic dimension will find this point difficult to grasp, thereby finding it necessary to postulate global content-schemata, text-grammars, and so on, conceptualized by analogy to the clause, but with no clear relation either to the linguistic system or to the discourse formations which are constructed through its systemic resources. This is the problem with the text-as-supersentence type of approach. These have two principal drawbacks for an adequate understanding of textuality: (a) the text is conceptualized, by analogy, in terms of purely sentence-internal semantic relations (e.g. textual macro-propositions of the kind proposed by van Dijk); (b) the text is conceptualized in terms of an *ad hoc* situationally based pragmatics of the utterance, derived from the literalization of certain classes of explicit performative verbs (Silverstein 1985:208). This exemplifies the problems of a purely top-down conception of text, as in many cognitive psychological models of text-processing and text-understanding. Thus, the literalization of the exclusively metonymic dimension results in a purely derivable progression of schematic structure elements according to some normative schema of cognitive (or other) development. This process of literalization, along with the exclusion of the metaphoric dimension, means that textuality gets talked about in terms of a set of initial schema and the operation of system invariants such that the developmental stages follow one another in a determinate sequence. It amounts to what van den Daele calls 'derivable change':

> Derivable change implies common items in a state A and a state B which serve as 'continuity' components in transformation. Continuity components are identity elements which provide a common substrate to change. (van den Daele 1976:71)

Those who literalize the metonymic dimension presume that categories derived metonymically (by reduction) from clause grammar provide such a common substrate. This may be so within limits for the experiential aspect of this relation. Here we see that the various stages of some experiential sequence imply a derivable progression of continuity elements, which may occur at the same level of analysis, or on higher or lower levels. Thus, the metonymic dimension implies either the subordination or emergence of categories, depending on which direction one goes in. The movement from clause to text entails that the feature in the text is subordinated or reduced to a determinate feature of the clause. Contrariwise, the obverse movement entails that the feature in the clause is de-subordinated while the feature in the text is subordinated. The restrictive top-down criteria critiqued here remain descriptive rather than productive because they fail to account for the patterns of use and the modes of deployment of the lexicogrammatical resources of the linguistic system. Those who have recourse to such criteria entirely miss the point that textuality is a consequence of the assembling of many locally functioning clause-internal relations and their interclausal linkages. The literalization of the metonymic dimension leaves us with a reductive view of text as no more than the an epiphenomenal global consequence of the successive sub-ordination of the linguistic system to higher-order schemata which are derived through the integration of the lexicogrammatical stratum to pre-given top-down interpretative schemas.

Different phases of discursive activity involve differences in both the kind and degree of the automatization (see indexical presupposi-tion) and/or de-automatization (see indexical creativity) of the relations between linguistic forms and their contexts of situation. To quote Halliday:

> The term 'de-automatization', though cumbersome, is more apt than 'foregrounding', since what is in question is not simply prominence but rather the partial freeing of the lower level systems from the control of the semantics so that they become domains of choice in their own right. In terms of systemic theory, the de-automatization of grammar means that grammatical choices are not simply determined from above: there is selection as well as pre-selection. Hence the wording becomes a quasi-semiotic mode through which the meanings of the work can be projected. (Halliday 1982:136)

Halliday's remarks suggest two distinct but related questions which need to be posed in connection with the development of a semiotically informed text semantics. First, how do automatized or de-automatized instances enact situationally specific, socially recog-nizable actions and action sequences? Secondly, to what extent is textuality a consequence of the discourse-level organization of text-internal lexicogrammatical relations, as derived from all four metafunctions?

The first question requires a systematic analysis of both lexicogrammatical forms and their functionally significant pattern-ings in discourse. Only in this way can a semiotics of texts relate distinct phases of discourse activity to the level of social interaction. The second question requires that we avoid the pitfalls of all those text-grammars which take as their starting point global or macro-level content-schemata, not related to lexicogrammatical patterns of realization, except, perhaps, at the level of certain obvious lexicalized referential or performative meanings in the clause.

The clause–text homology can help us better to understand the metafunctional unity and the partial formal overlap of clause-level and discourse-level functions and relations. In the above analysis, the distribution and co-patterning of interpersonal selections in mood, modality, modulation and related features, interclausally related, illustrates the pervasive indexical character of discourse. The interaction of the four dimensions of our analysis shows, albeit partially, how particular kinds of social actions and their entextualizations are framed and enacted by distinct phases of discursive activity, which have specific presupposed and/or entailed social and interpersonal consequences.

Appendix 1: Mood analysis of clause-level selections in Texts A and B

1a	I	am		a 17-year-old virgin
	Subject	Finite: Tense	Predicator	Complement
	Mood: Declarative		Residue	
	Proposition			

1b	Subject Ellipsis ('I')	am		very scared
	Subject	Finite: Tense	Predicator	Complement
	Mood: Declarative		Residue	
	Proposition			

2a–b	I	have	never	been	brave enough to try sexual intercourse
	Subject	Finite: Tense	Polarity: Negative; Modality: Usuality	Predicator	Complement
	Mood: Declarative			Residue	
	Proposition				

3a–e	Could	you	please	give	me	some idea as to how I will feel, what will happen, and what to expect when I finally share my body with another?
	Finite: Tense; Modality	Subject	Modal adjunct	Predicator	Complement	Complement
	Mood: Polar interrogative			Residue		
				Proposition		

B1a–b	I	can't	tell	you	how you'll feel about your first experience of intercourse
	Subject	Finite: Modality; Polarity	Predicator	Complement	
	Mood: Declarative			Residue	
	Projecting clause				Projected clause
	Proposition				

B2

So much	depends on	how ready you are emotionally for the experience, and the type of relationship you have with your partner
Subject	Finite: Tense	Predicator	Complement
Mood: Declarative		Residue	
Proposition			

B3a–c

From the sound of things	you	have	not	yet	been	in a situation where …
Adjunct: Modal scopal relationship	Subject	Finite: Tense	Polarity: Negative	Mood adjunct	Predicator	Adjunct
	Mood: Declarative				Residue	
Proposition						

B4a–b

There	is		nothing brave about trying sex
Subject	Finite: Tense	Predicator	Complement
Mood: Declarative		Residue	
Proposition			

B5a–d	it	often	takes		more courage to wait until you know the time is right for you
	Subject	Modal Adjunct	Finite: Tense	Predicator	Complement
	Mood: Declarative			Residue	
		Proposition			

B6a	In the right relationship,	a loving sensitive male	will	take	things	gradually
	Adjunct: Modal scopal relationship	Subject	Finite: Tense; Modality	Predicator	Complement	Adjunct
		Mood: Declarative		Residue		
		Proposition				

B6b	you	will	progress	naturally
	Subject	Finite: Tense; Modality	Predicator	Adjunct
	Mood: Declarative		Residue	
		Proposition		

Appendix 1 – continued

B7a–b	You	may	care to take a look at	the excellent book *Will I Like It?* by Peter Mayle (Hutchinson, 1978)
	Subject	Finite: Modality	Predicator	Complement
		Mood: Declarative		Residue
			Proposition	

Notes

1. A first version of this chapter was presented at the International Spring Colloquium of the Applied Linguistics Research Working Group at Glendon College, York University, Toronto (22–24 April 1988). I am most grateful to the organizers of the conference for making this occasion possible. In particular, I should like to acknowledge the stimulating discussions I had then with Michael Gregory and Elissa Asp on the arguments presented here. Selected aspects were also presented at the meeting of the Newtown Semiotic Circle (Sydney) held on 1 June 1988. Those present included Gunther Kress, Jim Martin, Steve Muecke, Chris Nesbit, Terry Threadgold and Theo van Leeuwen. I am most grateful to all of these individuals for the valuable discussion they provided. In its present reincarnation, I have incorporated substantial revisions in the light of theoretical developments that have occurred in the intervening years. In any case, the Global Modal Program was the central notion in the first version.

2. My use of the term 'thematic' here refers to Lemke's (1983:160–161) distinction between text-specific thematic systems and intertextual thematic systems. Thematic systems combine the notions of lexical-taxonomic relations and ideational-grammatical relations in order to specify a cline from text-specific to intertextual thematic systems. Importantly, this concept is to be distinguished from the traditional systemic-functional notions of 'Theme' and 'thematic development' which pertain to the textual metafunction.

3. Lemke (1990a:198–204) distinguishes between activity structure and thematic formation as two dimensions of discourse and its entextualizations. Silverstein (1997) makes a similar distinction between denotational text and interactional text as two different dimensions of textual meaning that are projected on to each other during the temporal unfolding of discourse. Both of these formulations have affinities with the principles adduced here.

4. See Baumann and Briggs (1997 [1990]:242–243) for the notion of entextualization.

5. I am assuming four metafunctional components involved in the internal functional organization of the lexicogrammar: the experiential, interpersonal, textual and logical. The theoretical basis concerning the metafunctional hypothesis is assumed rather than spelt out in this chapter. Detailed accounts are available in Halliday (1979), Martin (1984) and Gregory (1987).

6. I am using the concept of discoursal phase as developed by Gregory (1995, 2001). Gregory writes: 'Phasal description distinguishes, at varying degrees of delicacy, stretches of discourse (continuously or discontinuously manifested) that share ideational, interpersonal, and textual consistency and congruity. Transitions out and/or into phases are signaled by changes in selections in one or more of the functions . . .

phases reflect the microinstantial situations of the discourse, the particular experiences, interactions, and medium relationships that the language is representing and/or creating' (1995:71).

7. Silverstein has formulated the distinction between linguistic function$_1$ and function$_2$ as follows: 'there is one sense in which language is "functional", inasmuch as its use seems to the natives to be potentially purposive, or actually effective, or the like, in their own individual experience. Let us call this goal-directed and sometimes goal-achieving categorization of occasions of use the function$_1$ of language ... But there is a contrasting sense in which language is "functional", inasmuch as by characteristic distribution of particular forms in certain contexts of use, these forms (or, rather, tokens of them) serve as specifically linguistic indicators (or indices) differentially pointing to (indexing) configurations of contextual features. Let us call this indexical quality of speech forms, or indexical mode of their signification, function$_2$' (Silverstein 1979:206).

8. See Halliday (1994 [1985]:124–129) for the terms Token and Value and their function in identifying clauses.

9. Some (not all) of the terms used in this analysis have been adapted from Habermas (1984 [1981]:273–337).

10. Bateson (1987 [1951]:217) has written of the instrumental subject as follows: 'Now, we ask, of what order is the conscious or unconscious proposition which guides the subject of instrumental experiments – the proposition which we may crudely verbalize for him as "the world is made up of contexts in which I can act instrumentally"? If we consider this statement, it is at once evident that the instrumental subject will, within certain limits, experience a world in which his propositions are apparently verified. Being an instrumental organism, he will meet the world instrumentally; he will seek out and respond to those contexts which are appropriately structured, and he will thereby reinforce his own belief that the world is an instrumental world.'

11. The notion of higher-order metacommunicative frame is located at the level of generic situation and thus constitutes part of the conditions of possibility of the Global Modal Program which is enacted. It resembles Parret's (1982:14) notion of the 'système de préconditions' at the level of metamodalizations.

References

Adam, Jean-Michel (1982) The macrostructure of the conventional narrative. *Poetics Today*, 3(4):135–68.

Bakhtin, Mikhail (1981) [1975] Discourse in the novel. In *The Dialogic Imagination: Four Essays*, ed. by Michael Holquist, Austin: University of Texas Press, 259–422.

Bateson, Gregory (1973) A theory of play and fantasy. In *Steps to an Ecology of Mind*. London: Paladin, 150–66.

Bateson, Gregory (1987) [1951] Information and codification: a philosophical approach. In *Communication: The Social Matrix of Psychiatry*, ed. by Jurgen Ruesch and Gregory Bateson, London: Norton, 168–211.

Bauman, Richard and Briggs, Charles (1997) [1990] Poetics and performance as critical perspectives on language and social life. In *Creativity in Performance*, ed. by R. Keith Sawyer, London: Ablex, 227–264.

Burke, Kenneth (1969) [1945] *A Grammar of Motives*. Berkeley: University of California Press.

Coward, Rosalind (1984) Have you tried talking about it? In *Female Desire: Women's Sexuality Today*, London: Granada, 133–142.

Davidse, Kristin (1991) Categories of experiential grammar. Unpublished Ph.D. thesis, Department of Linguistics, Katholieke Universiteit, Leuven.

Fabbri, Paolo (1998) *La svolta semiotica*. Rome: Laterza.

Foley, William A. and Van Valin, Robert D. (1984) *Functional Syntax and Universal Grammar*. Cambridge: Cambridge University Press.

Gregory, Michael (1987) Metafunctions: aspects of their development, status, and use in systemic linguistics. In *New Developments in Systemic Linguistics*, Vol. 1: Theory and Description, ed. by M. A. K. Halliday and Robin Fawcett, London: Pinter, 94–106.

Gregory, Michael (1995) Generic expectancies and discoursal surprises: John Donne's 'The Good Morrow'. In *Discourse in Society: Systemic Functional Perspectives*, ed. by Peter H. Fries and Michael Gregory, Norwood, NJ: Ablex, 67–84.

Gregory, Michael (2001) Phasal analysis within communication linguistics: two contrastive discourses. Chapter 10 of this book.

Greimas, Algirdas J. (1983a) Le savoir et le croire: un seul univers cognitif. In *Du sens II: essais sémiotiques*, Paris: Seuil, 115–133.

Greimas, Algirdas J. (1983b) De la colère: étude de sémantique lexicale. In *Du sens II: essais sémiotiques*, Paris: Seuil, 225–246.

Greimas, Algirdas J. (1983c) Pour une théorie des modalités. In *Du sens II: essais sémiotiques*, Paris: Seuil, 67–91.

Greimas, Algirdas J. and Fontanille, Jacques (1991) *Sémiotique des passions: des états de choses aux états d'âme*. Paris: Seuil.

Gumperz, John J. (1992) Contextualization revisited. In *The Contextualization of Language*, ed. by Peter Auer and Aldo di Luzio, Amsterdam: John Benjamins, 39–53.

Habermas, Jürgen (1984) [1981] *The Theory of Communicative Action. Volume 1: Reason and the Rationalization of Society*. Thomas McCarthy (trans.), London: Heinemann.

Halliday, M. A. K. (1979) Modes of meaning and modes of expression: types of grammatical structure and their determination by different semantic functions. In *Function and Context in Linguistic Analysis. A*

Festschrift for William Haas, ed. by D. J. Allerton, Edward Carney and David Holdcroft, Cambridge: Cambridge University Press, 57–79.

Halliday, M. A. K. (1980) Text semantics and clause grammar: some patterns of realization. In The *Seventh LACUS Forum 1980*, ed. by James E. Copeland and Philip W. Davis, Columbia, SC: Hornbeam Press, 31–59.

Halliday, M. A. K. (1982) The de-automatization of grammar: from Priestley's 'An Inspector Calls'. In *Language Form and Linguistic Variation: Papers Dedicated to Angus Macintosh*, ed. by John Anderson, Amsterdam: John Benjamins, 129–159.

Halliday, M. A. K. (1994) [1985] *An Introduction to Functional Grammar*, 2nd edn. London: Edward Arnold.

Hanks, William F. (1996) Exorcism and the description of participant roles. In *Natural Histories of Discourse*, ed. by Michael Silverstein and Greg Urban, Chicago: University of Chicago Press, 160–200.

Hasan, Ruqaiya (1988) Offers in the making: a systemic-functional approach. Macquarie University, Sydney: School of English, Media and Linguistics. Mimeo.

Hasan, Ruqaiya (1992) Rationality in everyday talk: from process to system. In *Directions in Corpus Linguistics. Proceedings of Nobel Symposium 82. Stockholm, 4–8 August 1991*, ed. by Jan Svartik, Berlin: Mouton de Gruyter, 257–271.

Holiday, Anthony (1988) *Moral Powers: Normative Necessity in Language and History*. London: Routledge.

Irvine, Judith T. (1996) Shadow conversations: the indeterminacy of participant roles. In *Natural Histories of Discourse*, ed. by Michael Silverstein and Greg Urban, Chicago: University of Chicago Press, 131–159.

Jakobson, Roman (1985) [1956] Metalanguage as a linguistic problem. In *Selected Writings: Vol. 7*, Berlin: Mouton, 113–121.

Kress, Gunther R. (1977) Tense as modality. *UEA Papers in Linguistics*, 5:40–52.

Labov, W. and Waletzky, J. (1967) Narrative analysis: oral versions of personal experience. In *Essays on the Verbal and Visual Arts*, ed. by J. Helm, Seattle: University of Washington Press, 12–44.

Latour, Bruno (1986) The powers of association. In *Power, Action and Belief*, ed. by John Law, London: Routledge & Kegan Paul, 264–280.

Leech, Geoffrey and Svartik, Jan (1975) *A Communicative Grammar of English*. London: Longman.

Lemke, Jay L. (1983) Thematic analysis: systems, structures, and strategies. *Recherches Sémiotiques/Semiotic Inquiry*, 3(2):159–187.

Lemke, Jay L. (1988) Discourses in conflict: heteroglossia and text semantics. In *Systemic Functional Approaches to Discourse*, ed. by James D. Benson and William S. Greaves, Norwood, NJ: Ablex, 29–50.

Lemke, Jay L. (1990a) *Talking Science: Language, Learning, and Values*. Norwood, NJ: Ablex.

Lemke, Jay L. (1990b) Technical discourse and technocratic ideology. In *Learning, Keeping and Using Language. Volume 2: Selected Papers from the 8th World Congress of Applied Linguistics, Sydney, 16–21 August 1987*, ed. by M. A. K. Halliday, John Gibbons and Howard Nicholas, Amsterdam: Benjamins, 435–460.

McGregor, William B. (1997) *Semiotic Grammar*. Oxford: Clarendon Press.

Martin, James R. (1981) How many speech acts? *UEA Papers in Linguistics*, 14–15:52–77.

Martin, James R. (1984) Functional components in a grammar: a review of deployable recognition criteria. In *Nottingham Linguistic Circular 13*, ed. by Michael Stubbs and Ronald Carter, 35–70.

Martin, James R. (1991) Intrinsic functionality: implications for contextual theory. *Social Semiotics*, 1(1):99–162.

Martin, James R. (1992) Macro-proposals: meaning by degree. In *Discourse Description: Diverse Analyses of a Fundraising Text*, ed. by W. C. Mann and S. A. Thompson, Amsterdam: Benjamins, 359–396.

Parret, Herman (1982) Eléments pour une typologie raisonné des passions. *Actes Sémiotiques: Documents du Groupe de Recherches Sémio-linguistiques* 4, 37.

Pike, Kenneth (1971) *Language in Relation to a Unified Theory of the Structure of Human Behaviour*. The Hague: Mouton.

Poynton, Cate (1988) 'The linguistic realisation of attitude: amplification as a grammatical prosody'. Unpublished manuscript.

Rodríguez-Navarro, Quereda, Luis (1993) *A Morphosyntactic Study of the English Verb Phrase*. Granada: Universidad de Granada.

Siewierska, Anna (1991) *Functional Grammar*. London: Routledge.

Silverstein, Michael (1979) Language structure and linguistic ideology. In *The Elements: A Parasession on Linguistic Units and Levels*, ed. by Paul R. Clyne, William F. Hanks and Carol L. Hofbauer, Chicago: Chicago Linguistic Society, 193–247.

Silverstein, Michael (1985) The functional stratification of language and ontogenesis. In *Culture, Communication, and Cognition: Vygotskian Perspectives*, ed. by J. V. Wertsch, London: Cambridge University Press, 205–235.

Silverstein, Michael (1987) [1980] The three faces of 'function': preliminaries to a psychology of language. In *Social and Functional Approaches to Language and Thought*, ed. by M. Hickmann, London: Academic Press, 17–38.

Silverstein, Michael (1997) The improvisational performance of culture in realtime discursive practice. In *Creativity in Performance*, ed. by R. Keith Sawyer, Greenwich, Conn.: Ablex, 265–312.

Silverstein, Michael and Urban, Greg (1996) The natural history of discourse. In *Natural Histories of Discourse*, ed. by Michael Silverstein and Greg Urban, Chicago: University of Chicago Press, 1–17.

Thibault, Paul J. (1989) Semantic variation, social heteroglossia and intertextuality: thematic and axiological meanings in spoken discourse. *Critical Studies*, 1(2):181–209.

Thibault, Paul J. (1991) Grammar, technocracy and the noun: technocratic values and cognitive linguistics. In *Recent Systemic and Other Functional Views on Language*, ed. by Eija Ventola, Trends in Linguistics Studies and Monographs, Berlin: Mouton de Gruyter, 281–305.

Thibault, Paul J. (1992) Grammar, ethics, and understanding: functionalist reason and clause as exchange. *Social Semiotics*, 2(1):135–175.

Thibault, Paul J. (1995) The interpersonal grammar of Mood and the ecosocial dynamics of the semiotic exchange process. In *On Subject and Theme: From the Perspective of Functions in Discourse*, ed. by Ruqaiya Hasan and Peter Fries, Amsterdam: Benjamins, 51–89.

Thibault, Paul J. (1999) Communicating and interpreting relevance through discourse negotiation: an alternative to relevance theory. *Journal of Pragmatics*, 31:557–594.

Thibault, Paul J. (forthcoming) The interpersonal enactment of agency in discourse: towards a social semiotically motivated account of modality and mood in English.

Thibault, Paul J. and van Leeuwen, Theo (1996) Grammar, society, and the speech act: renewing the connections. *Journal of Pragmatics*, 25:561–585.

Threadgold, Terry (1997) Critical literacies and the teaching of English. In *Constructing Critical Literacies: Teaching and Learning Textual Practice*, ed. by Sandy Muspratt, Allan Luke and Peter Freebody, Cresskill, NJ: Hampton Press, 353–385.

van den Daele, Leland D. (1976) Organization and transformation. In *The Developing Individual in a Changing World. Volume 1: Historical and Cultural Issues*, ed. by Klaus F. Riegel and John A. Meacham, The Hague: Mouton, 68–78.

van Dijk, Teun A. (1979) Recalling and summarizing complex discourse. In *Textprocessing. Textverarbeitung*, ed. by Wolfgang Burghardt and Klaus Hölker, Berlin: Walter de Gruyter, 49–118.

Walkerdine, Valerie (1985) On the regulation of speaking and silence: subjectivity, class and gender in contemporary schooling. In *Language, Gender and Childhood*, ed. by Carolyn Steedman, Cathy Urwin and Valerie Walkerdine, London: Routledge & Kegan Paul, 203–241.

4

The Flow of Information in a Written English Text[1]

Peter H. Fries

Introduction

Over the last 25 years, I have devoted considerable time to exploring a Systemic Functional approach to discourse analysis. In particular, I have focussed on the phenomena which systemicists assign to the textual metafunction. These phenomena are discussed in Systemic theory primarily under the headings of *thematic structure* (with its associated functions *Theme*[2] and *Rheme*) and *information structure* (with its associated functions *New* and *Given*). I would like to take this opportunity to demonstrate the usefulness of these concepts for the analysis of text by applying them to the description of one particular text – a fund-raising letter on behalf of a political action committee called Zero Population Growth.

Theoretical concepts

Before beginning the actual analysis of the text it is necessary to present the theoretical concepts to be used. Systemic Functional Grammar distinguishes three systems within the textual metafunction which correlate with one another but which are nevertheless distinct concepts. These are thematic structure, information structure and reference. The first two systems assign structural functions to the clause. The third system is an aspect of cohesion and does not assign structural functions.

Thematic structure

The grammatical functions Theme and Rheme result from choices made within the thematic system. Halliday has defined Theme in the following terms:

The English clause consists of a 'theme' and a 'rheme' ... [the theme] is, as it were, the peg on which the message is hung ... The theme of the clause is the element which, in English, is put in first position ... (Halliday 1970:161)

The Theme is a function of the CLAUSE AS MESSAGE. It is what the message is concerned with: the point of departure for what the speaker is going to say. (Halliday 1985:36)

The Theme functions in the structure of the CLAUSE AS MESSAGE, a quantum of information; the Theme is the point of departure for the message. It is the element the speaker selects for 'grounding' what he is going to say. (Halliday 1994:34)

It is useful to notice that 'pegs', 'points of departure' and 'grounding what one is going to say' are semantic notions and are the basic core of the definition. The statement that Theme occurs in first position in English is a realizational statement for English, not a definition of the notion of Theme. This point needs some further discussion because there are some complications in the way this principle plays out in specific examples. Specifically, the Systemic model claims that the English lexicogrammatical system falls into three major subsystems which are called *metafunctions*. (See Halliday 1970, 1994 for further discussion.) These three metafunctions are the experiential (which concerns the way the speaker uses the clause to represent the world), the interpersonal (which concerns the way the speaker uses the clause to act on the addressee) and the textual (which concerns the way the speaker indicates how the clause being produced is to be related to the linguistic and non-linguistic context). The Theme includes everything at the beginning of the clause up to and including the first constituent that comes from the experiential metafunction.[3] In practice, this means that clauses may have complex Themes which derive from up to three metafunctions, and each of these can itself be complex. Figure 4.1 presents Halliday's (1994:55, Figure 3.13) example of a maximally extended clause Theme. In Figure 4.1, the first portion of the clause that derives from the experiential metafunction consists of the words *the best idea*. The Theme of this clause, then, extends from the word *well* up to and including the word *idea*.

Finally, the definitions quoted from Halliday describe Theme as an element of structure of the clause. Elsewhere, Halliday makes it clear that he believes other structures – such as clause-complexes (1985:56–59) and nominal and verbal groups (1977:183 and

Well	but	then	Ann	surely	wouldn't	the best idea	be to join the group?
Continuative	structural	conjunctive	vocative	modal	finite	topical	
			interpersonal			experiential	
Textual							
Theme							Rheme

Figure 4.1 A maximally extended clause Theme

1985:158,166 and 176) – also have thematic structures. Indeed Martin (1992a:436ff.) suggests that larger structures such as paragraphs and texts have thematic structures which he calls hyper-Themes and macro-Themes. In much of my work (Fries 1981, 1995b; Fries and Francis 1992), I have found it useful to treat thematic structures within independent conjoinable clause-complexes. This structure consists of an independent clause together with all hypotactically related clauses which are dependent on it. The independent conjoinable clause-complex is very similar to the T-unit of American educational literature (see Hunt 1965), and so I often use the term 'T-unit', since it is so much shorter.

Since the Hallidayan definition of Theme is so often interpreted as really referring to 'topic',[4] and since the relation of Theme to the traditional notion of topic is tenuous and indeed the very notion of topic is problematic at best,[5] I have generally avoided referring to Theme as meaning 'what the clause is about'. Thus, I have described Theme (Fries 1995b) in the following terms: The Theme of a T-unit provides a framework within which the Rheme of that T-unit can be interpreted.[6] This description is intended to parallel Halliday's while avoiding any interpretation as 'topic'. Bäcklund (1989:297), while describing the uses of initial infinitive clauses, uses terminology which provides a good sense of what I intend for the meaning of Theme. She says: 'In written text these [= initial purpose] infinitive clauses may be said to reflect the imaginary reader's questions, or rather, they indicate which potential question the writer has chosen to answer.'

Text 1 illustrates the use of thematic information to provide a framework to use to interpret the remainder of the clause:

Text 1:
1. What does the term *culture* mean throughout this book?
2. <u>As used by anthropologists</u>, the term *culture* means any human behavior that is learned rather than biologically transmitted. (Gregg 1985:2)

In Text 1, the author is obviously aware that the word *culture* is often used with radically different interpretations from the one she intends to use. By placing the restriction *as used by anthropologists* first in sentence 2, she 'prevents' the response 'That's not what *culture* means to me.'[7]

Information structure

The second theoretical construct which is relevant to this discussion is information structure. Information structure involves the division of what is said into units of information and the signaling of which portions of those information units contain the newsworthy information. In the spoken language, units of information are signaled by the location of tone group boundaries, while the location of tonic prominence indicates the culmination of the information that is being presented as New. (One important implication of this fact is that since the information unit is indicated through intonation and rhythm, there is no necessary relation between information units and clause structure.) Halliday defines New information as 'information which is being presented by the speaker as ... not recoverable to the listener' (1985:277 see also 1994:298). New information is contrasted with Given information, which is defined as 'information which is being presented by the speaker as recoverable ... to the listener' (1985:277 see also 1994:298). I prefer to rephrase the definition of New positively, as 'information which is being presented as "newsworthy"'. (Indeed, this rephrasing is in keeping with Halliday's intent, since he elaborates on the meaning of New by saying, 'The meaning [of New] is: attend to this; this is news' (1985:277 and 1994:298). (The revised description of New has the added advantage of being quite different from the description of the third factor which will be discussed later – the notion of participant identification.)

Several issues need to be emphasized at this point. (1) The location of the tonic accent indicates the *culmination* of the New. However, New information may extend forward (to the 'left') in the clause. Thus, the tonic foot will be at least a portion of the information presented as New, but the tonic foot may not include *all* the information presented as New. Indeed, in some cases, the entire clause may present New information. (2) Like all other aspects of language, the choice of what to present as newsworthy in a given message is up to the speaker. It cannot be predicted with certainty by an external observer. Thus, even if we know that the listener knows a certain bit of information, and we also know that the speaker knows that the listener knows that information, we cannot with certainty say that that bit of information will be presented as Given. Point 2 is illustrated in Text 2:

Text 2:
// 4 ∧ in /*this* job / Anne we're // 1 working with / *silver* / ∧ // (Halliday 1985:283)

Text 2 is the initial sentence of a conversation in which a job trainee is being oriented to a new job working as a clerk in the gifts department of a department store. If we look at the information from the trainee's point of view, and ask what information is in fact unfamiliar to her, we find that the sentence contains *no* unfamiliar information. She knows her name, she knows she is there to work at a job, and she sees silver all around her. However, even though the sentence contains no unfamiliar information, some of the information is *being presented* as news, i.e. as New. The sentence is divided into two tone groups (tone group boundaries are marked by //). Each tone group contains one tonic syllable (marked in italics). This division indicates that there are two bits of information in the sentence. It turns out that in this sentence the New information is restricted to the single words which contain the tonic syllables. In this context the listener is told to recover the notions of 'job', 'working', etc. The newsworthy parts of the message lie in 'this' and in 'silver'.[8]

Participant identification

Participant identification refers to the ways the various participants are introduced and referred to in the development of a text. In Text 3, for example, Alice has the task of introducing two new participants (*a book* and *a newspaper*) into the discourse, while Betty needs to refer to one of those participants (*the book*) as already on stage and in attention

Text 3:
Alice: I have a book and a newspaper. Which do you want?
Betty: Could you give me the book?

Alice achieves her task by introducing the participants with indefinite articles, while Betty achieves her task by referring to the participant with a definite article. Many linguists describe the use of the indefinite article as introducing a referent which is not recoverable from the context, while definite articles are said to introduce referents which are recoverable from the context. Of course, these wordings introduce an ambiguity, since 'recoverability' is often used to describe the difference between Given and New information. (See Halliday's definitions above.) Since the two concepts are similar (indeed, some linguists such as Chafe (1992:270; 1994:7) link the two concepts in essential ways), this is a serious ambiguity. In the case of participant identification, we are concerned with referential identity. In the case of information structure, referential identity is not a primary focus. We are rather concerned with what is presented as 'news'. One way to avoid the confusions inherent in the different interpretations of the term 'recoverable' is to avoid that term altogether. I have already chosen to use the term 'newsworthiness' to describe the meaning of New in information structure. In the issue of participant reference, I will follow Martin (1992a) in distinguishing *presenting* and *presuming reference*. Presenting reference introduces new referents into the discourse, and, in English, is associated with indefiniteness. Presuming reference, on the other hand, introduces participants whose identities are familiar to the audience, and, in English, is associated with definiteness.

Interactions among thematic structure, information structure and participant identification

We now have three different sets of concepts, each defined in its own terms and presented as if they were unrelated to one another. While it is important to realize that they differ inherently, it is also important to realize that they correlate with one another. Many linguists (including Halliday 1967, 1985, and Chafe 1980, 1984, 1994) have noted that each new intonation contour signals a new chunk of information (or new information unit, to use Halliday's term). Similarly, Halliday (1967:200–201, 1985:274) and Chafe (1984:437, 1994:65–66) note an unmarked correlation between the clause and the information unit.[9] Finally, several linguists note a general tendency for the last major constituent of the clause to receive a tonic accent. Halliday talks about this as the unmarked location of the tonic syllable. Crystal (1975:23) found that the tonic fell on the last lexical item of the clause about 80 per cent of the time. Tench (1990:497) found the tendency even higher in newscasts. That is, there seems to be a general correlation between rhematic status (more specifically, last position in the clause) and New information. At the other end of the clause, most Themes are presented as Given information, and often contain presuming reference. It would be wrong, however, to assume that the correlations between these concepts are perfect. Many Themes (particularly marked Themes) are pronounced as separate tone groups (see Text 2 for an example) and thus are presented as expressing New information, and while most Themes do contain presuming reference, many do not. Similarly, while Rhemes usually are presented as containing New information, many are not so presented. (Indeed, Davies 1989 points out the placement of Given information in the Rheme as a cohesive device.)

Discourse effects of Theme and Rheme

So far my presentation has focussed on clause-internal phenomena, and I have ignored the discourse consequences of these phenomena. The descriptions of the meanings of textual phenomena have always been difficult because the meanings are totally language-internal, and thus difficult to grasp and illustrate. In my work on Theme, I have tried to provide a better 'fix' on the meaning of Theme by a three-pronged approach. (1) I have tried to describe strategies for the development of texts which would lead one to make certain items of information thematic in specific contexts (Fries 1995b). (2) I have tried to connect thematic content with perceived meanings of texts (Fries 1981), or perceived functions of texts (Fries 1995a). (3) I have tried to contrast the effect of giving information the status of Theme with the effects of information which has been given other sorts of status (Fries 1981).

Points (2) and (3) can be seen in the following hypotheses which lay behind the discussion in Fries (1981):

(1) If a text segment is perceived as having a single method of development, then the words which contribute to the expression of that method of development will occur thematically within the T-units of that text segment.

(2) If a text segment is perceived as expressing a single point, then the words which contribute to the expression of that point will occur within the Rhemes of the component T-units of that text segment.

(3) The perception of a nominal item as topic of a text segment is unrelated to the thematic or rhematic placement of the references to that item.

The model used here is a correlational model.[10] No claim is intended that every text segment must have a single simple method of development or must express a single point, or must have a simple nominal topic. Indeed, many people object to using the notion of a single method of development or single point, since many text segments do not have such phenomena. Even in these more complicated text segments, however, the intent of my basic hypothesis remains; Themes and Rhemes of clauses and clause-complexes are used for different purposes. As part of specifying the uses of thematic information, it is useful to examine a longer text which is not so uniform as the ones I previously examined. I have primarily examined written texts because I suspect that the differences between the uses of thematic and rhematic information will be most prominent in writing.[11]

First, let me discuss why I believe that the differences between thematic and rhematic information will be prominent in written English – particularly writing which is intended to mimic the patterns of spoken language. We have already said that New information is information which is being presented as 'newsworthy', and that in the spoken language, the culmination of the New information is signaled by the location of the tonic accent. Of course, in the written language, there is no accent, and thus a major means of signaling New information is lost. What alternatives exist within the written language to signal 'newsworthiness'? Perhaps the most obvious means are graphic signals such as underlining, capitalization, the use of colored ink or the use of different typefaces or sizes. In addition there are considerations such as paragraphing and page layout. Most of these means are used with restraint in more formal writing. (Editors often do not approve of the extensive use of capital letters or underlining for emphasis.) As a result, writers in these formal contexts are restricted to using other means to indicate what is 'newsworthy'. Two major resources come to mind: (1) writers sequence the information in their texts so that readers have the relevant background information in their attention as they read each new sentence;[12] (2) writers tend to sequence the information presented in each sentence so that, where possible, the New information is placed where the unmarked tonic accent would be in the spoken sentence. That is, writers will tend to place New information toward the end of the clause, thus strengthening the correlation of New with Rheme.

Theme, N-Rheme and discourse goals

To summarize, we are assuming that in written language there is a correlation between thematic position and Given information on the one hand, and rhematic position and New information on the other. I wish to explore the notion that writers use position at the end of the clause to indicate the newsworthy information to their readers, and that they use the beginnings of their clauses to orient their readers to the message which will come in the rest of the clause.

Systemicists already have a good term ('Theme') for the first clause-level constituent at the beginning of the clause. However, we need a term for the end of the clause. Rheme is too inclusive, since in Halliday's terminology it includes everything that is not Theme.

Since we are interested in the unmarked association of Rheme with New, and since New typically is associated with the last constituent of the clause, we can coin the term *N-Rheme* to indicate the last constituent of the clause.

Because of its association with New, the N-Rheme typically expresses the core of the newsworthy part of the clause,[13] that is, the part of the clause that the writer wants the reader to remember. As a result we should expect the content of the N-Rheme to correlate with the goals of the text as a whole, the goals of the text segment within those larger goals, and the goals of the sentence and the clause as well. On the other hand, the Theme is the orienter to the message conveyed by the clause. It tells the reader how to understand the news conveyed by the clause. As a result, we should expect the choice of thematic content to have a less obvious relation to the overall goals of the text or text segment. For example, if we are examining a text which has a problem-solution structure, we should expect the meanings to change as the text moves from the description of the problem to the description of the solution. Both the thematic content and the N-Rhematic content should change. However, the content of the N-Rhemes should be more obviously connected with the goals of each text portion. For example, in the section which describes the problem, the N-Rhemes should have an obvious connection with what is wrong, while in the section which describes the solution, the N-Rhemes should have an obvious connection with what was done to solve the problem. The Themes of the problem section, on the other hand, might well concern different aspects of the item which is causing the problem (say, an engine which is not functioning properly), while the Themes of the solution section might concern notions such as the relative temporal order of the actions taken in solving the problem.

Analysis of the ZPG letter

I wish to take as my text a fund-raising letter sent out by the political action group Zero Population Growth (henceforth ZPG). I have chosen this text because a number of alternative analyses have been published in Mann and Thompson (1992). These analyses provide relevant resources and interesting comparisons with the approach taken here. The text of the letter is provided in Appendix I, while Appendix II contains the same letter with items labeled to facilitate reference. The numbering system preserves the numbering assigned by Mann and Thompson, but adds information to preserve paragraphing and clause information. Each new paragraph has been assigned a capital letter and each punctuated sentence has been given a number. Each non-embedded clause in each sentence has been given a lower case letter and placed on a separate line. The logo, the date and other information associated with the genre of letter writing have also been assigned capital letters and numbers even though they do not clearly constitute clauses, sentences or paragraphs. Since not every item that has been assigned a number is actually a sentence, I will refer to numbered items as Segments. (Thus, 'Segment 7' refers to clauses 7a and 7b.) The Theme of a clause is written in small capitals, while the N-Rheme of the clause is indicated by italics. All underlining is in the letter.[14]

The letter was written by an officer of ZPG to people who were on her mailing list, usually because they had already contributed money. That is, the audience was presumed to be already sympathetic. But sympathetic as the audience might have been, the author still needed to persuade the readers to contribute money to this particular project, and she chose to take an advertising approach to the task. This is not the only approach which could have been used, but it is not an unusual one. The approach she took is basically one of first motivating a request, and then expressing that request.[15] How can she motivate her request? Two points are obvious: (1) she must show a need for money; and (2) she must show the value of her project. Since the author is writing to an audience that she presumes is already sympathetic with the basic issue, she can assume that her readers agree that overpopulation is an issue. As a result, she does not emphasize that idea. Rather, she spends her effort on describing the value of this particular project. One way of showing the value of a political action project is to show the effects it has had. Relevant effects for a political action group are of two basic types: (1) getting the message heard (so that political forces can be brought to bear); and (2) influencing decisions made by political officials. Thus, the author should show the effects of ZPG on three audiences: public officials (who make decisions), members of the media (who can get information out to the public) and the public (who can affect decisions that the public officials make). The need can be demonstrated by showing (a) that harmful things are happening to the organization because of the lack of funds, or (b) the organization could be much more effective if it had more funds to take advantage of opportunities which are being presented at this time. This appeal can be made more dramatic by adding a note of urgency. (Most fundraising letters do their best to get the audience to send the money *now*, and therefore contain some reference to the urgency of the appeal.)

A couple of other general factors in the situation also affect this letter. First, in our society requests are better received if they are personalized. That is, letters are more successful if they are seen as coming from some person (or group) and as showing that the addressee has some personal stake in the success of the group. (Composition textbooks are sensitive to this factor and often suggest students develop a 'you-orientation' in writing business letters.) As a result, we should expect that the author of this fund-raising letter will try to involve the reader, and will try to make the organization more obvious as a group of people. Finally, the request can't be too direct. The author cannot merely say 'Send money!' From what has been said here, we may hypothesize that the letter will generally emphasize the following meanings:

(1) The value of the project.
(2) The reactions of non-ZPG people. This description will include the reactions of the three primary groups mentioned above.
    (a) public officials
    (b) members of the media
    (c) the public.
(3) The need for help.
(4) The urgency of the need for help.
(5) Some means of personalizing the appeal. This will include mentioning the people behind ZPG, as well as including references to *I, you* and *we*.

Since meanings 1–4 relate to the goals of the text, we predict that they will regularly be found in the N-Rhemes rather than the Themes of the component clauses. Such meanings will include descriptions of the problem, appraisals (see Martin 1992b, 2000) and mentions of people who are important to judge the effectiveness of ZPG. By contrast, meanings related to the personalizing the appeal (meaning set 5) do not form part of the goals of the text, so words which express these meanings will not regularly occur within the N-Rhemes of the text.

Items 1–4 on the list above describe a number of meanings which can be seen to be important for the functioning of a fund-raising letter, particularly one which attempts to raise funds for a political action group. That is, the list applies to the purposes of the text as a whole. Since the goals of the various portions of the text may vary, we also need an interpretation of the text which describes the goals of each of its parts. Rhetorical Structure Theory (or RST), as developed by William Mann and Sandra Thompson (see, for example, Mann and Thompson 1985 and 1986), provides just such an interpretation. RST analysis describes a text as composed of a number of text portions. Each text portion (except the largest) is related to at least one other text portion by one of a small list of relations such as antithesis, concession, etc. The resulting combination is then seen as a larger text portion, which has a nucleus and satellite structure. Finally, each relation is seen as deriving from a goal which the author wishes to achieve by adding the satellite to the nucleus. Appendix III presents an analysis of the ZPG letter published in Mann, Matthiessen and Thompson (1992). It provides a detailed interpretation of certain aspects of the ZPG text, one which relates explicitly to the presumed goals that the author had in creating this text. Finally, I should note that it was done by others independently of my work, and without consideration of thematic and N-Rhematic structures.

Since their analysis concerns relations between clauses and larger portions of the text, Mann, Matthiessen and Thompson have not treated those aspects of this letter which concern its structure as a letter. For example, Segments 1–3 – the ZPG logo, the date and the address to the reader – are missing from their analysis. Rather they have focussed on the body of the letter. They find that the body of the letter expresses two requests. The first request is expressed in Segments 4–23, and the second request is expressed in Segments 29–30. The nucleus of the first request is Segment 22. Segments 4–21 and 23, then, constitute two motivations for the reader to comply with the request expressed in 22. Within the first motivation section (Segments 4–21), there is again a nucleus-satellite structure, with Segments 11–16 constituting the nucleus of the motivation, and groups 4–10 and 17–21 constituting the satellites. In this case, the two satellites each provide evidence to support the claims in 11–16. Within the group which includes Segments 4–10, Segments 4–6 provide a background for Segments 7–10. Segments 4, 5 and 6 are in a Sequence relation and in fact constitute a small narrative. But, of course this narrative is the beginning of a section intended to motivate the reader to comply with a request to send money. Let us examine what happens in that narrative.

4. AT 7:00 A.M. ON OCTOBER 25, our phones *started to ring.*
5. CALLS jammed our switchboard *all day.*
6a. STAFFERS stayed *late into the night,*

6b. answering *questions,*

6c. and talking *with reporters from newspapers, radio stations, wire services and TV stations in every part of the country.*

The information which is emphasized in this passage seems to begin with activity (*started to ring*) and then moves into the duration of that activity (*all day*) and the range of that activity (*with reporters from newspapers . . . in every part of the country*). One of the interesting aspects of this small narrative is the absence of action on the part of *we* (= ZPG). That is, while *started to ring* describes an activity, it is the phones, not the people, that engage in that activity. Further, we know that phones ring in response to someone else calling. Though *jamming* is a material process, it is the nominalized process *calls* that is the actor. To uncover the people involved in this process, one must infer something such as *people called us.* Again, the ZPG is the goal of the action and is seen to respond to the actions of others. Finally, *stayed* (in 6a) is not an activity but a relational process. It is only when one gets to clause 6b that one finds a human connected with ZPG actually doing something – answering questions – and even that activity is clearly done in response to some other person. In the light of all the reactive meanings in the previous clauses, one could very well interpret the last clause ((6c) *talking with reporters . . . country*) also as ZPG personnel reacting to others outside the organization.

Indeed, in Segment 7, the author does refer to the previous narrative as a response:

7a. WHEN WE released *the results of ZPG's <u>1985 Urban Stress Test</u>,*

7b. WE had *no idea we'd get such an overwhelming response.*

In fact this reference is located at the very end of Segment 7 (the N-Rheme of both the clause and the sentence), where it receives a natural prominence. Further, the term *overwhelming* is used to describe the response. What justification have we been given for this description? The reactive nature of ZPG in the narrative has already been pointed out. The author has prepared us for 'overwhelming' by consistently placing information which would lead to that judgment in the N-Rhemes of the component clauses.[16] In clauses 5 and 6a *all day* and *late into the night* indicate the great extent of the reaction. The N-Rheme of 6c details the wide range of the reaction. We are given a list of the major news media. Such a list has much the same effect as saying 'all the major news media'.

Segment 8 explicitly repeats the evaluation of the response described in Segment 7:

8. MEDIA AND PUBLIC REACTION has been *nothing short of incredible.*

Mann, Matthiessen and Thompson describe the relation between Segments 7 and 8 as one of Restatement. But there is a difference between the two segments. In Segment 7 the grammar of the main clause focusses on the surprise the response caused. (*We'd get such an overwhelming response* is an embedded clause within the noun phrase *no idea we'd get such an overwhelming response.*) Clearly, the notion of surprise *had no idea* is grammatically prominent here. Segment 8 focusses exclusively on an evaluation of the response (*nothing short of incredible* is an attribute of *media and public reaction*). It is of interest to note that in this context, receiving an overwhelming reaction to an activity is good, since the goal of the organization is to affect people's lives. Doing something which people react to is therefore an indication of being effective.

Lest that message be lost on the reader, the author goes on in Segments 9 and 10 to elaborate on the nature of that reaction:

9. AT FIRST, THE DELUGE OF CALLS came *mostly from reporters eager to tell the public about Urban Stress Test results and from outraged public officials who were furious that we had 'blown the whistle' on conditions in their cities.*

10. NOW WE are hearing *from concerned citizens in all parts of the country who want to know what they can do to hold local officials accountable for tackling population-related problems that threaten public health and well-being.*

Again, the N-Rhemes are devoted to the elaboration of the range of response engendered by the report. Segments 9 and 10 consist of single clauses. Segment 9 is coded as a metaphorical motion, with the source of the calls coded as a directional source, while Segment 10 is coded as a mental perception, again with the source being coded as a direction. In both cases, the N-Rhemes of the clauses are entirely devoted to an elaborate description of the sources of the calls – that is, the people who are doing the calling. Again we are given a list and it is seen to include the people whom ZPG might well consider important to affect (i.e. reporters, public officials and concerned citizens).

Clearly, it is obvious from the content of the N-Rhemes of Segments 4–10 that the author is emphasizing the great reaction engendered by the release of the ZPG Urban Stress Test. At this point, a large reaction is good. One would expect this from the general mode of argumentation used by other letters in similar situations, and one can see this value in the wording of this portion of the ZPG letter.

However, the letter undergoes a change at this point. Mann, Matthiessen and Thompson indicate this change by saying that Segments 11–16 constitute the nucleus of the motivation of the request. Segments 11–12 form a background for Segment 13. Segments 11–13 are in a concessive relation to Segments 14–16 and finally, Segment 12 elaborates Segment 11, while clause 11b elaborates 11a. How are these relations reflected in the thematic and N-Rhematic structures of these segments?

We see that the Themes in Segments 11–13 all refer to the Urban Stress Test. The Urban Stress Test is being elaborated in this passage, and this portion of the letter focusses on the various attributes of the Urban Stress Test. This effect is achieved by repeatedly placing references to the Urban Stress Test within the Themes of each clause, which has the effect of making the ZPG Urban Stress Test the method of development of this portion of the letter. The N-Rhemes, on the other hand, contain the new information about the elaborated item. In this case, the N-Rhematic information gives a general description of the nature of the test (in 11a), emphasizes the work that went into developing the test (in 11b), gives a more detailed description of the test (in 12), and describes who might use it (in 13). All these attributes are quite useful in helping the reader understand the nature of the test, and in pointing out the quality and usefulness of the test.

11a. ZPG's 1985 URBAN STRESS TEST, 《F.11b》, is *the nation's first survey of how population-linked pressures affect U. S. cities.*

11b. created *after months of persistent and exhaustive research*

12. IT ranks 184 urban areas *on 11 different criteria ranging from crowding and birth rates to air quality and toxic wastes.*

13. THE URBAN STRESS TEST translates complex, technical data *into an easy-to-use action tool for concerned citizens, elected officials and opinion leaders.*

At this point in the letter, the author apparently feels that she has established the basic argument as to the effectiveness of the organization and the usefulness of the Urban Stress Test. She then turns to an argument to establish the need for further support. While she has to demonstrate that the organization is doing well, she cannot afford to imply that the organization is so effective that it no longer needs help. That is, she needs to prevent the response 'If the organization has done so well so far, why does it need my money right now?' She does so at this point by distinguishing between having a tool and using it well. Mann, Matthiessen and Thompson describe the relation between 11–13 and 14–16 as Concession. Thus this portion of the text has roughly the meaning of 'Though we have this marvelous tool [implying that we don't need help], we still need your help.' Certainly, the author emphasizes the truth of Segment 14 and devotes Segment 15 to supporting it. The author must emphasize the notion of need at this point, and it can be seen that the N-Rhemes of the various clauses do contain meanings which relate to that notion.

14a. BUT TO USE it *well,*
14b. WE urgently need *your help.*
15a. OUR SMALL STAFF is being swamped *with requests for more information*
15b. AND OUR MODEST RESOURCES are being stretched *to the limit.*
16. YOUR SUPPORT NOW[17] is *critical.*

Clause 14a implies a distinction between having the test and using it well (with *well* receiving emphasis as the N-Rheme of the clause). Similarly, the N-Rheme of 14b contains *your help* as the object of *need*. Clauses 15a and 15b seem to provide evidence to support the statement in 14b. The N-Rheme of 15a (*with requests for more information*) encoded as the Actor of the process of *being swamped* links the great reaction described in Segments 4–10 to the present problems of ZPG. The harmful aspect of the great reaction is also emphasized in 15b by placing *to the limit* in the N-Rheme of its clause as an Adverbial of the verb *being stretched*. It is worth noting again that the N-Rhemes do not necessarily contain *all* the New information in the clause. Thus in Segment 14b, the New information would probably include *urgently need* in addition to *your help*. Similarly, the New information in 15a would include *swamped*, and the New information in 15b would include *stretched* in addition to the italicized portions of those clauses. Thus, while the N-Rheme of these clauses does not exhaust the New information contained in the clause, each N-Rheme does contain at least a part of the New information.[18]

The negative effects described in clauses 15a and 15b are applied directly to aspects of ZPG. (*Our small staff* is goal of *being swamped*, and *our modest resources* is goal of *being stretched*.) So, in this passage, we see that the good results of the reaction mentioned at the beginning of the letter have their bad aspects for ZPG.

Finally, in Segment 16, *critical* is coded as an attribute of *your support now*, with *critical* emphasized by being made N-Rheme of the clause. As in the case of Segments 7 and 8, Mann, Matthiessen and Thompson suggest that Segments 14 and 16 are in a restatement relation, and indeed, these clauses provide very similar information. However, these segments have rather different information structures and emphasize different aspects of the message. *Your help* is N-Rheme in 14b; *your support* is Theme in 16. *Urgently* is neither Theme nor N-Rheme in 14b, but *critical* is N-Rheme in 16. The clause Theme of 14b is *we* (= ZPG). This sets up clauses 15a and b, which describe the reason why help is needed and continue the thematic content of the Theme of 14b (14b... *we* ... 15a *Our small staff* ... 15b ... *our modest resources* ...).

All of the clauses in Segments 14–16 emphasize meanings which can be seen to relate to the need of ZPG for funds by placing these meanings within the N-Rhemes of the component clauses. By contrast, Mann, Matthiessen and Thompson say that the next sequence of Segments (17–21) reverts to providing evidence for Segments 11–16. The evidence the author has chosen to present seems largely to concern the way the Urban Stress Test may be used and how the ZPG can profit from the reader's help. The information relevant to these aspects of the meaning is regularly placed within the N-Rhemes of the component clauses. (Again, the information functioning as New in some of the clauses includes more than merely the final clause-level constituent of the clause. In particular, the New information of Segment 17 begins with the verb *arm* and the New information in 21b probably includes *need*. The point remains, however, that the information placed in the N-Rheme forms at least a part of the core of the New information in each clause.)

17. ZPG's 1985 Urban Stress Test may be *our best opportunity ever to get the population message heard.*

18. With your contribution, ZPG can arm our growing network of local activists *with the materials they need to warn community leaders about emerging population-linked stresses* <u>before</u> *they reach the crisis stage.*

19a. Even though our national government continues to ignore *the consequences of uncontrolled population growth,*

19b. <u>we can act to take positive action *at the local level.*</u>

20. Every day decisions are being made by local officials in our communities *that could drastically affect the quality of our lives.*

21a. To make sound choices in planning *for people,*

21b. both elected officials and the american public need *the population-stress data revealed by our study.*

In Segment 20 the N-Rheme is a relative clause which forms a part of the Subject, but which has been placed within the N-Rheme of its clause. The effect of this structure is to place information describing the practical effect of these decisions (and by implication the practical effect of informing the officials who are making these decisions about the effects of population stress) into the N-Rheme of the clause. The passage ends with an assertion of need. But this time the need relates officials and the public to the data revealed by the ZPG study. (Compare clause 14b which relates *we* to *your help*.) Since Segments 17–21 provide evidence for the claims made in Segments 14–16, it is implied that the officials and public won't get the help they need unless the reader gives the help that ZPG needs.

Hard on the heels of that assertion of need follows the real pitch of the letter, Segment 22:

22. PLEASE MAKE a special contribution to Zero Population Growth *today*.

The note of urgency which has already been sounded in clauses 14b (*urgently*) and 16 (*now* and *critical*) is echoed in the N-Rhematic placement of *today*. (Note that clauses 14b and 16 are closely tied to Segment 22 in that they form part of the nucleus of the motivation for Segment 22 in the Mann, Matthiessen and Thompson analysis. As a result, any note of urgency which these two clauses invoke is likely to be carried over to the request which they motivate.)

Mann, Matthiessen and Thompson say that Segment 23 provides an additional motivation for the request expressed in Segment 22. The ideas of urgency and need are continued in Segment 23, in *immediately* in 23a, and *in the hands of those who need it most* in 23c. Again, both of these meanings constitute the N-Rhemes of their respective clauses.

23a. WHATEVER YOU GIVE – $25, $50, $100 or as much as you can – will be used *immediately*
23b. to put the Urban Stress Test *in the hands of those who need it most*.

Mann, Matthiessen and Thompson see Segments 28–30 as a postscript, an add-on which makes a second request. They see Segment 29 as a background for Segment 30, and the last clause of Segment 30 (30c) providing a means by which the actions in clause 30b are to be achieved.

29. THE RESULTS OF ZPG'S <u>1985 URBAN STRESS TEST</u> were reported as a top news story *by hundreds of newspapers and TV and radio stations from coast to coast.*

30a. I *hope*

30b. YOU'll help us monitor *this remarkable media coverage*

30c. BY completing *the enclosed reply form.*

Since Segment 29 is to provide background for Segment 30, in which the media coverage is to be mentioned, it is only natural to describe that media coverage in the background sentence and to emphasize the nature of that coverage. While it is not necessarily part of the role of this sentence in its immediate context to emphasize the wide range of reportage, it is definitely consistent with the purpose of the letter as a whole to do so, and indeed, the N-Rheme of Segment 29 echoes clause 6c by listing the major news media, and thereby implies the great extent of that coverage. (Here again is a complication of the general picture which is being investigated. Clearly the news media, having been mentioned before, are unlikely to be the focus of the New. Readers of this passage are more likely to place tonic accent on *top* or on *news* thus emphasizing *as a top news story* rather than the list of news media. Yet, the appropriateness of the wide range of coverage for the goals of the letter cannot be ignored and must be considered at least partially responsible for including such an extensive list (rather than using a short noun phrase to refer to all the news media). Also, note that the author could have reversed the order of these adverbials, but chose to mention the news media last. I believe that this order has the effect of emphasizing the news media.) Segment 30 contains an indirect request (30a and b) followed by a specification of the means by which that request is to be satisfied. Clause 30c – the one which specifies the means by which the request is to be satisfied – occurs as the N-Rheme of the entire punctuated sentence and thus is given a prominent position.

One interpretation of these facts is to say that the author feels that the request described in Segment 30 is too small to require a separate motivation. That is, once the readers perceive the need, they are likely to comply with the request. However, there is another way of looking at Segment 30. The prominence of 30c, occurring as it does at the end of its sentence, and the nature of the relation between 30c and the rest of Segment 30, implies that 30c is a request itself. Indeed, the relation between clauses 30b and 30c can be viewed as a metaphorical realization of Motivation—Request. Clause 30b describes ZPG's goal (= monitoring this remarkable media coverage). If the readers agree with this goal then they will be more likely to comply with the request that they fill out the reply form.

Regardless of how we interpret Segment 30, this segment provides the only true exception within the letter to the notion that the N-Rheme contains informationally prominent material. Clause 30b contains the N-Rheme *this remarkable media coverage* which refers to the reports mentioned in Segment 29 and so is not likely to be presented as New information. Rather *monitor* is more likely to be the core of the New information.

The N-Rheme of clause 30c (*the enclosed reply form*) appears to present a similar situation. The reply form is known from the physical context, it is physically present, thus the reference to it does not convey new information. Yet, a reading of clause 30c with the accent on *completing* sounds unlikely in this context. Several factors contribute to this fact. First, only a few requests are likely to be made concerning reply forms in this context. That is, the author is likely to ask the reader to *fill out* or *send in* or *complete* the reply form, not to *throw it away*, etc. Thus, the verb itself is moderately predictable in this context. Further, the author's suggestion is made in the context of another more urgent request – to write out (= complete?) a check. Thus, we may perhaps take the entire clause *by completing the enclosed reply form* as the New information. Thus, clause 33c constitutes another example in which the N-Rheme contains a portion of the new information, even though the particular information expressed in that N-Rheme is well known to the reader.

Summary

The discussion so far has been phrased in terms of a detailed examination of the ZPG letter from the point of view of each clause. Let me change the approach to try to summarize the trends in this text. Several bits of evidence point to the fact that in contrast with Themes, N-Rhemes are being used as a position of emphasis, and that the information placed within the N-Rhemes relates directly to the general goals of the text. Table 4.1 presents all the Themes and N-Rhemes of this text.

First, some general comments about Table 4.1. There are 34 clauses in the body of this letter. Of these 34 clauses, eight are non-finite clauses,[19] and do not have topical Themes, so only 26 of the clauses have topical Themes. By contrast, all 34 clauses present new information somewhere in them, thus there are 34 N-Rhemes.

Table 4.1 Themes and N-Rhemes in the ZPG letter

	Theme	**N-Rheme**
B.4.	AT 7:00 A.M. ON OCTOBER 25,	started to ring.
B.5.	CALLS	all day.
B.6a.	STAFFERS	late into the night,
B.6b.		Questions
B.6c.	AND	with reporters from newspapers, radio stations, wire services and TV stations in every part of the country.
C.7a.	WHEN WE	the results of ZPG's 1985 Urban Stress Test,
C.7b.	WE	no idea we'd get such an overwhelming response.
C.8.	MEDIA AND PUBLIC REACTION	nothing short of incredible!
D.9.	AT FIRST, THE DELUGE OF CALLS	mostly from reporters eager to tell the public about Urban Stress Test results and from outraged public officials who were furious that we had 'blown the whistle' on conditions in their cities.
E.10.	NOW, WE	from concerned citizens in all parts of the country who want to know what they can do to hold local officials accountable for tackling population-related problems that threaten public health and well-being.
F.11a.	ZPG'S 1985 URBAN STRESS TEST,	the nation's first survey of how population-linked pressures affect U.S. cities.
F.11b.		after months of persistent and exhaustive research
F.12.	IT	on 11 different criteria ranging from crowding and birth rates to air quality and toxic wastes.
G.13.	THE URBAN STRESS TEST	into an easy-to-use action tool for concerned citizens, elected officials and opinion leaders.
G.14a.	BUT	well,
G.14b.	WE	your help.
H.15a.	OUR SMALL STAFF	with requests for more information
H.15b.	AND OUR MODEST RESOURCES	to the limit.
I.16.	YOUR SUPPORT NOW	critical.
I.17.	ZPG'S 1985 URBAN STRESS TEST	our best opportunity ever to get the population message heard.
J.18.	WITH YOUR CONTRIBUTION,	with the materials they need to warn community leaders about emerging population-linked stresses before they reach the crisis stage.
K.19a.	EVEN THOUGH OUR NATIONAL GOVERNMENT	the consequences of uncontrolled population growth,

K.19b.	WE	can act
K.19c.		at the local level.
L.20.	EVERY DAY	that could drastically affect the quality of our lives.
L.21a.		sound choices
L 21b.		in planning for people,
L.21c.	BOTH ELECTED OFFICIALS AND THE AMERICAN PUBLIC	the population-stress data revealed by our study.
M.22.	PLEASE MAKE	today.
N.23a.	WHATEVER YOU GIVE –	Immediately
N.23c.		in the hands of those who need it most.
P.29.	THE RESULTS OF ZPG'S 1985 URBAN STRESS TEST	by hundreds of newspapers and TV and radio stations from coast to coast.
P.30a.	I	hope
P.30b.	YOU	this remarkable media coverage
P.30c.		the enclosed reply form.

Table 4.2 Summary of meanings expressed in Themes and N-Rhemes in the ZPG letter

	Expressed within Theme		Expressed within N-Rheme	
	Grammatically prominent	Grammatically non-prominent	Grammatically prominent	Grammatically non-prominent
Establishing interpersonal involvement	12	0	2	2
I	1	0	0	0
You	4	0	1	0
We = staff & members of ZPG	7	0	1	2
Appraisals	5	0	21	3
ZPG organization, staff, resources	5	1	0	1
Urban Stress Test	4	1	0	2
Population problem			1	7
Media, government officials or public	3	0	6	2
Other	2		9	

Table 4.2 summarizes the meanings which are expressed in the Themes and the N-Rhemes of the ZPG letter. In this summary, a distinction is made between those meanings which are grammatically prominent and those which are not grammatically prominent. In the case of nominal groups, meanings which are expressed in some

function (such as Head, or Deictic) of the dominant nominal group are considered to be grammatically prominent. Meanings which are expressed in some embedded construction within the nominal group (such as *our* in *the population-stress data revealed by our study*, or *we* in *no idea we'd get such an overwhelming response*) are considered to be grammatically non-prominent. If the structure is a prepositional phrase, any meaning which is expressed in the preposition or directly in the structure of the nominal group which functions as Complement of the preposition will be considered grammatically prominent. Only one phrase-complex occurred within this text (i.e. the N-Rheme of Segment D.9). This is a paratactic phrase-complex, so this complex is simply treated as two prepositional phrases. If the structure is an embedded clause, then the items which directly fill the elements of structure of the clause are considered grammatically prominent.

Of the 26 Themes in this text, one is a prepositional phrase and one is a prepositional phrase-complex; a third is an embedded clause. The topical Themes of the other 23 clauses are nominal groups. As is to be expected the structures which occur within the N-Rhemes are much longer and more complex, and include adverbial groups, nominal groups, verbal groups, prepositional phrases, a prepositional phrase-complex, and an embedded clause.

Twelve (that is, almost one-half) of the nominal Themes of this letter are devoted to establishing an I–you relationship with the audience. (Indeed, in seven of these Themes *I, you* or *we* is the Head of the group.) By contrast only four N-Rhemes make any reference to *you* or *we* at all, and two of those references are buried grammatically.

Only five of the clause Themes of the letter contain words and phrases which appraise. By contrast, within the N-Rhemes, appraisal items dominate. Twenty-one of the 34 N-Rhemes contain appraisal items which are grammatically prominent. An additional three N-Rhemes contain appraisals which are not grammatically prominent. It should be noted that in eleven of these N-Rhemes appraisal seems to be the *focus* of the N-Rheme. Table 4.3 presents these examples.

In addition to the eleven examples in Table 4.3, two N-Rhemes consist of extensive lists (B.6c, *with reporters from newspapers, radio stations, wire services and TV stations in every part of the country*, and F.12, *on 11 different criteria ranging from crowding and birth rates to air quality and toxic wastes*). These lists are extensive enough to constitute appraisals themselves, even though one of them does not contain any *words* that appraise. Thus, thirteen of the 34 N-Rhemes *focus* on appraisal.

Table 4.3 N-Rhemes which focus on appraisal

B.5.	all day
B.6a.	late into the night
C.7b.	no idea we'd get such an overwhelming response.
C.8.	nothing short of incredible!
F.11b.	after months of persistent and exhaustive research
H.15b.	to the limit
I.16.	critical
I.17.	our best opportunity ever to get the population message heard.
L.20.	that could drastically affect the quality of our lives.
M.22.	today
N.23a.	Immediately

Mentions of the ZPG organization, its staff and its resources, and of the Urban Stress Test, occur primarily with the Themes of the clauses. It should be noted that three of the thematic mentions of the Urban Stress Test occur within a section of the letter which describes the nature of that test (Segments F.11–G.12). By contrast, mentions of the population problem occur only within the N-Rhemes, and they are typically not grammatically prominent (as might be expected of information that the writer assumes her readers agree with her on). Mentions of the groups of people that ZPG should influence – the media, the public and government officials – typically occur within the N-Rhemes of the clauses and are regularly grammatically prominent.

Even where Themes and N-Rhemes contain similar information, that information is being used in different ways. For example, temporal adverbials appear both thematically and N-Rhematically. However, these adverbials have quite different effects in the two positions. Table 4.4 lists the clauses which contain thematic temporal adverbials.

Table 4.5 contains all the clauses of the ZPG text which contain temporal adverbials in the N-Rhemes of the clauses.

In Table 4.4, with one exception (that in Segment 20, which I wish to return to later), the adverbials are being used to locate the clause in time. One Theme, *when* in clause 7a, is a structural Theme and is required to be initial in its clause. As a result, I do not wish to lay great store on the fact that it is thematic.[20] In the remainder of these examples, the temporal adverbial seems merely to locate the action described in the rest of the clause. It is not a major part of the news. This is true even in cases in which the initial adverbial is separated from the remainder of its clause by a comma (as in Segments 4 and 9),

Table 4.4 Thematic Temporal Adverbials

4.	AT 7:00 AM ON OCTOBER 25, our phones started to ring.
7a.	WHEN we released the results of ZPG's 1985 Urban Stress Test,
9.	AT FIRST, THE DELUGE OF CALLS came mostly from reporters eager to tell the public about Urban Stress Test results and from outraged public officials who were furious that we had 'blown the whistle' on conditions in their cities.
10.	NOW we are hearing from concerned citizens in all parts of the country who want to know what they can do to hold local officials accountable for tackling population-related problems that threaten public health and well-being.
20.	EVERY DAY decisions are being made by local officials in our communities that could drastically affect the quality of our lives.

Table 4.5 N-Rhematic Temporal Averbials

5.	Calls jammed our switchboard *all day*.
6a.	Staffers stayed *late into the night*,
11b.	created *after months of persistent and exhaustive research*,
22.	Please make a special contribution to Zero Population Growth *today*.
23.	Whatever you give – ... – will be used *immediately*

and so can be seen to require a focus of information. (In fact, when I read Segments 10 and 20 aloud, I also tend to emphasize the initial adverbials. As a result, these can be seen to convey important information. However, that information seems to be used to orient the reader to the message which follows – the function that we have been hypothesizing for the meaning of Theme.)

By contrast, the temporal adverbials in Table 4.5 seem to constitute an integral part of the message. One might say that this impression results from the different nature of the adverbials. For example, the first three clauses contain adverbials of extent (*all day*, *late into the night* and *after months of persistent and exhaustive research*). However, the other two adverbials (*today* and *immediately*) locate the action in time, and convey meanings similar to the ones expressed by the adverbials in Table 4.5. However, there is a great difference in the effect of the use of *today* and *immediately* in Segments 22 and 23 from the use of *at 7:00 AM on October 25* (in Segment 4), *at first* (Segment 9), or *now* (Segment 10). In Segments 22 and 23, the adverbials are much more an integral part of the message. There is an urgency about the use of these words in this context that the other examples do not convey. Note that the urgency is not merely conveyed by the nature of the words themselves. That is, the same words, used in a different way would not have the same effect. Note the difference between saying 23 and 23i:

23. Please make a special contribution to Zero Population Growth today.

23i. Today, please make a special contribution to Zero Population Growth.

Example 23i simply does not have the same urgency that Segment 23 has.[21]

Finally, as my third point, let me return to the five Segments (mentioned above) which contain appraising terms in their Themes. These are given in Table 4.6. The examples in Table 4.6 are exceptional in that the Themes contain words which appraise. Do these examples constitute counter-examples to the basic hypothesis that the N-Rheme of the clause generally contains appraisals while the Themes do not? The answer is 'no', for the N-Rhemes of these clauses also contain appraisals. Indeed, the N-Rhemes of these clauses contain information which is much more relevant to the goal of the clause in its context. For example, the purpose of Segment 9 is to elaborate on the nature of the public and media reaction mentioned in Segment 8. *The deluge of calls* is a cohesive phrase referring back to and evaluating the reaction mentioned in Segment 8, while the list of callers is given in the N-Rheme of Segment 9. Clauses 15a and 15b provide similar examples. Segment 14 asserts that we need help, and Segment 15 describes why that help is needed. *Our small staff* and *our modest resources* (from Segment 15) again involve cohesive reference together with evaluation, while the main point of the clauses is the swamping with requests and the stretching to the limit – the information that is found within the Rhemes of the two clauses.

Segment 16 is slightly different. Here *now* modifies *support*, and since *support* has been made Theme, *now* is also included as part of

Table 4.6 Appraising terms in the Themes

9.	AT FIRST, THE DELUGE OF CALLS came *mostly from reporters eager to tell the public about Urban Stress Test results and from outraged public officials who were furious that we had 'blown the whistle' on conditions in their cities.*
15a.	OUR SMALL STAFF is being swamped *with requests for more information*
15b.	AND OUR MODEST RESOURCES are being stretched *to the limit.*
16.	YOUR SUPPORT NOW is *critical.*
20.	EVERY DAY decisions are being made by local officials in our communities *that could drastically affect the quality of our lives.*

the Theme. It is worth noting, however, that Segment 16 contains *critical* as N-Rheme, a word which clearly contains an urgent evaluative meaning which is directly relevant to the purpose of that clause.

Segment 20 is, perhaps, more interesting. In the discussion of the clauses in Table 4.4, Segment 20 was exceptional in that it contained a temporal Theme which clearly communicated a sense of urgency. However, let us look at the structure of that clause more closely. It is reproduced below:

20. EVERY DAY <u>decisions</u> are being made by local officials in our communities *<u>that could drastically affect the quality of our lives</u>*.

The underlined portions constitute a single noun phrase that has been separated by placing the relative clause at the end of the including clause. If we examine this relative clause, we see that it contains the 'emotive' term *drastically*. Further, it describes the practical effect of the decisions. That is, the relative clause describes the urgent importance for us of the decisions which are being mentioned. Thus, Segment 20 fits into the pattern that we have already seen in this letter: the N-Rhemes of the component clauses express ideas that involve some emotive judgment, and show the importance of what is being discussed for the reader. Segment 20, however, contains two portions which convey that sort of information: the postposed relative clause, and *every day*. Given the content of that segment, the author had to choose which meaning was most important to emphasize, and chose to emphasize the effect of the decisions on the lives of the readers. I believe that she could very well have chosen to emphasize the urgency via the frequency. She could have chosen to write:

20i. Decisions that could drastically affect the quality of our lives are being made by local officials in our communities every day.

But that wording would have had another effect. (Notice that although placing the relative clause at the beginning increases the 'weight' and complexity of the Subject and thus the flow of the resulting sentence is rather unusual, the resulting construction is far from ungrammatical. That is, we cannot explain the appropriateness of the actual wording of Segment 20 merely by referring to sentence internal concerns.)

In summary, then, all of the five clauses in Table 4.6 contain N-Rhemes which are directly relevant to the goals of their respective clauses. Indeed, most of those N-Rhemes contain strongly evaluative terms such as *to the limit, critical* and *drastically*. In other words, the importance to the goals of these clauses of the information in their N-Rhemes seems to outrank the evaluative meanings which appear in their Themes. Thus, there seems to be a hierarchy of relevance to the goals of these segments with the highest-ranking information appearing in the N-rheme of the clause.[22]

In the interests of ease of investigation, I have taken a particularly rigid approach to the notion of information. Something either is or is not 'newsworthy', and I considered placement in the N-Rheme to be the indicator of 'newsworthiness' in writing. In spite of that rigid approach, there is a general correlation of newsworthiness and placement within the N-Rheme. In only one of 34 clauses was there a true exception to this tendency. One case was doubtful. In several other clauses the New information included more than merely the N-Rheme. This last situation is merely a complication of the picture, however. By contrast, information placed thematically in the clauses was never informationally prominent in a way paralleling the role of the N-Rheme. In other words, the author of the ZPG letter clearly used thematic and N-Rhematic position in the clause for different purposes. The content of the N-Rhemes regularly concerned information which related to the purposes of the text, of the text segment and of the sentence and clause of which it was a part. On the other hand, the content of the Themes, even when they were separated from their main clauses by commas, regularly did not relate to the purposes of the text and text segments. Rather the content of the various Themes served as orienters to the information contained in the clauses. Comparing the information placed in the two positions helps us develop a better sense of the operation of each one separately.

Appendix I

Dear Friend of ZPG:

At 7:00 a.m. on October 25, our phones started to ring. Calls jammed our switchboard all day. Staffers stayed late into the night, answering questions and talking with reporters from newspapers, radio stations, wire services and TV stations in every part of the country.

When we released the results of ZPG's <u>1985 Urban Stress Test</u>, we had no idea we'd get such an overwhelming response. Media and public reaction has been nothing short of incredible!

At first, the deluge of calls came mostly from reporters eager to tell the public about Urban Stress Test results and from outraged public officials who were furious that we had 'blown the whistle' on conditions in their cities.

Now we are hearing from concerned citizens in all parts of the country who want to know what they can do to hold local officials accountable for tackling population-related problems that threaten public health and well-being.

ZPG's <u>1985 Urban Stress Test</u>, created after months of persistent and exhaustive research, is the nation's first survey of how population-linked pressures affect U.S. cities. It ranks 184 urban areas on 11 different criteria ranging from crowding and birth rates to air quality and toxic wastes.

The Urban Stress Test translates complex, technical data into an easy-to-use <u>action tool</u> for concerned citizens, elected officials and opinion leaders. But to use it well, we urgently need your help.

<u>Our small staff is being swamped with requests for more information and our modest resources are being stretched to the limit.</u>

Your support now is critical. <u>ZPG's 1985 Urban Stress Test</u> may be our best opportunity ever to get the population message heard.

With your contribution, ZPG can arm our growing network of local activists with the materials they need to warn community leaders about emerging population-linked stresses <u>before</u> they reach the crisis stage.

Even though our national government continues to ignore the consequences of uncontrolled population growth, <u>we can act to take positive action at the local level.</u>

Every day decisions are being made by local officials in our communities that could drastically affect the quality of our lives. To make sound choices in planning for people, both elected officials and the American public need the population-stress data revealed by our study.

<u>Please make a special contribution to Zero Population Growth today.</u> Whatever you give – $25, $50, $100 or as much as you can – will be used immediately to put the Urban Stress Test in the hands of those who need it most.

Sincerely

Susan Weber
Executive Director

P.S. The results of the ZPG's <u>1985 Urban Stress Test</u> were reported as a top news story by hundreds of newspapers and TV and radio stations from coast to coast. I hope you'll help us monitor this remarkable media coverage by completing the enclosed reply form.

Appendix II: ZPG text – Analysed by non-rankshifted clauses

Key:

SMALL CAPS	indicate the Theme of the clause.
Italics	indicate the N-Rheme of the clause.
<u>Underlining</u>	as in the original.

Numbering

Capital letters indicate paragraphs.
Arabic numbers indicate punctuated sentences or other segments.
Small letters indicate clauses within a sentence.

B.4. AT 7:00 A.M. ON OCTOBER 25, our phones *started to ring.*

B.5. CALLS jammed our switchboard *all day.*

B.6a. STAFFERS stayed *late into the night,*

B.6b. answering *questions*

B.6c. AND talking *with reporters from newspapers, radio stations, wire services and TV stations in every part of the country.*

C.7a. WHEN WE released *the results of ZPG's <u>1985 Urban Stress Test</u>.*

C.7b. WE had *no idea we'd get such an overwhelming response.*

C.8. MEDIA AND PUBLIC REACTION has been *nothing short of incredible!*

D.9. AT FIRST, THE DELUGE OF CALLS came *mostly from reporters eager to tell the public about Urban Stress Test results and from outraged public officials who were furious that we had 'blown the whistle' on conditions in their cities.*

E.10. NOW, WE are hearing *from concerned citizens in all parts of the country who want to know what they can do to hold local officials accountable for tackling population-related problems that threaten public health and well-being.*

F.11a ZPG's <u>1985 URBAN STRESS TEST</u>, ⟪F.11b⟫, is *the nation's first survey of how population-linked pressures affect U.S. cities.*

F.11b. created *after months of persistent and exhaustive research*

F.12. IT ranks 184 urban areas *on 11 different criteria ranging from crowding and birth rates to air quality and toxic wastes.*

G.13. THE URBAN STRESS TEST translates complex, technical data *into an easy-to-use <u>action tool</u> for concerned citizens, elected officials and opinion leaders.*

G.14a BUT to use it *well.*

G.14b. WE urgently need *your help.*

H.15a. <u>OUR SMALL STAFF is being swamped *with requests for more information*</u>

H.15b. <u>AND OUR MODEST RESOURCES are being stretched *to the limit.*</u>

I.16. YOUR SUPPORT NOW is *critical.*

I.17. <u>ZPG's 1985 URBAN STRESS TEST</u> may be *our best opportunity ever to get the population message heard.*

J.18. WITH YOUR CONTRIBUTION, ZPG can arm our growing network of local activists *with the materials they need to warn community leaders about emerging population-linked stresses <u>before</u> they reach the crisis stage.*

K.19a. EVEN THOUGH OUR NATIONAL GOVERNMENT continues to ignore *the consequences of uncontrolled population growth.*

K.19b. <u>WE can *act*</u>

K.19c. <u>to take positive action *at the local level.*</u>

L.20.   EVERY DAY decisions are being made by local officials in our communities *that could drastically affect the quality of our lives.*

L.21a.   To make *sound choices in planning for people,*

L.21b.   BOTH ELECTED OFFICIALS AND THE AMERICAN PUBLIC need *the population-stress data revealed by our study.*

M.22.   <u>PLEASE MAKE a special contribution to Zero Population Growth *today*.</u>

N.23a.   WHATEVER YOU GIVE – 《N.23b》 – will be used *immediately*

N.23b. $25, $50, $100 or *as much as you can*

N.23c.   to put the Urban Stress Test *in the hands of those who need it most.*

O.24.   Sincerely

O.25.   [SIGNATURE]

O.26.   Susan Weber

O.27.   Executive Director

P.28.   P.S.

P.29.   THE RESULTS OF ZPG'S <u>1985 URBAN STRESS TEST</u> were reported as a top news story *by hundreds of newspapers and TV and radio stations from coast to coast.*

P.30a.   I *hope*

P.30b.   YOU'll help us monitor *this remarkable media coverage*

P.30c.   by completing *the enclosed reply form.*

Appendix III

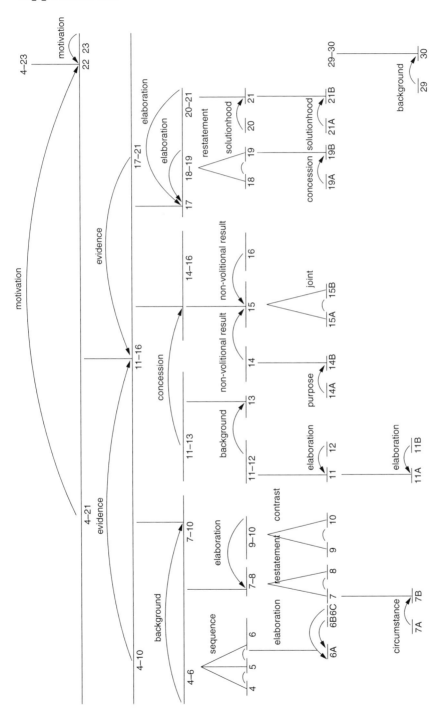

Notes

1. This chapter has been affected by the responses of a number of audiences including the Spring 1988 meeting of the Applied Linguistics Working Group at York University in Toronto, the Summer School in Linguistics at Jyväskylä in 1989, the Technical University of Berlin, the English Department at the University of Birmingham, the London Institute of Education and the Mini International Systemic Congress at Nottingham. I would like to thank William C. Mann and Sandra A. Thompson for extensive critical comments on an earlier version of this chapter. While I am sure that they disagree with many aspects, I hope they will see their influence. Finally, Christian Matthiessen has also contributed substantially to the nature of the chapter. A paper derived from an early version of this paper entitled 'On Theme, Rheme and discourse goals' was published in Malcolm Coulthard (ed.), *Advances in Written Text Analysis*, London: Routledge & Kegan Paul, 1994, 229–249.

2. In this chapter, I will follow the convention of capitalizing terms which refer to grammatical functions. This convention will be essential when terms are used both in a non-technical sense and as a technical term for a grammatical function. Thus, *New* refers to a grammatical function, while *new* refers to something which is being introduced for the first time (i.e. is unfamiliar). While there is a strong correlation between the two, these are not the same notions. See Fries (1998/2001) for an extended discussion of the difference.

3. More specifically, the Theme is the first constituent which 'has a function in transitivity' Halliday (1994:53). Transitivity is one aspect of the experiential metafunction.

4. Note for example that the lengthy argument of Huddleston vs. Matthiessen and Martin turns in large part on this very matter. See Huddleston (1988, 1991) vs. Martin (1992c), Martin and Matthiessen (1992) and Matthiessen and Martin (1991).

5. See the discussion of topic in Brown and Yule (1980).

6. See also Winter (1977:475) for a similar wording when describing the meanings of Theme and Rheme.

7. It is often pointed out that the term *anthropologists* is cohesive with the term *culture*, a word that is part of the title of Gregg's book and forms the major topic of the book. However, that cohesive tie does not seem to be essential to the nature and operation of the Theme in this instance. The author could have mentioned any prominent group of people who have an irrelevant interpretation of the word *culture*. Thus, she could just as well have begun with wording such as 'As used in layman's language, the term culture refers to ...' Had she taken this approach, she would have been required to devote a second sentence to contrast the irrelevant use by the other group with the relevant interpretation used by anthropologists.

8. Presenting familiar information with tonic accents is often explained away by referring to 'contrastive accent'. However, Lambrecht (1994) provides sufficient evidence that such a simple explanation is not possible in many cases. See also Fries (1998/2001) for a similar discussion.

9. Chafe (1994:65–66) finds that about 60 per cent of his intonation units are single clauses.

10. A correlational model is actually too simple. For example, it is highly likely that thematic content will correlate with the structure of the text, and, further, thematic status in particular structurally important sentences in a text segment will correlate with perception of a nominal constituent as topic. I am using the simple correlational model first in order to get a rough approximation.

11. Certainly, such a study could be carried out on spoken text, but the results would probably differ. The interest in N-Rheme arose here from the limited tools available to writers to signal emphasis, and the hypothesis that one major tool which they use is word order. Since speakers have a number of additional tools available to them to signal their emphases, one would suspect that the correlation of N-Rheme and emphasis would not be as great in the spoken language.

12. Fries (1993) attempts to use the analysis of systematic repetition in a short text to predict the perception of New information.

13. Saying that the N-Rheme is the newsworthy part of the clause should not be taken to imply too close an association between the N-Rheme and the placement of the tonic accent. Although the initial reason for positing N-Rheme lay in the unmarked placement of the tonic on the last major constituent of the clause, there are a number of reasons which lead speakers to deviate from that pattern. First and most frequently, the New information may include more than merely the grammatical unit which includes the tonic syllable. Thus, in the text under discussion later in this chapter, Segment 15a is *Our small staff is being swamped with requests for more information*. Though the N-Rheme of this segment contains only *with requests for more information*, the New extends forward to include *is being swamped* also.

A more interesting complication of the situation occurs when the latter part of a clause is predictable based on some earlier portion. Segment 4 of the ZPG text is *At seven A.M. on October 25, our phones began to ring*. In this case *began to ring* conveys little new information, since phones normally do little else. As a result, *began to ring* is unlikely to contain a tonic accent. Since the argument for the absence of tonic accent concerns a clause-*internal* redundancy, and not a cohesive tie to some prior text segment (compare the examples discussed in Davies 1989), the information presented in this phrase is still considered to be part of the New information. Indeed, since this segment constitutes the first sentence of the letter, the entire clause is news and *started to ring* describes the first event of the narrative. As a result, this N-Rheme is considered to be closely related to the goals of the text and of the text segment of which it is a part. (See Chafe 1994: Chapter 9 for an interesting discussion of similar issues.)

14. It should be noted that this letter is typical of written English in that most clause Themes are simple Themes. That is the clause Themes of this letter typically contain only information from the experiential metafunction. The four exceptions to this generalization are C.7a (*when we*) and K.19a (*Even though our national government*) in which structural Themes precede the topical Themes; and D.9 (*At first, the deluge of calls*) and E.10 (*Now, we*), in which continuative Themes precede the topical Themes.

    Finally it should be noted that non-finite dependent clauses do not have normal thematic structures.

15. Winter (1992:147–148) points out the intimate relation between imperatives and motivations:

    We are, so to speak, linguistically free human beings; we have a very strong tendency to why-question any imperative. The rule runs something like this: if an imperative is *not* preceded by a reason, then this reason is predicted as the next clause. If, however, the reason *does* precede the imperative, then it is linguistically complete and no longer predicts the reason to come: [emphasis in the original]

16. It has already been pointed out that the New information in a clause may not be restricted to the content of the N-Rheme. The whole of Segment 4 is clearly New information. Similarly, we can reasonably say that *jammed* in Segment 5 and *stayed* in Clause 6a would most likely form part of the New information in those clauses.

17. I have interpreted *now* as an adverbial within the nominalized clause *your support*, largely since the letter seems to me to constitute a plea for immediate support (e.g. note the emphasis on *today* in Segment 22 and other references to urgency.) Another possible interpretation of this structure would be to interpret *now* as an adverbial (in a slightly unusual position) within the including clause (roughly parallel to *Now your support is critical*). Both analyses seem reasonable in the context. The analysis presented here is not affected by the different interpretations.

18. Chafe (1992:290 and 293) analyses *small* and *modest* as expressing new information on the grounds that these ideas have not previously been implied in the letter. While I would agree that these ideas have not been implied, I believe that they are not *presented* as New information. Rather they are included in order to increase the plausibility of the information which *is* being presented as New, i.e. that the staff is being *swamped with requests* ... and the resources are *being stretched to the limit*. One piece of evidence that *small* and *modest* are *not* being presented as New is that they can easily be omitted with little damage to the function of these clauses in the context.

19. See Halliday (1994) for the conditions under which non-finite clauses are analysed as clauses, rather than infinitive or participial phrases.

20. While one cannot draw major conclusions on the basis of the placement of *when* within its clause, we can move up a level and examine the relative placement of the two clauses within the T-unit in Segment 7. At the level of T-unit, the entire clause 7a serves as a temporal adverbial for Segment 7. Further, it functions as Theme for the T-unit by setting the time-frame for the event depicted in that T-unit. In other words, when considered as a whole, Segment 7 fits the pattern of the effects of the thematic placement of temporal adverbials established by the other clauses in Table 4.4.

21. It is worthy of note that most fund-raising letters contain some identifiable request such as this one, and the sentence which expresses that request will usually contain a temporal adverbial in the N-Rheme. A survey of 21 fund-raising letters shows that all letters contained at least one identifiable request. Some letters contained more than one request so that the corpus contained a total of 26 requests. Of these 26 requests, four requests made no mention of time. The remaining 22 made at least one reference to time. One contained two references to time. As a result, the corpus contained 23 references to time. *Today* (with fourteen occurrences) and *now* (with six occurrences) were the most frequently used temporal adverbials in the data. Two temporal adverbials were neither Theme nor N-Rheme. Four temporal adverbials were placed within the themes of their clauses, while seventeen temporal adverbials occurred in the N-Rhemes of their clauses.

22. This approach is reminiscent of the notion of communicative dynamism discussed by Firbas (1982).

References

Bäcklund, Ingegerd (1989) *To sum up*: initial infinitives as cues to the reader. In *Proceedings from the Fourth Nordic Conference for English Studies, Helsingør, May 11–13, 1989*, ed. by Graham Caie, Kirsten Haastrup, Arnt Lykke Jakobsen, Jørgen Erik Nielsen, Jørgen Sevaldsen, Henrik Specht and Arne Zettersten, Department of English, University of Copenhagen, 289–302.

Brown, Gillian and Yule, George (1980) *Discourse Analysis*. Cambridge: Cambridge University Press.

Chafe, Wallace L. (1980) The deployment of consciousness in the production of a narrative. *The Pear Stories: Cognitive, Cultural, and Linguistic Aspects of Narrative Production*, ed. by Wallace L. Chafe, Norwood, NJ: Ablex, 9–50.

Chafe, Wallace L. (1984) How people use adverbial clauses. *Proceedings of the Tenth Annual Meeting of the Berkeley Linguistics Society*, Berkeley, Berkeley Linguistics Society, 437–449.

Chafe, Wallace L. (1992) The flow of ideas in a sample of written language. In Mann and Thompson (1992):267–294.

Chafe, Wallace L. (1994) *Discourse, Consciousness and Time: The Flow and Displacement of Conscious Experience in Speaking and Writing.* Chicago: University of Chicago Press.

Crystal, David (1975) *The English Tone of Voice.* London: Edward Arnold.

Davies, Martin (1989) Prosodic and non-prosodic cohesion in English. *Word*, 40:255–262.

Firbas, Jan (1982) Has every sentence a theme and a rheme? *Language Form and Linguistic Variation*, ed. by John Anderson, Amsterdam: John Benjamins, 97–115.

Fries, Peter H. (1981) On the status of theme in English: arguments from discourse. *Forum Linguisticum*, 6:1–38.

Fries, Peter H. (1993) On repetition and interpretation. In *New Horizons in Functional Linguistics*, ed. by S. K. Verma and V. Prakasam, Hyderabad: Booklinks Corporation, 69–102.

Fries, Peter H. (1995a) Themes, methods of development, and texts. In *On Subject and Theme: From the Perspective of Functions in Discourse*, ed. by Ruqaia Hasan and Peter H. Fries, Amsterdam: John Benjamins, 317–359.

Fries, Peter H. (1995b) Patterns of information in initial position in English. In *Discourse in Society: Functional Perspectives*, ed. by Peter H. Fries and Michael Gregory, Norwood, NJ: Ablex, 47–66.

Fries, Peter H. (1998/2001) Issues in modeling the textual metafunction a constructive approach. Paper delivered at the 25th International Systemic Congress, Cardiff, July 1998. In *Patterns of Text: In Honour of Michael Hoey*, ed. by Mike Scott and Geoff Thompson, Amsterdam: John Benjamins, 83–107.

Fries, Peter H. and Francis, Gill, (1992) Exploring theme: problems for research. *Occasional Papers in Systemic Linguistics*, 6:45–60. Also in *Systemic Functional Linguistic Forum*, 1(1):51–63.

Gregg, Joan Young (1985) *Communication and Culture: A Reading Writing Text.* Belmont, CA: Wadsworth.

Halliday, M. A. K. (1967) Notes on transitivity and theme in English: Part 2. *Journal of Linguistics*, 3:177–274.

Halliday, M. A. K. (1970) Language structure and language function. In *New Horizons in Linguistics*, ed. by John Lyons, Harmondsworth, Penguin, 140–164.

Halliday, M. A. K. (1977) Text as semantic choice in social contexts. In *Grammars and Descriptions*, ed. by Teun A. van Dijk and Janos Petöfi, Berlin: Walter de Gruyter, 176–255.

Halliday, M. A. K. (1985) *An Introduction to Functional Grammar.* London: Edward Arnold.

Halliday, M. A. K. (1994) *An Introduction to Functional Grammar* (2nd edn). London: Edward Arnold.

Huddleston, Rodney (1988) Constituency, multi-functionality and grammaticalization in Halliday's functional grammar. *Journal of Linguistics*, 24:137–174.

Huddleston, Rodney (1991) Further remarks on Halliday's functional grammar: a reply to Matthiessen and Martin. *Occasional Papers in Linguistics*, 5:75–129.

Hunt, Kellogg (1965) *Grammatical Structures Written at Three Grade-Levels*. Champaign, IL: NCTE.

Lambrecht, Knud (1994) *Information Structure and Sentence Form: Topic, Focus and the Mental Representations of Discourse Referents*. Cambridge: Cambridge University Press.

Mann, William C., Matthiessen, Christian M. I. M. and Thompson, Sandra A. (1992) Rhetorical structure theory and text analysis. In Mann and Thompson (1992), 39–78.

Mann, William C. and Thompson, Sandra A. (1985) Assertions from discourse structure. *Proceedings from the Eleventh Annual Meeting of the Berkeley Linguistics Society*, Berkeley: Berkeley Linguistics Society, 245–258.

Mann, William C. and Thompson, Sandra A. (1986) Relational propositions in discourse. *Discourse Processes*, 9(1):57–90.

Mann, William C. and Thompson, Sandra A. (eds.) (1992) *Discourse Description: Diverse Linguistic Analyses of a Fundraising Text*. Amsterdam: John Benjamins.

Martin, James R. (1992a) *English Text: System and Structure*. Amsterdam: John Benjamins.

Martin, James R. (1992b) Macro-proposals: meaning by degree. In Mann and Thompson (1992), 359–395.

Martin, James R. (1992c) Theme, method of development and existentiality: the price of reply. *Occasional Papers in Linguistics*, 6:147–183.

Martin, James R. (2000) Beyond exchange: appraisal systems in English. In *Evaluation in Text: Authorial Stance and the Construction of Discourse*, ed. by Susan Hunstan and Geoffrey Thompson, Oxford: Oxford University Press, 142–175.

Martin, James R. and Matthiessen, Christian (1992) A brief note on Huddleston's reply to Matthiesen and Martin's response to Huddleston's review of Halliday's *Introduction to Functional Grammar*. *Occasional Papers in Linguistics*, 6:185–195.

Matthiessen, Christian and Martin, James (1991) A response to Huddleston's review of Halliday's *Introduction to Functional Grammar*. *Occasional Papers in Linguistics*, 5:5–74.

Tench, Paul (1990) *The Roles of Intonation in English Discourse*. Frankfurt am Main: Peter Lang.

Tench, Paul (1996) *The Intonation Systems of English*. London: Cassell.

Winter, Eugene O. (1977) Replacement as a function of repetition: a study of some of its principal features in the clause relations of contemporary English. #77–70,036, Ann Arbor MI: University Microfilms.

Winter, Eugene O. (1992) The notion of unspecific versus specific as one way of analysing the information of a fund-raising letter. In Mann and Thompson (1992), 131–170.

5

Intrastratal and Interstratal Relations in Language and Their Functions

David G. Lockwood

Introduction

In its various specific models, the stratificational theory of language attempts to deal with the diverse facts of language structure with a few essential relationships used repeatedly in relatively few relational patterns. The present chapter aims to survey the fundamental relations among them and to discuss the more specific varieties of them all, as proposed for special purposes by various researchers.[1]

It has been the aim of most stratificational linguists to develop a precise notation for linguistic structure. This notation has been intended to mirror each linguistic relationship with an element termed a NODE. These nodes are then connected among themselves by lines often treated as representing wires of some sort. In view of this practice, much stratificational discussion of the relations in language has been couched in terms of nodes representing the relations and the various configurations into which these nodes can enter. As a result, the discussion of the relations themselves and the notations associated with them have traditionally gone hand in hand. Although the author is certainly aware of the theoretical difference between actual relations and specific notations which seek or claim to represent them, the common custom is followed here. This fact is explicitly mentioned here lest an unconscious adherence to a usual custom mislead those unfamiliar with this convention into thinking that relations and notations really are treated as the same thing in this framework.

The first major section of the chapter deals with the syntagmatic relations, commonly known as AND RELATIONS. This is followed by a section on the paradigmatic or OR RELATIONS. The concluding section then devotes some attention to an exploration of how such ideas lead us beyond the purely stratificational model.

Syntagmatic relations

The term SYNTAGMATIC has been commonly used for a fundamental linguistic relation at least as far back as Saussure's *Cours* (1916/1959). In the established stratificational notation, this kind of relation is symbolized by a triangle. It has been virtually universally conceded, furthermore, that two fundamental subtypes of this relation are necessary: the ORDERED AND specifies a linear sequence, as when A is followed by B, while the UNORDERED AND specifies the simultaneous occurrence of A in combination with B. Figure 5.1 shows these fundamental types of nodes. In the work of Peter A. Reich (1973), these nodes and the relations corresponding to them are sometimes termed CONJUNCTION (for the unordered AND) and CONCATENATION (for the ordered variety).

The most obvious uses or functions of these nodes appear in the representation of syntactic relations within a particular layer or stratum of linguistic structure, a very significant type of intrastratal relation. There are many examples of the uses of each of these relations on various strata. In the four most widely discussed strata, namely the SEMEMIC, LEXEMIC, MORPHEMIC and PHONEMIC, examples of both ordered and unordered syntagmatic relations are shown in Figure 5.2. Straightforward examples are available for all possibilities except the sememic use of the ordered AND. The classic view of stratificational semology disfavors the use of linear order on the sememic stratum, this being seen as one of several major distinctions between stratificational semology and Chomskyan 'deep structure' (and its successors). There have been various proposals to use linear order in such structures, from an early one by Reich (1968) to a later one by Lamb (Personal Communication). Both have proposed imposing a linear order within what is here termed the EVENT CLUSTER – the typical semological realizate of a clause. These proposals, however, have remained controversial and have never passed into the general canon of common stratificational usages.

Although the AND relations can be seen as epitomizing syntagmatic and therefore intrastratal relations, AND relations also have important roles in the treatment of interstratal relations. This is especially true in the series of patterns traditionally termed SIGN

Figure 5.1 Basic AND nodes

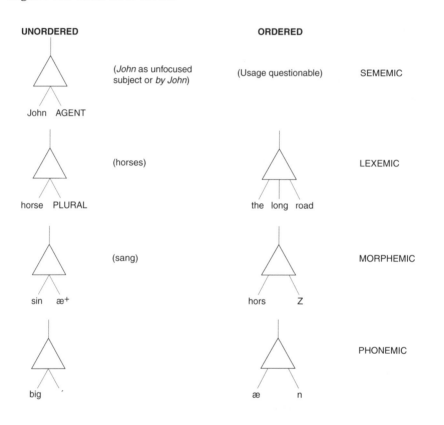

Figure 5.2 Tactic functions of AND relations by strata

PATTERNS. These have the function of 'spelling out' units the size of tactic units of a particular stratum in terms of elementary units capable of relation more directly to the stratum below. The units spelled out in this way are classically termed EMIC SIGNS – thus SEMEMIC SIGNS, LEXEMIC SIGNS, MORPHEMIC SIGNS and PHONEMIC SIGNS – and the elementary units that spell them out are termed ONS – thus SEMONS, LEXONS, MORPHONS and PHONONS. In general, both ordered and unordered AND relations can occur in a

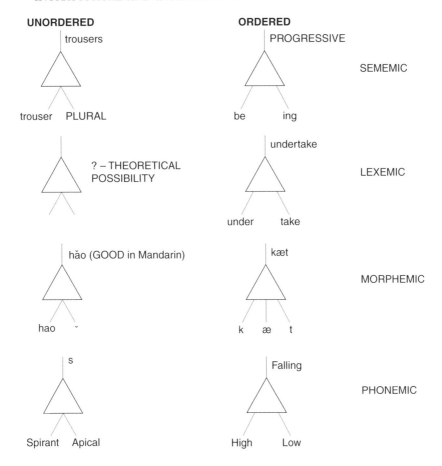

Figure 5.3 AND relations in sign patterns (composite realization)

sign pattern, as illustrated in Figure 5.3. While the ANDs in a tactic pattern can be seen as depicting the syntagmatic relation of TACTIC COMPOSITION, the usual term for the relation depicted by the same ordered ANDs in a sign pattern is COMPOSITE REALIZATION.

Discussion of interstratal relations also brings us to the matter of relations in an upward orientation. In general, there is no strong case for upward ANDs in tactics (though some have proposed their use), but such relations have often been used to deal with the interstratal relationship termed PORTMANTEAU REALIZATION, allowing a single emic sign to realize two or more tactic units (EMEs) in combination. Such ANDs apparently need to be used in the treatment of individual portmanteau phenomena – where the portmanteau relation applies to just one example (or perhaps a few individual examples), as when English *well* occurs instead of **goodly* as the manner adverb

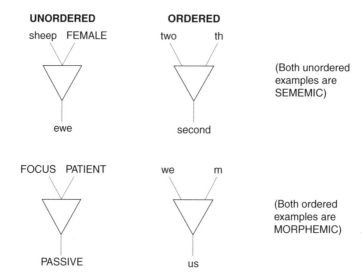

Figure 5.4 ANDs in upward function in some individual portmanteaus

corresponding to *good*. More systematic patterns of portmanteau relationship may lend themselves to a treatment involving the tactics also. A few examples of individual portmanteaus are presented in Figure 5.4.

In the view adopted here, it should be noted, the UPWARD versus DOWNWARD occurrence of a given type of node is regarded as a matter of different uses or functions of the same type of relationship. What may be termed the ORIENTATION of a node (a dimension subsuming the particular terms UPWARD and DOWNWARD) is thus treated as a less essential difference than that between an ordered and an unordered node, or that between a syntagmatic (AND) node and a paradigmatic (OR) node.

Beyond the fundamental kinds of ANDs, there are several other nodes used by some stratificationalists that can arguably be seen as special kinds of ANDs. The longest-used of these is the diamond node, introduced by Lamb and his associates at the Yale Linguistic Automation Project around 1967[2] to show the connections between tactic patterns – those patterns that show intrastratal relations – and realization patterns – those that show interstratal relations. In a slightly earlier formulation from Lamb (1966b), upward ANDs – normally unordered[3] – were used for this purpose. It was soon realized, however, that the upward AND properly characterizes only the encoding-oriented part of tactic/realizational relations. For decoding relations, we need to have the AND in a sideways orientation such that the tactic + lower realizational connections can result in an upward signal in the realizational portion. So the ordinary diamond at (a) in Figure 5.5 can be seen as an upward AND for encoding purposes, but as a sideways AND for decoding purposes. The four-sided shape of the diamond further allows a single realizational signal from above to be realized simultaneously as a tactic specification and an emic unit. This would be applicable, for instance, to a situation where interrogation is simultaneously signaled by a special word-order construction and also by a marked intonation pattern. Part (b) of Figure 5.5 shows this kind of diamond and its encoding and decoding interpretation. The possibility of four distinct connections in cases such as this justifies the four-sided shape of the diamond node.

Just a little later,[4] the ENABLER NODE was introduced to provide conditions for context-sensitive alternations. Earlier attempts to treat such conditions have involved the use of upward ANDs. The enabler is essentially a special type of upward AND which allows – but does not in itself require – the selection of a certain option when conditions to which the enabler further connects are satisfied. Since the detailed discussion of the enabler crucially involves its interaction with the nodes that specify choices – paradigmatic relations – the extended discussion of this node is deferred until the nodes treating these choices are introduced. The enabler is mentioned here only to affirm that it is a variety of AND node.

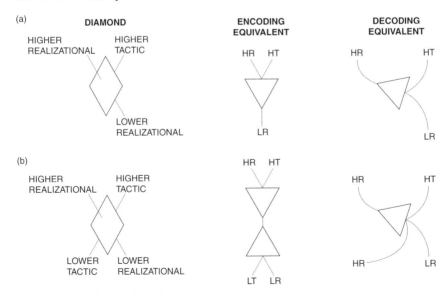

Figure 5.5 Diamond nodes

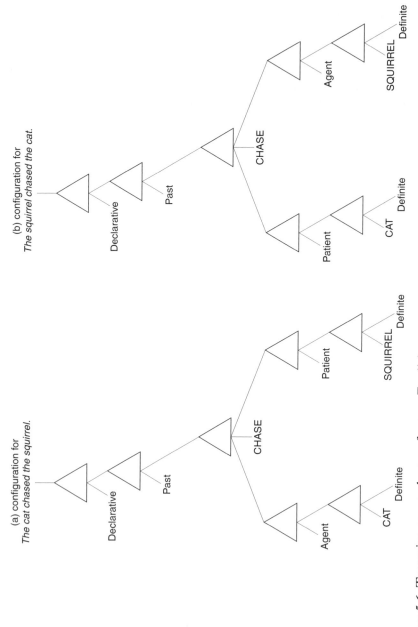

(a) configuration for
The cat chased the squirrel.

(b) configuration for
The squirrel chased the cat.

Figure 5.6 Tentative event clusters for two English sentences

Another special kind of AND node was proposed in the unpublished work of two stratificationalists in the early 1970s. By sheer coincidence, these people, Ilah Fleming and the present author, conceived of this node in a similar way and independently suggested the same graphic means of representing it. This node, here termed the ASSOCIATIVE AND developed as one response to a problem which arises in relating a non-linear semology to an (at least largely) linear grammatical structure. According to the earlier conception presented in Lockwood (1972), for instance, the semological structures for the sentences *The cat chased the squirrel* and *The squirrel chased the cat* are those shown in Figure 5.6. Since all the nodes in either of these configurations are unordered downward ANDs, it is implied that all the sememic signals for one of these sentences are simultaneously made available to the next lower stratum, where the surface syntax (more or less) is treated.[5] Since configurations (a) and (b) contain exactly the same sememes, it would appear that the grammatical system would receive the same set of signals for these two sentences, despite the obvious contrast between them, and despite the differences in the particular connections shown in the two diagrams. If the grammatical syntax did receive all these signals simultaneously, and received nothing else, it would be completely unable to distinguish one of these possibilities from the other.

In practice, there have been various responses to the problem presented by this situation. Gleason (Personal Communication), for example, has proposed that the grammatical system should simply be allowed to have reference to the entire semological configuration. If this is allowed, the differences are indeed obvious, and the problem disappears. This approach makes a considerable compromise, however, and it turns out to be incompatible with the notion that the semology and the grammar are simply parts of a larger network of relationships which can be put into operation by the specification of a few kinds of signals running through this network. Those who have wanted to stick more closely to the latter conception have therefore had to seek alternative solutions. Varying uses of ordered ANDs in the semology have been proposed at various times by both Reich (1968) and Lamb (Personal Communication), but others have seen such uses as rather arbitrary and troublesome. The associative AND, as proposed by Fleming and the present writer, can be seen as a special type of unordered AND distinct from the simple simultaneous conjunction node. This node, represented by both originators by a shaded triangle, is used for those ANDs that specify relations between event sememes like ^{S}/chase/ and various associated participants, such

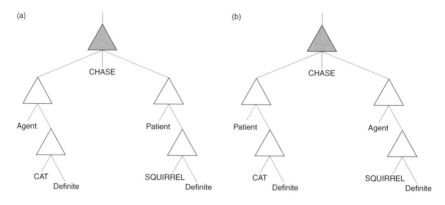

Figure 5.7 Event clusters using associative ANDs

as the sememes marking the roles of AGENT and PATIENT, which then occur in a simultaneous AND-relationship with their associated entity sememes, such as ^{S}/cat/ and ^{S}/squirrel/ in the example already cited (see Figure 5.7). With relation to the grammatical syntax, an associative AND can be seen as arbitrarily sequential, in that it is capable of activation in any sequence depending on when the grammar calls for it. In the examples here, for instance, the grammatical syntax (lexotactics in the usage of Lockwood 1972), in the absence of additional signals calling for special constructions, will be ready for the agent first, as unmarked subject, and then the event sememe (realized as a verb), and finally for the patient as object. If a FOCUS ELEMENT were present simultaneous with the patient, the lexotactics would take the patient as subject, the event as a passive verbal phrase, and finally the agent in a prepositional phrase with 'by'.

   In the opinion of the present author, the most viable alternative to the use of associative ANDs in such instances is the approach originated by Sullivan (1976). In this approach, signals for roles are given a different hierarchical order designed to ensure that signals will not reach the grammatical system all at the same time. The obvious advantage of this approach is that it does not require the postulation of a special additional node such as the associative AND. The more disturbing aspect of it is that it appears to require the assignment of hierarchy which might not otherwise be motivated by considerations of the semology. If this objection should prove to be illusory, Sullivan's approach could easily eliminate the need for an associative AND altogether.[6]

   While the associative AND can be seen as a special variety of

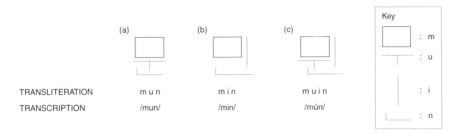

	(a)	(b)	(c)
TRANSLITERATION	m u n	m i n	m u i n
TRANSCRIPTION	/mun/	/min/	/mün/

Figure 5.8 Examples of Korean writing (Han'gul)

unordered AND, there is evidence that some aspects of the treatment of non-spoken varieties of language require the introduction of different varieties of ordered ANDs. The linearity of spoken language allows only one dimension, so any elements not simultaneous occur in a before/after relationship.

Written language, on the other hand, uses a two-dimensional medium, so that marks can be ordered vertically as well as horizontally. An example of such a possibility is available from the Han'gul writing system used for Korean. Each of the three examples shown in Figure 5.8 shows an orthographic syllable as represented in this system. In example (a), the three marks have a purely vertical arrangement, but in (b) and (c) there are examples of both horizontal and vertical arrangement. The overall system is most fully illustrated by (c) in Figure 5.8.

It shows the four letter-positions possible for the orthographic syllable all filled. In this scheme, the initial consonant letter (which is obligatory) may be followed by one or two vowel letters. Vowel letters of one class – they always have a long horizontal stroke – come under the initial consonant letter; vowel letters of a second class – all with a long vertical stroke – come to the right of the consonant or the consonant + vowel complex. The final consonant, which is not actually obligatory, though it always occurs in these examples, comes below the preceding parts. The treatment of the graphotactic properties of these various graphemes would seem to require one to recognize a distinction between a horizontally ordered AND and a vertically ordered one. The overall system could be shown as in Figure 5.9, with a small H or V inside the ordered AND node indicating whether it specifies a horizontal or vertical order.[7] It could be argued, however, that these examples are pertinent only on a graphetic level and not graphemically, since the vertical-vs.-horizontal arrangement of two graphemes is automatically predictable from their shapes, and so can never distinguish different written messages.

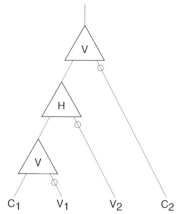

Figure 5.9 The structure of the Korean orthographic syllable

It should be noted that gestural language – such as the various kinds of sign language – involves a three-dimensional medium. From this it follows that it might be necessary to specify order in a front/ back axis as well as in a horizontal and a vertical axis in dealing with these types of language. It would be interesting to know if actual examples from some type of sign language can be cited to concretely demonstrate this necessity.

In summary, within this first major section of the chapter, it has been noted that the fundamental syntagmatic nodes – the unordered and ordered ANDs – have downward functions in dealing with both intrastratal relations (tactics) and interstratal relations (realization). Such AND nodes also have upward realizational functions in the treatment of miscellaneous occurrences of portmanteau realization. Special varieties of AND relations include diamonds, enablers, associative ANDs, along with varieties reflecting different types of ordering in non-spoken media.

Paradigmatic relations

Saussure proposed that syntagmatic relations be opposed to what he termed **ASSOCIATIVE** relations (1959:123), but Hjelmslev renamed the latter **PARADIGMATIC** (1961:39).[8] In the stratificational notation, a bracket lying on its side has been the established notation for a paradigmatic (or OR) relation. This node can be seen as representing an option or choice within the structure of language. Fairly early in the history of Lamb's notation, it came to be recognized that a kind of ordering can be said to apply to OR nodes as well as to ANDs. This order, it must be emphasized, has nothing at all to do with linear

Figure 5.10 Basic OR nodes

sequence, but it rather relates to the precedence of one possible choice over one or more others. Figure 5.10 presents the two nodes with Reich's alternative terms for them (1973). In the unordered case, A and B are simply presented as two options with equal possibility. With the ordered OR, however, A will occur if possible – that is, if it is allowed by the other nodes found in the overall configuration – and otherwise B will occur.

The function of an OR, *par excellence*, is the paradigmatic function, which like the construction function of the AND belongs in the tactics as a part of the intrastratal relations. It can be seen in combination with the AND in Figure 5.11. Here the OR on the left represents the

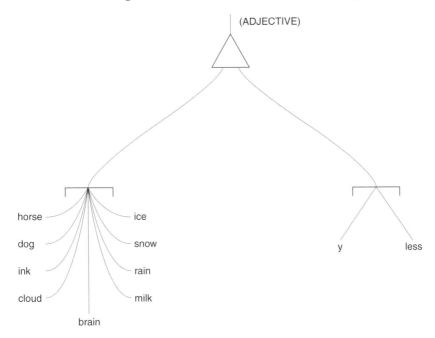

Figure 5.11 Unordered ORs in tactic structure

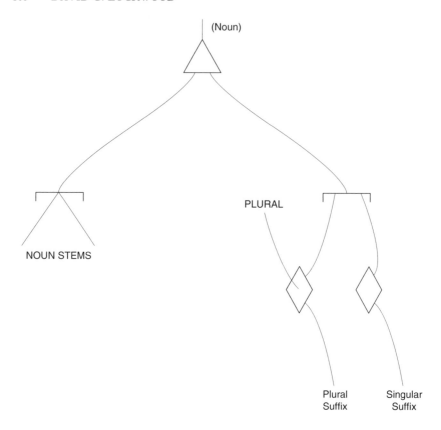

Figure 5.12 An ordered OR in tactic structure

morphological class of bases (all of them noun roots in this example) which can combine with the English suffixes spelled -*y* and -*less*, and the right-hand OR shows this class of suffixes. Ordered ORs can also be used in tactic patterns, as illustrated by Figure 5.12, which represents the number suffixes in a language like Italian, where there are overt suffixes for both singular and plural. There, the syntax needs an overt signal only for the marked plural category, and the morphology can automatically supply the singular suffix in the absence of a plural signal.[9]

In addition, both unordered and ordered ORs are used to represent the alternation of allo-units, as depicted in Figure 5.13. This usage brings us to a possible difficulty, in that Lamb's early work (e.g. 1964a:107) made a major point about the difference between an emic unit and a true class. Lamb criticized the traditional Neo-Bloomfieldian definitions of phonemes and morphemes as classes, since an emic unit like one of these can be said to occur (on its

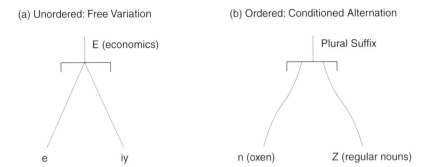

Figure 5.13 Downward ORs in diversification

particular level of abstraction) whenever one of the allo-units associated with it occurs (on a lower level). The same is not true, however, for a true class, as generally understood in mathematics and as needed elsewhere in linguistics. There a class can be said to occur only when every one of its members occurs. While it is certainly important to maintain Lamb's basic insight in this matter, it still seems that an OR relation is involved in both cases. The essential difference seems to involve whether the OR is in the tactics (where it represents a classification), or in the realizational description (where it represents an alternation).

The use of ORs for alternation brings up the issue of conditioning, which allows us to return to the question of enabling nodes, the details of which were deferred in the previous section. In general, an ordered OR cannot occur without control from some kind of upward AND node, but in the model adopted here there are three varieties of such controls applying to various situations. These varieties are depicted in Figure 5.14. In the realizational portion, the possibilities are an upward AND in the case of portmanteau realizations, or an enabler in the case of conditions from the tactics of the same stratum. In the tactics, the choices at ordered ORs are conditioned directly – or sometimes indirectly – by diamond nodes leading to the onic units of the stratum above.

As to the enabler specifically, this node was introduced in Sullivan (1969), a dissertation on Russian phonology and morphology. As stated previously, this node indicates that a particular option is permitted, but not required, if the condition to which it is attached is satisfied. For a demonstration of how this node might be preferred to an ordinary upward AND in cases of conditioned alternation, consider Figure 5.15. The diagram at (a) uses the upward AND in a fashion proposed in the middle 1960s, while the diagram at (b) uses the

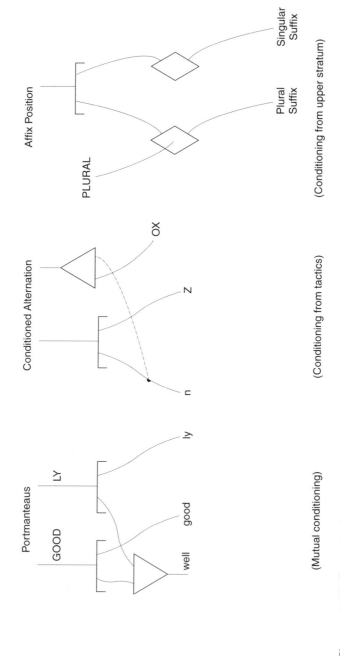

Figure 5.14 Control of downward ordered ORs

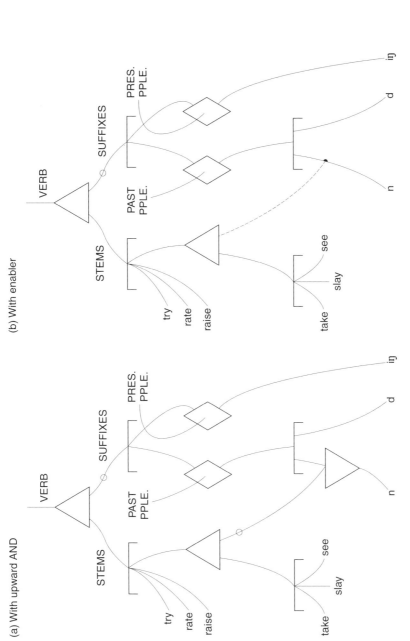

(a) With upward AND

(b) With enabler

Figure 5.15 Treatment of conditioned alteration

enabler. The alternation depicted is that between /n/ (in combination with any of *take, slay* or *see*) and /d/ (under other circumstances) as a realization of the past participle suffix in standard English. In the version with the upward AND, the conditioning line prompted by the occurrence of *take, slay* or *see* is shown (by the small circle on it) to be optional. The condition will be relevant, that is, just in case the suffix is taken, but otherwise it will not be relevant. Notationally, the major difference in the (b) version is that the enabler occurs and is connected by a dashed line, and no optionality is indicated. The dashed line is understood to work only in the downward direction: a signal down to *take, slay* or *see* will prompt its activation, but one upward from /n/ will not. This, plus the fact that the enabler does not in itself **require** a choice to be taken, removes the need for the indication of optionality in such a case.

While the enabler does not by itself require a choice to be taken even though its associated conditions are satisfied, in combination with an ordered OR its effect is to require the choice as a result of the properties of this kind of OR. In diagram (b) in Figure 5.15, /n/ has to be taken as a realization of the past participle morpheme if any of *take, slay* or *see* is present because the ordering of the OR means that the branch with precedence will be taken if possible; so if /n/ is enabled here it must be taken, and /d/ can occur as the realization of this suffix only when the condition is not satisfied. In other situations, however, an enabler can be combined with an unordered AND as in Figure 5.16, which differs from part (b) of Figure 5.15 only

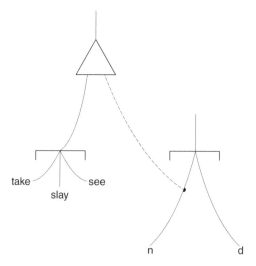

Figure 5.16 Enabler with unordered OR (enabling but not requiring)

in the substitution of an unordered OR for an ordered one. In this case, we could get /n/ only if *take*, *slay* or *see* preceded the past participle suffix, but we could also get /d/ in that situation. It would be appropriate to make use of the nodes in this fashion if, in some dialect, /n/ and /d/ were in free variation in the presence of these particular roots, and /d/ were the only possibility under other conditions.

Returning now to the functions of OR nodes, a very important additional function of the unordered OR is its occurrence in an upward orientation. This is not only a possibility, but a very ordinary occurrence in both tactic and realizational descriptions. In tactics, the upward OR allows a unit, construction or class to be used in more than one position without repetition. Its use is therefore a valuable aid in capturing generalizations. The examples in Figure 5.17 demonstrate the usefulness of this node in tactics. All three diagrams in the figure are attempts at representing the simple sentences *See the dog* and *The dog ran*. The version at (a) is equivalent to a simple listing of the two possibilities, and the words *the* and *dog* are repeated, so that they are not explicitly shown to be two occurrences of the same unit. In the version at (b), the upward OR is used twice to make the identity of these two words completely explicit. In the version at (c), furthermore, the fact that *the* and *dog* occur in that order in both examples is captured by positing an additional construction (obviously a kind of NOUN/NOMINAL PHRASE) and showing, via a single upward OR, that it functions as part of either of the larger constructions. We could, of course, generalize still further from the version in (c) by elaborating the membership of such classes as Imperative Verbs, Determiners, Nouns and Past-tense Verbs.

In realizational description, the upward OR is used to show the phenomenon of **SYNCRETIZATION**: the coincident realization of two or more units of one level by just one unit on the level below. One such usage is shown in the top part of Figure 5.18, labeled the **MORPHEMIC ALTERNATION PATTERN**. There the two morphemes, verbal ^{M}/well/ FOR A LIQUID TO RISE TO THE SURFACE and nominal ^{M}/well/ A HOLE IN THE GROUND FROM WHICH WATER IS OBTAINED, are shown to coincide in the single morphemic sign ^{MS}/wel/. These two must be kept apart as morphemes because of their distinct inflectional possibilities. Upward ORs of the same sort are also found abundantly in a sign pattern, as shown in the lower half of Figure 5.18. The upward ORs above the morphons (= morphopho-nemes) ^{MN}/w/, ^{MN}/l/, and ^{MN}/e/ show that the same unit functions as part of various different morphemic signs as they are spelled out.

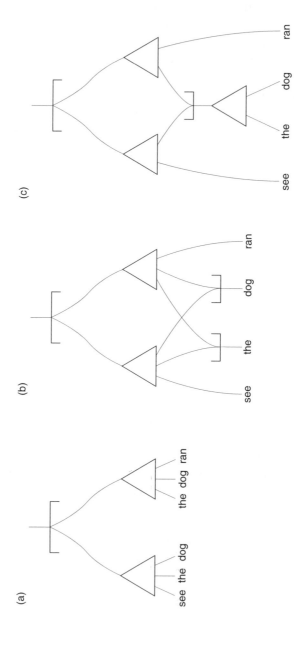

Figure 5.17 Representations of *See the dog* and *The dog ran*

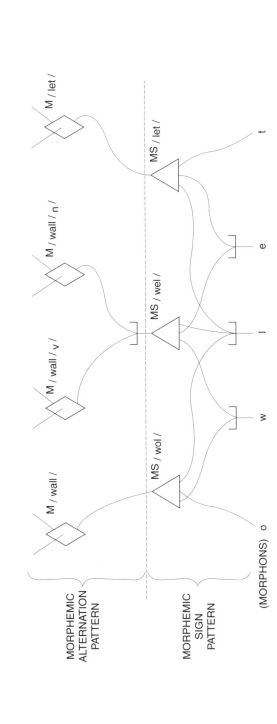

Figure 5.18 Realizational uses of upwards ORs

Just as some special and less commonly recognized types of ANDS were discussed in the previous sections of this chapter, there are some special kinds and uses of OR relations to be treated as well. The one that fits most readily into the overall picture is the upward use of the ordered OR. In the conception adopted in this chapter, this is not a distinct type of node, it should be recalled, but only a particular function of a node already identified. An ordered OR in such a function, however, was not included in the formulation of the notation in Lamb (1966b) or Lockwood (1972). Cases for such a usage emerged from Herrick's work on writing systems, but it would be applied to other structural subsystems just as readily as to the linguistic study of written language. The case for the upward ordered OR in such situations is presented by Herrick (1984:158).

Figure 5.19 shows an application of the upward ordered OR in a sign pattern dealing with a simple three-vowel system. The more conventional account at (a) uses an unordered OR in upward function to show that the **PHONON** (a componential unit of the phonology sometimes alternatively termed a **SINGULARY DISTINCTIVE FEATURE**) VOCALIC can form part of any of the phonemic signs /a/, /i/, /u/. The alternative account at (b) shows an ordered OR in combination with an unordered one in this function. Here the left-hand branch is the 'elsewhere' branch and the right-hand one is the preferred. For encoding purposes, there would be no significant difference between these two accounts. In using the configuration in the upward direction for purposes of decoding, however, one would want to check first whether an occurrence of the vocalic phonon was accompanied by an additional component (FRONT or LABIAL) or not, and the decoding as the unmarked vowel /a/ should be used only when both /i/ and /u/ explicitly fail for the lack of this additional component. Such an example seems to offer evidence that an upward function for ordered ORs is justifiable at least for such cases as this in various sign pattern configurations.

Another kind of proposal which needs to be discussed is that for the use of AND/OR nodes, as originally proposed by Reich (1970, 1973). Such nodes are represented in a way that combines the triangle characteristic of the AND with the bracket characteristic of the OR, as shown in the examples in Figure 5.20. The labels in the figure also indicate Reich's alternative names for these nodes: INTERCATENA-TION for the ordered version and INTERJUNCTION for the unordered version (1970:168, 173).

The discussion of these nodes is presented as a part of the consideration of OR nodes because such nodes can be seen as ORs

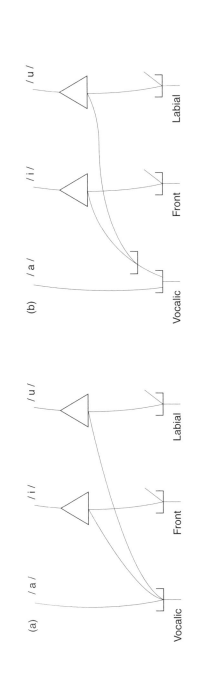

Figure 5.19 Components of a three-vowel system

a) Ordered AND / OR = INTERCATENATION

(b) Unordered AND / OR = INTERJUNCTION

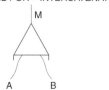

Figure 5.20 AND/OR nodes

which are **inclusive** rather than **exclusive** in nature, since one can take one of the options involved or any combination of them. It should be mentioned, however, that the ordering involved in these nodes is strictly of the type associated with AND nodes. It is a matter of linear order, and does not in any way involve precedence. Crucially, if one takes only one branch from an ordered AND/OR, no precedence among the possibilities is assumed. This much is in fact suggested by the **CATENATION** (rather than **JUNCTION**) in Reich's terms for the ordered AND/OR, and this could be considered an advantage of his kind of terminology, since the alternative term 'ordered AND/OR' is just not clear about what variety of order is meant.

From the beginning of the discussion of these nodes, it has been clear that the information included in either one of them can always be represented by a configuration of several of the more ordinary ANDs and ORs in combination. The simplest such case is presented in Figure 5.21, with four basic nodes. It should be noted, however, that when the AND/ORS have three, four or more branches, the number of basic nodes needed in the alternative configurations increases considerably. In such cases, it is not even always easy to figure out the simplest way to represent the possibilities, even though some representation using only basic nodes is always possible. Still, the AND/OR notation could simply be used as a notational shorthand for the more complex configurations which would otherwise appear, though Reich argued against this interpretation when he introduced these notational alternatives (1973:103–107).

One of the main arguments against the acceptance of AND/OR nodes, however, has long been that the cases in natural language where they would be usable are so rare as to make them hardly necessary in view of the availability of alternative representations of

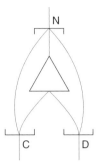

Figure 5.21 Alternative representation of Figure 20(b)

the facts in any case. Since the late 1970s, however, James Copeland has argued that such nodes are appropriate for vast parts of what will here be termed the **CONCEPTUAL SYSTEM**, the system which organizes concepts within overall human cognition.[10] If his conclusions are correct, it may be that such relations are commonplace in this system, even if they are not necessary in what we could term 'language proper'.

Copeland's most essential point has to do with the way to represent an individual concept in terms of what logicians term its **INTENSION** (its set of defining properties) and its **EXTENSION** (the enumeration of the individual items or concepts which serve to instantiate it). Traditionally, the situation can be represented as in part (a) of Figure 5.22, with an upward unordered AND for the intension – indicating that each of the defining properties of the concept must occur in order for it to be properly identified – and a downward unordered OR for the extension (seen as a class of individual instances). Copeland has argued that in ordinary usage a concept should be represented as in part (b) of Figure 5.22, where AND/OR nodes are used for both intension and extension. His argument for the upward AND/OR for intension is fairly straightforward: while in strict scientific usage all properties of the intension must be observed to define a concept, the more common everyday usage normally extrapolates from a few properties in making an identification, so it would not require the observation of all of them. His argument for the downward usage is somewhat more difficult, in that he simply observes that all members or several can be in our awareness even if we ultimately speak of only one at a given time.

So if Copeland is right about this, AND/OR relations may be very common indeed in the conceptual system, which is an essential auxiliary to language even if we do not choose to define it as a part of language proper.

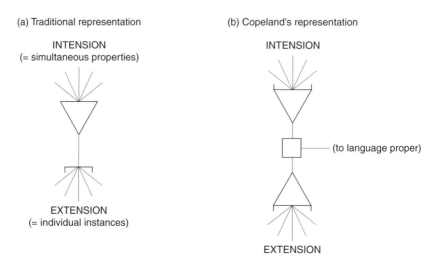

Figure 5.22 Concepts in relation to intension and extension

His presentation of the extension as an AND/OR – equivalent to an inclusive OR – raises a further question about whether we really need truly exclusive ORs or not. Further, is it possible that realizational ORs for emic units are exclusive while classificatory ORs in general need not be? These questions are raised here, even though the author is not at all sure how they should ultimately be answered.

Another possible variety of OR is the small circle for optionality, which has been used in Figures 5.9 and 5.15. This can be seen simply as a shorthand notation for the optionality represented more explicitly in part (a) of Figure 5.23, corresponding to the abbreviated form seen in part (b) of the same figure. When Reich introduced this notation, however (1973), he argued that it should be seen as representing an independent element. Full discussion of the arguments here is beyond the scope of this chapter. If this optionality element is taken as a separate element of structure as Reich has suggested, however, it could be seen as a special type of OR node, inasmuch as a choice is still involved.

The OR relation, then, is of crucial importance in the treatment of both interstratal and intrastratal relationships, and varieties of this relation occur in both upward and downward orientation in both of these areas. Further, a strong case can be made for the use of the ordered OR in an upward orientation, at least in sign patterns. Since the AND/OR can be seen as an inclusive variety of OR, it is treated under this heading, and so is the optionality element, if indeed it is to be used as anything more than an abbreviation.

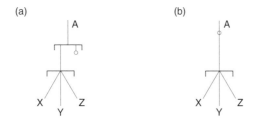

Figure 5.23 Representations of optionality

Broader considerations

The foregoing discussion has sought to establish that AND and OR relations are very important to any discussion of language structure. It has further sought to explore some of the varieties and particular usages of such relations, with special regard to the work of stratificational linguists and various systems of nodes proposed by them.

The broader issue that can now be examined is the place of relations in general in the structure. The early work of Lamb (1964a, 1964b, 1965 for instance), in common with the views of others such as Charles Hockett (1961), saw language as a system of elements with relations between them. In this view, both the elements and the relations seemed to be essential. By the middle of the 1960s, however, Lamb had come to adopt the Hjelmslevian view that 'a totality does not consist of things but of relationships' (from Lamb 1966a:8). This means that language does not contain true elements, but only relations to relations to relations.

It is not difficult to demonstrate the point that linguistic relations are not just more important than units, but that they are the only essential elements of a linguistic system. The standard demonstration runs as follows:

Take a common linguistic unit, for instance the morpheme *cat* in English. As a unit, this morpheme connects, for one thing, to a set of pronunciations. In this case, that is quite a simple matter, though at some level one would need to deal with details about the degree of aspiration of the initial /k/, the release or non-release of the final /t/, and so on. For another thing, this morpheme has a set of connections to meaning. The primary such connection would doubtless be some such thing as 'a carnivorous mammal (*Felis catus*) long domesticated and kept by man as a pet or for catching rats and mice' (Mish 1984). There would also be alternatives referring to other felines as well as connections to such idiomatic combinations as *bearcat, cat-of-nine-tails, cattail,* and *catfish.* Thirdly, this morpheme would have certain relations to the morphotactics of the English language, the pattern of relations that specifies how morphemes combine to form grammatical words. These connections would include primarily the fact that this morpheme may function as a stem in the general noun construction, which makes it capable of inflection for number. They would also include its function as a base for such an adjective as *catty,* and various other possibilities. Suppose, however, that we specify all of these relations in full detail. In doing so, the argument runs, we have specified everything we can about it. The unit we started with has been exhaustively characterized in terms of its relationships elsewhere, and it then ceases to be essential as a part of the structure of the language. Such a unit is therefore only a convenient label to aid the reader of our account of the language. It contributes no essential content to the description, so it is not of any crucial importance to this description itself. By extension, such an argument can apply to any linguistic unit, and this demonstrates that only relations, and not units, are essential in the structure.

As a result of arguments of this type, the predominant view among those stratificationalists influenced by Lamb's work is that in the last analysis a language is indeed a system of relationships. This viewpoint is found, for example, in the work of Sullivan and of Reich as well as that of the present writer. This is true despite the fact that we all speak of various labeled points of reference in a language as if they were really things, recognizing that the English language, if not all languages, leaves us no reasonable alternative if we want to be even partially understood.

Still, many linguists – apart from others strongly influenced by Hjelmslev – find this point difficult to understand. Their common-sensical question is 'How can you have relations without things to relate?' Even among stratificationalists, Ilah Fleming, whose views have been influenced by Gleason, M. A. K. Halliday and various tagmemicists as well as by Lamb, explicitly points out that her system is to be viewed as one with units as well as relationships. Although such a view undoubtedly has a strong intuitive appeal, items do not really seem to be any more essential in her model than in those of Lamb and others, given that all the essentials can be spelled out in terms of relations. When we speak of intuitive reactions, in any case, it must be remembered that we are not speaking directly about linguistic structure, but rather about people's conscious ideas about such structures, and such ideas must be sharply distinguished from the actual structures. It would seem that, even if we find it of great interest to explore the psychological questions involved with native reactions to language and folk ideas about language, we must admit that linguistic structure *per se* would only be one ingredient of such an investigation. Those more competent in the area of cognitive psychology than the present writer could then study the notion of linguistic units in relation to more general considerations of that discipline.

As to the question of the need for things to be related, it could be said that language ultimately does relate to things of sorts, such as routines of speaking and writing, to mention only those involved in encoding on the expression side. In connection with the present discussion, however, the point is that all such things are matters of SUBSTANCE (in the Hjelmslevian sense – 1961 *passim*), and as such they are outside of language. But language itself, not including this substance, can profitably be seen as consisting of a network of relationships.

In conclusion, the view of the present writer is that relations are not just in language, but they make up the totality of language. Once the relations in any language have been exhaustively treated, the structure of that language has also been totally characterized.[11]

Notes

1. The very latest introduction to this general approach is found in Lamb (1999), where a contrast is made between the neuro-cognitive approach advocated by Lamb today and the more traditional approach described as a form of 'analytical linguistics'. Lamb does not argue that analytical approaches such as that seen in earlier stratificational work are invalid, but he simply points out that they have different aims than his most recent work.
2. The diamond node first appeared in print in Bennett (1968).
3. In cases of anataxis, the conventions proposed in the *Outline* suggested that the upward ANDs involved be ordered.
4. See the further discussion under 'Paradigmatic relations' later in this chapter.
5. In Lockwood's model (1972), this lower stratum is termed the **LEXEMIC**, contrasted with the still lower **MORPHEMIC STRATUM**, which deals almost exclusively with word-internal relations. In Fleming's model, however, the functions of these two strata are both handled by the morphemic stratum, in a broader sense (1979:307–308; 1988; see also Cope 1994).

6. The same approach was incorporated in various later works of Sullivan's (e.g. 1980) and in the work of some of his students (e.g. Pope 1975, Coleman 1982).

7. The Korean example is based on the introductory remarks on the Korean writing system contained in Luckoff (1982) (xv–xxx). These particular examples were confirmed by the late Professor Seok Choong Song of the Michigan State University linguistics faculty, whose aid is hereby gratefully acknowledged. The particular stratificational interpretation offered here is the responsibility of the present author. See Herrick (1969) for a somewhat different approach to different types of ordering.

8. It would be hoped, however, that Hjelmslev's rich glossematic theory of language will be remembered for much more than this minor terminological innovation. (See Lamb 1966b, 1980.)

9. In view of the evidence for overt singular suffixes in such (historically borrowed) nouns as *cactus*, *stratum* and *phenomenon*, an overall analysis of modern standard English morphology would have to include a singular suffix morpheme, even though its unmarked realization would be zero.

10. These arguments were initially presented in Copeland and Davis (1980) and Davis and Copeland (1980). Copeland is given credit for them since he is the one who has been working explicitly in the stratificational model, whereas Davis's contribution to their overall collaboration came from a more eclectic viewpoint.

11. This insistence is not intended to disparage the conclusion that it is useful to speak about units as well as relations in the discussion of linguistic models. Ilah Fleming, a strong advocate of units, was present at an oral presentation of this piece and her rejoinder to this concluding section was essentially to affirm that units are useful. The present writer agrees completely on utility, but does not believe that this utility means that they are essential parts of the model, because their utility is a purely practical, not a theoretical matter. Perhaps the disagreement between Fleming and the present writer is more on whether a proper theory must necessarily include everything that is practically useful.

References

Bennett, David C. (1968) English prepositions: a stratificational approach. *Journal of Linguistics*, 4:153–172. (Reprinted in Makkai and Lockwood, eds., 1973, 277–306.)

Coleman, Douglas Wells (1982) Discourse functions of the active-passive dichotomy in English. Unpublished dissertation, University of Florida.

Cope, Pamela (1994) *Introductory Grammar: A Stratificational Approach.* Dallas: Summer Institute of Linguistics.

Copeland, James E. and Davis, Philip W. (1980) A stratificational approach to discourse and other matters. In *Sixth LACUS Forum 1979*, ed. by William C. McCormack and Herbert J. Izzo, Columbia, SC: Hornbeam Press, 255–263.

Davis, Philip W. and Copeland, James E. (1980) Knowledge, consciousness, and language: some possible sources of discourse phenomena. *Rice University Studies*, 66(2):101–123.

Fleming, Ilah (1979) Discourse from the perspective of four strata. In *Fifth LACUS Forum 1978*, ed. by Wolfgang Wölck and Paul L. Garvin, Columbia, SC: Hornbeam Press, 307–317.

Fleming, Ilah (1988) *Communication Analysis: A Stratificational Approach*, *Vol. 2*. Dallas: Summer Institute of Linguistics.

Herrick, Earl M. (1969) Orderedness and stratificational 'AND' nodes. Paper read at the Annual Meeting of the Michigan Linguistic Society, Central Michigan University, October (revised mimeographed version distributed by the author).

Herrick, Earl M. (1984) *Sociolinguistic Variation: A Formal Model*. University, AL: University of Alabama Press.

Hjelmslev, Louis (1961) *Prolegomena to a Theory of Language*, English translation of *Omkring Sprogteoriens Grundlægelse* (revised version) by Francis J. Whitfield. Madison: University of Wisconsin Press.

Hockett, Charles F. (1961) Linguistic elements and their relations. *Language*, 37:29–53.

Lamb, Sydney M. (1964a) On alternation, transformation, realization, and stratification. *Georgetown University Round Table*, 15:105–122.

Lamb, Sydney M. (1964b) The sememic approach to structural semantics. In *Transcultural Studies in Cognition*, ed. by A. Kimball Romney and Roy G. D'Andrade, *American Anthropologist*, 66(2):57–78. (Reprinted in Makkai and Lockwood, eds., 1973, 207–228.)

Lamb, Sydney M. (1965) Kinship terminology and linguistic structure. In *Formal Semantic Analysis*, ed. by E. A. Hammel, *American Anthropologist*, 67(5):37–64. (Reprinted in Makkai and Lockwood, eds., 1973, 229–257.)

Lamb, Sydney M. (1966a) Epilegomena to a theory of language. *Romance Philology*, 19:531–573.

Lamb, Sydney M. (1966b) *Outline of Stratificational Grammar*. Washington, D.C.: Georgetown University Press.

Lamb, Sydney M. (1980) Louis Hjelmslev's position in genetic and typological linguistics. *Travaux du Cercle Linguistique de Copenhague*, 20:49–63.

Lamb, Sydney M. (1999) *Pathways of the Brain: The Neurocognitive Basis of Language*. Amsterdam: John Benjamins.

Lockwood, David G. (1972) *Introduction to Stratificational Linguistics*. New York: Harcourt Brace Jovanovich.

Luckoff, Fred (1982) *An Introductory Course in Korean*. Seoul: Yonsei University Press.

Makkai, Adam and Lockwood, David G. (eds.) (1973) *Readings in Stratificational Linguistics*. University, AL: University of Alabama Press.

Mish, Frederick C. (ed.) (1984) *Webster's New Collegiate Dictionary*. Springfield, MA: Merriam-Webster.

Pope, Roger Wayne (1975) Active and passive voice in English and Russian: a contrastive analysis. Unpublished M. A. thesis, University of Florida.

Reich, Peter A. (1968) Order in deep structure. Paper presented at the Annual Meeting of the Linguistic Society of America, New York, December.

Reich, Peter A. (1970) A relational network model of language behavior. Unpublished dissertation, University of Michigan.

Reich, Peter A. (1973) Symbols, relations, and structural complexity. In Makkai and Lockwood, eds., 1973, 92–115. (Originally appeared as a report of the Linguistic Automation Project of Yale University, May 1968.)

Saussure, Ferdinand de (1916/1959) *Course in General Linguistics*, translation of *Cours de linguistique générale* by Wade Baskin, New York: Philosophical Library.

Sullivan, William J. (1969) A stratificational description of the phonology and inflectional morphology of Russian. Unpublished dissertation, Yale University.

Sullivan, William J. (1976) Active and passive sentences in English and Polish. *Papers and Studies in Contrastive Linguistics* (Poznan, Poland) 5:117–152.

Sullivan, William J. (1980) Syntax and linguistic semantics in stratificational theory. In *Syntax and Semantics, Vol. 13: Current Approaches to Syntax*, ed. by Edith A. Moravsik and Jessica R. Wirth, New York: Academic Press, 301–327.

PART TWO

APPLICATION

6

Memory and Discourse

Stephen A. Tyler

> *... an immediate conclusion is seen in the premises by the light of common sense, and where that is wanting, no kind of reasoning will supply its place.*
>
> Thomas Reid

In his *Confessions*, St. Augustine tells us that human knowing is only synecdochic, for human speech occurs in time.[1] God's word is timeless and could not be a linear sequence of sound. It is a whole and eternal. Linear temporality cannot comprise the whole, and that is why the word became flesh, for we could not otherwise understand it (*Confessions* X1:7). In speaking of speech Aristotle observes that: 'none of its parts has an abiding existence, when once a syllable has been pronounced it is not possible to retain it, so naturally as the parts do not abide, they cannot have position' (*Categoriae* 5). Speech is not a proper whole, but in *Categoriae* 13–15 he speaks of simultaneity as reciprocal dependence where each part involves the other whether the other is actually present or not, as in such terms as x is double of y, x is half of y, or of species of the same genus distinguished by the same method of division. These are all wholes whose parts do not abide in the present, are not present in the present, but are nonetheless wholes whose parts interrelate, not lineally but simultaneously. In his commentary on Aristotle, Hamilton adds that a whole once constituted, though it be constituted sequentially, may be simultaneous in memory (1895b:912).

I invoke these ancients here as a means of drawing attention to the interplay among time, sequence, simultaneity, parts, wholes, discourse and memory as topics intimately involved in the discourse about discourse. The ancients are conjured for another reason – to remind readers that much of what we now call discourse analysis is little more than a rediscovery of what these ancients called rhetoric.

Discourse structure, like the *dispositio* of rhetoric, is concerned with the arrangement of parts relative to a larger whole; semantic memory is clearly the modern equivalent of *memoria*, one of the principal parts of rhetoric; and the current interest in inference and implication is obviously paralleled by the concepts 'argument' and 'demonstration' in the rhetorical tradition. Even something so modern sounding as 'conversational implicature' has its ancient equivalent in the concepts *ethos* and *pathos* which had to do with the speaker's judgments about the hearer's participation.

Some things are, of course, omitted. Significantly, modern studies have no equivalent of the *inventio*, the speaker's means of finding ideas to talk about. Its absence in contemporary discourse analysis signifies the fact that modern work is reader/hearer oriented. It reflects the contemporary bias toward written forms which provide linguists with visual objects to analyse. It also reflects their long-standing prejudice against intentionality. Writing made it possible for authors to control and manipulate their intentions in a way that speakers in oral dialogue could not. Authors could sustain occult or ambiguous intentions through irony or by shifts of voice without the accountability of hearer intervention. Flight from intentionality as a source of interpretation derives from the reader's suspicion of the author's 'true' intentions and marks the recognition of the author as a kind of 'trickster'. Obscurity of authorial intention has been the justification for the necessity of interpretation and consequently for the enhancement of the reader's role at least since Aristotle's *De Interpretatione*, and reflects, as does that work, the problematic character of writing.

Writing made it possible for the reader to dispense with the author's intentions in another way. Because texts always say both more or less than authors intend, authors do not have full control over their texts. They are dupes of the text. Readers arrogate to themselves an understanding of a text superior to that of its authors, an understanding which the author has only limited rights to contradict.

We come, then, to a paradox at the heart of contemporary discourse analysis. One cannot *analyse* oral discourse as discourse, for in order for analysis to work, it must have an object that can be dismantled and reassembled. Discourse analysis consequently first transforms all oral discourse into written text in order to analyse it. It must first destroy what it seeks to analyse. A written transcription of oral discourse is no longer oral discourse as it was created and understood by participants; it is an object created to be analysed by non-participants for reasons that are remote from those that usually motivate participants. What relation this object and its analysis has to the understanding of participants is problematic at best. This is not to say that analysis must recreate the understanding of participants, for that would entail an explication of common sense that is neither possible nor necessary. What need would it fulfill? If participants are able to understand oral discourse without the benefit of linguistic analysis, what need could they have of analysis? Analysis seeks its justification, then, not in practical application, but in the loftier *telos* of theory. Here is another contrast with the ancients, who though often as singular in their pursuit of abstract knowledge as any contemporary linguist, yet grounded rhetoric in the real world of practical action.

Schemata: discourse ready-mades

Scheme, schema, schemata, frames, or words to that effect, have joined the list of hegemonic invocations in cognitive and linguistic studies, replacing the former rule of 'rule' in our conceptual kingdom. The terms scheme, schema and schemata are usually attributed to Bartlett (1932), but actually derive from rhetoric, where *schemae* and *figurae* referred to the making of tropes by fixed formulae. Apart from attesting once again to the unacknowledged rhetorical tradition, these terms signify a general retreat from grammar as an axiomatic deductive system. Interest in schemata points to a concern for preformed units of comprehension and production that are not entirely fixed and that are not just names for syntactic categories, such as 'noun', 'verb' and 'phrase', nor single words. Schemata are 'ready-mades' with 'options' rather in the way a Cadillac is a Chevy with all the trimmings. They are, in other words, constituted wholes whose parts interact with one another by means of the whole of which they are parts. As signs, their representational mode is indexical and their colligational mode is synecdochic (see Thought picture 6.2 later in the chapter).

   In the past, linguists have treated this group of collocations under the general rubric of 'idioms', or 'frozen expressions', as forms of fixed multilexical construction whose meanings are not mechanically predictable by part-part summation. Such forms, however, are merely one kind of schematic ordering. They are of the type whose parts and their relations are fixed, such as: 'I mean ... ', 'gimme a break ... ', 'take a break ... ', 'break a leg ... ', 'stick 'em up ... ', 'get off my back ... ', 'he went 'n ... ', and so on. Some are complete utterances, but by far the greater number are parts of larger utterances. Although they are fixed, even the most frozen expression has the as yet unrealized possibility of optionality, of deletion or expansion, and it is this capability that characterizes the majority of schemata.

Some schemata are indexed by a key term or terms, all other terms being optional. Who does not immediately recognize 'if — then'; '— is to — as — is to —'; '— as — as—'; 'the more — the less —'; 'the — -er, — the — -er —'. Key-term schemata are so predictable that they enable hearers to anticipate what is coming and at the same time economize the speaker's effort in hanging together the bits and pieces that eventually make up his utterance. It is as if, when in talk we come to a schema, the rocky road of discourse opens into a broad, smooth highway which we speed along with ease, and that is why most talk – and writing, too – is not novel, but consists of long stretches of freeway interspersed with construction detours. Easy idioms bridge the gaps and comfortable metaphors ease us through the traffic.

From this point of view (a nicely built, but much-used bridge), discourse is not so much a matter of grammatical constraint – at least in the usual sense of grammar – but of the stitching together of schemata into a rhapsody in very much the way the rhapsodists of oral traditions have always done, and for the same reasons: schemata are much closer to the form of inner speech and thought than are sentences and propositions (see Ong 1982; Lord 1960). Oral discourse, and thought too, are orders of schemata to which grammatical conventions are attached. Grammar is an optional add-on.

Key-term schemata need not have the quasi-sequential or part-propositional ordering of the previous examples, but may be thought of instead as instances with simultaneous possibilities of realization. This is not so much a key word as such, but an index to a family of possible schemata. This, in fact, is a very common form of what I call the 'family scheme' as illustrated by the 'nice' and 'problem' families

'nice':	'it's nice'
	'it's kinda nice'
	'it's real nice'
	'it's sorta nice'
	'it's quite nice'
	'it's so nice here'

'it's so nice of you to —'
'how nice'
'whata nice —'
'hava nice —'
'that's a nice —'
'that's not nice'
'it's not nice to —'
'wouldn't it be nice if —'
etc.

'problem':

'whatcher problem?'
'gotta little problem?'
'— gotta little problem with —'
'— have a problem'
'— having a problem with —'
'— having problems'
'the problem (with that) is —'
'there's only one little problem —'
'that's one helluva problem'

'that's a $\left\{\begin{array}{c}\text{real hard}\\\text{big}\\\text{bad}\end{array}\right\}$ problem'

'whatsiz problem?'
'is that ever a problem!'
'is it ever a problem for you to —?'
etc.

Some of these are relatively fixed, but most have optional expansions or transformations of one sort or another. The point is, though, that the key terms – 'nice' – and 'problem' – are foci. Around each is a cluster of common expressions which the focal terms index but do not themselves represent. 'Nice' and 'problem' are synecdoches of the expressions in which they commonly function as focal parts.

Other key-word schemata are more directly 'keyed' to parts of discourse than to situations. Consider, for example, discourse 'openers' such as 'What I would like to find out more about is your operation', Sue's opening line in the Sue/Kay interview (see Appendix at the end of this book). This is a prominent member of a family of openers. Some of its more commonly used congeners are:

'what I intend to talk about is —'
'what I would like to try to explain is —'

'what I have in mind is —'
'what I am going to speak about is —'
'what interests me is —'
'what I want to ask you about is —'
'what I mean to explain is —'
'what I wanted to speak to you about was —'
etc.

These are all keyed to the opening of one or another kind of speech event, some to speeches or talks, others to chats, and still others to conversations. Some can be used almost universally in any kind of speech situation ranging from opening an interview to seizing an opening in a conversation, discussion, argument, or debate. All, however, are indexed by the 'what I —' key term and have the effect of providing reasonable context for what is to follow.

Consider, too, the schema '— for example', in the paragraph preceding the examples above. 'For example' is a phrase that indexes exemplification and ties what is to follow with what has gone before as illustrative instances of a general case. It was known in the books of rhetoric as the *exemplum*, and was tied to the argument part of the *dispositio*. 'The following —' has a similar linking function and may also be used argumentatively. 'Follow' itself indexes another set of bridges – consequential ones. The most common of these in the Sue/Kay discourse is 'so' (about 30 instances), as in 'so I thought —', 'so I said —', 'so I figured —'.

'So —' and other schemata may function as conclusions or summary paraphrases of what has preceded. They may also be used as 'turn-keepers,' indexing no inferential connections between what has gone before and what is now to come, as in 'so, well listen —', or even as openers in 'so tell me what you —'. In all of these cases they have a common function of giving the appearance of connectedness of discourse either within the discourse itself or by means of the distribution of speaker/hearer roles, but they also alert us *to the fact that* schemata share an important feature with words – they are context dependent at the same time as they are makers of contexts. They mean different contexts and their different contexts mean differently. 'So I thought X' need not mean that my thinking 'X' is actually directly the conclusion or consequence of whatever preceded 'so I thought X', it may only index *the fact that* I've got more to say and am using this schema *to hold the floor* until I *figure out* what, or how to, or if I should say next.

Contrast this situation with 'empty schemata' which are 'meaningless' and whose function is to give the appearance of meaningful grammatical connection between parts of a sentence. In the preceding paragraph I used, in addition to the tired but useful schemata 'to hold the floor' and 'figure out', an empty schema – 'the fact that —' schema. In the sentence 'this alerts us to the fact that etc.', 'the fact that' is there not because there is a fact, but because one has to be alerted *to* something, and in the sentence 'it may only index the fact that —', 'the fact that' is there because an index indexes something. Not all 'fact thats' are so empty, for they may signify 'evidence of consequence', as in 'the fact that he fell means he slipped', but most 'fact thats' are as empty as 'at this point in time' of Watergate infamy, signifying flabby speech and insipid prose. Other examples of 'format' (Goodman 1971) abound in speech and prose. Consider, 'the thing is that —', 'in terms of —', 'from the point of view of —', 'well maybe I —', 'to sorta,' 'n' those sortsa things —', and those other wretched members of the 'fact family': 'in fact —', 'fact is —', 'the fact of the matter is —', 'the true facts —', 'factually speaking —', 'from a factual point of view —'.

These are not far removed from pure 'gap fillers', meaningless phonation meant to exclude other speakers as in : 'you know?' or 'I mean —', or 'you know what I mean?', or 'like', 'like well', or – in a paroxysm of gap filler – 'you know what I mean, like well —'. In a more charitable mood we interpret these as the speaker's urgent plea for us to complete in thought or speech what neither of us knows or can say as an index of the known but ineffable.

(Well) I think that, it seems to me that, I believe that I should have thought that this discussion is sufficient introduction to the use of schemata in the Sue/Kay discourse. It remains to say only that schemata – even of the gap filler type – are part of the poetry of oral discourse. They have rhythmical functions either in the words and phrases of utterances themselves or as means of 'making time' for the harmony that is expressed in the speaker's and hearer's synchronous coordination of gesture, body position, body tension and gaze (see Tannen 1984:152–159). I suggest, then, that the list that follows be read in the manner of a poem, aloud and perhaps polyphonically with different readers starting at different intervals, as in singing rounds. This will as closely as possible approximate to our sense of different voices clamoring for our attention as we speak and listen. Following is a list of schemata used in the Sue/Kay interview/conversation:

What I would like to find out about
that you are having done
you see
find out what happens to
find out more about
I have a similar problem
you've got a real problem
the problem is
having tremendous problems
I don't have a problem
going to do something about it
well, maybe I
so, tell me what
my friend who
that was great
does that mean
everyone going like this
someone else pay for it
didn't you notice
(well) I mean
everything else
and stuff
and stuff like that
and all sortsa stuff
and all that other stuff
and all that kinda stuff
you can't even
there are other things
like (I, maybe, well)
it's like
can you like
just time and money
just not even
I just
let's just
I always wanted
I only wanted
get this thing fixed
someone told me that
you really should get
I am sort of
I sort of
sort of

Those sort of
(n') that sort of
That's a real sort of
It's all sort of
It sort of
(n') all sorts of
— sort of like —
to figure out how
They may have to, they may not (maybe yes, maybe no)
I got around it
if that's all straight
gonna look real funny
straighten that up
an that's all
be put asleep
that's nothing
I don't know
able to breathe out of
a lot
right
yeah, right
that's right
they're right
(and) you know
I'm tired of
I was tired of
in fact
the fact that
get rid of
(even) went in for
to see what
or something
(or) something like that
this way
the real good stuff
I swear
it was when
I wish I could
go in and get a total overhaul
(and) things like that
instead of saying
it seems to me
I don't like (it)

but luckily
I've got a great reason
it happens to be
in an automobile accident
I really didn't realize
what (a) state I was in
but, had I known
(know(n)) what he was doing
I hadn't thought (of it like that)
it's a good thing
I'm thinking ahead
whole outlook on life
and things
and everything
who knows
we heard a story
couple weeks ago
difficult child
always getting in trouble
long lost relative
I learnt right off
would last in
and then I'd
whip it off
I just couldn't stand it
I've thought about this for awhile
it's all in your head
(I know) it sounds like
really stay with you
long enough for
out of the blue
Do you know what
to move over
so that it
torn away from
I must be totally
basically it's like
the reason
the thing is that
Imagine this
all those years
all at once

way to go
and besides
This better be a — that's all I can say
That's all I can say
This better be a
maybe you should
they do feel
gonna feel like
what's wrong with you
drop the subject
be real rational about this
that's about the only
(I mean) other than
(he said) just — forget it
and at least
I'm not gonna admit to that
I haven't been able to breathe for years
ah that's a shame
it's gonna be a new experience
for the first time (in your memory)
I was hoping that
go really low
or whatever
where — comes from
what they figure is
going to surface
now that
have you ever
it's an OK book
I wouldn't use it
open up a whole new world
all make sense
I didn't do it
you are the person in charge
whatever you punch in
it has a mind of it's own
it's magic
that's nice
sort of nice
it's nice for
see, so it's nice
gave up on me

can't do anything
taken care of
life can be OK (beautiful)
black and blue
when I came out of
up for

Inventio: where do topics come from?

Discourse also indexes action schemata. These may be represented in the mind not just in propositional agent/patient form, but as visual images, sensorimotor patterns, or in a rebus combining elements of verbal, visual and motor patterns. Consider, for example, what we might call the central topic of the Sue/Kay discourse – Kay's nose and what is to happen to it. The conversation uses the 'nose rebus' as a base schema which establishes and maintains discourse coherence. The nose is Kay's; it's to be changed, to be broken, to be operated on, to be straightened, to be made handsome. All of this, and more besides, is commonplace knowledge about noses and what can be done to them. These are mostly agent/patient schemata in which the nose is the recipient of some action. They are the basis for much of Sue's questioning. She makes inferences from the nose rebus about problems with noses, who fixes problem noses, how it is done, what it means to be a patient, the subject of an operation, and who performs the operation. These, and others, provide the content of her questions and comments. For example: (22) 'You couldn't breathe through the ... '; (45) 'Do they have to break your nose ... '; (58) 'Are they going to put you to sleep ... ;' (70) 'Are you going to be black and blue ... ;' and (115) '... probably pretty swollen'. All of these are based less on what Kay says, though that is also part of the condition for saying them, than on what Sue knows about noses; you breathe through them, they get broken, operations are performed on them, broken noses are accompanied by bruises and swelling, and so on. There is, in other words, a readily available account of reasonable action relative to noses that Sue uses as the *inventio* for her questions. Here the concept 'nose' functions as a 'topic' in exactly the same way as the *topoi* of classical rhetoric. It is a commonplace (*locus, topos*) in memory which is capable of suggesting a collection of indexical particulars. Consequently, we can say that it is this topical structure, this nose schema, that already provides the possibility of a coherent conversation. Its principle of organization is that of a substance (noun) and its accidents (attributes) or, in other words, the qualities and relations of a subject. This is the underlying conception of a semantic network (Quillian 1966), but it was first worked out in detail by Aristotle in *De Memoria*, and later by Hamilton (1895a:899–900) among others. The essential idea is that there is a concept ('nose') and what may be predicated of it. The predications (what may be said of noses) are the accidents or qualities, functions, characteristics and attributes of noses in general. These constitute what one can say about noses and thus are not only the source of information about noses that speakers and hearers use in saying things about noses; they are also, at least in part, the structure of what can be said.

In this same way Kay uses other schemata to organize her account. First of all, her narration has the predictable overall narrative structure of setting, complication and resolution. Within this larger structure she uses various related episodes. Line 213, for example, introduces a story within a story (see Sacks and Schegloff 1974). Sue, too, uses the story schema at 199: 'There's some guy ... we heard a story ... '. Kay also shifts frequently from narrative voice to dramatic dialogue: (13) 'my friend who is a nurse said, "listen ..."'; (16) 'I said, ...'; (35) '... sure, you've got a real problem ...'; (38) 'so I said, well ...'; (50) 'well, listen, is it ...'; (53) 'he said, "Well, OK."'

Apart from such narrative and story schemata, the first part of the discourse is organized by another schema, that of the interview. The interview schema is a type of exchange between speakers where one is in the role of interviewer, the other in the role of interviewee. The interviewer asks questions. The interviewee responds with answers that are supposed to be relevant to the question asked or to its presuppositions. In addition to asking questions, the interviewer has rights of summation, supplementation, clarification, emphasis and overall direction, as well as the duty to assess the quality of cooperation, relevance, quantity and general quality of the interviewer's contributions, though all of these may be shared with or challenged by the interviewee. The interviewee's questioning rights are largely limited to clarification and challenge, in the fullest sense of 'What do you mean by that question?'

Interviews fall into two broad types with respect to these characteristics: friendly and cooperative, and hostile and adversarial, rather like the different roles of defense and prosecution in forensic discourse. Cutting across these distinctions are two other characteristics: an interview may have an agreed-upon agenda that both speakers more-or-less adhere to, or it may have no specific agenda apart from a rather broad and undefined topic that both speakers agree to explore together. The first part of the Sue/Kay discourse is a cooperative and explorative interview. Finally, the interview has a fairly rigid pattern of turn-taking. Overlapping turns are less prevalent than in a conversation (see Sacks and Schegloff 1974). The general expectation is that one person asks a question relevant to the agenda, then the other answers that question with relevant and sufficient information (see Grice 1971). This can take the form of a direct response, a clarification, a reinterpretation of the question, a challenge to the interviewer's rights to and reasons for asking, or a parry in which the interviewee declares the question improper or unanswerable without saying so. The interviewer's next question must then be relevant to the answer or to the agenda, and so on.

At approximately line 188 a different form of exchange emerges. Here the discourse shifts from interview format to the looser organization of a conversation. The question/answer schema breaks down and Sue takes a more active role as contributor who does more than just ask questions. Sue begins to build on, amplify and complete Kay's utterances. As shown, for example, in Figure 6.1. In jazz

```
192–193   K: ... 'and things like that'.⌐
          S:                            └ 'personality, too'.

188–189   K: ... 'whole outlook on life'.⌐
          S:                             └'your demeanour'.

220–21    K: ... 'not cute.'⌐
          S:                └'instead of cute'.

224–25    K: ... 'and then I'd ...'⌐
          S:                        │ 'Then breathing became more
                                    └ important.'

233–34    K: ... 'This kid with ...⌐
          S:                        └'runny nose'.

273–78    K: ... 'die because you've got
                             ⌐a nose'               ⌐
          S:                 │'chokes on a piece│   ⌐of food'  ⌐
          K:                 └                  │   │'operation'│

          K: ...  ⌐'a disgusting way to go ...'   ⌐
          S:      └'you've have to be very careful'.│

          K: ...  'this could possibly happen'⌐
          S:                                   └'on chocolate mousse' ...
```

Figure 6.1

parlance, Sue takes off on a 'riff', a thematic variation on what Kay is saying. In common speech, we might observe here that they are 'getting it on', 'getting into it' or 'relaxing into it' as each picks up a piece of the theme and creates a virtuoso improvisation in harmony or contrapuntally with the other's utterance.

All of this signals that the discourse has moved from the style and structure of the interview to that of a conversation. It is now marked by freer and partly overlapping turn-taking, looser topical co-ordination between speakers, and flights of interpretive play on both meanings and implications. Cohesion is no longer a function of thematic exploration of the literal content of the nose schema, but is one of figural transformations of that content. This is a move from what might be called the central area of the nose schema to its periphery where 'looser' associations predominate, where breath and nose are no longer linked by the 'serious implications' of 'nose is what you breathe with' and 'obstructions in the nose cause problems of breathing', but are linked instead by 'breathing through different nostrils is a Yogic technique that affects the mind' (199–210, 327–378), and the humorous implications that flow from that. That is, instead of being something that needs blowing, the nose blows the mind.

Coherence is also accomplished by a kind of associative chaining rather than by repetition of previous content as the old information to be built on. The patterning of thematic repetition is replaced by associative novelty. Note, too, that utterances here are characterized by hyperbole (264–268), conceits (327–378), and parables (199–210) in place of description or of exposition by argument and example. Each speaker also makes fuller use of enthymemes rather than the material implications and presuppositions which were the predominant inferential means in the interview part of the discourse. In sum, both speakers rely less on the *inventio* of the nose rebus and more on the possibilities of verbal play created by the discourse itself.

De Memoria

Contemporary linguists, like their ancient counterparts, the rhetoricians, invoke memory or knowledge structures as part of the system of discourse comprehension. Here, too, linguists and psychologists have largely reinvented much that was already fully established within the rhetorical tradition (see Ong 1958; Yates 1966). There are, of course, interesting differences. The rhetorical tradition, for example, understood memory as a source of information for speech production; contemporary linguists understand it primarily in its role in comprehension. This difference in perspective – production on one hand, comprehension on the other – is a shift in focus from the speaker/writer to the hearer/reader, and signifies the transition from a context of oral discourse to one of writing. This contemporary emphasis on the passive consumer of print is the consequence of having an object in the form of a written text and has the effect of displacing the speaking subject as the creator of discourse in favor of the autonomous text itself or of the omniscient interpreter. It thus expresses that antipathy toward authors/creators of all kinds that has constituted so much of the theme of alienation in Western thought. It also reflects the resistance to writing as an occult practice that reveals only inasmuch as it conceals. This ambivalence to the text as an occult document requiring interpretation is responsible for enhancing the role of the interpreter at the expense of both text and author. It is the condition that creates linguists and the condition that linguists create, the condition that Derrida (1967) both documents and exemplifies. The emergence of the interpreter, which Peirce's theory of signs so clearly signified, is part of the glorification of the role of the disengaged, objective observer that both characterizes the age of science and is its central problem.

Two dominant themes have characterized memory research from its beginnings in Greek thought to the present. They are 'time' and 'representation'. The latter is a metaphoric implicate of 'space', of objects in space, and refers to the manner of 'coding' information ('memories') about objects in the world. 'Time' implicates a family of concepts having to do with remembering and forgetting, with 'retention' of memories or their 'vividness' (Aristotle, *De Memoria*, Hume 1888, 2.1.1), or 'recoding' (Seamon 1980:101), or 'depth of processing' (Craik and Lockhart 1972). To put it differently, 'time' has to do with the qualities or accidents of an object. Memory research thus recapitulates the general Indo-European linguistic schema of predication of a noun (= real object) and what can be said of it (= its contingencies or accidence).

A third topic relating to 'will' in the 'act' of remembering is the source of the difference between merely having memories and remembering. This volitional aspect of remembering has always been the subject of conscious mnemonic systems or 'artificial memory' in the rhetorical tradition. In its pathological form of 'forgetting as repression', it has been the focus of psychoanalytic research, as the tale of volition unconsciously thwarted and repressed. We thus have the concept of will ambiguously marked, so to speak; positively as conscious remembering, but negatively as artifice and as that which obscures true, unconscious significance.

Will apart, most thinking about memory is dualistic. With respect to time, memories are either 'vivid' or 'faded' in older terminology and common speech, or in the less vivid language of modern research, 'short-term' or 'long-term', or in the somewhat less contemporary usage of James (1890), 'primary' or 'secondary'. Short-term memory is itself sometimes divided into 'working short-term memory' and peripheral or unused short-term memory, thus indexing a sense of focus that articulates with will in its contemporary reading as 'awareness' or 'attention span'. Working short-term memory is focussed attention, consciously controlled by the will; peripheral short-term memory is unwilled, unconscious, and, in some understandings at least, doomed to sudden death. There is also an unspoken bias that connects short-term memory almost exclusively to the processing of ongoing external sensory stimulations, that is to say, with the present. Long-term memory, on the other hand, is only indirectly involved in the present. It is the past itself. The duality of memory research derives from an unspoken opposition in time between the present and the non-present. All that is non-present derives from the present (see Derrida 1967:6–26).

Representation, too, is dualistic. The rhetorical tradition distinguished between *res* ('thing') and *verba* ('word') as modes of representation, a distinction that continues today in the differences between 'visual' and 'verbal' images (see Paivio 1971), and 'episodic' and 'semantic' memories (Tulving 1972). These distinctions in turn reflect a deeper issue that underlies all 'dual coding' theories, namely, the distinction between 'contingent' knowledge and 'necessary' knowledge. Both representation and time acknowledge a transformation of the present as a re-presentation that moves from more to less vivid or from short-term to long-term. The presented is coded and recoded in successive re-presentations that move from iconic to indexical or symbolic images, in the case of visual or episodic representation, and from the sounds of words to concepts in the case of verbal or semantic memory. The transition from present to past is thus at the same time a movement from concrete to abstract representation. These conditions are illustrated in Thought picture 6.1.

Among the overtly dualistic treatments of memory are those of Bergson (1912), Russell (1921:167) and Ayer (1956:134–142). Bergson distinguished between 'habit memory' and 'pure memory'. The former was a 'mere motor mechanism', the latter the remembering of an actual event in one's past. Russell kept the same

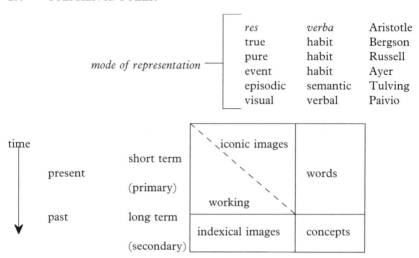

mode of representation		
res	*verba*	Aristotle
true	habit	Bergson
pure	habit	Russell
event	habit	Ayer
episodic	semantic	Tulving
visual	verbal	Paivio

Thought picture 6.1 Generalized cognitive memory model with dual coding (visual, verbal) and dual term (present, past)

distinction but called pure memory 'true memory', the recalling in imagery of a personal experience. Habit memory for Russell was a kind of verbalization, as in 'knowing by heart'. Ayer discriminated between 'habit memory' and 'event memory'. Habit memory he characterized as 'being able to do something' or as 'knowing a fact'. Event memory was the remembrance of a particular occurrence. A part of the distinction involved in all of these cases is that between memories for occurrences and memories of non-occurrences. Stated in this way the latter seem hardly to qualify as memories, hence Russell's expulsion of them from the domain of true memory. It reveals a bias in favor of personal experience. Habit memory, by contrast, is only indirectly – if at all – derived from personal experience. What basis is there in our personal experience for remembering that 'cows calve', 'sows farrow' and 'mares foal'? Pure memory is more 'real' than habit memory because the latter is only a kind of 'hearsay'. My memory of the world, of reality is my experience of it derived from my perceptions of it. My true memory is thus a kind of perception of a past event in the present. All of my other memories were never really presences, but are only knowing how to do something or remembering some collection of words. It is clear that the philosopher's distinction between habit memory and true memory is nothing more than the ancient distinction between *verba* and *res*. So, too, with the psychologist's distinction between episodic and semantic memory.

There is, however, a problem in the way these pairs of concepts correlate with the underlying distinction between contingency and necessity. The problem is signified by Tulving's 'episode' and Ayer's 'event'. Episodes and events are not proper substances (*res*); they involve action and motion and are thus attributes of substances rather than substances. Nor is semantic memory a proper substance. It is only indirectly derived from experience, being instead what is given by the facts of language. Its content corresponds to analytic propositions whose meanings are functions of the structure of language rather than images of things in the world. Although semantic memory is thus *verba* and not *res*, it nonetheless has the necessity of an analytic proposition. In the case of Ayer's 'event', the problem is 'how can the merely contingent facts of my personal experience be necessary?' This reflects not only a different understanding of the kind of reality that is necessary, it also implicates a different interpretation of the foundational sensory allegory, suggesting in place of static 'pictures' of things something more like action, movement, and change, an imagery of the motor and kinesthetic rather than the visual. In short, events, episodes, habits and semantic memory are all *verba* and contingent, and consequently illusions rather than realia.

In the original Aristotelian distinction, only visual metaphors counted as representations of reality, and that is why philosophers and psychologists continue to speak of events and episodes as if they were visual pictures of substance rather than qualities of substance. How else are we to understand the use of the common term 'representation' for all? The same is true of verbal memory. It is written about as if it were an object of some kind, though few are ready to specify the shape or locus of this *lingua mentis*. In effect, philosophers and psychologists have kept the ancient distinction between substance and accidence, but have confounded its implications. They are victims of an Indo-European linguistic bias that connects nouns, substances, reality, presence and visual perception as mutually implicated concepts.

The underlying issue (to use another favorite piece of mythology) has to do with the conservation of objects. All memory theories speak of memories as if they were objects or substances of some sort that are conserved over time. Memory is the conservation of an object, and that is why memories can be 'stored', 'fade', leave 'traces' and 'decay'. We generally understand movement and change as Aristotle did – as attributes of objects, not as objects themselves. The conservation of objects is their *identity* in *differences* of motion and time. In simple terms, we say something is the same (identity) when we see it in different times and changed circumstances. Observers apart, conservation thus entails three conditions, one of identity, and two of difference: object, motion and time, respectively. These, in turn, are metaphoric implicates of the sensory modalities of vision, kinesthesia (proprioceptive and tactile), and verbal/auditory, respectively. Representation, then, is not dualistic, it is triadic.

This is an implication that could well have been drawn from Peirce's semiotics, but is actually worked out in other places. Consider, for example, Don Locke's (1971:47) treatment of memory as consisting of three kinds: factual memory, as 'remembering that'; practical memory, or 'remembering how to do'; and personal memory, or 'remembering some specific person, place, thing, or incident from personal experience'. These distinctions parallel Ryle's analysis of knowing, but they also recapitulate the ancient divisions of rhetoric symbolized by *verba*, *ergon* (activity, motion) and *res*, which are themselves sensory allegories of 'saying', 'doing' and 'seeing'. Factual memory, as defined by Locke, consists in remembering what is given by or in language; remembering 'how to do' (practical memory) obviously refers to action; and personal memory is the remembering of things witnessed, things once really present in the rememberer's experience. In the analysis of meaning these quite obviously parallel the distinctions among sense, pragmatics and reference.

The memory model of Atkinson and Shiffrin (1968) is similar to Locke's. It has three memory structures: a sensory register; a short-term store; and a long-term store. These are linked by rehearsal and coding. Information is transferred to the long-term store by rehearsal in the short-term store. The model has been modified in subsequent publications in response to criticism concerning the connections between 'stores' and 'processes', but the triadic structure has been retained and widely used in research. In the present context, it is the mode of representation in these three stores that is interesting, for it is clear that their modes of representation correspond to the representational modes of the sign types, iconic, indexical and symbolic. The sensory register represents iconically, the short-term store represents indexically, and the long-term store represents symbolically. The model, in other words, recapitulates Peirce's semiotic categories, which are themselves allegorical recapitulations of Aristotle's three categories of *anima*.

Recoding is also triadic. The distinction between short-term memory and working memory, for example, is not just a distinction of focus and time, it is also a distinction of relative transformation. Non-focal short-term memory consists of relatively untransformed sensory information; working memory deals with information already transformed and is not restricted to contemporary sensory information. Long-term memory is further transformed and can be independent of current sensory information. To speak of 'depth of processing' (Craik and Lockhart 1972) is only another way of talking about the transformation of information as it moves from one store or level to another. It is a less interesting way of speaking of vividness. Both recoding and depth of processing are ways of talking about identities within differences in a manner analogous to Peirce's sign types. Moreover, they correspond to the antique distinctions *sensus*, *imaginatio* and *intellectus*. They are also aspects of time, not just of present and past as in Thought picture 6.1, but of present, past and future. Symbolic, long-term memory is not really oriented to the past in the way we usually think memory is; it is the future, what the future is made of – reconstructions of the past.

The implication is clear; memory contains as part of itself what we would normally call thinking and sensing. The latter are neither separate from nor coordinate with memory; they are aspects of memory. Now we can perhaps understand why the Greeks made Mnemosyne the Queen of the Muses.

The intersection of the dimensions 'time' and 'representation' yields Thought picture 6.2. At the iconic and indexical levels there are sensory-specific representations. That is, each sensory modality has its own images and patterns, but all follow a similar course of transformation. In addition, kinesthetic representations are partially integrated with visual representation at the indexical level, and both visual and kinesthetic are integrated at the symbolic level by a higher order mode of representation which represents itself and all lower order modes of representation. It is a *sensorium communis*, a *lingua mentis*, a *summa essentia locutio*, an interior *locutio*, 'language', the 'word', the *logos*.

Each sensory modality has a metaphoric implicate. Verbal/auditory has time or *verba*; visual has space or *res* (that which has extension in space and identity in time); and kinesthetic has motion, change, action, function, work or *ergon*. Moreover, each dimension of time or manner of representation has a characteristic mode of tropic ordering. Iconic representation is metonymic, the mechanical juxtaposition of part-to-part. Indexical representation is synecdochic, the organic relation of part-to-whole. Symbolic representation is metaphoric, the relation of whole-to-part. The symbolic can

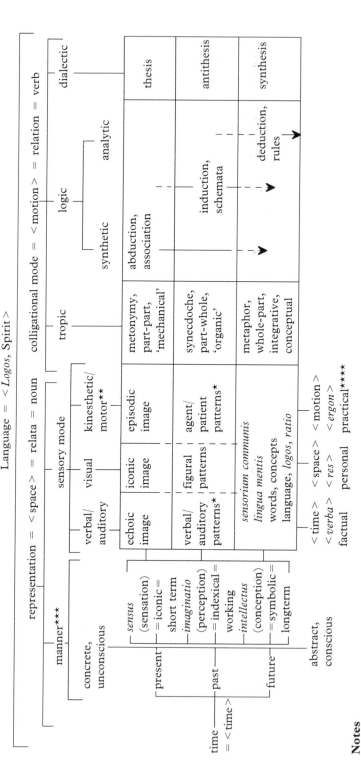

Notes

* verbal/auditory patterns include: melody, rhythm, movement, frequency, intensity; figural patterns include: shape, dimension, orientation; agent–patient patterns include movement, orientation, rhythm, frequency and intensity.
** kinesthetic-motor includes tactile and proprioceptive sensory modes.
*** manner of substituting appearances = recoding = memory stores = depth of processing = time.
**** Don Locke's memory types (1971).
Taste and smell are excluded because they do not make representations.
Words in < > are metaphoric implicates.

Thought picture 6.2 Triadic model of memory as a *loci communis* for metalepsis and *inventio*, or 'How the World Becomes a Fable' recapitulate in its own form all of the sign functions of the other levels but cannot recapitulate what they transform after they have transformed it. Finally, each manner of representation has a more-or-less correspondent mode of logical ordering. Iconic has associativity; indexical has schemata; and symbolic has rules, or in Peirce's terms, abduction, induction and deduction.

This account implies that Thought picture 6.2 can be read in several different contexts. Most obviously, it is about memory, how memories are coded, transformed and integrated, but it is as well a pictorial story of perception, of how percepts are sensorially coded, transformed and integrated in the movement from sensation to conception, from concrete to abstract, from unconscious to conscious. It can also be read developmentally as the child's transition from kinesthetic to visual to verbal modes of thought. It is an outline of sensory integration in the development of thought, perception and memory. Each sensory modality does not develop in isolation, but is always interacting with other modalities and that integration produces cross-modal integrative systems characteristic of each major developmental stage. So too with thought, which achieves its highest integration in the emergent symbolic system of language, of thought 'properly speaking'. It strongly implies that thought is immanent in this highest level of integration rather than something that precedes it or transcends it. Moreover, it does not so much reduce thought and perception to memory as to make all three different aspects of a single, unifying process. It purports to be a unified model of perception, thought, memory and development.

Thought picture 2 can also be read metaphorically in several ways. It recapitulates Reid's (1895) mental powers of man, Peirce's triadic system of signs and McLean's (1973) concept of the triune brain, which are all, in turn, variforms of Aristotle's founding allegory of the three forms of *anima*. It is a metaphor of the three tropes, metonymy, synecdoche and – here is its irony – of metaphor itself; and of the three modes of inference, abduction, induction and deduction; and of the three means of sign, colligation, association, schemata and rules. It epitomizes the dialectic, both in its implication of progressive unification, sublation, abstraction and emergence, and in its implicit ordering of the relations among sign types. Without going into detail, it understands iconic and indexical signs as inverses of one another, for an iconic signifier is determined by its signified, but an indexical signifier determines its signified. Iconic and indexical are thus related to one another as thesis to antithesis. Their opposition is neutralized in the symbol whose signifiers and

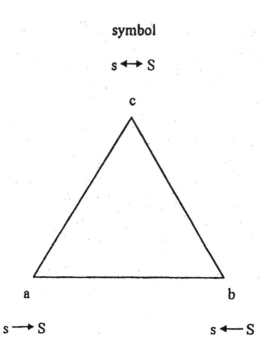

symbol

Notes: s = signified, S = signifier.
'a' is the inverse of 'b', and 'c' is the sublation of 'a' and 'b'.
The dialectic thus 'rationalizes' the order of signs.

Thought picture 6.3 Dialectical relation of constitutive signs

signifieds are mutually constituted and reciprocally determinative. We thus have the familiar structuralist triangle of Thought picture 6.3.

Just as the sign functions iconic, indexical and symbolic are variforms of *sensus*, *imaginatio* and *intellectus*, the Latinized versions of Aristotle's three forms of *anima*, so too are the sensory modalities metaphorical implicates of Aristotle's semantico-grammatical categories. Verbal/auditory is 'time,' and *verba*, visual is 'space' and *res*, kinesthesia is 'motion', 'movement', 'action', 'function', 'work' or *ergon*. These are reflexes of the underlying categorical distinctions between substance (*ens per se*), the first category, and the other nine categories which are all attributes (*ens per accidence*) of the first category.

Other metaphoric implicates can be worked out, but enough have been given to suggest the persistence of an episteme, of a structure of foundational concepts which keep getting reinvented. In that sense, the rediscovery of Aristotle in the Middle Ages is itself a sort of allegory of this whole cyclical history, so that what passes for memory functions in discourse analysis in linguistics and cognitive science today is only another rediscovery of the rhetoric of the Stagirite.

I note now a final harmony between past and present. Thought picture 6.2 is itself a memory system – at least for me. It functions as *inventio* and *topoi*. It is an organization of places (*loci*) for ideas as concepts, imitating, but poorly, the memory systems of Bruno and Lull, being like them a system of memory *loci* whose *locus* is memory itself (see Yates 1966:173–230). It tells us why we persist in searching for the location of memory in the brain, as if it were a granary in a farmyard, and each memory a needle in a haystack, and why that is as compelling as it is peculiar.

The preceding picture of memory focusses on representation, but has little to say about memory in discourse or communication. The following is a brief account of the integration of discourse from the speaker's point of view, or more appropriately, his point of speech. It is based on the musical analogy of melody and harmony, the former being a sequence of units in time, the latter the synchronous or simultaneous or non-temporal integration of different 'spatial' positions. Although these correspond to what linguists have some-times referred to as the syntagmatic and paradigmatic axes of language, they are used here not in the context of language as a whole, but with respect to some part of discourse. I omit discussion of other forms of synchrony, of the integration of unsaid thoughts or processes outside of the focal pattern, even though these contribute to the composition of utterances as surely as counterpoint and polyphony do to music.

As in music, our sense of discourse orderliness is given by theme and variation, a pattern of repetition with change, of identity with difference, corresponding more-or-less to the linguist's categories of theme and rheme, 'old' information and 'new information'. In a related sense we can say that it is given by the integration of prospect – what will be said – and retrospect – what was said. These, in turn, correspond respectively to long-term memory and short-term work-ing memory. The relation of units – words, phrases, sentences, breath groups, the linguist's 'beads on a string' – is metonymic, synecdochic and metaphoric. The speaker's 'saying' is informed by an emergent whole which is reconstituted in memory as 'the said', and becomes the condition for the speaker's continuing to 'say' or for his silence.

Consider the following simple case of someone saying the ABCs. Assume that the conditions for saying them are appropriate: the speaker can speak them, her saying them is preceded by an intention to say them, and her intention includes an apprehension of the ABCs which is complete enough for us to say: 'She knows them'. This apprehension is not the whole sequence of the ABCs; it is 'ABC ... go on in the same way to ... Z'. That is, it is an inchoate whole whose parts are incompletely articulated (in both senses). In saying the ABCs she articulates this whole but never makes it present as a whole, for it emerges as the metaphoric relation of a whole to its parts. We would not say, for example, that the whole was either A or Z or anything in between. Nor would we say it was the presence of the whole sequence, since that is never present in the way it might seem to be if we wrote out the sequence on paper. It is, then, an emergent whole different from its parts but it is never articulated as a whole or in one or all of its parts. Nonetheless, it can become itself a part in some other utterance, as in, for example, 'say your ABCs ten times'.

Moreover, the speaker's saying of each separate letter is conditioned by the context of that letter, which is the correct saying of the sequence to that point and the anticipation of some part of the sequence that is to follow. Saying 'E', then, is enabled by the memory of having said A–D, with something like an echoic memory or feedback of B–C–D, the rehearsal of F–G–H, and the anticipation of I–Z. That is to say, when the speaker says 'E', she has other things than 'E' on her mind that make saying 'E' possible. This 'saying E' is illustrated in Thought picture 6.4.

In these senses, saying the ABCs is analogous to saying any other sentence or part of a large discourse. It is, of course, too simple and mechanistic to be like real speech. All of its units, for example, have roughly equal prominence and can thus be linked unambiguously by metonymic association, unlike the layered units of syntax which are synecdochically induced. But, even in this simple case of saying or singing the ABCs there are rhythmical and breath groups which are synecdochic structures (see Halliday 1967; Liberman and Prince 1977; Ladd 1980; Thompson 1980). For example, one variant of singing the ABCs has what is shown in Figure 6.2.

Here the metonymic sequence of letters is broken into schemalike groupings which are in part imposed by the necessity of breathing, but are also arbitrary rhythms reflecting protosemantic orderings in the grouping of signs alone. Note that each rhythm group is divided into beats of accented and unaccented parts, and of prolonged and shortened sounds thus,

A-B-Ć – Ď-E-F-G – Ḣ-I-J-K – Ĺ-M-Ṅ-O-Ṗ – Q-Ṙ-S-T – Ú-V̇ – W-Ẋ-Y-and Ź –

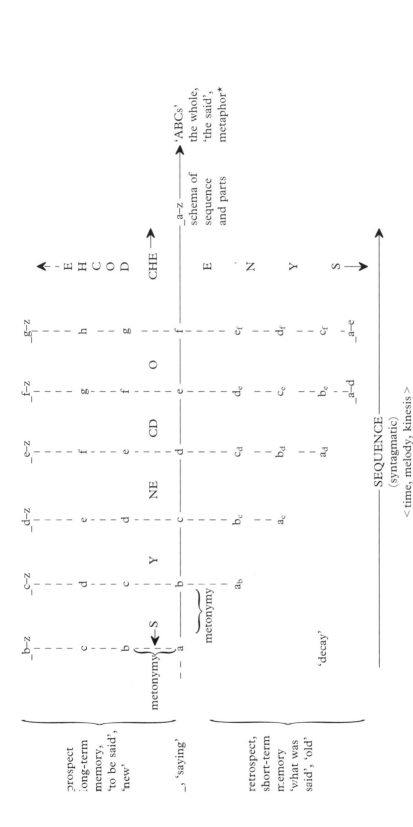

Thought picture 6.4 'Simplest case' integration of discourse

Notes:
★ the Aristotelian sentence as *logos*.
< > words are metaphoric implicates.
_ indicates 'conditions for saying'.[2]

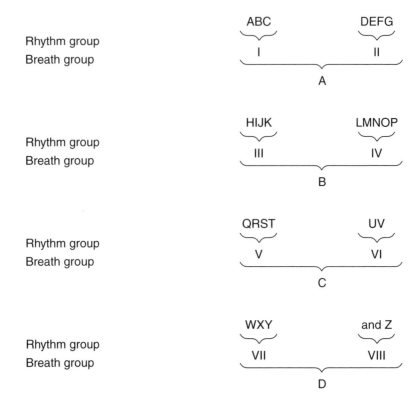

'Now I know my ABCs/Aren't you proud of me?'

Figure 6.2

In these groupings we see the emergence of a kind of 'protosyntax', which breaks up the lineal sequence of the letters, not just by grouping them into adjacent groups, but by bringing them together as constituents of groups that are non-adjacent. The grouping overthrows the adjacency aspect of metonymy.

Other groupings perform a similar function. In addition to breath groups and rhythm groups, this example also has a rhyme scheme and accent groups. With the exception of rhythm group III above, all rhythm groups end in a prolonged [î] sound, as do the concluding lines. Accent groups consist of accented or stressed letters in the same breath group. In the ABCs, as outlined above, we have the syntaxlike groupings of Thought picture 6.5.

The elements in Thought picture 6.5 are not, like beads on a string or links in a chain, confined to strict temporal sequence; they are constituents of simultaneously retrospective and prospective groups whose elements are both separated in sequential time and

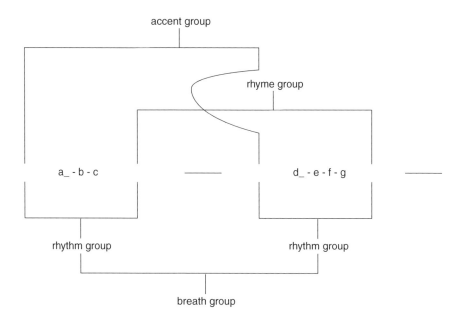

Thought picture 6.5: Prosodic groupings in the 'ABC' song

synchronously conjoined. Linguistics has traditionally understood such disjacent constituency as the province of syntax. The argument here, however, is that all such groupings are only superficially grammatical; they are instead mnemno-semantic schemata (see Chafe 1980; Halliday 1967; Thompson 1980). They are similar to the phrasal groupings that constitute commonsense knowledge and function as basic information units in discourse.

Phrasal schemata are also rhythmic. They tend to be broken into breath groups or prosodic groups marked by rising and falling tones, and accentual groups not unlike those of the ABC example. Consider the selection shown in Figure 6.3 from the Sue/Kay tape. The rhythm of lines 24–26 is something like:

24. DAAH DAHda DAHda daDAHda daDAHda REST
25. DAHda DAHda DAHda REST DAHda REST
26. da REST dada DAHdaDAHdaDAHda REST

Even this brief sample chosen at random illustrates the way prosodic features mark schemata. In line 24 each phrase (terminally marked by | or ||) is a piece of rhythmic format: 'so I thought', 'I mean', 'there are other things wrong with me'. So, too, in line 25: 'so 1 figured', 'like, well', 'that's just'. And in lines 26 and 27 there are: 'so, but (I)',

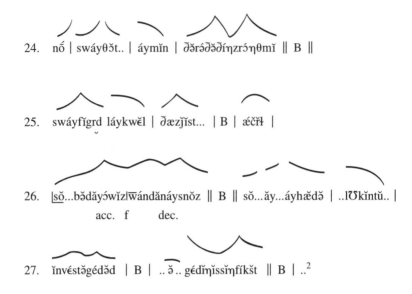

24. nő | swáyθɔ̌t.. | áymĭn | ðɔ̌rɔ́ðɔ̌ðíηzrɔ́ηθmĭ ‖ B ‖

25. swáyfĭgrd láykwĕl | ðæzjĭst... | B | ǽčřɬ |

26. |sǒ...bɔ̌dăyɔ́wĭz|w̄ándănáysnŏz ‖ B ‖ sǒ...ăy...áyhǽdɔ̌ | ..lʊ̌kĭntŭ.. |
    acc. f   dec.

27. ĭnvéstɔ̌gédɔ̌d | B | ..ɔ̌.. gédĭ̞ṇissĭ̞ṇfíkšt ‖ B | ..²

Figure 6.3

'I always wanted a nice nose', 'so I had a' 'look into' or 'I had a look into', 'getting this thing fixed'. Their unitary wordlike character is clearer in the phonetic transcription than in ordinary print. Their prosodic patterns mark them off from one another, though that is obviously not the whole function of prosody in communication. The point is that schemata are often rhythmically and tonally defined units of information similar to those of the ABC example. They are not, of course, fixed musical patterns, for that would prevent us from using stress and intonation to focus attention on different points of a schema when needed as is shown in Figure 6.4. That is, 'I'm going to HIT you!' vs. 'I'm going to hit YOU!' vs. 'I'M going to hit you.'

ámɔ̌ńitcŭ vs. ámɔ̌ńitcŭ vs. ámɔ̌ńitcú.

Figure 6.4

Moreover, I do not suggest that rhythm is important only in the word. As meaningful in conversation and other forms of oral discourse is the synchronization of movement and utterance that gives a conversation, for example, its pace and rhythm. Speakers' turns are synchronized with the perception of beats, accents and rests as are movements displaying the hearers' attention and involvement.

How we as speakers and hearers attend to or fail to attend to these features of synchrony is a sign of how we feel about ourselves, the speaker/hearer, what is being said, or all three. They are, then, part of our construction – our memory – of what was said. They may be used to dismiss utterly the cognitive content of what was said, as when we attend more carefully to how someone speaks than to what she says as a surer guide to her meaning.

Returning to the memory picture of Thought picture 6.4, we can illustrate how Kay and Sue use different schematic forms in accomplishing their interview/conversation. As speaker, Kay uses the macro-structure 'The story of having my nosed fixed' as the whole toward which her utterances work. Implicated substories are generated as parts of this larger whole, such as 'how noses are' (9–36, 81–110), 'how my nose got to be the way it is' (147–168), 'what the doctor will do' (39–79), 'how things will be afterwards' (112–144, 179–198, 319–379). Each of these is part of a larger story. They correspond to setting, complication, resolution and evaluation, and unfold in the manner of a Proppian folktale.

As the page numbers above indicate, however, Kay's story does not develop as a straightforward sequence of related substories or episodes in the manner of a written narrative or well-known folktale. It is, instead, cumulative and cyclical. Substories appear in disconnected parts, separated by other substories or parts of substories, and they are recycled as topics or themes in other stories. She uses the mode of *sorites*, the 'heaping up' of bits of information in a manner reminiscent of Ezra Pound's ideogramic method of heaping together the components of thought. Part of this drift from a straight narrative line arises from Kay's following out incidents and observations peripheral to the main story of the moment. She drifts into new stories tangential to her main narrative instead of repressing them in favor of tighter narration. Part of this drift is due to Sue's questions which pick out themes for emphasis or identify implications that lead to new divergences. The 'interruptions' of interviews and conversations work against ordered exposition and fixed narration of a single story, particularly when the interviewer or conversational partner has a different story in mind. Part of the drift is also verbal play, especially in the latter parts of the conversation where 'absurd' associations or implications became the focus in place of exposition and narration. Here it is no longer story and narration or even dramatic narrative, but a cooperative exchange of witty and exaggerated comic situations. The two cooperate not so much in creating a story as in making the story a metaphoric source of amusing possibilities.

These different 'drifts' – from interview to topic-oriented conversation to verbal play – are marked by different incidences and types of 'interruption'. From lines 1 to 100, there are only two speaker overlaps. All other speaker turns occur at phrase boundaries or at appropriate speaker silences in the form of turns at the end of an idea sequence or as cooperative fill-ins or repetitions when the speaker is stuck. Sue, in effect, helps the story along by interrupting only in the interests of clarification, emphasis, flow and as a sign of empathetic listening. In the next 100 lines there are, by contrast, ten overlaps, not all of which are strictly cooperative from the standpoint of narrative flow and clarity. In the next 100 lines there are fifteen overlaps, and most of them are 'playful' metaphoric 'take-offs'.

From the hearer's point of view, the outline of memory in Thought picture 6.4 illustrates how each speaker is able to interrupt the other, complete the first speaker's sentence in a word or phrase and go on to a new and implicated topic. The hearer knows where the speaker is going before she gets there. The hearer anticipates the other's destination – 'gets her drift' as we say – arrives there first, interrupts, and sets off on a new journey. This reflects 'hearing for meaning' or 'getting the gist' of an utterance which is not dependent on having the whole utterance in all its parts in mind as such. It is a meaning 'for now' which is sufficient to present purposes.

Thought picture 6.4 also makes clear the organization and role of schemata themselves. The whole utterance or story may be a schema, or their parts may be schemata. The implication here is that the units of utterances and stories are themselves schemata operating at different constructional levels, all the way from the relatively fixed format of idioms, common expressions and metaphors to such larger units as routines, episodes, plots, stories, genres, narration and exposition. Very little in discourse can be accounted for metonymically as the mechanical conjunction of parts. There is no smooth, step-by-step, inductive transition from sensory signal to concept. The sensory signal itself is a sign only in a schematic context. The past (= schema) always precedes the present (= iconic sign) and makes its future context. The movement then is not just from sense to concept *via* percept but from concept to sense via percept or from percept to concept or percept to sense. This, of course, parallels, in part, the distinction between thoughts, perceptions, and memories that are 'data driven' or processed from the 'bottom-up' (inductively) vs. those that are 'concept driven' or processed from the 'top-down' (deductively). Both are mediated by schemata, and the consequence is that concepts are neither built-up analytically as generalizations abstracted from data nor understood by reductive analysis to concrete particulars.

Concluding objection

This 'picture of memory' is consistent with the kind of physicalist understandings of memory that have predominated in memory research, and that is the surest sign that it is wrong. It portrays memory as an instance of the conservation of objects. Our memories are like objects subject to the ravages of entropy. They 'decay', they 'fade', they 'disappear' from mind, they leave 'traces', they can be 'stored', they can be 'retrieved', sometimes even after they have been 'lost' or 'repressed'. We like to think of memory not only as a collection of *loci*, of places where memories are stored, but as a place itself, having a *locus* in the brain. This whole vast and persistent metaphor of objects and places is a peculiar metaphor for memory, which, after all, is more intimately implicated by time than by space and its congeners of objects in places. It is part of a tradition of speculation that ties memory to writing and visualization, to the idea of representation, whether of the cruder sort known as images or of the subtler variety called symbols. The idea of representation makes sense only in a context of writing and visualization, of the spatialization of sound. It confirms us in that false analogy between the behavior of bodies and the behavior of minds which encourages us to think of memory on the model of a physical transaction. When we think of memory for sound rather than the memory of visual pictures of sound the idea of representation is less persuasive. What could be re-presented in the case of sound? An echo? A vibration? (ibid. (Reid 1895:536)). Unlike images, the idea of sound does not implicate spatial representation, it implies instead, time, which is not a thing, has no dimensions, and cannot be perceived. It is reasonable, then, that memory for speech is neither representation nor the conservation of an object. We would do better to think of memory as the conservation of time rather than the conservation of an object. We would no longer think of memory as if it were the recurrence of a thing known before, an object identical in two different times – past and non-past. Rather than differences in time confirming identity of objects, differences in objects would only confirm differences in subjects, but no difference in time. We would no longer think of time as a locus or container and we would no longer speak of 'being on time' or 'being in time', but of 'being time', and we would find it stranger to say 'I am an object' than to say 'I am time'. Who knows, we might even be able to hear the voice of God.

222 • STEPHEN A. TYLER

Notes

1. Conventions used in this analysis:
   - ..   short pause
   - ...   long pause
   - ....   deletion
   - ′   primary stress
   - ¢   secondary stress
   - ⌐   raised pitch on phrase
   - ⌐   lowered pitch on phrase
   - ‖   end of phrase
   - | B | breath in middle of a phrase
   - ‖ B ‖ breath at end of a phrase
   - f   forte
   - acc.   accelerated speech
   - dec.   decreasing speech rate
   - []   overlapping speech, two people talking at once
   - ⌐   second speaker attaches utterance to first speaker's uncompleted utterance

2. Note that this thought picture gives a different value to the concepts 'metonym' and 'metaphor' than that in Jakobson (1960). Jakobson restricts metonymy to the syntagmatic axis and metaphor to the paradigmatic axis, but there is no more reason for identifying sequence and metonymy than for equating simultaneity and metaphor. In Thought picture 6.4, both metaphor and metonymy are treated as either simultaneous or sequential. Historically, the idea of metonymy – as association – was sometimes thought of as the 'chain' of elements in a sentence (as, for example, in Hume) and sometimes under the name of 'suggestion' as the 'chain' of thoughts and memories apart from the strict lineal sequence of words in the sentence. The latter might interfere with the train of thought and expression, but the former were the train of thought and expression. The latter were also poetic and rhetorical means and were opposed to 'plain style'. For further discussion of this point, see Tyler (1987), Chapter 1, 'Epode'.

References

Aristotle (1928) *Categoriae,* and *De Interpretatione.* In *The Works of Aristotle, Vol. I,* ed. by W. D. Ross, Oxford: Oxford University Press.

Aristotle (1973) *De Memoria,* trans. by G. R. T. Ross, New York: Arno Press.

Atkinson, Robert C. and Schiffrin, R. M. (1968) Human memory: a proposed system and its control processes. In *Psychology of Learning and Motivation, Vol. 2,* ed. by K. W. Spence and J. T. Spence, New York: Academic Press, 176–212.

Augustine, St. (1950) *Confessions*. New York: Dutton.

Ayer, Alfred J. (1956) *The Problem of Knowledge*. New York: Penguin Books.

Bartlett, Frederic Charles (1932) *Remembering: A Study in Experimental and Social Psychology*. London: Cambridge University Press.

Bergson, Henri (1912) *Matter and Memory*. London: Allen & Unwin.

Chafe, Wallace (1980) The deployment of consciousness in the production of a narrative. In *The Pear Stories*, ed. by Wallace Chafe, Norwood, NJ: Ablex, 9–50.

Craik, Fergus I. M. and Lockhart, R. J. (1972) Levels of processing: a framework for memory research. *Journal of Verbal Learning and Verbal Behaviour*, 11:671–84.

Derrida, Jacques (1967) *L'Écriture et la difference*. Paris: Seuill.

Goodman, Paul (1971) *In Defense of Poetry*. New York: Vintage Press.

Grice, Paul (1971) Logic and conversation. In *Syntax and Semantics* 3, ed. by P. Cole and J. Morgan, New York: Academic Press, 43–58.

Halliday, M. A. K. (1967) *Intonation and Grammar in British English*. The Hague: Mouton.

Hamilton, Sir William (1895a) Note D: contribution to a history of the doctrine of mental suggestion or association. In *The Philosophical Works of Thomas Reid, Vol. 2*. Edinburgh: James Thin, 888–910.

Hamilton, Sir William (1895b) On the theory of mental reproduction: outline of a theory of mental reproduction, suggestion, or association. In *The Philosophical Works of Thomas Reid, Vol. 2*. Edinburgh: James Thin, 910–917.

Hume, David (1888) *Treatise on Human Nature*. Oxford: Clarendon Press.

Jakobson, Roman (1960) Concluding statement: Linguistics and poetics. In *Style in Language*, ed. by T. A. Sebeok, Cambridge: MIT Press, 350–378.

James, William (1890) *The Principles of Psychology*. New York: Dover Press.

Ladd, Robert D. (1980) *Intonational Meaning*. Bloomington: Indiana University Press.

Liberman, M. and Prince, A. (1977) On stress and linguistic rhythm. *Linguistic Inquiry*, 8:249–336.

Locke, Don (1971) *Memory*. New York: Doubleday.

Lord, Albert B. (1960) *The Singer of Tales: Harvard Studies in Comparative Literature*, 24. Cambridge: Harvard University Press.

McLean, Paul (1973) A triune concept of the brain and behavior. In *The Hincks Memorial Lecture*, ed. by T. Boag and D. Campbell, Toronto: University of Press Toronto.

Ong, Walter J., S.J. (1958) *Ramus: Method and the Decay of Dialogue*. Cambridge: Harvard University Press.

Ong, Walter J., S.J. (1982) *Orality and Literacy: The Technologizing of the Word*. London: Methuen.

Paivio, Allan (1971) *Imagery and Verbal Processes*. New York: Holt, Rinehart.

Quillian, M. R. (1966) *Semantic Memory*. Cambridge, MA: Bolt, Beranek, & Newman.

Reid, Thomas (1895) *Essays on the Active and Moral Powers of Man, Vol. 3.* In *The Works of Thomas Reid*. Edinburgh: James Thin.

Russell, Bertrand (1921) *Analysis of Mind*. London: Allen & Unwin.

Sacks, Harvey, and Schlegoff, E. (1974) A simplest systematics for the organization of turn-taking for conversation. *Language*, 50(4):696–735.

Seamon, John G. (1980) *Memory and Cognition*. Oxford: Oxford University Press.

Tannen, Deborah (1984) *Conversational Style*. Norwood, NJ: Ablex.

Thompson, H. S. (1980) Sentence stress and salience in English: theory and practice. Palo Alto: Palo Alto Research Center, photocopy.

Tulving, Endel (1972) Episodic and semantic memory. In *Organization of Memory*, ed. by E. Tulving and W. Donaldson, New York: Academic Press, 282–404.

Tyler, Stephen A. (1987) *The Unspeakable: Discourse, Dialogue, and Rhetoric in the Postmodern World*. Madison: University of Wisconsin Press.

Yates, Frances (1966) *The Art of Memory*. Chicago: University of Chicago Press.

7

Highlighting in Stratificational-Cognitive Linguistics

David G. Lockwood

The scope of highlighting

The text which forms the basis of this the *Second Rice Symposium in Linguistics and Semiotics* contains several examples of the use of special grammatical devices to direct attention to a particular aspect of the situation being spoken about in a given clause. Consider the following:

(1) I was taken to the hospital (ll. 170–171)
(2) now you have to have really good reasons (ll. 165–166)
(3) What I would like to find out more about is your operation (that you are having) (ll. 1–2)
(4) (then) they want to be put asleep (l. 65)

In example (1), we see the semological patient (*I*) selected as the grammatical subject along with the use of passive voice to direct more attention upon that patient than would be found in the active equivalent.

In example (2), the initial placement of the temporal element *(now)* can be seen as again drawing special attention to this part of the situation.

In example (3) we see a device commonly called the **PSEUDO-CLEFT**, which directs a kind of attention to *your operation* by beginning the clause with the coreferential pronoun *what* and placing the phrase as complement of a copular verb. A related construction not found in the text is the **CLEFT,** which could be exemplified by the paraphrase *It's your operation that I would like to find out more about.*

Finally, example (4) illustrates attention directed to the grammatical subject *(they)* via the use of strong accent.

These uses all involve various ways of picking out certain participants or circumstantial elements in clause structures and marking them in particular ways to direct, as already suggested, some special kind of attention to them. The term **HIGHLIGHTING** is offered as a generic term for these devices. The purpose of this chapter is to trace the history of treatments of this set of devices in textual structure according to the tradition of stratificational-cognitive linguistics. Where possible, the devices discussed are illustrated from the Symposium Text [at the 1984 Rice Symposium], though further examples are sometimes needed.

Stratificational-cognitive treatments of highlighting

This section surveys the treatments of these phenomena found in the tradition of stratificational-cognitive linguistics beginning in the 1960s. Lamb (1964) was the first publication outlining his approach to semology.

Early treatments

The small amount of material on this subject in the early stratificational literature is generally restricted to the treatment of passive forms. The popularity of the active/passive distinction as an illustration in early transformational grammars makes it quite understandable why this was the first variety of highlighting to be tackled by stratificationalists. They wanted to show that such clause types could be related in a linguistic description without resort to transformational devices.

Two treatments of the passive date from the middle of the 1960s. Both of them use one form or another of **SEMOLOGICAL NETWORK**, a configuration posited in those years for structures on the sememic stratum by both Lamb and Gleason. Later on, when Lamb began to use the term **NETWORK** for a configuration of relationships dealing with various structural strata, Gleason proposed the alternative term **RETICULUM** for this more limited sort of configuration (1968:271, 275n).[1]

The only published examples referring to this problem are found in Hockett (1966), a work which developed out of a series of lectures which Hockett gave at the 1964 Linguistic Institute at Indiana University, Bloomington. Since Hockett characterized himself as describing Lamb's practice of the time (1966:170ff.), it can be presumed that a degree of personal communication between the two underlay these versions. Some examples of what Hockett termed **SEMON NETWORKS** for declarative, interrogative, active and passive versions of *The man shot the tiger* are presented in Figures 7.1–4.[2]

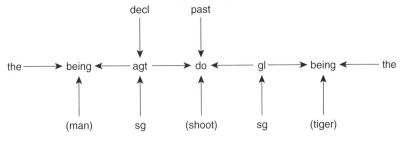

Figure 7.1 Hockett's Semon Network for *The man shot the tiger* (slightly modified from Fig. 40, p. 182, Hockett 1966)

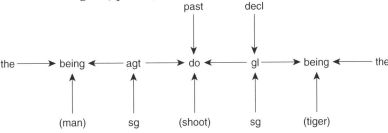

Figure 7.2 Hockett's Semon Network for *The tiger was shot by the man* (Fig. 41, p. 183)

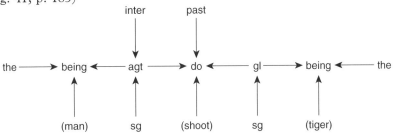

Figure 7.3 Hockett's Semon Network for *Did the man shoot the?* (Fig 42, p. 183)

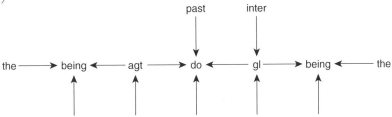

Figure 7.4 Hockett's Semon Network for *Was the tiger shot by the man?* (Fig. 43, p. 183)

According to the hypothesis underlying these examples, 'the difference ... between active and passive is interpreted as a difference of arrangement of exactly the same semons' (Hockett 1966:180–181). Specifically, the difference is assumed to center on whether the **DECLARATIVE** or **INTERROGATIVE** semon characterizing the sentence type is attached to the **AGENT** semon (as in Figures 7.1 and 7.3) for the actives, or to the **GOAL** semon (as in Figures 7.2 and 7.4) for their passive counterparts.

Hockett did not comment extensively on these or the other eighteen examples he presented over the space of five and one-half pages, but some of his further examples show, if one tries to carry their principles further, that the treatment of the active/passive voice distinction offered here cannot be readily extended to other types of examples. The items in Figures 7.5–7.7 illustrate the treatment of relative clauses. These specific examples all illustrate active declarative principal clauses containing an active relative clause. On the basis of the examples in Figures 7.2 and 7.4, one could readily produce networks for the equivalents with passive principal clauses. But the active/passive distinction is by no means confined to principal clauses. It is also possible in subordinate clauses, as illustrated by such examples as:

(5) I saw the man by whom the tiger was shot.
(6) The people by whom I was taken to the hospital were kind.

This model of the passive, however, seems to have no way to represent such types, since relatives and other subordinate clauses do not have any token of the declarative or interrogative elements associated with their agents and goals, and the placement of *Decl* or *Inter* is the only way actives can be distinguished from passives in this model, as Figures 7.1–7.4 demonstrate.

No alternative treatments of the English active-passive distinction occur in the published material of this period. Lamb presented a somewhat different treatment, however, in his lectures in a Linguistic Institute course in Stratificational Grammar offered at the University of Michigan, Ann Arbor, in the summer of 1965. Figures 7.8–7.10 show sememic networks of the type he was using at that time.[3] These networks differ from those exemplified by Hockett in that some of the arrows connecting the elements have distinctive labels. In particular, the Declarative and Interrogative elements have arrows labeled 'PRED' (meaning 'PREDICATION') pointing to the associated event sememe, and arrows labeled 'TOPIC' pointing to whatever will be the grammatical subject. The roles of agent and goal

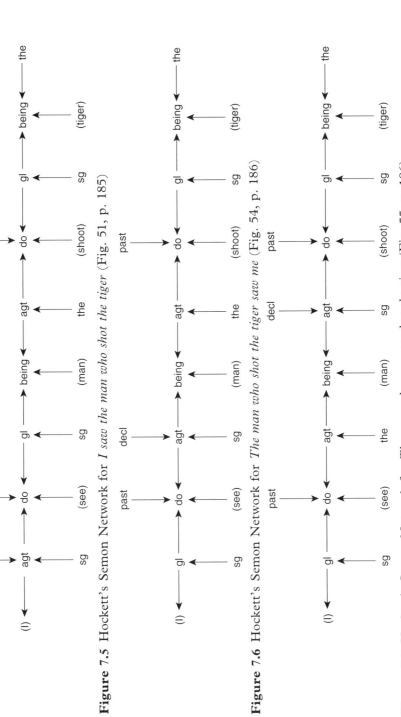

Figure 7.5 Hockett's Semon Network for *I saw the man who shot the tiger* (Fig. 51, p. 185)

Figure 7.6 Hockett's Semon Network for *The man who shot the tiger saw me* (Fig. 54, p. 186)

Figure 7.7 Hockett's Semon Network for *The man who saw me shot the tiger* (Fig. 55, p. 186)

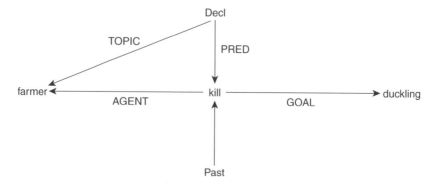

Figure 7.8 Lamb's Sememic Network for *The farmer killed the duckling*

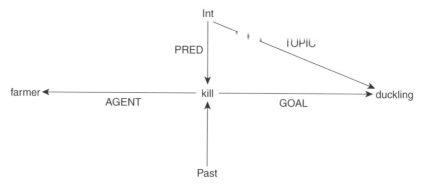

Figure 7.9 Lamb's Sememic Network for *Was the duckling killed by the farmer?*

are also distinguished by different arrows rather than different sememes. Figures 7.8 and 7.9 show the treatment of a declarative active and an interrogative passive clause. From these, it can easily be deduced how a declarative passive and an interrogative active would be treated. Figure 7.10 shows the treatment of a relative clause, which like those in Hockett's examples contains neither a declarative nor an interrogative element. For all this it is not difficult to see how we might get a network for such an example as *The farmer who ate the duckling killed it* using this model, but it still does not have a ready way to show a passive relative clause, as in such an example as *The prince ate the duckling that was killed by the farmer*.

Nevertheless, the recognition of some kind of a separate element for TOPIC represents an advance over the earlier version. Given this, only one more innovation is required to allow passive relatives to be handled: alongside the declarative and interrogative sememes already recognized, we need a **RELATIVE** sememe with its own

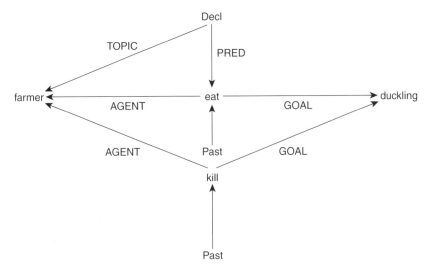

Figure 7.10 Lamb's Sememic Network for *The farmer who killed the duckling ate it*

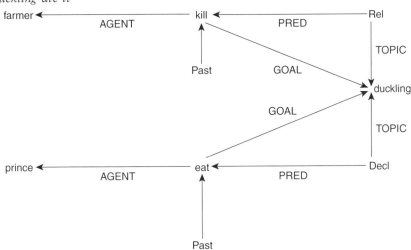

Figure 7.11 A modified form of Lamb's Sememic Network designed for example with a passive relative clause: *The duckling that was killed by the farmer was eaten by the prince*

PREDICATION and **TOPIC** arrows, as suggested in the application of Figure 7.11. This small additional step provides for the active/passive distinction in relative clauses as well as in principal clauses.

At this early stage of the theory, however, it was not at all easy to show how the relations between semology and the ordinary syntax of the lexemic stratum were to be formalized. The relationship was supposed to be handled by so-called semolexemic realization rules. But such rules were generally characterized only in rather vague terms and it was not until somewhat later that the interaction of realizations with the tactics was clarified. The model presented in Lamb (1966), namely, explicitly showed that realizational relations at various strata have to interact with the tactics of the stratum of realization, indicating a further advance in the theory beyond the earlier stage.

This clarification provided the key to handling this realization problem. However, literature published between 1966 and 1970 contains no treatment of either the active/passive distinction or any other type of highlighting in English.

It has to be said that there was one published application of stratificational principles to highlighting phenomena in Ata Manobo, a language of Mindinao in the Philippines. It was the work of Virginia M. Austin, a student of Gleason at the Hartford Seminary Foundation. The published version of her master's thesis (Austin 1966) is devoted to three sorts of highlighting in this language. It deals not only with their occurrence and realization, but also seeks to relate these phenomena explicitly to their functions in discourse. **FOCUS** in this treatment is an obligatory phenomenon at the clause rank, and is placed on either an actor, a goal, a referent or an accessory. The focus selection is realized by verbal inflection as well as by special particles marking nominal forms or special suppletive pronoun forms. The phenomenon of **EMPHASIS** also applies at the clause rank, but it is optional and may sometimes apply to more than one item in the same clause. It is realized quite regularly in Austin's material by a postposed particle. **ATTENTION** is an obligatory characteristic, like focus, but it is realized on the rank of paragraph rather than in the clause: each paragraph has a single item under attention through its duration. The treatment of attention shows it to be realized by any of several devices, including initial position and special particles.

Later treatments

Due to the lack of explicit and full treatments of types of highlighting in the literature, the discussion of these matters in Lockwood (1972) (written primarily in 1970) had little previous work to draw upon. This textbook did, however, treat two varieties of highlighting in some detail: the passive and the cleft construction. Some other types were also mentioned in passing. The treatment of these phenomena was based on the assumption that a special sememe should be associated with each of them. For the passive, the participant functioning as the grammatical subject was marked with a sememe labeled **FOCUS**.[4] The label **TOPIC** (though it had been used for subject selection by Lamb in some of his unpublished material) was adopted for highlighting via the cleft construction, the sememe of this name being attached to the participant or circumstantial element to be highlighted by placement in the *It BE ....that* frame.

It is important to note that the focus element was postulated only for marked subjects, as in *John was given the book* or *The book was given to John*, and not for active subjects, as in *Bill gave John the book*. Such an analysis can be viewed as a small forward step, in that it captured the notion that the active forms are in some sense more basic than their passive counterparts, and it does this without positing any kind of derivational relationship between these forms. The topic sememe, on the other hand, is needed whenever a cleft construction occurs, since cleft constructions are always marked.

The focus element in English could accompany either what was termed a **GOAL**, as in *The book was given to John*, or a **RECIPIENT**, as in *John was given the book*, but no other participants or circumstantials. The topic, on the other hand, was capable of optional occurrence on one participant or circumstantial in the clause, triggering its realization in the *It BE ....that* frame. The occurrence of these sememes and semotactic diagrams dealing with their placement were presented in section 5.2 of Lockwood (1972), (which discusses predication structure), while their syntactic realization via the lexology was handled in section 5.3 (which discusses the realization of focus and topic).

Figures 7.12–7.15 show the semotactic traces for four of the examples discussed earlier. The next two figures then summarize details of the formal realization of the sememes **FOCUS** and **TOPIC**. Figure 7.16 shows that ^{S}/Focus/ portmanteaus with either ^{S}/Goal/ or ^{S}/Recipient/. The resultant sememic sign ^{SS}/Passive/ is then realized by a combination of three factors: (1) by subject selection, (2) by an occurrence of ^{L}/be/ in the proper position in the verb phrase, and (3) by an occurrence of the past-participle lexeme ^{L}/en/ on the following verbal form. Figure 7.17 shows that the sememe ^{S}/Topic/ leads to a construction involving the *It BE ....that* frame, with the accompanying sememes being realized in that frame.

Lockwood (1972) concentrated its attention on relating agnate clauses such as actives and passives and the various topicalized clauses with their non-topicalized counterparts. It focused its

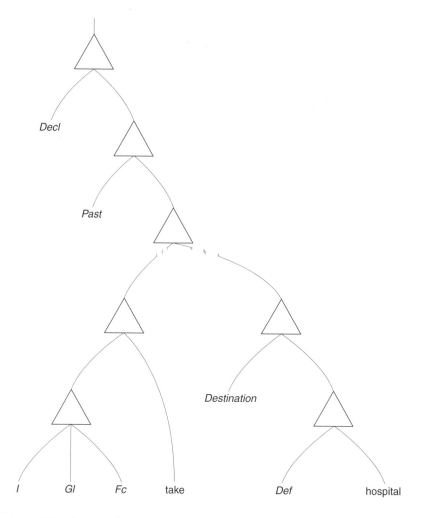

Figure 7.12 A trace for *I was taken to the hospital* (Appendix 000, based on the principles of Lockwood (1972) Chapter 5)

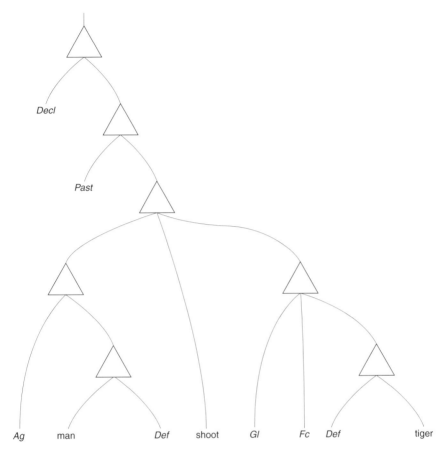

Figure 7.13 A trace for *The tiger was shot by the man* (see Fig. 2.7, based on Lockwood, Chapter 5)

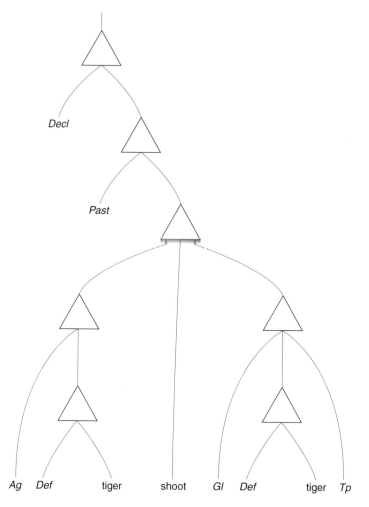

Figure 7.14 A trace for *It was the tiger the man shot* (based on Lockwood, Chapter 5)

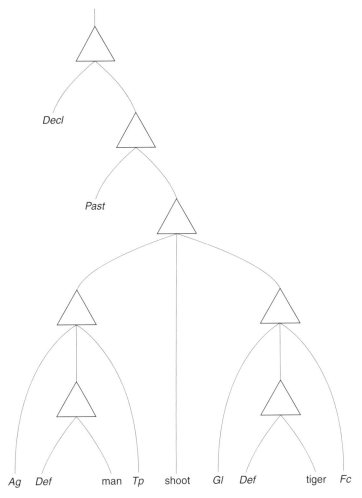

Figure 7.15 A trace for *It was by the man that the tiger was shot* (based on Lockwood, Chapter 5)

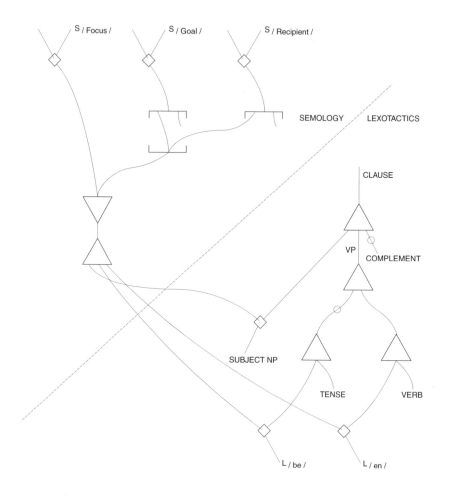

Figure 7.16 Realization of focus (refined from Lockwood, Fig. 5.11, p. 153)

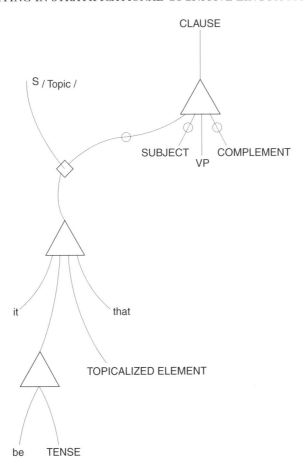

Figure 7.17 Realization of topic (based on Lockwood, Fig. 5.15, p. 157)

primary attention on the paradigmatic relations between clauses and the syntagmatic relations within them. However, it contained no mention of the relevance of highlighting to the structure of texts, even though certain aspects of such an overall aim were mentioned in the relevant chapter, especially in section 5.5 ('The Two Strata of Semology').

The first stratificational writer to call explicit attention to the discourse relevance of some of these matters in relation to English-language material was William J. Sullivan. In a series of papers beginning in the later 1970s, Sullivan treated the English passive in a manner roughly similar to that proposed by Lockwood. He explicitly noted that his passive sememe (labeled ψ for 'psychological focus') connected further to 'discourse block' considerations. Details on these considerations remained unspecified, but it was important to see these matters finally given explicit mention in the literature. Sullivan's most complete statement of this phenomenon said that his treatment 'identifies the semotactic difference between active and passive as a relative difference of hierarchical dominance between agent and patient evoked by a set of discourse block environments' (1980:322).

Figures 7.18–7.20 are based on Sullivan (1980), which represents the latest available version of his views on the subject.[5] Figure 7.18 is his semotactic diagram for some common actives and passives, based on his Figure 6 (p. 322), and Figures 7.19 and 7.20 are the traces resulting from this diagram for the examples *The farmer killed the duckling* and *The duckling was killed by the farmer*.

Apart from Sullivan's explicit mention of the discourse relevance of the active/passive distinction, the main difference between his treatment and that seen in Lockwood involves Sullivan's assumption of a difference of hierarchical dominance between the active and passive voices.[6]

Sullivan's teachings on this matter also inspired two of his graduate students at the University of Florida to work on passives. Roger Pope wrote an M.A. thesis (1975) contrasting the implementation of the active/passive distinction in English and Russian using a stratificational model based on Sullivan's teaching and on a pre-publication version of Sullivan (1976), finding the systems to be parallel regarding nine points but contrastive regarding five others, which are mostly at the less abstract levels of lexology and morphology. Douglas Wells Coleman wrote a dissertation and published some related papers after he received his Ph.D. The dissertation (1982) dealt with the discourse functions of the active/passive distinction in English, finding 'that the primary function of the active-passive dichotomy is control of thematization' (1982:144). The first of the related papers dealt with the conditioned vs. contrastive status of passives (1983), arguing that while many passives show contrast with active counterparts, others are conditioned by the absence of an agent. The second paper was less obviously related, dealing with idiomaticity in relation to the question of the autonomy of syntax (1984), but many of its examples involved the difference between idioms and their literal counterparts regarding the possibility of passivization. This paper also went beyond just active/passive to cite parallel examples involving marked themes and topics.

Further details regarding the discourse correlates of the high-

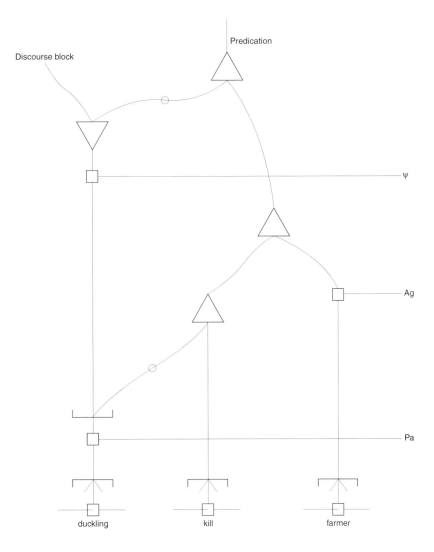

Figure 7.18 Sullivan's Semotactic Diagram for some active/passive examples (Sullivan 1980, Fig. 6, p. 322)

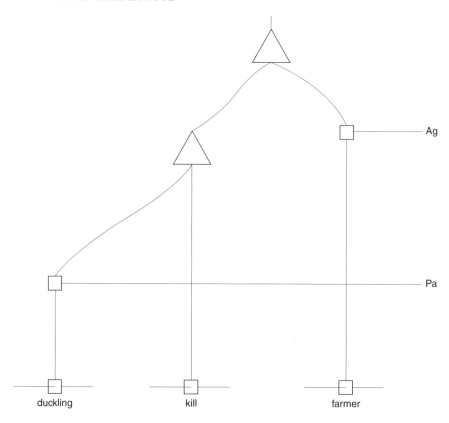

Figure 7.19 Trace from Figure 7.18 for *(The) farmer killed (the) duckling*

lighting elements of English were investigated in the 1980s by Copeland and Davis (1980, 1981 and Davis and Copeland 1980). This investigation was later continued by Copeland working independently (1983, 1984). For the purpose of the present discussion, the most important paper in this series is Copeland and Davis (1981), originally delivered in the summer of 1980 under the title, 'Identifiability and Focal Attention in an Integrated View of Discourse'. Under 'identifiability', the authors reviewed and clarified points made in earlier papers involving a scale of categories from GIVEN to NOVEL, correlated with such matters as the occurrence of articles and pronominalization in English. These matters are important for discourse in general, but they do not relate directly to highlighting.[7] In the remainder of the paper, however, they discuss the correlates of focus in the sense of Lockwood (1972), and of topic in a sense which is at least relatable to the one used by Lockwood.

The foundation for this treatment was their definition of the

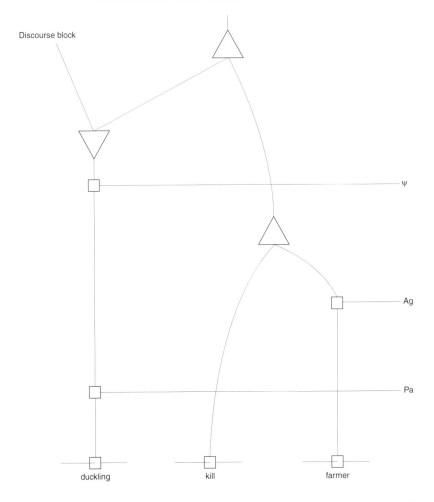

Figure 7.20 Trace from Figure 7.18 for *(The) duckling is killed by (the) farmer*

THEME/RHEME distinction in conceptual terms. THEME was identified with 'those terms of the utterance that are present in the Listener's gnostology' (1981:127). Then RHEME was defined as constituting those portions of the message that 'are constructed and thereby added to the Listener's system, sense being made of them via their connections with the theme' (1981:127). It should be noted that this usage does not coincide totally with Halliday's use of the same terms. Halliday (1994:37) defines Theme in conceptual terms as 'the element which serves as the point of departure of the message; it is that with which the clause is concerned'. This point of departure function is often Given information and hence present in the 'listener's gnostology' but that is not necessarily true. (See Halliday 1994:59 and 299–300, and Fries 1981, 1995:57.) On a formal level, Hallidayan Theme is identified in English as the initial element of the clause (1994:37). For this reason, we need different terms for Hallidayan Theme/Rheme and the Copeland-Davis usage. Copeland (1983) introduces the Greek forms THEMA/RHEMA (Boost 1955) for his conceptually defined version. The latter usage is adopted here to minimize confusion.

The discussion of Thema/Rhema then sets the stage for the treatment of TOPIC, which Copeland and Davis define as 'the term in the utterance on which the Listener is asked to place his focal attention' (1981:130). More specifically, they say that it is a selection within Thema/Rhema. Finally, they identify FOCUS as a matter of focal attention within the propositional content of an utterance, and identify the realization of focus in the same terms set forth in Lockwood (1972): the focused participant is realized as the grammatical subject, at least in a language such as English. Their discussion of topic is exemplified primarily from German. Their overall discussion gives the general impression that they are using the term 'topic' to deal with the whole range of highlighting phenomena apart from Focus, with expression via the initial element selection, the cleft, or the pseudo-cleft, and possibly even contrastive accent placement. The contribution of Copeland and Davis in the area of highlighting is summarized in Table 7.1.

Table 7.1 Summary of the treatment of focus and topic by Copeland and Davis (1981)

Term	Definition	Realization
FOCUS	Portion of role/event prepositional structure selected for focal attention	Grammatical Subject
TOPIC	Portion of Thema/Rhema selected for focal attention	Initial (*Vorfeld*) Placement [German]

An integrated view

This section sketches the main points of a view originally prepared for a revision of the semology chapter in Lockwood (1972). This revised text was used in packet form for classes in the 1980s, but the projected second edition of the textbook was never published. It is a revision and expansion of the view of highlighting found in the original published work.

The first revision made is a simple matter of terminology: the former term GOAL (going back at least to Bloomfield 1914) is replaced with PATIENT, applied to the participant which serves as the grammatical object in unmarked situations. The designation GOAL, if it is to be used at all, seems better suited to the destination of a movement. This new usage is, furthermore, in line with that of some other stratificationalists (e.g. Sullivan 1980), as well as with the usage of other linguists such as Chafe (1970).[8]

A more important revision is the inclusion of THEME, essentially in the sense proposed by Halliday (1967–68, 1985, 1994), among the highlighting phenomena treated. This inclusion means that the rudiments of three of the five highlighting phenomena mentioned in the first part of this chapter are now treated. The treatment of focus has not been changed in any substantial way: it is viewed as optionally available for patients and recipients, and as realized by the selection of the expression for the focused participant as the grammatical subject, along with the use of a passive form of the verb phrase.

As for theme, this phenomenon appears to be readily capable of integration with the original treatment of topic. It seems most convenient to treat theme as an obligatorily present sememic element, with its marked vs. unmarked varieties distinguished by whether or not a special conceptual element is being realized by the thematic selection. The occurrence of theme in these contexts is summarized by the following statements:

> MARKED THEME occurs under special cognitive circumstances in association with (a) a circumstantial clause element, or (b) a participant other than the agent, or (c) an agent when marked focus occurs on some other participant.
> UNMARKED THEME occurs in the absence of marked theme, coming (a) on the focused participant, if there is one, or else (b) on the agent, which constitutes the unmarked subject.

Then topic is viewed as a stronger variety of the theme. This view is based on the fact that its realization in the cleft structure is typically at the beginning of the clause,[9] and further on the fact that the elements that can occur as theme (at any rate in declarative main clauses) can alternatively be topicalized.

Figure 7.21 summarizes the thematization options in the fashion used in the version described above. Figure 7.22 is a fuller diagram showing the more formal details as applied to a particular type of event cluster. Finally, Figure 7.23 gives a schematic form of the

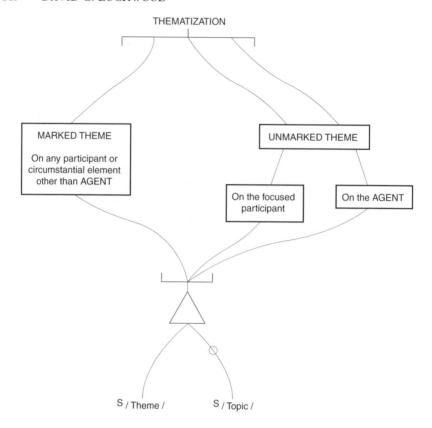

Figure 7.21 Schematic diagram for thematization in declarative principal clauses

clause syntax at the lexotactic level, indicating how the theme and topic sememes are realized, along with the realization of focus.

Further extensions

Since there is still a good deal of work to be done on the subject of highlighting from the standpoint of stratificational-cognitive linguistics, it seems appropriate to conclude this chapter with a list of the major tasks remaining for the investigation of these aspects of English discourse.[10]

First, we need further exploration of the relations between topic and theme, particularly in interrogative and subordinate clauses, where there appear to be more restrictions than in declarative principal clauses. Next, we obviously need to extend the formal treatment to pseudo-cleft constructions and to cases of marked accent

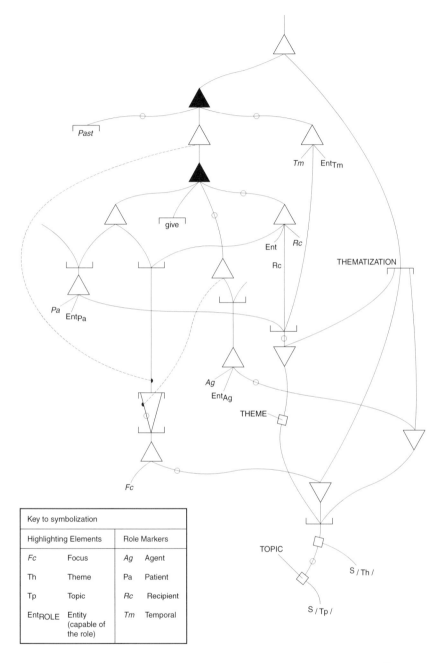

Key to symbolization

Highlighting Elements		Role Markers	
Fc	Focus	*Ag*	Agent
Th	Theme	*Pa*	Patient
Tp	Topic	*Rc*	Recipient
Ent_{ROLE}	Entity (capable of the role)	*Tm*	Temporal

Figure 7.22 Formal diagram for Focus, Theme, and Topic with ^S/give/

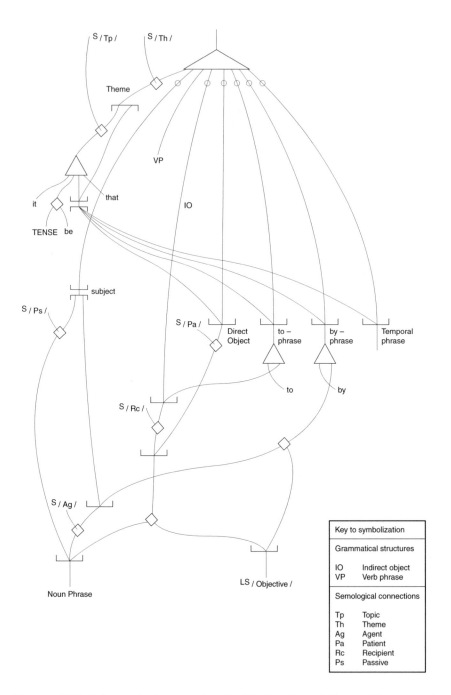

Figure 7.23 Schematic diagram for the Realization of Focus, Theme and Topic in English Lexotactics

placement. Both of these extensions pertain to the semotactics and its relation to the ordinary syntax, as embodied in the lexology of some stratificational models.

Also, we need to extend the work begun by Copeland and Davis on the conceptual correlates of the various highlighting elements. For one thing, these extensions would require one to pinpoint more precisely the origin of a marked focus or topic selection in the conceptual system. Copeland and Davis have spoken in terms of particular parts of the conceptual apparatus activated or to be activated. We now need to carry the work to the point of showing just how semological elements of focus and topic get activated on the basis of these conceptual facts. Furthermore, we need to differentiate their 'topic' category so as to arrive at an understanding of what appear to be several distinct highlighting elements grouped together in their usage.

An example pointing out the last-mentioned need can be cited from the Symposium Text. Consider the example cited in the first section of this chapter for the pseudo-cleft construction: *What I would like to find out more about is your operation (that you are having)* (ll. 1–2). It seems quite clear that we could not arbitrarily substitute for it the paraphrase cited in the same section to exemplify the cleft: *It's your operation that I would like to find out more about*. The interviewer could not have started out in that way, and neither could she have started out with a further paraphrase using the simple theme: *Your operation, I would like to find out more about*. Furthermore, in this example a marked placement of the sentence accent would not have been an available option, since the most neutral form of the clause would have the accent there in any case: *I would like to find out more about your* **operation**.

On the other hand, as suggested in Part 2 of Halliday 1967–1968, a different type of suprasegmental highlighting might be used with the same order of words to give special prominence to *operation* via a suspended rather than a falling terminal intonation. This seems to be the only one of the various highlighting possibilities that could have alternatively been used to open the interview. This fact indicates, then, that themes, clefts and pseudo-clefts have different occurrences in discourse, so that we must distinguish them in our accounts, even if there are other contexts where two or more of them may occur as alternatives.[11]

The discussion of the above two paragraphs is an application of a very old and very basic technique of linguistic investigation: the substitution test. This test can obviously be used in many places in the task of untangling the highlighting varieties with regard to their contextual appropriateness.

A further resource for stratificationalists seeking to extend their formulations of highlighting is the work of other linguists in this and related areas. Some of the most valuable work along these lines has been done by M. A. K. Halliday and his followers in the systemic school. For example Halliday makes quite specific suggestions about the difference between the meaning of the cleft (which he terms the PREDICATION option) and that of the pseudo-cleft (which he calls the IDENTIFICATION option, with further subvarieties). His discussion involves specifically the following pair:

(7) *It was John who broke the window.* (PREDICATION)
(8) *John was the one who broke the window.* (IDENTIFICATION)

His claim is that the prominence in (7) is thematic, meaning that 'John and nobody else is the topic of this sentence', whereas in (8) the prominence is cognitive, meaning 'John and nobody else broke the window' (1967–1968:236).

While these conclusions may or may not be correct in the long run, they at least are a useful point of departure for future work. Further exploration, then, could take these suggestions of Halliday along with the work of Copeland and Davis, and attempt to either show that Halliday's conclusions are correct, while at the same time indicating what this means in Copeland and Davis's schema, or else show how and why these conclusions have to be modified and how the modifications fit into the Copeland/Davis model.

If Halliday's suggestions concerning the cognitive vs. thematic difference between pseudo-cleft and cleft constructions prove to be correct, a terminology for fitting the distinction into the framework of stratificational semology comes readily to mind. What Lockwood (1972) termed topic could be termed THEMATIC TOPIC ($^S/Tp_{TH}/$, realized via the cleft construction), while the further type realized by the pseudo-cleft could be termed the COGNITIVE TOPIC ($^S/Tp_{CG}/$). In addition to simple theme and focus, as discussed previously, we would also need a semological element to deal with the marked placement of accent. The term CONTRAST, suggested by Chafe (1976), is perhaps as useful as any of the possibilities. If these ideas are adopted, we have the schema summarized in Table 7.2. This can at least be used as a point of departure for further explorations along the lines suggested above. In addition, details of the tactic occurrence and co-occurrence of such elements within the semotactics need further elaboration. All these things are needed to bring us closer to a more adequate account of highlighting within the stratificational framework.

Table 7.2 Summary of a treatment of five types of highlighting in English

Semological elements	Realization	Example (HIGHLIGHTED ITEM IS UNDERLINED)
FOCUS	Subject selection + passive voice	*I was taken to hospital*
THEME	Initial placement (in declarative principal clause)	*Now you have to have really good reasons.*
THEME + THEMATIC TOPIC	Cleft construction	*It's your operation that I would like to find out more about.*
THEME + COGNITIVE TOPIC	Pseudo-cleft construction	*What I would like to find our more about is your operation.*
CONTRAST	Contrastive accent placement	*They want to be put asleep.*

Notes

1. This term was also used in a course on Stratificational Grammar taught by Gleason at the 1967 Linguistic Institute at the University of Michigan, Ann Arbor.

2. Parenthesized labels such as (man) were assumed to stand for whole complexes of ultimate semological constituents or SEMONS. The original version of Figure 7.1 (Hockett's Figure 40) showed (man) broken down into the semons ^{SN}/adult/, ^{SN}/male/, and ^{SN}/human/, but such details were omitted elsewhere. Here a similar simplification has been made in Figure 7.1 to make it parallel to the other examples quoted. These semon labels should be read 'the semon adult', 'the semon male', and so on. Their labeling follows a system introduced in Lamb (1966), according to which each name assigned to a structural unit has its label enclosed in slant-lines with a preceding suprascript indication of the kind of unit involved. The first letter indicates the stratal system involved: S(ememic), L(exemic), M(orphemic), P(honemic). If it is the only letter, the unit is an -eme [a unit relating to the tactics of the stratum]: sememe, lexeme, morpheme, phoneme; the second letter N indicates an -on [an elementary unit of the stratal system]: Semon, Lexon, Morphon, Phonon; the second letter S indicates an emic sign [a composite of -ons less abstract than an -eme]; Sememic Sign, Lexemic Sign, Morphemic Sign, Phonemic Sign. For further explanation of these terms and notations see Lamb (1966):18–21, 56–7 or Lockwood (1972):14–27.

3. These diagrams have been taken from the writer's course notes.
4. This use of the term 'focus' is based primarily on a tradition observable in grammars of Philippine languages (see Pike 1963, Austin 1966), where it refers to a phenomenon roughly comparable to voice in European languages, though typically with greater complexity regarding the types of participants that can be highlighted by it. This usage of the term should not be confused with another usage (inherited from the Prague School), in which the same term designates highlighting via the placement of the strongest accent and intonation center in the clause.
5. Sullivan (1976) compares and contrasts the English active/passive distinction with analogous distinctions in Polish. Sullivan (1977), delivered at the Michigan State University Metatheory Conference of the same year, treats the interaction of the English passive with the phenomenon termed 'raising' in the Chomskyan literature.
6. In Sullivan's diagrams, the participant to be realized as the grammatical subject forms one immediate constituent of the predicational construction, and the other constituent includes the event sememe and any other participant(s). Such an analysis is a way of tackling certain problems which arise from the need to relate an unsequenced semological representation to an essentially sequenced grammatical representation.
7. It should be emphasized that the GIVEN-to-NOVEL hierarchy of identifiability in the work of Copeland and Davis is not identical to the GIVEN/NEW distinction found in systemic work (e.g. Halliday 1967–1968, 1985). The latter, unlike the former, does have relevance for questions of highlighting.
8. Neither of these terms, it must be admitted, is completely problem-free, because to some 'patient' suggests a more strictly semantic sense in which the object associated with a verb like *caress*, *kill* or *hit* would be seen as true patients because the action has some physical effect upon them, while others like those associated as objects of *see*, *hear* or *smell* would be classified differently because they as not similarly affected. It should be made clear that a broader construal of 'patient' is intended here. The systemic tradition also labels some grammatical objects as 'range', as in *Mary is playing <u>tennis</u>*, *Tom was visiting <u>relatives</u>*, or *Ann had <u>a hot shower</u>*, where the objects (underlined) do not refer to things that either are acted upon or result from the action. At the level under discussion, the stratificational hypothesis is that finer distinctions are not needed, though they may be appropriate at a more abstract level. In personal communication, Lamb has suggested that in the final analysis virtually every transitive verb would have to be viewed as having somewhat different semantic roles associable with its subject and object. This consideration raises the difficult question of how fine a subclassification is appropriate.
9. Peter Fries points out (personal communication) that there is data that requires a greater separation between themes and topics than was

suggested in this analysis. For instance, such variations on one of these examples as *Yesterday it was your operation that she wanted to find out about* (Temporal as marked Theme, but Prepositional Axis as Thematic Topic) and *Yesterday, what she wanted to find out about was your operation.* (similar but with Cognitve Topic). The association of theme with the types of topic is therefore not an absolute, though it may be the unmarked situation, and it may only allow circumstantial elements like Temporals and Locationals to occur as separate Themes in such examples.

10. It should be noted that three more recent textbook treatments either omit mention of highlighting altogether (Lamb 1999) or treat it only in a very limited way (Fleming 1988; Cope 1994). The book by Cope, intended as a fairly elementary introduction to the approach developed by Fleming, does contain (in its section 4.6, 'Focus, Emphasis', pp. 39–40) a brief but useful summary of some highlighting devices with examples in English and three other languages, but without any detailed formalization of them. Fleming's more detailed book does little more.

11. According to Peter Fries (personal communication), Collins (1991) has studied the occurrence of some constructions involved in English highlighting, namely the cleft and pseudo-cleft, and would therefore be an important and valuable resource to anyone trying to develop and refine this model.

References

Austin, Virginia M. (1966) *Attention, Emphasis, and Focus in Ata Manobo. Hartford Studies in Linguistics*, No. 20. Hartford, CT: Hartford Seminary Foundation.

Bloomfield, Leonard (1914) *An Introduction to the Study of Language.* New York: Henry Holt.

Boost, Karl (1955) *Neue Untersuchungen zur Wesen und Struktur des Deutschen Satzes: Der Satz als Spannungsfeld.* Berlin: Akademie-Verlag.

Chafe, Wallace L. (1970) *Meaning and the Structure of Language.* Chicago: University of Chicago Press.

Chafe, Wallace L. (1976) Givenness, contrastiveness, definiteness, subject, topics, and point of view. In *Subject and Topic*, ed. by C. N. Li, New York: Academic Press, 27–55.

Coleman, Douglas Wells (1982) Discourse functions of the active-passive Dichotomy in English. Unpublished dissertation, University of Florida.

Coleman, Douglas Wells (1983) Conditioned and contrastive status of passive focus. *Southwest Journal of Linguistics*, 6:64–77.

Coleman, Douglas Wells (1984) Idiomaticity and the autonomy of syntax in stratificational grammar. *Southwest Journal of Linguistics*, 7:26–46.

Collins, Peter C. (1991) *Cleft and Pseudo-Cleft Constructions in English.* London: Routledge.

Cope, Pamela (1994) *Introductory Grammar: A Stratificational Approach.* Dallas: Summer Institute of Linguistics.

Copeland, James E. (1983) Linguistic creativity and the langue/parole distinction. In *LACUS Forum IX*, ed. by John Morreall, Columbia, SC: Hornbeam Press, 159–168.

Copeland, James E. (1984) Texture and cohesion: some complementarities in systemic and cognitive linguistics. In *LACUS Forum X*, ed. by Conrad Bureau *et al.*, Columbia, SC: Hornbeam Press, 85–95.

Copeland, James E. and Davis, Philip W. (1980) A stratificational approach to discourse and other matters. In *LACUS Forum VI*, ed. by Herbert J. Izzo and William C. McCormack, Columbia, SC: Hornbeam Press, 255–263.

Copeland, James E. and Davis, Philip W. (1981) An integrated view of discourse. In *LACUS Forum VII*, ed. by James E. Copeland and Philip W. Davis, Columbia, SC: Hornbeam Press, 122–137.

Davis, Philip W. and Copeland, James E. (1980) Knowledge, consciousness, and language: Some possible sources of discourse phenomena. *Rice University Studies*, 66(2):101–124.

Fleming, Ilah (1988) *Communication Analysis: A Stratificational Approach*, Vol. 2. Dallas: Summer Institute of Linguistics.

Fries, Peter H. (1981) On the status of theme in English: arguments from discourse. *Forum Linguisticum*, 6:1–38.

Fries, Peter H. (1995) Patterns of information in initial position in English. In *Discourse in Society: Functional Perspectives*, ed. by Peter H. Fries and Michael Gregory, Norwood, NJ: Ablex, 47–66.

Gleason, H. A., Jr. (1968) Contrastive analysis in discourse structure. *Georgetown University Roundtable 1968*, pp. 39–63. Reprinted in Makkai and Lockwood, eds., 1973, 258–276. [*Page references are to the reprint.*]

Halliday, M. A. K. (1967–1968) Notes on transitivity and theme in English. *Journal of Linguistics*, 3:37–81, 199–244, 4:179–216.

Halliday, M. A. K. (1985) *An Introduction to Functional Grammar.* London: Edward Arnold.

Halliday, M. A. K. (1994) *An Introduction to Functional Grammar*, 2nd edn, revised. London: Edward Arnold.

Hockett, Charles F. (1966) *Language, Mathematics and Linguistics* (Janua Linguarum, Series Minor, No. 60). The Hague: Mouton.

Lamb, Sydney M. (1964) The sememic approach to structural semantics. *Transcultural Studies in Cognition*, ed. by A. Kimball Romney and Roy G. D'Andrade, *American Anthropologist*, 66(2): 57–58. (Reprinted in Makkai and Lockwood, (eds.), 1973, 207–228).

Lamb, Sydney M. (1966) *Outline of Stratificational Grammar.* Washington, D. C.: Georgetown University Press.

Lamb, Sydney M. (1999) *Pathways of the Brain: The Neurocognitive Basis of Language.* Amsterdam: John Benjamins.

Lockwood, David G. (1972) *Introduction to Stratificational Linguistics*. New York: Harcourt Brace Jovanovich.

Makkai, Adam and David G. Lockwood (eds.) (1973) *Readings in Stratificational Linguistics*. University, AL: University of Alabama Press.

Pike, Kenneth L. (1963) A syntactic paradigm. *Language*, 39:216–230.

Pope, Roger Wayne (1975) Active and passive voice in English and Russian: a contrastive analysis. Unpublished M. A. thesis, University of Florida.

Sullivan, William J. (1976) Active and passive sentences in English and Polish. *Papers in Studies in Contrastive Linguistics* (Poznan, Poland), 5:117–152.

Sullivan, William J. (1977) Raising: a stratificational description and some metatheoretical considerations. *Second Annual Metatheory Conference Proceedings, 1977*, Department of Linguistics, Michigan State University, 47–92.

Sullivan, William J. (1980) Syntax and linguistic semantics in stratificational theory. In *Syntax and Semantics, Vol. 13: Current Approaches to Syntax*, ed. by Edith A. Morvcsik and Jessica R. Wirth, New York: Academic Press, 301–327.

8

Interpreting Discourse

Sydney Lamb

This chapter discusses interpretation as a mental process, one that takes place in the brains of speakers of a language. Accordingly, the linguistic system is treated as a neurocognitive system, locatable in the brain of the speaker. To some not familiar with the recent history of linguistics it may seem that such an approach is so obviously appropriate that its adoption hardly seems worth mentioning. Yet in the context of contemporary linguistics this approach is distinctively that of a small (but perhaps growing) minority. Most linguists still cling to the view of a language as some kind of social system or as an abstract system shared by all members of a 'speech community'. That kind of linguistics, which comes in many varieties, may be called 'analytical linguistics', since its primary concern is the analysis of things people say or write. The alternative I adopt, which may be called 'neurocognitive linguistics', while naturally sharing an interest in the things people say and write, is concerned mainly with using this information as evidence for the neurocognitive systems of people which underlie and are responsible for their ability to speak and to interpret speech.

Linguistic processing and traveling activation

We may distinguish three ways of treating linguistic processes like those of speaking and interpreting. The first, commonly adopted in analytical linguistics, is simply to ignore them – sometimes with the excuse that the job of linguistics is to account for 'competence' but not 'performance'. The second is in terms of high-level abstractions like 'speaking' along with 'as if' descriptions using symbolic representations: it is *as if* the speaker replaces certain symbols by certain other symbols in forming utterances. (Some may believe that our brains actually perform such symbol-manipulating operations.) The third approach, adopted here, is an account in terms of operations in the cognitive system of the person speaking or interpreting.

It has been demonstrated elsewhere (e.g. Lamb 1999) that a person's neurocognitive system is a vast network, ultimately analysable as a network of neurons, but usually described at a more abstract level, using nodes (technically, 'nections') which, according to the current hypothesis, are implemented neurologically as cortical columns (Lamb 1999:Chapter 17). In describing linguistic processes according to the neurocognitive approach, therefore, we can speak in terms of (1) movement of activation through the network from node to node and (2) various operations that alter the form of the network, including especially the strengthening of connections.

The movement of activation in the network can follow many different pathways, some of which are depicted in Figure 8.1. Using this diagram we can follow the paths of activation for a large variety of processes (and we could do still more if the diagram were filled out to show the cognitive subsystems in greater detail). A very frequent occurrence in everyday life is the production of an utterance by someone about something observed visually: *Waiter, my fork is dirty.* Activation has traveled from the visual system to the conceptual to lexical to phonological recognition, to phonological production, to

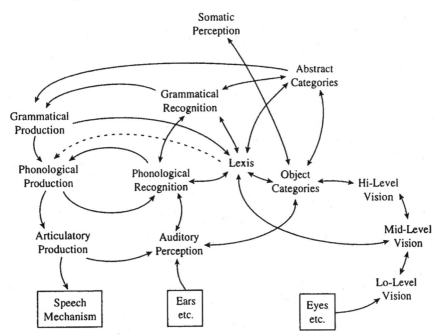

Figure 8.1 Some cognitive subsystems and their interconnections

the organs of speech production. Another person hears a spoken report of something seen by someone else: in the waiter's system, activation travels from the ears to the auditory system to the phonological to lexical to conceptual to visual. Activation may then travel to his planning and process-controlling subsystems (not shown in the figure), which will activate appropriate muscles in his body in an appropriate sequence – he takes action in response to his comprehension of the report. Similarly, you may use Figure 8.1 to help you think about others of the numerous possibilities for the traveling of activation from subsystem to subsystem.

On the other hand, we must guard against interpreting such diagrams too simplistically. For example, major semantic processes include the semantic interpretation of lexemes and the choice of lexemes to convey ideas the speaker or writer is trying to express. Activation goes from lexemes to concepts in the former case and in the latter from concepts to lexemes. But activation does not really travel just in one direction except in the simplest cases: there is often interactive bidirectional processing between levels. In the process of choosing a way to express an idea, for example, the traveling of the activation often does not just go from the semological level to the lexemic level, as a simplistic model might have it. It goes back and forth. The writer tries out alternative possibilities. What is happening in this process? Each such trial involves the travel of activation from lexemic to sememic, giving the writer an experience of what that particular provisional wording 'sounds' like – actually, it is the experience of activation of the particular semological connections which that lexeme provides. The process continues, commonly with a trial-and-error strategy, one lexeme after another, until a semological representation including a desired connotation is arrived at. It is bidirectional processing, another example of how such processing is altogether prevalent in our thinking processes (see Lamb 1999: Chapter 8). Similarly, we can play with what may be called 'outer semantics' – for example, alternative images that will be promoted by different conceptualizations that are activated by different wordings. We can even activate an entire realm of associations, such as Shakespeare's Hamlet, by saying 'Something is rotten in the state of Texas' or 'To thine own self be true'.

Linguistically guided structure building

There is much more going on in ordinary interpretation of discourse than meets the eye at first glance. When we receive speech or writing, we interpret it. That much is easy to say. But just what does the process of interpretation consist of?

In the phonological and lexical regions of the neurocognitive system, it is a process mainly of *recognizing*. The receiver of a message typically has nodes for all the phonemes and lexemes occurring in the text, and for these levels the process of interpreting is like that of perceiving in other modalities. The nodes for the phonemes and lexemes are automatically activated as the message is received. They then pass activation on to the next higher level of integration. This is recognition, a largely passive and uncreative process. For sentences with complex syntax it is likely that we engage in a more elaborate process, activating also our phonological *production* system and using the *inner speech* loop, allowing us to keep the sentence 'alive' in our minds while we complete the more difficult recognition process – made difficult by the demands imposed on our immediate memory by the syntactic complexity.

But if we consider what commonly goes on at the semological levels, we find a quite different interpretive process, and one which requires considerably more cognitive activity than just satisfying thresholds of nodes and putting the phonological production system into operation. For in the interpretation of texts containing information that is new to us, we have to incorporate the new information into our cognitive systems – or else simply not remember it – and incorporating new information means building connections (see Lamb 1999:Chapter 12). Since in the simple situation, involving no new morphemes or lexemes, the distinction between recognition and structure building is not needed, it has tended to be overlooked by linguists. Overlooking it can give rise to the illusion that higher level representations (that is, at any level higher than raw phonetic) are carried somehow in the message itself. This illusion, for example, is present in the common metaphor according to which messages convey information. They do not – they are just sounds.

The interpretation of a text, including the short texts commonly received in conversation that is not just idle chit-chat, therefore includes constructing: building or strengthening connections. Each interpreter – and that can include also the producer of the text – constructs an internal representation of its content as understood in accordance with how it fits into the previously existing network of information.

This process of new structure building occurs also at levels other than the sememic, but less often. It occurs in the lexical system when a new lexeme is encountered and accepted. This process, lexicalization, goes on regularly in the lives of intellectuals who read texts or hear lectures on topics outside their specialties, for such lectures often contain lexemes that are new to such a listener. Recruitment of lexical nections occurs especially often for students, who are learning new lexemes quite regularly along with the new concepts which they represent. This process of structure building at the lexemic level is not really an uncommon occurrence for ordinary adults of various walks of life, even though it occurs for only a quite small percentage of the text processed by them. For children, on the other hand, this building process takes place much more commonly. It is an essentially creative process, much more so than that of putting new sentences together out of existing lexemes, since it is one of building new structure, not just exercising existing structures. One important contrast between these two processes is that every time the former occurs, the creative one, it changes the generative power of the system, the set of possible texts that can be produced. Here we are talking about something quite different from the so-called 'creativity' which some analytical linguists have talked about in recent decades, enchanted by our ability to form new combinations of words using existing syntactic structures – actually a rather prosaic ability in comparison, comparable to going through a cafeteria line and selecting a new meal that one has never eaten before.

We may also distinguish the type of lexeme building which makes use of existing morphemes, such as *get into trouble* (a lexeme which gets built at some point during childhood for typical English speakers), from the relatively more creative process that involves building new morphemes. Young children engage rather frequently in the latter process, adults far less often. And for very young children there is also the process of new phoneme formation. Thus there is no real boundary between language acquisition and the ordinary use of language. Language acquisition is a process of structure building, and it can continue throughout life. It tends to proceed gradually from lower to higher levels but this is only a tendency. Even adults sometimes make changes of pronunciation, and such changes can involve structure modification as low as the level of articulatory production.

But in the semological systems, structure building and structure modification can occur in the interpretation of virtually any information-bearing sentence, except where the listener is not paying attention to what is said or does not understand or does not remember. But if he remembers, that information received and remembered takes the form of newly built structure.

Let us now take a look at a narrative text which will illustrate these and other points.

An illustrative narrative

Sue's narrative about a nasally treated case of hyperactivity, a portion of the text that served as data for the symposium at which the original version of this piece was presented, can be broken down into meaningful discourse units as largely marked by intonation, as follows, with parenthetical comments at the right on lower-level discourse processing (Appendix to this book, lines 199–209):

0	There's some guy ... we	(Aborted introduction)
1	We heard a story, a couple of weeks ago.	(New Introduction)
2	of this...this family.	(Establishing topic)
3	And there was a young child in the family.	(Main character)
4	A young boy.	(Editing previous line)
5	And he was he was having tremendous problems in school,	
6	he was a very difficult child,	
7	he was too active, and he was always getting in trouble, and and um	
8	A long lost relative, came into this family. And	(Edited out by intonation)
9	who had been to India.	
10	and studied with some of the Eastern mystics.	
11	And ... so he suggested to this child,	
12	that he stuff cotton, up the right side of his nose.	
13	And so they stuffed cotton, up the right side of his nose. (laughter)	
14	And his personality, completely changed.	
15	He became this very passive, nice, docile, child, ...	
	(Interrupted by K)	

Notes: This passage is punctuated in accordance with intonation as follows:
Period indicates sentence-final intonation contour (drop).
Comma indicates steady final contour or dip (non-sentence final).
Heavy phrasal accents, indicating the new information in each phonological phrase, as
Halliday (1994) defines new information, are not shown, although Halliday's given–new
distinction is altogether relevant to the topic of this chapter.

A sentence-ending is normally followed by a capitalized initial word of the next sentence, but lines 9 and 10 are exceptions, as shown not by intonation but by grammar. Line 9 begins a relative clause that belongs within the sentence of line 8. The 'And' shown edited out between lines 8 and 9 is capitalized, as it suggests the start of a new sentence. But then Sue evidently decided instead to continue with a relative clause. That line 10 still continues this sentence is more strongly shown. It not only lacks a subject, continuing the predicate of the preceding line, it also has 'studied' rather than 'had studied', indicating that it is the second main verb in a compound verb phrase with a single occurrence of 'have' (the first part of the perfect marker) and with the past-participle ending (the second part) on each of the two verb stems of the compound verb phrase. That is, the grammatical form of line 10 suggests that the sentence-final intonation of line 9 is to be edited out, so that the edited version would be

9–10　who had been to India and studied with some of the Eastern
mystics.

Each numbered line represents a phonological phrase or a sequence of such phrases that closely cohere on the basis of grammatical structure. These may be taken as the units to be processed at the conceptual level by the interpreter. The first is assigned the number 0 since it is broken off by the speaker as an aborted introduction. She then begins again with what we may label line 1. We may accordingly take this line as the starting point for our study of the interpretive process.

The outset of the interpretation does not correspond directly to any actual phrase of the text, since it is not provided by text as such in the way we are accustomed to from linguistic analysis of lower levels of structure. Rather, it represents the information we have, as interpreters, about who is telling the story, together with the fact that a story is being told: We have an instance of speaking, and we know that speaking necessarily involves a speaker and something said; and we know that this particular woman named Sue is the speaker and that what is said is the text to come. All of this conceptual information, which is essential for the interpretation of the 'We' in line 1, gets registered in the system of a normal English-speaking observer as Sue begins to tell the story. It comes not from the text but from the discourse situation itself.

This example illustrates the important principle that conceptual information can and often does come from other sources than the lower linguistic levels.

We may now proceed with the first lines of the narrative. The representations shown below are in lines labeled with numbers corresponding to the line numbers given above and with stratal identifiers 'M' and 'L' for morphemic and lexemic, respectively. But a little explanation is needed. The morphemic level in neurocognitive linguistics is not the same as that of analytical linguistics. For analytical linguistics the morphemes are the units resulting from analysis of morphological material down to their minimal units. So for example, *heard* would be analysed as representing the morpheme *hear* plus the past tense morpheme. But different criteria apply in neurocognitive linguistics, in which we are attempting to represent as faithfully as practically possible the linguistic information system of the typical individual. And a typical English-speaking individual has heard the word *heard* so many times that he cannot fail to have it registered as a single unit within his system. The same is true of *weeks*, which thus has to be recognized as a single neurocognitive morpheme even though its plural ending is perfectly regular, and even though granting it that status causes the inventory of morphemes recognized to be less economical and in fact full of redundancies. For while elimination of redundancy is prized in analytical linguistics, cognitive realism is prized in neurocognitive linguistics (for further discussion, see Lamb 1999:170ff.).

In the lexemic and morphemic representations, the lexemes/morphemes are separated by spaces. This convention differs from that commonly used for morphemic representation in analytical linguistics, which uses either space or hyphen for morpheme boundary, depending on whether or not it is also a morphological word boundary. For the lexemic representation, morphological word boundaries are irrelevant, and hyphens do not represent lexeme boundaries. Thus *a-couple-of* is one lexeme.

M1   we heard a story a-couple-of weeks ago
L1   we past hear a story a-couple-of week pl ago

It is apparent that the morphemic and lexemic representations are largely alike, and the question naturally arises as to whether all these elements are really distinct. In my opinion it remains an open question in neurocognitive linguistics. We can identify certain differences between morphemic and lexemic. The morphemic level recognizes morphological word boundaries while the lexemic does not and would in fact be hindered by them. For example, the past tense element is part of the same morphological word as the main verb stem, or the auxiliary if present; but the lexemic past tense element occurs with the entire verb phrase. Other differences are also seen in the verb tense system, such as the perfect tense element, a single element on the lexemic level, but realized morphemically as two distinct morphemes, *have* and the past-participle morpheme, occurring in two different morphological words, as in *have taken*. On the other hand, for many lexemes, like *story*, there is no distinction other than the fact that from the morphemic point of view it can constitute a morphological word by itself, while the lexemic level recognizes no such units as words. It may be that, at least in the neurocognitive systems of many people, the same node serves for *story* at both morphemic and lexemic levels. Of course, we must still recognize various complex lexemes that include *story* as a component, such as *sob story*. In any case, for the remaining analysis given below, we will not show morphemic (nor phonological) representations.

Returning now to the morphemic and lexemic representations for the first two lines, shown above, the symbols identify elements – nodes – in the neurocognitive system which are recognized by a typical English-speaking interpreter in the process of interpretation. The recognition takes the form of activation of these nodes.

Now what about the conceptual level? Well, that is quite a different matter. In the first place, we can't just add a line for conceptual representation because it is not linear. A linear representation works for the morphemic and lexemic levels because we get a linear sequence of morphemes which largely match those of the groups of phonemes which realize them, and the same is largely true also of lexemes, though less so. Thus in the example above we identify a lexeme *past* and place it before the verb even though it is (with less frequent verbs) realized as a suffix. Why? Because from the lexemic point of view the past tense element (like tense lexemes in general) occurs with the entire verb phrase.

But the conceptual representation is not linear, except in that there is a linear sequence of events in narratives and personal or other histories and the like, and often a linear logical sequence of ideas in other kinds of texts. But the concepts involved in an event are all there simultaneously. On the other hand, we can also observe that the concepts corresponding to the lexemes get activated in sequence as the lexemes are activated. So to this extent there is some linearity of activation of concepts, as a preliminary stage of building the conceptual representation.

A second factor making conceptual representations far more problematic is the very important fact that, to be cognitively realistic, they need to show the difference between recognition and structure building. Recognition applies to material that is already present in the system, as in the case of the morphemic and lexemic representations. Such material is there just to identify a location or locations in the previously existing network – that which must be already present in order for this piece of discourse to be understood and the point(s) at which the new information is attached.

A third problematic aspect of conceptual representation is that we cannot really say with any assurance what gets represented in any given person's conceptual system as a result of interpreting some sentences, since there are often multiple possibilities. Take, for example, sentence 1. Will the typical interpreter remember that Sue heard the story a couple of weeks ago, or just that she heard it, perhaps recently? And will they remember that it was someone else besides her, maybe several other people, who also heard it? After all, she said, 'We heard a story...', but without identifying who else also heard it. So we can say that, as with non-linguistic perception, we are given many possibilities (on an ongoing basis) to register new information in our conceptual system; and we are generally quite selective about what we actually choose to register from among the abundant possibilities that keep streaming in.

Notice also another important difference between lexical and conceptual information: This person named 'Sue' who is talking is, of course, not just any Sue but a particular person, one of perhaps a dozen individuals with that name who are represented within the assumed typical personal cognitive system. Thus the label *'Sue'* is applicable at the morphemic and lexemic levels, and only one lexeme *Sue* needs to be recognized in the system. But in the conceptual system there must be a separate element for each individual represented there and that element might be connected not just with one name but with multiple alternative designations (such as 'Miss Jones', 'that blonde lady', etc.). This is one aspect of a larger problem: It is not just personal names, but also nouns in general that have this problem, and not just nouns but also verbs (see below). In the example *we heard a story*, what is the conceptual representation corresponding to *a story*? It is not just STORY (small capitals are used here for conceptual representations), for STORY is the *category* of stories, and this is just one member of the category, a new one. It is identified as such by the use of the indefinite article, and that identification gets confirmed by the following sentences as they relate the story. If this one gets remembered it will be registered in the conceptual system as a new entity, a member of the category of stories, but differing from other members of the category in various ways, including the fact that it was heard from Sue on this occasion and especially that it contains a particular cast of characters and sequence of events.

Similarly, this instance of hearing is just one instance, one event belonging to the category HEAR. A category of events can be called a process; each event is an instance of the process, generally identified linguistically by an entire clause with its specification of participants and time and possibly location and other matters. And the bare process, the category of all those events, is represented linguistically by just the bare verbal lexeme. Similarly, but differently, a category of things is represented by just a noun lexeme, while a particular member of the category is identified by a noun phrase.[1]

A further general problem is that concepts do not have their own symbols, so anything we do to represent them symbolically is likely to be misleading. Now of course, people do talk with one another about concepts. How is this possible, if they don't have their own symbols? Well, this is where language comes in. They do have a way of being represented symbolically, through the lexemic representations that are connected to them, or in the case of new concepts, for which new connections to lexemic representations can be formed. But such lexemic representations are in no way to be confused with the concepts themselves, for a given concept can be represented by different lexemic representations (Sue, Miss Jones, that blonde lady, Harry's girlfriend, etc.), and a given lexeme (like *story*) can represent different conceptual entities. So in any case the attempt to represent concepts symbolically is artificial and necessarily flawed. How, then, do we handle them within the information systems of our minds? We don't represent them symbolically at all, except indirectly though the use of language. Instead, they are represented in the connectivity of the neurocognitive network.

So in line 1, *a story* invites the interpreter to recruit a new node and to attach it to the category STORY. This new node represents a new instance of a story, a new member of the category.

The principle of structure building carries with it the complementary principle that the text has to be considered in relation to previously existing knowledge of the interpreter. Thus morphemic and lexemic decoding requires the presence of internal representations of the morphemes and lexemes involved. Their presence is what makes decoding at these levels a process of recognition.

At the conceptual level, the processing of the interpreter normally involves both recognition and structure building. The interpretation of each information unit of the text involves adding new information to an already existing web of informational connections, and its understanding depends upon the prior existence of that existing information. The structure building would be impossible without the knowledge of where to build the new structure. We have all had the experience of hearing a discourse on a topic that 'goes over our heads'. The meaning of that idiom in neurocognitive terms is that our cognitive systems lack certain connections (those for certain conceptual and lexical nections) needed to enable us to know where to build new connections to represent the new information. Hence the only thing we remember is that we heard someone talking about something abstruse.

The interpretation of line 1, for a typical speaker of English as interpreter, necessarily involves connections to the certain concepts that must already exist in that speaker's information system in order for the phrase to be understood, as shown in Table 8.1.

Table 8.1 Knowledge prerequired to understand line 1

Text item	Meaning, as previously existing concept(s)
We	speaker and (unspecified) other(s)
heard	the concept HEAR with its properties
story	the concept STORY with its properties

Now the concept STORY carries with it (in the conceptual systems of ordinary speakers of English) certain well-established properties: There will be characters and a sequence of events. These properties have become connected with STORY through numerous prior examples. This is part of the conceptual syntax – in this case STORY has its own little tactic structure: A story presupposes characters and events. As with tactic constructions at lower levels it is a generalization which has specific instantiations, in this case specific stories. The new node for this story will have further nodes added to it as the story is received and interpreted. The conceptual syntax that has been built around stories provides the expectation not only that characters will be introduced but also that there will be a series of events.

Line 2 introduces some characters:

L2   of this family.

The receiver does not yet know whether 'this family' includes all the characters or only some of them. Noun phrases representing new persons or things are commonly introduced by an indefinite determiner (as in 'there was a family'); whereas the definite article indicates that the entity is one assumed to be already present in the conceptual system of the receiver. In line 2 we have 'this', generally known as a demonstrative but functioning here as an indefinite determiner, an introducer of a new item. Its meaning may be roughly indicated by the paraphrase 'a certain'. Its conceptual representation is the operation of adding new structure. The function of the determiner is to specify that the structure building operation is to be performed while that of the noun to which it is attached (in this case *family*) identifies the place where the new structure is needed: It is attached as a new instance of the category FAMILY.

Let us now continue with the next portion of the text. Line 3 introduces a particular member of the family, 'a young child', and this phrase is then edited by line 4, 'a young boy', which although it consists of three words supplies only the additional information that the 'child' of line 3 is male. Since line 4 is being taken as an editing of line 3, these two lines are equivalent to an assumed edited version 'And there was a young boy in the family.' The edited representation might be assumed to result from an editing process performed as an early stage of interpretation. Since it was told in real time the speaker is unable to go back to edit as one would if working with a text on paper. The editing is thus the responsibility of the hearer, who is given cues to guide the process by the teller of the story as it is told. An alternative interpretation is to analyse line 4 as an afterthought supplying additional information, in this case only the additional information that the child introduced in line 3 is a male. Different interpreters might well differ on this point, but it would make no significant difference in the result.

Lines 3–4 (edited)
    Items recognized:
        L and there past be a young boy in the family .

C CONTIN. TIME-0 EXIST INDEF YOUNG BOY MEMBER-OF
    FAMILY-1
Constructive processes at conceptual level:
    New node attached to category BOY and to properties YOUNG
    and MEMBER-OF FAMILY-1

In the conceptual representation of items recognized, CONTIN. is
an abbreviation for CONTINUING. It represents the conceptual
representation of *and*, which indicates that the narrator is continuing
to the next discourse unit. For TIME-0 see below.

In lines 3–4 we see another example of the typical use of the
indefinite article – to introduce a new nominal item. From the
foregoing discussion it is apparent that introducing a new item is an
invitation to the interpreter to perform an operation of building new
structure. It is common for 'definite' to be marked by the definite
article and for 'indefinite' to be marked by the indefinite article, but
of course these are far from being the only markers of that distinction.
When a nominal occurs with the definite article, the latter signifies
that a particular member of the set labeled by that nominal is
intended whose exact identity, moreover, is assumed to be known or
knowable to the receiver of the clause. The indefinite article, as in
John gave a book to Henry, usually introduces a new entity into the
discourse, only partially identified. In this example, taken by itself,
the only identification provided is that the entity is a book. Here the
process of interpretation involves adding this new entity to the conceptual system and connecting it to the category of books, the category
named by the nominal with which the indefinite article occurs. If the
following sentence reveals, let us say, the name of the book, then
the receiver of the text, as part of the process of understanding it,
connects that newly added entity with a new property, its name. The
other end of this new connection to the name must, of course, be that
same entity introduced in the previous sentence. The conceptual representation of that entity is present just once in the conceptual
system, but it is represented twice in the linguistic expression.

Thus the structure of the content of a coherent discourse is a single
network in which each participant is present just once, but typically
with multiple connections to events and other properties while the
expression side of the discourse has multiple occurrences of
realizations for each participant, on the order of one occurrence for
each such connection. Each such occurrence after the first is typically
'definite' as marked by a definite article or by a pronoun.

Lines 3–7 have in each finite clause the past tense element, and lines 5 and 7 have also the progressive lexeme (whose morphemic representation consists of *be* together with the suffix *-ing* on the following verb form). But at the conceptual level there is only one occurrence of a past time element here, labeled 'TIME–0', the beginning time of the events of the story (see also below). It goes with the whole series of clauses, disregarding clause and sentence boundaries. But as the surface syntax of English requires a tense marker with every finite verb, this 'past' marker is repeated in every clause of this portion of the text. That does not mean that its repeated occurrences are just redundant, since they provide cohesion, helping to indicate that all of these clauses go together as one portion of the narrative. Its reoccurrence in line 7 with no intervening 'then' or 'and' or the like is what tells the English-speaking receiver that we are still within the same tense unit, the one already in effect just as the repeated occurrence of a case-number-gender ending on successive adjectives in a Latin or Russian noun phrase signifies that the separate adjectives are all part of the same noun phrase, which as a phrase is in that case and number and gender just once, as a whole.

Line 5
  Items recognized:
    L and he past progr have tremendous problem -pl in school .
    C CONTIN. TIME–0 BOY–1 GREATLY HAVE-PROBLEMS IN SCHOOL
  Constructive operations:
    Build connection from (just recruited node) BOY–1 to properties representing having problems in school
Line 6
  Items recognized:
    L he past be a very difficult child.
    C TIME–0 BOY–1 BE GREATLY DIFFICULT-CHILD
  Constructive operations:
    Further connection built from BOY–1 TO DIFFICULT-CHILD
Line 7a
  Items recognized:
    L he past be too active,
    C TIME–0 BOY–1 HYPERACTIVE
Constructive operations:
    Further connections from BOY–1 TO HYPERACTIVE
Line 7b
  Items recognized:
    L and he past progr always get-into-trouble .

C CONTIN. TIME–0 BOY–1 PROG FREQUENTLY GET-INTO-
  TROUBLE
Constructive operations:
  Further connections from BOY–1, or possible reinforcement
  of the connection to HYPERACTIVE

As mentioned above, the time of the outset of the story is indicated
as TIME–0. Similarly, as the events unfold, their sequence is given,
furnishing the interpreter with indications of their relative times.
They can be indicated as TIME–1, TIME–2, and so forth. Although
the time element TIME–0 is present only once in the network built for
the interpreted story, it keeps getting recognized in each of several
clauses in which its lexemic representation occurs. It must be
understood that as the information structure is a network of relations,
different occurrences of the same symbol in the conceptual
representation do not signify different elements or different
occurrences of one element, only multiple connections to one and
the same element.

Likewise, the symbol 'BOY–1' is what I have chosen to represent
the boy of our story in the conceptual network. As a particular entity
it gets a specific node in the network, which is connected to the
general concept BOY. It is present only once in the network. After all,
the boy is only a single entity. By contrast, in natural language
representations as in notation systems based on natural languages,
that which represents him occurs repeatedly (thus *a young child* in
line 3, *a young boy* in line 4, *he* in line 5, line 7 (twice), *this child* in line
11, etc.). A single concept, but repeated and differing expressions.

The node being labeled BOY–1 enters the network as the result of
decoding line 3, at that point as the conceptual representation of *a
young child*. It is the indefinite article which expresses the fact that we
are here concerned with a new node. The definite article would have
signified an already existing node.

The process in 7b is an instance of the process GET-INTO-
TROUBLE. It furnishes an example of a concept whose realization
requires three separate words. (Similarly, as already noted, the
progressive aspect lexeme is realized as two separate morphemes, *be*
and *-ing*, appearing in two separate words, which in line 7 are
separated by 'always'.) We also have an additional temporal
specification, *always*, which in fact does not carry the actual meaning
ALWAYS at all but rather the meaning FREQUENTLY; it is supplied as
additional specification to narrow down that provided by the
progressive element.

The suggestions given above about constructive operations at the conceptual level are not in any way to be considered conclusive. Different interpreters will build different internal structures to represent the information being received, and only those with very agile memories and intensely applied attention are likely to build all the connections suggested above. For many, perhaps all of the information given in lines 5 to 7 would just be remembered as the assertion that this child was hyperactive. In this case there would be just the connection to HYPERACTIVE established from the new node BOY–1 (attached to the category BOY at lines 3–4).

Line 8 introduces a new character, and with him an event. Further information is provided about this character by lines 9 and 10. In other words, these two lines invite the receiver to attach additional connections to the new node recruited for this character as a result of interpreting line 8. Here I will give just the lexemic representation, the record of lexemes recognized by the interpreter:

8 L and a long-lost relative past come into this family ,
9 L who past perfect be to India
10 L and perfect study with some of the Eastern-mystic -pl.

The form *long-lost* in line 8 provides an example of multiple function, a phenomenon that occurs with great frequency not only in linguistic interpretation but also in perception generally. This form is at one and the same time a representation of the lexeme *long-lost*, evidently chosen as a good lexeme for a story because of its connections to many other stories and also includes the past-participle element. It is really the past-participle element which carries the dual function; first, as part of the lexeme *long-lost* and second as a signal of the past perfect tense, which is seen again, with its complete representation (i.e. with *have*) in line 9. The function of the past perfect tense here is to establish the time of this relative's sojourn in India as prior to TIME–0.

We now continue with lexemic representations of the next few lines:

11 L and so he past suggest to this child
12 L that he stuff cotton up the right side of he -'s nose .
13 L and so they past stuff cotton up the right side of he -'s nose .

In line 13, the pronoun *they*, as a definite form, refers to persons already introduced, and in the plural. Since the only other persons already introduced are the members of the family, not otherwise identified, they must be the ones referred to. Continuing,

14   L and he -'s personality , completely past change .
15   L he past become this very passive , nice , docile , child ,

Secondary interpretation

The discussion of interpretation above has dealt with primary interpretation. To the actual participants in a typical conversation, however, it is the secondary interpretation that is of greater interest. Let us here at least acknowledge secondary interpretation by means of a few brief remarks.

First, the typical interpreter might well infer from lines 9 and 10 that what was studied was some form of yoga. This inference could come from the combination of two items of information from the primary interpretation: (1) the location IN INDIA of the process STUDY and (2) the third participant (which for STUDY is the teacher), *some Eastern mystics*. This example illustrates what is meant here by secondary interpretation.

The observation of the process of secondary interpretation points up perhaps with particular clarity how helpful it is to view the person's knowledge system as a relational network, for secondary interpretation involves activating pathways from the concepts identified in the primary interpretation, leading to thoughts which thus get activated, often as a result of the confluence of activations from multiple concepts within the system. In the above example, some interpreters would reach the concept YOGA as the confluence of activations stemming from the concepts STUDY, IN INDIA and EASTERN MYSTICS. For other interpreters, of course, such activation may not occur, and such minor differences in secondary interpretation make little difference in most situations – so little, in fact, that different interpreters present within the same conversational group are normally unaware of it.

Another noteworthy example of secondary interpretation is provided by Kay's reaction to the narrative, which interrupts its ending. Kay's secondary interpretation of the concluding events of the story is that the boy is unable to breathe as a result of having the cotton stuffed up one nostril. This interpretation might well occur in only a minority of receivers of this narrative, as it ignores the normally present awareness that another nostril is still available for that function. Perhaps Kay's secondary interpretation stems from the fact that, as she has explained earlier in the conversation, in her own case there is only one nostril functioning properly in breathing.

Further variety in secondary interpretation of the conclusion comes from the lexeme *docile*, which has such different semantic properties for different people that some receivers conclude that the outcome of the unorthodox treatment was beneficial, since the hyperactivity was evidently cured, while others conclude that it was harmful to the boy, since docility is an undesirable quality. In fact these opposite conclusions were arrived at by different linguists attending the 1984 Rice Symposium at which this text was discussed, and there were very strong opinions expressed in support of the opposing interpretations. Correlated with this difference was a difference in the pronunciation of the word: The strongest argument for the harmfulness of this treatment was from a linguist who pronounced the word with the so-called 'long o' in the first syllable and the 'long i' in the second, concurrently with a relatively heavy stress on the second syllable, while those who considered the treatment beneficial pronounced it with the so-called 'short o' (as in *doctor*) and with a very weak second syllable. I must say that the former pronunciation has a much more negative feeling to me than the latter. Here we are dealing with connections from phonological to conceptual information.

Many additional possibilities exist for secondary interpretation of the events of the story and as already suggested, these possibilities will tend to vary widely for different interpreters, far more so than for primary interpretation. The reason is that secondary interpretation involves the activation of a larger portion of the conceptual system, not just the points immediately connected to lexemes, so that individual differences in knowledge and interests play a greater role.

Some interpreters with an interest in right brain and left brain phenomena, for example, will follow a pathway of thought like that suggested later in the text by Sue (some of them before, others not until after, having that possibility pointed out by her), which may lead to the likely explanation of why the treatment was successful in curing the hyperactivity as well as, indeed, why it was too successful as appraised within the information systems of those who came to that conclusion. This line of thought may lead further, for some secondary interpreters with scientific curiosity, to hypotheses relating to the influence of right and left nostril breathing on left and right brain activity, respectively. Everything depends on the individual conceptual system, including not only the information already present in it but also the kinds of interests and curiosities which help to control its operation.

Some conclusions

There are many things of linguistic interest that can be said upon observation of even so small a text as the one discussed here. The foregoing remarks, which constitute just the first tentative steps toward a neurocognitive understanding of discourse interpretation, barely touch on a very few of them.

The conclusions given below are a summary of certain principles that we have discussed and perhaps justified (or, if already well known, perhaps further supported):

(1) There is no such thing as the meaning of a text apart from an interpreter. And meaning is not conveyed by a text, as the usual metaphor would have us believe. Rather, elements of the text activate meanings in the minds of interpreters.

(2) The processes which must be performed for interpretation include (i) recognition, (ii) building of new structure and (iii) finding structure elements which conform to recognized criteria (in the case of questions, not illustrated above).

(3) A text cannot be interpreted except by virtue of information already present in the system before the text is received (or produced). Understanding of a text consists of relating the results of its decoding to the already present information.

(4) A text cannot be interpreted except by constructing a content representation which is connected, while being built, to those parts of the interpreter's internal information system which constitute the already existing information. As the process goes on, the newly constructed information from one portion of text becomes existing information for additional portions to follow. The meaning representation of the text consists of new nodes with connections to those of the previously existing relational network. That is, interpretation is a process of constructing information, in the form of new network connections.

(5) Conceptual structure can also be built on the basis of information from modalities other than language, such as visual perception.

(6) The linguistic-conceptual system of every person is different from that of every other person. There is therefore no possibility of perfect communication through language.

(7) The meaning constructed by the receiver of the text is the same as that constructed by the sender only if the two have identical information systems (i.e. never).

Note

1. This use of the terms 'event' and 'process' differs from that of some other linguists including those who have been using the misnomer 'events' for what is here (and in Systemic Functional Grammar) called 'process'.

References

Halliday, M. A. K. (1994), *An Introduction to Functional Grammar*, 2nd edn. London: Edward Arnold.

Lamb, Sydney M. (1999) *Pathways of the Brain: The Neurocognitive Basis of Language*. Amsterdam: John Benjamins.

9

Prosody and Emotion in a Sample of Real Speech

Wallace Chafe

The discussion that follows is a preliminary attempt to examine some of the ways emotions and attitudes are expressed prosodically as people engage in a conversation. While there have been countless studies of prosody and a smaller number of studies directed at the relation between prosody and affect, data from ordinary conversations has been conspicuous by its absence. Despite this neglect, the naturalness and ubiquity of conversational language suggest that there ought to be important things to learn from it with respect to emotions, and prosody would seem to be the main channel for emotional expression.

As might be expected, the most extensive and valuable work relating prosody and emotion has been experimental, with the usual sacrifice of naturalness for a rigorous methodology. One popular technique has used actors to simulate standard emotions like anger, sadness, or joy, and to test how well subjects can identify those emotions from their acoustic signals (e.g. Bezooyen 1984). But the most detailed and ramified experiments were those conducted by Klaus Scherer and his collaborators during the 1970s and 1980s. A useful summary of that work is available in Goldbeck, Tolkmitt, and Scherer (1988). A review of these and other studies is more than can be accommodated within this chapter, but it is worth quoting the last-mentioned article to the effect that 'a close collaboration between psychology and the language sciences will be required to disentangle the complex web of factors that determine human vocal expression' (p. 137). What follows is an exploratory contribution to that disentanglement in the framework of discourse analysis.

As I use the word here, *prosody* includes variations in the following dimensions of physical sound and its perception:

Fundamental frequency (F0), perceived as pitch
Intensity, perceived as loudness
Duration (tempo, lengthening, pausing, etc.)
Voice quality (creaky voice, whispering, laughing, etc.)

The relations between sound and perception are not yet well understood. Because it is easier to make physical measurements than to establish their perceptual correlates, I will base prosodic markings and graphic displays here on the former. But what our brains do with physical inputs under the influence of context and expectations may in the end be more relevant than the physical phenomena themselves. The representations provided here should thus be regarded as only approximations to the full story.

Any attempt to discuss prosody in a written format inevitably raises a problem to which there is no good solution. The examples I cite would be a great deal more meaningful if they could be heard. I have added occasional prosodic markings to the transcripts when they are relevant to the discussion, and I have provided selected displays of F0, and in a few places intensity. These devices may help the reader to imagine the sounds, but they are a poor substitute for the sounds themselves.

In a broad perspective, I believe that prosody performs at least four distinguishable functions in discourse (Chafe 2000). Two of them involve discourse *organization*, and two what can be called the *evaluation* of discourse elements, in two different senses of evaluation. With respect to discourse organization, prosody delimits units such as words, phrases, sentences, and topics as people organize what they are saying on-line. At the same time prosody shows the relations such units bear to their larger contexts, as when rising pitches at the ends of phrases indicate more to come, falling pitches indicate closure, and so on. With respect to evaluation, some elements stand out as more prominent than others in terms of new information, contrast, emphasis, and the like. But another kind of evaluation involves emotions and attitudes, and they will be our chief concern here.

Because prosody performs these several functions, a particular prosodic pattern cannot usually be explained on the basis of one of them alone. It can be a challenge to sort these functions out, and to interpret aspects of prosodic patterns in terms of them. It is important also to remain aware that emotions do not occur in isolation, but in combination with whatever ideas are being expressed. It may thus be futile to try to segregate some particular aspect of prosody and assign some emotional 'meaning' to it alone. Its effect may differ, depending on the ideas with which it is associated.

In the course of this discussion I will suggest that particular prosodic phenomena express a generalized heightening of emotional involvement, and also sometimes specific affective attitudes. I will relate these suggestions to what was happening in the discourse, but I realize that such interpretations will strike some readers as overly dependent on introspection. I am myself convinced that the human sciences were held back during the twentieth century by an unwillingness to take introspective evidence seriously, although that unwillingness permeated psychology more thoroughly than linguistics. In the future it may become possible to validate degrees and perhaps even types of emotional arousal through brain imaging. Even then, however, it will remain necessary to relate emotions to the content of language, and that will always require that we understand, as best we can, the nature of that content. For now I can only hope that for many readers my descriptions of what was happening in this conversation will have a ring of plausibility.

For the most part I will restrict the discussion to F0 and its perceptual correlate in pitch. One aspect of F0 that will be relevant will be its range, typically within the domain of an intonation unit (Chafe 1994:53–70), but sometimes within a larger segment of speech. As the minimum F0 in that range I will sometimes make use of what I will call the prefinal baseline, exclusive of any final fall that descends into unmeasurable creaky voice. This prefinal baseline is typically the lowest F0 associated with given information (Chafe 1994:71–81), or with a weakly accented element such as the indefinite article. In addition to range and baseline, I will point out certain places where a rise-fall contour on some element assigns a more localized emotional involvement to that element alone. And in addition to F0, I will point out a few places where lengthening, rhythm and intensity also contribute to the expression of affect. These, as well as voice quality, clearly play important roles in emotional expression, and they deserve more attention than I will give them here.

The conversation that is studied in a variety of ways in this book is well suited to an investigation of prosody and emotion. The main speaker, Kay, had what might be called an expressive voice, in the sense that her prosody was quite varied and communicated numerous fluctuations in emotional involvement. The conversation was initiated by the other speaker, Sue, as follows. (I use accent marks only when they are relevant to the discussion. An acute accent shows a rise in pitch, a grave accent a fall, and a circumflex accent a rise-fall. The equals sign shows a prolongation of the preceding segment.)

1.S   ... What I'd like to find out more about .. is .. your operation.

2.   ... That you're having. {laugh}

3.K   ... My nô = se [operation.]

4.S   [Yes .. your nose] operation.

Evidently Sue knew of Kay's pending operation and had decided to introduce it as a topic of conversation. She did that in 1–2, and in 3 Kay confirmed her familarity with this topic. The square brackets in 3 and 4 show overlapping speech, with Sue confirming the nature of her inquiry before Kay had fully completed her own confirmation.

If one were to read 3 in an emotionally neutral way, on the basis of nothing more than the written words *my nose operation*, one could imagine it as spoken with either of two prosodically distinct patterns. One would have a rising pitch on *nose*, followed by a further, phrase-final rise at the end of *operation*. That contour is suggested by the question mark in:

My nose operation?

Spoken in that way, 3 would have asked for confirmation of the specific operation Sue had in mind. With a different prosody, the peak on *nose* would be followed by a fall that continued to the end, as suggested by the period in:

My nose operation.

Spoken in that way, 3 would simply have expressed Kay's confirmation of this topic.

What Kay actually said differed from both these alternatives, although it had more in common with the second. The word *nose* was spoken with a rise-fall contour, the peak of which reached 396 Hz, well above Kay's range when she was speaking in a more matter-of-fact way. Figure 9.1 traces F0 on the words *my nose*. (Because Sue overlapped Kay's next word, *operation*, no tracing of F0 could be made for that word.) The word *nose* was also prolonged, occupying more than half a second, as compared with Kay's average rate of about 150 ms per syllable.

The idea of Kay's nose had not been activated up to this point in the conversation, and was thus a new idea. We would expect it, then, to be uttered with a higher F0 than *my*, which expressed the already active idea of Kay herself, and *operation*, which expressed an idea that

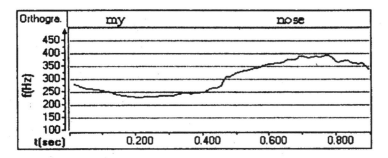

Figure 9.1 F0 in *my nose* in 3

had just been activated by Sue. We will see, however, that in less involved utterances Kay expressed new ideas with F0 levels no higher than about 260 Hz. Why did *nose* rise to almost 400 Hz?

Kay was expressing her recognition and acceptance of a newly introduced topic, but it was also a topic that must have been emotionally loaded for her. This operation promised to be a major event in her life. Sue's introduction of it as a topic of conversation must have aroused in Kay a feeling that can be described with terms like arousal, excitement, or involvement. I will make frequent use of the last of these terms, identifying places in the conversation where Kay showed what I will call heightened involvement. We will see that such involvement was consistently expressed with heightened pitch, and typically with an expanded F0 range extending over the domain in question. Expressive lengthening, as with the word *nose*, may also contribute to this effect.

To show that the environment of the pitch-raising in 3 was not unique, I can mention an analogous example that was cited in Chafe (2000), repeated here:

1.W   What was that about a-
2.   ... remember there was a-
3.   ... some man that,
4.   ... showed up at the door there,
5.   ... at the Ab Roth place.
6.M   Oh thât was up thêre.
7.   At that Ab Rôth place.

The woman labeled M had just concluded a topic that had to do with members of her family, and W then introduced something he remembered from a previous conversation, involving 'the Ab Roth place', where M had lived briefly as a child, and where some extraordinary events had taken place. In 6, M responded with heightened pitches on *that* and *there*, as well as on the name *Roth* in 7. As in Kay's case, there was a sudden recognition and uptake of a new and emotionally loaded topic. In such cases the range of F0 may extend well beyond that which characterizes a speaker's less emotional discourse, but we will see that this is only one of many discourse phenomena that can have this effect.

For purposes of comparison it is helpful to look at Kay's less involved speech, taking as an example another early segment of this conversation, transcribed in 16–17. F0 in this segment is traced in Figure 9.2, with the two intonation units identified by number at the top:

16. So I thought well,
17. ... I would get it ... cosmetically ... changed.

The maximum F0 here was 263 Hz on the second syllable of *cosmetically*. The minimum was 148 Hz at the end of that same word. The range was thus 115 Hz, typical of Kay's range under conditions of minimal involvement.

To look more fully at the segment in which Kay began to develop the topic of her nose operation, we can add the portion that immediately preceded 16–17. The entire passage 10–17 showed a restrained level of involvement, though, as we will see, involvement was not entirely lacking even here. F0 is traced in Figure 9.3, where it can be seen that, with one exception in 13, everything remained within the approximately 150 to 265 Hz range that characterized Kay's uninvolved speech.

10. ... Well,
11.12. ... mâybe I should prèface this thing whŷ I want it done.
13. ... First of all;
14. I want it for cosmètic reasons.
15. ... I'm sort of tired of everyone going like this to my nose.
16. So I thought well,
17. ... I would get it ... cosmetically ... changed.

In 10–12 Kay summarized the topic she was about to develop, reasons for the operation, postponing an answer to Sue's request that she describe what she was having done and the condition she would be in. In 13–15 she summarized the cosmetic reason, and in 16–17 her tentative decision to take care of that problem. None of what she said here was highly involving, and the restricted pitch range throughout this segment reflected that.

Conspicuous in Figure 9.3, nevertheless, is the rise to 320 Hz that occurred during the first word of 13:

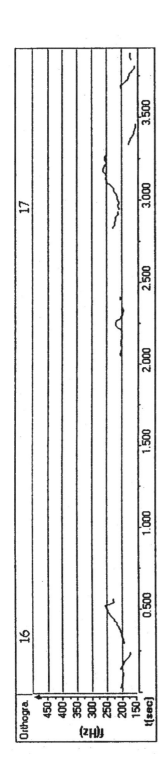

Figure 9.2 F0 in 16–17

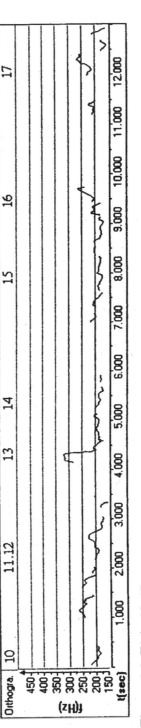

Figure 9.3 F0 in 10–17

13.   ... Fîrst of all,

Among other things, prosody can signal the initiation of a new topic
or subtopic. In 13 Kay introduced the subtopic of cosmetic reasons
for her operation. It might be that the heightened prosody on *first*
simply reflected this aspect of discourse organization. I would like to
raise the possibility, however, that the very act of anticipating a new
topic may create at least a mild degree of emotional involvement. If
so, the heightened pitch at the beginning of 13 provides an example
where both discourse organization and at least some degree of
involvement are in play.

It is worth noticing also that the baseline during the sequence 13–
15, at about 165 Hz, was elevated slightly above the 150 Hz
characteristic of Kay's uninvolved speech. If that difference has any
significance, it suggests that the involvement created by initiating a
new topic can extend over a segment longer than a single word, or
even a single intonation unit. This slightly raised baseline may be a
small piece of evidence that prosodic expression can be gradient
rather than categorical. Perhaps the small baseline difference of 15
Hz reflected a small heightening of involvement associated with the
new subtopic. Whether prosody and its effects are gradient or
categorical continues to be an important question.

But even before 13, when 11.12 summarized what was to come,
involvement was not totally absent. Rather than being extended over
several intonation units, it was restricted here to transient, highly
localized elements:

11.12. ... mâybe I should prèface this thing whŷ I want it done.

Of interest is the fact that both *maybe* and *why* showed a rise-fall
pattern, whereas *preface* showed only a fall, as can be seen in Figure
9.4. We can notice that *maybe* and *why* expressed subjective,
emotionally tinged judgments, whereas *preface* did not. *Maybe*
qualified the factuality of Kay's statement. There was no certainty
that she should 'preface this thing' as she did, and deciding to do so
was a value judgment. *Why* expressed a contrast with Sue's request,
in mild opposition to Sue's agenda. It was also significantly
lengthened, occupying 640 ms, almost as much time as the 765 ms
taken up by the entire four syllables of *preface this thing*. Lengthening
can be another manifestation of contrast. Unlike these two subjective
judgments, *preface* simply stated Kay's plan for organizing the topic,
an emotionally neutral idea. The prominence it did have resulted
from its participation in new information, not from involvement.

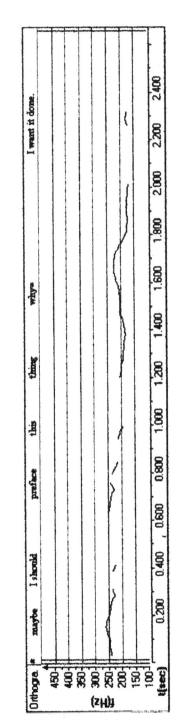

Figure 9.4 F0 in 11.12

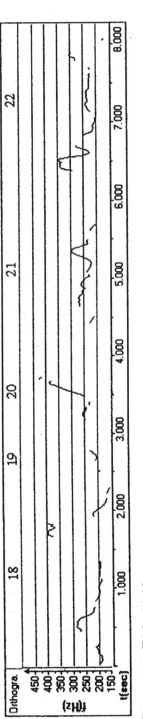

Figure 9.5 F0 in 11.12

Examples like these, and there are many of them, suggest that a rise-fall contour can be associated with a single brief element that is emotionally tinged, whereas a simple fall lacks the same affective force. The involvement associated with *maybe* and *why* was limited to what those words alone conveyed, minor blips within an otherwise emotionally restrained segment of Kay's talk.

The level of involvement increased substantially in 18–22, as can be seen in Figure 9.5:

18.   And then sômeone told me that I hâd a problem;
19.   you sée?
20.   ... That was grêat.
21.   ... My friend who's a nûr–se said,
22.   ... lîsten you've got a deviated sèptum.

Kay had for some time thought that the shape of her nose was something she wanted to correct, but for various reasons, including the unwillingness of her insurance company to pay for cosmetic surgery, she had done nothing. Then came this new and exciting discovery that she actually had a medical problem, a deviated septum, that would be covered by her insurance. She hoped that her surgeon might be persuaded to correct the cosmetic problem while he was correcting the medical one. The excitement attached to this discovery was manifested in a greatly increased F0 range. There were two peaks in the neighborhood of 400 Hz and a third at about 350 Hz. The overall range was about 250 Hz, as compared with about 115 Hz for minimally involved passages.

This sequence began with 18, whose F0 is traced in Figure 9.6:

18.   And then someône told me that I hâd a problem;

Like the *why* in 11.12, the *had* in 18 was contrastive. What it contrasted with was the implied idea that she *didn't* have a medical problem. But the *had* in 18 reached 400 Hz, whereas the *why* in 11.12 reached only 225 Hz. Evidently the contrastiveness of *had* was superimposed on the heightened involvement of the entire 18–22 passage. It can be noted that the word *someone* in 18 also showed a rise-fall contour, but with a lesser peak of about 290 Hz. The idea of this someone was new but not contrastive. In addition to its newness, however, its rise-fall contour gave the idea of that person a subjective coloring that would not have been present if it had been pronounced with a simple fall. Kay's prosody expressed a special interest in this person, who, as we learn, contributed as both a friend and a nurse to the solution of her twin problems.

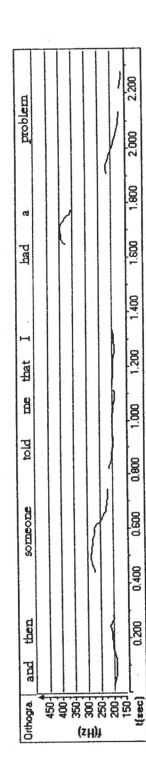

Figure 9.6 F0 in 18–22

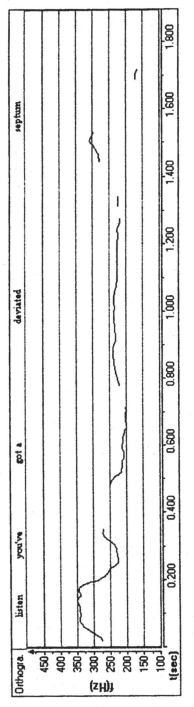

Figure 9.7 F0 in 18

In 20 the word *great* was pronounced with a rise-fall that reached 392 Hz, about the same level as *had* in 18, or for that matter *nose* in 3.

20. … That was grêat.

Great, of course, expressed Kay's highly positive evaluation of the news she had received. Up to this point, then, it appears that a peak in the neighborhood of 400 Hz was associated with a maximum of emotional involvement.

The sequence 21–22 expanded on 18:

21. … My friend who's a nûr–se said,
22. … lîsten you've got a deviated sèptum.

The *someone* of 18 was now identified as *my friend who's a nurse*, and *a problem* was clarified as a *deviated septum*. Of interest is the fact that 22 contained the first of many direct quotes, with an F0 shown in Figure 9.7. Direct quotes are frequently uttered with a higher pitch than surrounding speech, in an iconic representation of the other voice.

The fall at the end of *septum* was comparable to other falls, with a low of 162 Hz. Since *listen* reached 354 Hz, the overall range was 192 Hz, well above the restrained norm. However, this intonation unit illustrates the value of distinguishing a prefinal baseline from the baseline established by a final fall. The lowest frequency before the final fall, on the indefinite article *a*, was 199 Hz, noticeably higher than Kay's typical baseline of approximately 160 Hz. This and similar examples suggest that a direct quote may be set off from surrounding speech by a higher prefinal baseline in addition to, or perhaps sometimes instead of, an expanded range. The difference is clearly visible in a comparison of Figure 9.7 with Figure 9.8, which shows F0 in 15, where there was an absence of any pitch-raising above the norm.

Kay's subsequent speech contained many direct quotes, some of them self-quotes as in 26:

26.K … Will someone else pây for it.

Here the prefinal baseline was raised to 221 Hz, the lowest point during the word *else*, with a peak of 415 Hz on *pay*, the highest pitch reached so far in Kay's speech. But it rose even higher in 27–28:

27.K … She said … sûre.
28.K … It's a mêdical problem.

Sure and *medical* reached 490 Hz and the prefinal baseline was 190

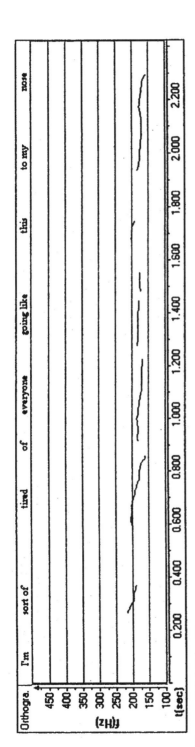

Figure 9.8 F0 in 15

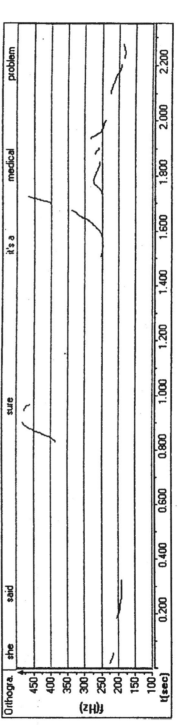

Figure 9.9 F0 in 27–28

Hz. The heightened pitch associated with a direct quote was accompanied by the gratifying information that her problem was a medical one, yielding a major increase in emotional involvement that is clearly visible in Figure 9.9.

Similar peaks reaching nearly 500 Hz occurred in the two instances of *no* that were answers to Sue's questions in 30–36, ascending to 490 Hz in 31 and 496 Hz in 36:

30.S   Didn't you notice you had a deviated septum?
31.K   ... Nô=,

   ...

34.S   you couldn't brea–the through the side
35.S   ... one side of your nose?
36.K   ... Nô=.

These two *no's* continued the unusually high involvement of 27–28. A general and potentially important finding is that emotional involvement, once produced, tends to persist through at least several intonation units, suggesting that emotions change more sluggishly than ideas of events and states and their participants, which are replaced during speech with great rapidity. Heightened involvement is slow to dissipate.

Lines 57–59 provide one more example of heightened pitch in a direct quote:

57.K   I just inquired and they said sûre.
58.K   ... You've got a real prôblem.
59.K   ... {laugh} Let's just fix that nòse up,

In 57 everything except the last word was at a normal level, hovering just below 200 Hz, but then the quoted *sure* jumped to 456 Hz, with *problem* in 58 at 395 Hz, and *nose* in 59 at 365 Hz. But in 59 pitch played another role, different from anything discussed so far. The contour that extended over all of 59 conveyed an attitude that Kay attributed to the hospital staff. We lack a terminology adequate to describe such attitudes, but what was conveyed by the prosody in 59 might be paraphrased as *let's just go ahead and do it; no problem*. (Obviously a more generally applicable characterization is needed.) Figure 9.10 traces F0, where this *no problem* attitude can be attributed to the combination of the rhythmic peaks in *let's, fix* and *nose* with the final rise on *up*.

It is instructive to turn from these reported conversations with the nurse and the hospital personnel, in which Kay exhibited a high level of involvement, to her conversations with the surgeon, who was

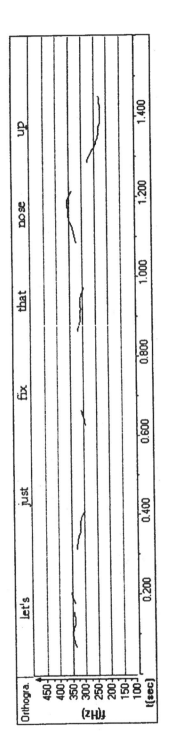

Figure 9.10 F0 in 59

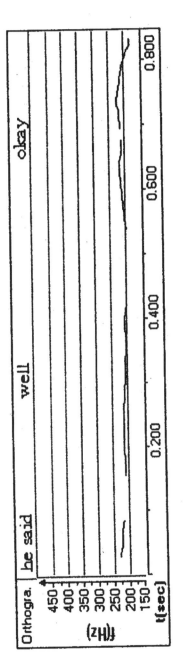

Figure 9.11 F0 in 94b

negative with respect to her cosmetic goals. Kay's own unenthusiastic attitude toward her interactions with him was manifested in several ways. She began in 68, for example, with less involved indirect speech:

68.   ... So um ... he said he côuldn't dô plastic surgery.

Unlike the earlier quotes, this one showed no raised baseline. Also noteworthy is the accelerated tempo of the words *he said he couldn't do*, which averaged about 100 ms per syllable, in contrast to Kay's normal tempo of about 150 ms per syllable. Added to the indirect quote and the low baseline, this acceleration captured Kay's lack of enthusiasm for what the surgeon told her.

In 74 she started to introduce her first direct quote from the surgeon:

74.K   And so he said well,

but she was immediately interrupted by a question from Sue:

75.S   ... Do they have to break your nose .. to correct your .. deviated septum?

which she answered in a matter-of-fact way in 76–81, remaining at her uninvolved baseline and within her normal range:

76.K. ... They may have to,
77.K. they may no–t.
78.K. ... But .. they do have to .. completely alter.
79.K. ... Insi–de .. at least.
80.K. ... They still have to change the whole shape.
81.K. .. So I'm sure that they're going to do something .. pretty drastic so,

Then she returned to her conversation with the surgeon, quoting her own questions and his replies:

82. ... uh– ... so I got arou–nd it by saying well,
83. ... listen.
84. ... Is it going to be straightened,
85. ... like that and he said yeah.
86. ... I said well what about this part.
87. ... You say that you cou–ld ... file that down a little bit.
88. He said we=ll,
89. .. okay.
90. ... {laugh} And I said well the=n,

91.   . . . if that's all straight,
92.   . . this is going to look really funny.
93.   . . . can you– . . . like straighten that up.
94a.   . . And so,
94b.   . . . he said well . . okay.

The first quote from the surgeon was his brief *yeah* in 85, followed by his grudging *well, okay* in 88–89, repeated in 94b. In 88 the lengthening of *well* and the following brief pause, together lasting 704 ms, captured the surgeon's suspenseful hesitation before his grudging agreement in 89. The highest F0 levels in the surgeon's statements in 89 and 94b were in the two occurrences of *okay*, but they reached only 236 and 221 Hz respectively. F0 in 94b is shown in Figure 9.11. This reduced prosody was Kay's way of expressing the surgeon's low level of commitment to her plan. She may have been conveying primarily the surgeon's negative affect, but certainly she herself was less than enthusiastic about his response.

Another reported conversation with the surgeon appeared in 125–130, precipitated by Sue's question in 120:

120.S . . . And how long afterwards are you going to . . . be . .
       black and blue or–
121.K I don't know.
122.   . . . I asked him if I could teach on . . . the following
       Monday.
123.   . . Since the operation's on Thursday.
124.   . . Would I be okay.
125.   . . . A–nd he said . . . yes.
126.   . . . But he said you wôn't be able to brêa–the,
127.   . . out of your nose.
128.   . . . So– . . but he said
129.   . . . uh . . . you haven't been able to breathe anyway {laugh}
       so–
130.   . . . whŷ nôt.

The first quote from the surgeon came in 125, where a 350 ms pause was followed by his peremptory *yes*. The continuation of his quote in 126–127 remained in the reduced range Kay assigned to his speech, with peaks on *won't* and *breathe* of only 272 and 225 Hz respectively. But then his attitude turned to humor in 129–130, and Kay captured this lighter mood with higher peaks of 320 Hz on both *anyway* and *so*, with intervening laughter. The ultimate answer to the question she posed in 122 appeared in 130. It was uttered with a

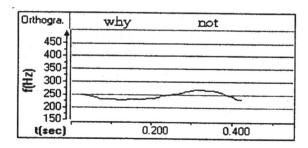

Figure 9.12 F0 in 130

varied contour that included a fall on *why* and a rise-fall on *not*, a combination that reflected the surgeon's more jocular attitude at this point, as shown in Figure 9.12.

We can turn now to something a little different, jumping to a point later in the conversation where Kay and Sue discussed the danger that might be involved in this operation. Kay suggested the following:

443.K ... Well,
444.   ... imagine this.
445.   .. I mean all those years you've been keeping yourself away from muggers,
446.   ... rapists,
447.   ... things like that,
448.   and then all at once,
449.   ... you die.
450.   ... Because you've got a nose op
451.S Choked on a piece of food.
452.K I mean that's a real ... sort of a ... disgusting way to go.

The climax of this little scenario came in 448–449. Figure 13 includes both intensity (top) and F0 (bottom) for this sequence.

448.   and then all at once,
449.   ... you= die=.

It is perhaps surprising that the highest F0, reaching 424 Hz, appeared in the word *all* in 448. The heart of this segment, however, was the threatening phrase *you die* in 449, where F0 in *die* reached no higher than 259 Hz. The emotion associated with *you die* was reflected in lowered, not raised pitch, reinforced by an ominous-sounding voice quality. But there were three other elements of prosody that added to this effect. One was the lengthening of both *you* and *die*, with *die* alone occupying 468 ms. Another was the

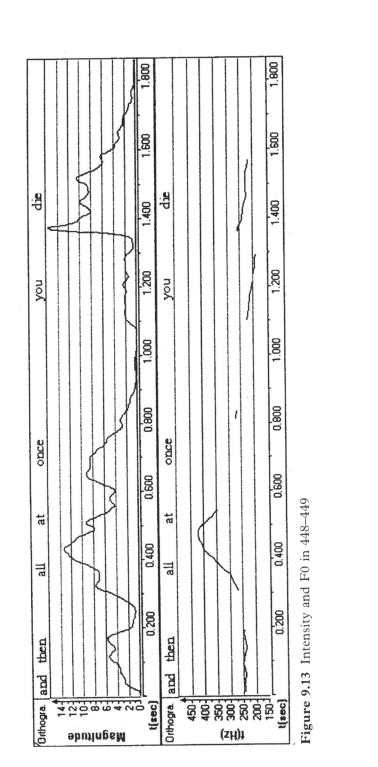

Figure 9.13 Intensity and F0 in 448–449

greater intensity of *die* that is visible in the upper part of Figure 9.13. A third was the falling contour that can be seen in both *you* and *die*, lending an air of inevitability to the dying event.

For an emotion of still another kind we can jump to a segment near the end of the conversation where Kay was describing her frustration with computers, specifically the tendency of her word processor to delete material against her wishes:

573.   ... Or .. when the paragraph goes ... off the page,
574.   when you're just trying to .. type in that ... little bit of information,
575.   and I'm screaming to Jim
576.   .. it just left.
577.   ... I didn't do it.
578.   ... I only wanted to put an A in there,
579.   instead of an E,
580.   ... and he keeps saying,
581.   ... you have .. you know .. you .. are the person in charge of this computer,
582.   .. and .. it only listens to whatever you punch in.

This sequence began with a restrained, matter-of-fact prosody, but then came the self-quote in 576–579, with the expanded range and raised baseline that are conspicuous in Figure 9.14:

576.   .. it just left.
577.   ... I didn't do it.
578.   ... I only wanted to put an A in there,
579.   instead of an E,

The peaks on *left, do* and *A*, were at 487, 466 and 411 Hz respectively. The baseline had a raised floor of 196 Hz during the word *there*.

Jim's quoted remarks in 581–582 provide an interesting contrast, with the F0 traced in Figure 9.15. The highest peak, 321 Hz, was reached in the third occurrence of *you* in 581.

581.K ... you have .. you know .. yóu= .. are the person in charge of this computer,
582.K .. and .. it only listens to whatever you punch in.

Noteworthy here is the steady rhythm at the end of 581, more visible in the graph of intensity in Figure 9.16, which is limited to the following words:

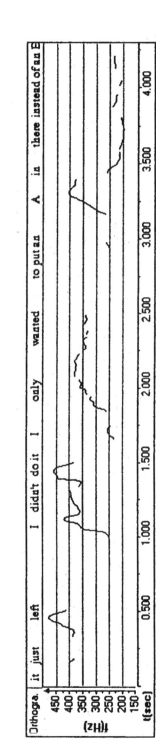

Figure 9.14 F0 on 576–579

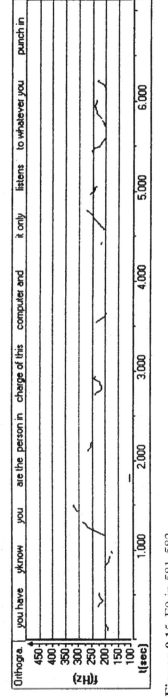

Figure 9.15 F0 in 581–582

the person in charge of this computer,

The accented syllables of *person, charge,* and *computer* were evenly spaced approximately 700 ms apart, as shown by the ticks.

In parallel fashion, the following words at the end of 582 were evenly spaced at approximately 350 ms, as can be seen in Figure 9.17:

you punch in.

By imitating Jim's speech in this way Kay conveyed his attitude of condescending instruction such as one might give a child: his careful explanation, one syllable at a time, of some elementary facts she ought to know.

To summarize, this attempt to discover a few of the ways prosody expresses emotions and attitudes in spontaneous conversational language has yielded the following observations. Over an intonation unit or longer segment it is important to examine F0 range, but it is often helpful to calculate it with respect to what I have called a prefinal baseline: the lowest F0 before a terminal fall. Matter-of-fact, uninvolved segments of speech are useful for establishing a reference range against which expanded ranges can be measured. An expanded range expresses heightened emotional involvement, but not the cause of that involvement. The content of what is being said can produce involvement in many ways, and the F0 range captures only the involvement itself. Among the open-ended factors that can stimulate involvement are the uptake of an emotionally charged new topic, the anticipation of a potentially life-changing experience, and frustration with recalcitrant equipment. Many conversations will have to be studied in this way before more general conclusions can be drawn.

An expanded range accompanied by a raised baseline is typical of quoted speech. On the other hand, negatively evaluated or discouraging speech may be quoted with a lowered baseline and a narrowed range. A rise-fall contour on a single element expresses localized involvement associated, for example, with elements that express either contrast or a subjective evaluation. There are numerous specific pitch contours that convey specific attitudes, but those attitudes are often difficult to categorize, and again they depend on the content of what is being said. They are expressed not only with patterns of F0, but also with patterned variations in intensity, timing, and voice quality. General points that were noticed here include a small amount of evidence that emotions and prosody are, at least in part, gradient and not categorical, and furthermore that emotions change significantly more slowly than the ideational content of

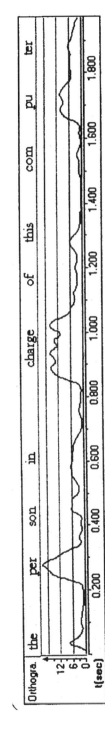

Figure 9.16 Intensity at the end of 581

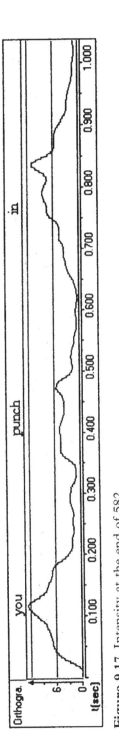

Figure 9.17 Intensity at the end of 582

language. Obviously this study has only scratched the surface, but I hope to have illustrated at least a few of the ways speakers use their voices to express their own and others' feelings.

Appendix

Conversation (Interview) between Sue and Kay:
videotaped and audiotaped at Rice University, 11/3/1983 (Chafe transcription)

1.S.	What I'd like to find out more about .. is .. your operation.
2.S.	... That you're having. {laugh}
3.K.	... My nose operation.
4.S.	Yes .. your nose operation.
5.S.	... You see I have a similar problem.
6.S.	... And I've been postponing doing something about it .. for a very long time.
7.S.	.. So tell me what you're having done and
8.S.	... what condition you're going to be in,
9.S.	.. when you're having it done.
10.K.	... Well,
11.K.	... maybe I should preface this thing
12.K.	why I want it done.
13.K.	... First of all,
14.K.	.. I want it for cosmetic reasons.
15.K.	... I'm sort of tired of everyone going like this to my nose.
16.K.	So I thought well,
17.K.	... I would get it ... cosmetically ... changed.
18.K.	And then someone told me that I had a problem;
19.K.	you see?
20.K.	... That was great.
21.K.	... My friend who's a nur–se said,
22.K.	... listen you've got a deviated septum.
23.S.	... {laugh}
24.K.	I said uch,
25.K.	... does that mean I can get my nose operated on?
26.K.	... Will someone else pay for it.
27.K.	... She said ... sure.
28.K.	... It's a medical problem.
29.K.	.. And they'll just
30.S.	Didn't you notice you had a deviated septum?
31.K.	... No–,

32.K.   I mean .. everything else is crooked and stuff,
33.K.   .. you can't even
34.S.   you couldn't brea–the through the side
35.S.   . . . one side of your nose?
36.K.   . . . No.
37.K.   . . . So I thought
38.K.   . . . I mean there are other things wro–ng with me,
39.K.   .. so I figured like well that was just . . . natural so,
40.K.   so . . . but I always wan–ted a nice nose.
41.K.   . . . So I . . . I had . . . uh . . . looked into investigated,
42.K.   . . . uh .. getting this thing fixed.
43.K.   . . . But it was a long time ago,
44.K.   .. so I couldn't do it.
45.K.   . . . And it was just . . . ti–me and,
46.K.   . . . money,
47.K.   and all that other stuff.
48.K.   . . . So– .. then I thought well,
49.K.   . . . it's about time I .. changed it.
50.K.   I got new insurance.
51.K.   . . . You see so I thought well,
52.K.   . . . and someone also this summer told me that,
53.K.   . . . um– . . . that he had .. the operation done.
54.K.   . . . And that .. you really should get it done,
55.K.   because you can brea–the better and all sorts of things .. so,
56.K.   . . . so when I went to the d . . . hospital this time,
57.K.   I just inquired and they said sure.
58.K.   . . . You've got a real problem.
59.K.   . . . {laugh} Let's just fix that nose up.
60.K.   . . . But I wanted
61.K.   .. you see then I had to figure out ho–w to get .. plastic
        surgery done it
62.K.   . . . also.
63.K.   So I said well I could trade .. art work,
64.K.   . . . uh .. {laugh} extra or I'd give money,
65.K.   . . . anything that once they were going to .. break my nose,
66.K.   . . . let's . . . do everything.
67.K.   . . . Why do it twice.
68.K.   . . . So um . . . he said he couldn't do plastic surgery.
69.K.   . . . So– . . . in the conversation with him,
70.K.   I just said .. well,
71.K.   . . . I mean I don't want to go pay somebody else,
72.K.   . . . a second time to break my nose again,

73.K.   ... to do this.
74.K.   And so he said well,
75.S.   ... Do they have to break your nose .. to correct your .. deviated septum?
76.K.   ... They may have to,
77.K.   they may no–t.
78.K.   ... But .. they do have to .. completely alter.
79.K.   ... Insi–de .. at least.
80.K.   ... They still have to change the whole shape.
81.K.   .. So I'm sure that they're going to do something .. pretty drastic so,
82.K.   ... uh– ... so I got arou–nd it by saying well,
83.K.   ... listen.
84.K.   ... Is it going to be straightened,
85.K.   ... like that and he said yeah.
86.K.   ... I said well what about this part.
87.K.   ... You say that you cou–ld ... file that down a little bit.
88.K.   He said well,
89.K.   .. okay.
90.K.   ... {laugh} And I said well the–n,
91.K.   ... if that's all straight,
92.K.   .. this is going to look really funny.
93.K.   ... Can you– ... like straighten that up.
94.K.   .. And so, ... he said well .. okay.
95.K.   And that's all I wanted done anyway.
96.K.   ... So far as plastic surgery's concerned.
97.K.   So he– ... did .. consent to it then so.
98.K.   ... I'm going to get this new nose.
99.S.   ... And what are .. are they going to put you to sleep when you have it done or,
100.S   ... do you have to be awake while it's being done?
101.K.   Well ... normally you're awake.
102.K.   ... A–nd ... if I understood it correctly,
103.K.   .. they're going to .. going to do it under .. general .. anesthetic.
104.K.   ... So that's okay–.
105.K.   ... So I'll be aslee–p.
106.K.   ... But .. uh– my friend,
107.K.   MA says that ... that all the doctors when they get their noses fixed,
108.K.   or corrected then
109.K.   ... they want to be put to sleep you see.

110.K. ... {laugh} But they tell these patients,

111.K. this is nothing.

112.S. {laugh}

113.K. ... Except that you see this hammer,

114.K. ... so,

115.K. ... whacking your face,

116.K. .. and that's sort of traumatic.

117.K. ... So MA told me not to get it done under uh .. local.

118.K. ... Cause it will hurt.

119.K. ... And uh– ... so?

120.S. ... And how long afterwards are you going to ... be .. black and blue or–

121.K. I don't know.

122.K. ... I asked him if I could teach on ... the following Monday.

123.K. .. Since the operation's on Thursday.

124.K. .. Would I be okay.

125.K. ... A–nd he said ... yes.

126.K. ... But he said you won't be able to brea–the,

127.K. .. out of your nose.

128.K. ... So– .. but he said

129.K. ... uh ... you haven't been able to breathe anyway {laugh} so–

130.K. ... why not.

131.S. ... How long have you not been able to breathe out of

132.S. ... is it is it the–

133.S. ... which side of the nose ... can't you breathe out of?

134.K. This side.

135.S. ... Out of your right side.

136.K. Mhm?

137.K. ... It's just collapsed.

138.K. ... I mean I just ... always thought that that's ... the way people .. breathed .. you know.

139.K. .. Sort of less

140.K. ... just .. use your mouth a lot.

141.K. ... To breathe.

142.S. {laugh} Uh huh yeah right.

143.K. {laugh} Right.

144.K. .. So ... I think it's uh .. the problem they say is that you get a lot of colds.

145.K. ... And stuff like that.

146.K. .. And,

147.K. ... and uh I'm tired of colds.

148.K. And in fact I said if .. this doesn't work,
149.K. ... I want my tonsils out.
150.K. ... If that doesn't work,
151.K. .. maybe a big pipe.
152.S. {laugh} Just
153.K. ... That's right.
154.S. Irrigation system.
155.K. In fact I was so desperate to g get rid of colds and,
156.K. ... coughing,
157.K. and all that other stuff,
158.K. that I even went in for .. new allergy tests.
159.K. ... So on the same da–y,
160.K. .. that I scheduled my operation I had ... sixty-two shots.
161.K. .. Up my arm,
162.K. ... to see what I was allergic to and
163.K. .... you know I just really want to breathe.
164.S. ... Did they tell you what you were allergic to?
165.K. ... All sorts of stuff.
166.S. Have you gotten–
167.K. .. Yes I'm
168.K. ... but I'm a good .. allergy patient.
169.S. ... They can treat ... every one of the allergies huh.
170.K. Yes.
171.K. After having all these diseases,
172.K. ... you see,
173.K. .. tuberculosis,
174.K. .. all that other stuff,
175.K. they said
176.K. ... that you're lucky.
177.K. ... {laugh} Because you can be treated,
178.K. and that's nice.
179.K. ... I mean the fact that I can get shots,
180.K. .. and that I don't have a problem,
181.K. ... is sort of nice.
182.K. ... And my allergists,
183.K. .. gave up on me.
184.K. .. Back in Pittsburgh.
185.K. .. Because they can't do anything anymore.
186.K. ... All these .. molds,
187.K. .. and mildews,
188.K. and stuff,
189.K. ... so .. if I get my allergies taken care of,

190.K. ... get my nose fixed,
191.K. ... keep my tonsils .. I think,
192.K. ... I think life can be okay. {laugh}
193.K. ... And then maybe,
194.S. This is going to be a big year.
195.K. ... also get a .. good nose,
196.K. yeah.
197.K. ... I am going to look .. black and blue though.
198.K. ... When I come out of this operation.
199.S. Probably pretty swollen?
200.S. ... All ... through
201.K. That's right.
202.K. ... So I have my sunglasses ready.
203.S. ... {laugh} Big ones that come
204.K. Yes.
205.K. ... But I s–m sort of
206.K. ... I think I'm I'm ready for this operation,
207.K. cause I nee–d like three days in the hospital for rest,
208.K. ... read cheap novels,
209.K. ... stuff like that.
210.K. ... So I'm up for ... convalescing,
211.K. ... I won't give my phone number out,
212.S. What kind of cheap novels are you going to read.
213.S. .. Harlequin romances or something like that to
214.K. .. Who knows
215.K. .. I think the Nurses.
216.S. .. {laugh} The Nurses?
217.K. {laugh} Yeah.
218.K. ... Something indefinitely general,
219.S. In between soap operas on television?
220.K. Well I don't like those soap operas.
221.K. So I could
222.K. .. I don't
223.K. .. I like reading better than watching TV I think.
224.K. ... So I .. I would rather read something like General Hospital but in
225.K. ... besides they can be more graphic in those books.
226.S. Big print and
227.S. ... yes.
228.K. ... They don't really ... uh do all that stuff.
229.K. .. So.
230.K. .. Besides you have to wait too long.

231.K. ... This way I can ... jump over paragraphs you see,
232.K. and get to the real good stuff.
233.S. Find out what happens .. to
234.S. ... yeah.
235.K. ... Instead of having to wait until tomorrow.
236.K. ... To get the information.
237.S. ... So how long have you had this.
238.S. .. Has it been since you were a kid?
239.K. ... I don't know.
240.K ... I ... I swear it was when my brother,
241.K. Jeff,
242.K. .. pushed me out of his .. bunkbeds,
243.K. .. when we were about ... two,
244.K. and .. three.
245.K. ... You see.
246.K. ... I think I broke my nose then but
247.K. ... my mother
248.K. ... maybe it's child abuse.
249.S. .. Child abuse? {laugh}
250.K. ... I don't know,
251.S. ... Let's make this statement on ... {laugh} TV right now.
252.K. ... That's right.
253.K. .. So—
254.S. .. Broker is the victim of child abruse {laugh} abuse.
255.K. ... That's right.
256.K. .. I mean I wish I could just go in and get a .. total .. body .. overhaul.
257.K. ... I mean I wish you could go in for sort of things like that but
258.K. ... you have to be—,
259.K. ... have aesthetic reasons.
260.K. .. They ask that instead of saying I don't like it,
261.K. ... it seems to me that's enough.
262.K. ... I don't like my ankles,
263.K. .. let's cut off,
264.K. ... a few inches,
265.S. ... {laugh} put in some new ones.
266.K. ... That's right.
267.K. ... But now you have to have really good reasons,
268.K. .. so luckily with my nose,
269.K. ... I've got a great reason.
270.K. ... It happens to be ... uh ... you know physical.
271.K. ... But it luckily it fits in there .. you see,

272.S. . . . Yeah I was always disappointed,
273.S. I was in an . . automobile accident,
274.S. about eight years ago,
275.S. and . . smashed . . . my mouth.
276.S. . . . And . . . when I was taken to the hospital,
277.S. I didn't really realize what state I was in.
278.S. And the . . plastic surgeon came in and,
279.S. . . completely reconstructed . . . my bottom lip.
280.S. . . But had I known what he was doing,
281.S. I would have asked to see . . a book . . of mouths first,
282.S. and pick out a new one.
283.S. I {laugh} . . was tired of my old one.
284.K. . . . I hadn't thought of it like that,
285.K. . . . well . . . I . . it's a good thing I don't like my nose.
286.K. . . . You see?
287.S. . . . I think your nose is perfectly fine.
288.K. . . . It's because you don't own it.
289.K. . . . You don't have to look at it all the time.
290.K. . . . No but it's all crooked,
291.K. and stuff like that,
292.K. . . . and it goes up,
293.K. . . and . . I mean I'm thinking . . ahead.
294.K. . . When I'm forty,
295.S. You mean it's not going to go up any more?
296.K. . . . That's right,
297.K. it's going to come down,
298.K. . . . a little bit,
299.K. . . . you see then I don't have to be a cute . . forty-year-old.
300.K. . . . In a few years.
301.K. . . You see it's going to be like
302.S. Well this is going to alter your appearance altogether.
303.K. . . It's going to . . alter my whole outlook on life.
304.S. Your demeanor and presence and everything.
305.K. . . That's right.
306.K. . . . That's right.
307.K. You never know.
308.K. . . . Dates,
309.S. Personality too,
310.K. and things like that right.
311.S. . . . Who knows.
312.K. . . . Maybe . . more . . higher enrollments,
313.S. . . . Higher enrollment in your classes,

314.K. ... They're going to come in and say look at that nose.
315.K. ... Anyway,
316.K. ... I'm sort of excited about this.
317.K. ... Cause I've waited a long time.
318.S. ... There's some guy,
319.S. we .. we heard a story a couple of weeks ago,
320.S. ... um ... of this ... this family.
321.S. And there was a young child in the family.
322.S. A young boy.
323.S. And he was .. he was ... having .. tremendous problems in school,
324.S. .. he was a very difficult child,
325.S .. he was .. too active,
326.S. and he was always getting in trouble and,
327.S. ... and um– ... a long lost relative .. came ... into this family,
328.S. .. and who had been to India.
329.S. .. And studied with some of the .. Eastern mystics and,
330.S. .. so he suggested to this child that he stuff cotton up the right ... side of his nose.
331.S. ... And so they stuffed cotton up the right side of his nose.
332.S. ... And {laugh} his personality completely changed.
333.S. He became this very passive,
334.S. ... nice,
335.S. docile,
336.S. child {laugh},
337.K. Yeah he had to writhe on the floor for a while,
338.K. .. he couldn't breathe.
339.K. ... {laugh} Good God.
340.K. ... Well well I as a kid,
341.K. .. I used to tape my nose down though.
342.K. ... Every night,
343.K. I would get this masking tape,
344.K. and I would ... put this ... tape on you see,
345.S. Was that .. to change the shape of it?
346.S. To .. flatten out your
347.K. That's right.
348.K. I thought it would hold it down.
349.K. ... Because everybody would go like this you know,
350.K. and say oh look at that cute .. Broker nose.
351.K. .. Well ... they you know like ... they
352.K. I wanted words like ... beautiful.
353.K. ... Gorgeous.

354.K. ... Great,

355.K. not cute,

356.S. Instead of .. cute,

357.K. ... So I I've learned right off that I've got to get a new nose.

358.K. ... But I would last in bed for about ... ten minutes.

359.K. ... With this tape.

360.K. .. You see and then I'd

361.S. Then breathing became more important.

362.K. Rip it off.

363.K. ... I'm surprised I just didn't have little welts going up my nose.

364.K. ... Uh but ... I just couldn't stand it so,

365.K. ... you can see I .. I've thought about this .. for a while.

366.K. ... I mean even though my mother complains,

367.K. and says it's because I had to blow my nose as a child,

368.K. ... my first reaction is why,

369.K. .. you see?

370.K. ... And ... and their ... their response to me blowing my nose was,

371.K. ... uh– ... stop blowing it.

372.K. ... Just stop.

373.K. ... It's all in your head.

374.K. ... Course then I'd ... try,

375.K. and I'd sort of be this

376.S. {laugh} Kid with the runny nose,

377.K. ... That's right.

378.K. ... That's right.

379.K. And I would have to apologize for blowing my nose,

380.K. and I kept thinking like ... oh– I'm mentally deficient,

381.K. because I ... I'm blowing my nose.

382.K. ... I mean I know it sounds like such a stupid subject,

383.K. but those sort of things really ... sort of last,

384.K. you see,

385.K. long enough,

386.S. They really stay with you,

387.S. that's ... yeah.

388.K. That's right.

389.K. Long enough for me just to ... out of the blue,

390.K. ... to have someone say,

391.K. ... well I had my nose operated on.

392.K. ... Why–.

393.K. .. You know.

394.K. ... It was because I had a deviated septum,
395.K. and then I just
396.K. ... it sort of fired.
397.K. .. It rekindled all that enthusiasm and.
398.K. .. Here I am.
399.S. ... Do you know what they have to do with a deviated septum?
400.S. .. Do they have to reconnect,
401.S. .. do they ... move
402.S. .. it's cartilage isn't it?
403.S. That they have to move over,
404.S. so that it
405.S. .. do they have to re–connect that .. to something?
406.S. ... That it has .. torn away from or s?
407.S. ... Do you know what they are doing?
408.K. ... Well,
409.K. .. it seems to me,
410.K. ... and I must be .. totally,
411.K. .. I'm hoping I'm wrong,
412.K. .. but I think they just take these poles,
413.K. .. and they just sort of ... make {laugh}
414.S. {laugh} ... They violently knock your
415.K. {laugh} ... That's right.
416.K. I think they're
417.K. ... basically it's like breaking inside,
418.K. .. I think.
419.K. ... Now,
420.K. ... and the reason I don't kn
421.S. But how do they reset it again.
422.K. ... Well,
423.K. ... they pack it.
424.S. ... Oh pack it.
425.K. They pack it and it resets.
426.K. ... And so it's like
427.S. So that's why you can't breathe,
428.S. until they take out the packing.
429.K. That's right.
430.K. .. You see so that's the only problem I foresee is that I
431.S. You can't brea–the for,
432.S. you have to breathe through your nose.
433.S. Right.
434.K. And ... and the thing is,

435.K. is if you choke on food,
436.K. I mean you could die.
437.K. ... Yeah.
438.K. ... In all these years,
439.S. Yes.
440.S. ... There's danger involved in this operation.
441.K. That's right.
442.S. High risk.
443.K. ... Well,
444.K. ... imagine this.
445.K. .. I mean all those years you've been keeping yourself away
from muggers,
446.K. ... rapists,
447.K. ... things like that,
448.K. and then all at once,
449.K. ... you die.
450.K. ... Because you've got a nose op
451.S. Choked on a piece of food.
452.K. I mean that's a real ... sort of a ... disgusting way to go.
453.S. You ought to be very careful .. for a period of time.
454.K. I know.
455.K. And it's Mu–rphy's law.
456.K. I know that this could possible happen,
457.S. On chocolate mousse,
458.S. or something like that {laugh}.
459.K. That's right.
460.K. And .. besides I .. can't taste anything,
461.K. So ... at least if I
462.K. .. I can go to cheap restaurants now,
463.K. ... because I can't taste anything.
464.K. .. I could be eating dogmeat,
465.K. .. and it wouldn't matter,
466.K. ... because .. I can't taste it.
467.S. ... Mm .. be an economical .. week.
468.K. .. That's right.
469.K. ... I .. I mean it may pay for my operation {laugh},
470.K. ... So ... I hope this .. this .. this better be a good nose,
471.K. .. that's all I can say.
472.S. ... Yeah,
473.S. maybe you should look at a .. book of noses.
474.S. .. Or something.
475.S. .. Before you go in.

476.K. No he doesn't want me to do that,

477.S. He doesn't want you to.

478.K. ... Because then he's going to feel like he's doing plastic surgery.

479.K. ... You see?

480.K. ... I mean I had a nose.

481.K. .. I mean I could draw him a nose.

482.K. ... That I would want.

483.K. ... But .. then I would may have to get other things done too.

484.K. ... I mean I do think that ... that the curve and things of your nose,

485.K. .. and it sort of goes with the rest of it.

486.K. ... Like I .. if I .. had a real pointy nose,

487.K. I'd have to have half my chin taken off.

488.K. ... You see,

489.K. .. or something like that.

490.K. ... So I can't be real radical about this,

491.K. .. I don't want someone looking at me and saying,

492.K. ... oh what's wrong with you.

493.K. ... You see.

494.K. .. I just don't want them to say what a cute nose.

495.K. ... In fact I'd like them to drop the subject. {laugh}

496.S. ... Just not even to notice your nose anymore?

497.K. That's right.

498.K. ... Let's .. just forget it.

499.K. ... So .... I don't know,

500.K. ... and that's about the only operation I've had.

501.K. ... I mean other than ... sort of .. foot reconstruction.

502.K ... And .. but ... but that was a real physical problem.

503.K. ... So this is the first time.

504.K. .. And and and at least this time when people say

505.K. ... why are you getting your nose fixed,

506.K. .. as a female,

507.K. they already think that it's because you want ... a nice nose you see.

508.K. ... Well .. they're right.

509.K ... But ... {laugh} but ... but I'm not going to admit to that,

510.K. ... Yeah.

511.K. ... So I immediately say,

512.S. ... I have a deviated septum.

513.K. ... Ah,

514.K. I can't breathe.

515.K. I haven't been able to breathe for years.
516.K. ... They say ah,
517.K. .. that's a shame.
518.K. ... See so,
519.K. ... it's nice.
520.K. ... And maybe it's Catholic guilt.
521.K. ... Something like that.
522.S. ... It's going to be a new experience.
523.S. ... Probably for the first time in your memory,
524.S. ... you'll be able to breathe out of both ... nostrils.
525.K. ... Yeah I was hoping that my voice was going to change.
526.K. Like I would go really lo–w or something.
527.K. ... That it would ... that I would sou–nd more like .. the way I
       hear it.
528.K. .. But ... uh .. after talking to uh Jim and
529.K. ... he just said forget it.
530.K. ... That's not where ... voice comes from or whatever.
531.K. ... Although he may be wrong.
532.K. ... See.
533.K. ... I mean maybe he's wrong.
534.S. ... Hey if you if these .. Eastern mystics are right,
535.S. ... you see what they figure is,
536.S. .. it's right and left brain .. kind of stuff.
537.S. .. so that ... the .. air that goes in your right nostril controls
       ... your left ... brain thinking.
538.S. ... Which is your more analytical .. intellectual kind of stuff?
539.S. ... And .. the air that goes in– ... the left side controls .. your
       right brain thinking.
540.K. ... So the more your artistic side.
541.S. ... Yeah.
542.K. ... Oh oh.
543.S. ... So this way your .. intellectual side is .. going to .. surface
       .. more.
544.S. ... Right?
545.K. ... {laugh} Oh God ... I'll be a renaissance professor
546.S. You're going to be a renaissance professor of art.
547.K. That's right.
548.K. .. You see now that I only have a right brain,
549.K. ... basically because I'm not using the left one right?
550.K. ... A–nd ... well have you ever read the book .. Drawing on
       the .. Right Side of the Brain?
551.S. A new dimension.

552.S. . . . Uh uh.

553.K. . . Well,

554.K. . . . it's an okay book,

555.K. . . . I mean I wouldn't use it,

556.K. . . uh–,

557.K. . . . it's nice for . . evening reading.

558.K. . . Sometimes but

559.K. . . . so I use my right hand.

560.K. . . . You see.

561.K. . . . And they do feel that . . you could . . . use . . y the right side of your brain . . . better.

562.K. . . . A–nd uh– . . . so this . . way,

563.K. maybe I'll learn how to use a computer now.

564.K. . . . Maybe it will all make sense.

565.S. Right it will open up a whole new wor . . . {laugh} world to you.

566.K. Instead of saying

567.K. . . bashing in there

568.K. . . hey . . you in there.

569.K. . . . send up {laugh} that information.

570.K. . . . Or stop saying things like doesn't compute,

571.K. or whatever you know,

572.S. . . . You'll invent the perfect one.

573.K. . . . Or . . when the paragraph goes . . . off the page,

574.K. when you're just trying to . . type in that . . . little bit of information,

575.K. and I'm screaming to Jim

576.K. . . it just left.

577.K. . . . I didn't do it.

578.K. . . . I only wanted to put an A in there,

579.K. instead of an E,

580.K. . . . and he keeps saying,

581.K. . . . you have . . you know . . you– . . are the person in charge of this computer,

582.K. . . and . . it only listens to whatever you punch in.

583.K. . . . But . . . I kno–w . . . that

584.S. It has a mind of its own?

585.K. That's right.

586.K. . . So maybe if I get . . the– left side working I'll

587.K. . . . I won't have to be bashing on the side of the computer again.

588.S. You won't have to be so

589.K. Violent with it.
590.S. Yes.
591.S. Violent with it.
592.K. ... Or or when in lithography it's
593.K. .. I won't say well it's magic,
594.K. .. while I'm teaching it.
595.K. ... You see.
596.K. ... Not that it's chemistry,
597.K. .. that it's magic.
598.K. ... So.
599.K. ... But if it doesn't work I'll ... {laugh} stuff the right side of
      my ... of my nose with stuff.
600.K. .. Okay?
601.K. ... So,
602.S. ... You would just take it out at night to sleep.
603.K. ... That's right.
604.S. ... I think we've finished.
605.K. Okay.
606.S. Let's call it 'The End.'

References

1. Bezooyen, Renee van (1984) *Characteristics and Recognizability of Vocal Expressions of Emotion.* Dordrecht: Foris Publications.
2. Chafe, Wallace (1994) *Discourse, Consciousness, and Time: The Flow and Displacement of Conscious Experience in Speaking and Writing.* Chicago: University of Chicago Press.
3. Chafe, Wallace (2000) The interplay of prosodic and segmental sounds in the expression of thoughts. In *Proceedings of the 23rd Annual Meeting of the Berkeley Linguistics Society, 1997,* ed. by Matthew L. Juge and Jeri L. Moxley, Berkeley: Berkeley Linguistics Society, 389–401.
4. Goldbeck, Thomas, Tolkmitt, Frank and Scherer, Klaus R. (1988) Experimental studies on vocal affect communication. In *Facets of Emotion: Recent Research,* ed. by Klaus R. Scherer, Hillsdale, NJ: Lawrence Erlbaum, 119–137.

10

Phasal Analysis within Communication Linguistics: Two Contrastive Discourses

Michael Gregory

Communication linguistics

The analyses presented here of a short story by Ernest Hemingway ('The Sea Change') and of part of the Sue–Kay interview conversation text are in terms of the particular development of systemic-functional linguistics I worked on with Karen Malcolm, Elissa Asp and others in the Linguistics and Stylistics section of the Graduate Programme in English at York University, Toronto. Insights from cognitive-stratificational linguistics are incorporated into a framework which has a special emphasis on the analysis of discourse, the linguistic exchange of message(s), seen as the most important aspect of the general human social phenomenon of communication. The analysis of discourse is considered the Alpha and Omega of descriptive linguistics, and the emerging framework is appropriately, if uninterestingly, called *communication linguistics*.

It had its origins not only in my early and continuing work on intralinguistic varieties, grammatical description and stylistics (see Enkvist, Spencer and Gregory 1964; Gregory 1965, 1967, 1972, 1974, 1978, 1982a; Gregory and Carroll 1978) but also, and more particularly, in the linguistic study of theatre I began in 1979–1980 (Gregory 1981/1982). There the concept of discourse *phase* was introduced. It was developed in the paper Malcolm and I wrote in 1981 on the spoken discourse of children as manifested in a video-taped situation (Gregory and Malcolm 1981). In this paper the related concept of *transition* was introduced and phase, as a micro-diatypic (micro-registerial in Halliday's terms) realization, was related, not necessarily isomorphically, to the nature of dynamic shifts in the *generic situation* of the language event. Both Malcolm and I have continued to develop and explicate the framework in papers presented to the *Ninth* and *Tenth International Systemic Workshops*, and the 1982 and 1983 meetings of the Linguistic Association of Canada and the United States, and of the Michigan Linguistic Society (Gregory 1982b, 1983, 1984a, 1984b; Malcolm 1983, 1984a, 1984b). Malcolm applied the framework to the conversational interchange, audio- and video-recorded, of both children and young adults (Malcolm 1985) and Asp has applied it to the Dylan Thomas prose piece 'Memories of Christmas' (Asp 1983 and 1984). She then investigated the gnostological and predicational nature of the phenomenon traditionally known as metaphor in data from both literary and non-literary texts (Asp 1985, 1992). Lynne Young has applied it to introductory university lectures in biology and has then extended it to include university lectures in other disciplines (see Young 1984, 1987/1988).

Theoretical perspective

Briefly, our theoretical perspective for the analysis of discourse is as follows: language is seen from a dual perspective, as activity and as code (see Figure 10.1). Seeing language as activity is the *dynamic* perspective; language is regarded as one type of behaviour in the general social sciences sense of the term: 'the actions and reactions of persons and things under specified conditions' (*The American Heritage Dictionary*). In other words, behaviour is manifested in situation. So language activity, a type of intentionally communicative behaviour, can be described in terms of three *planes of experience*: *situation*, *discourse* and *manifestation*.

Situation is, to use a current expression, where we are coming from as encoders in communication and to which we have ultimate interpretive recourse as decoders. It is the instantial referential realm: with an *ideational* component (see Halliday 1973, 1978; Gregory 1980), the real or imaginary persons, things, the incidents and states they're involved in; and an *interpersonal* component, their interactional interests, intents and attitudes. Such components are the stuff of the communicative impetus, the source of *messages*. In previous work within this framework the systemic tradition of using situation as the locus of generalization was followed. In the light of discussions at the *Second Rice Symposium on Linguistics and Semiotics* this has been changed, and situation is more appropriately viewed as a plane

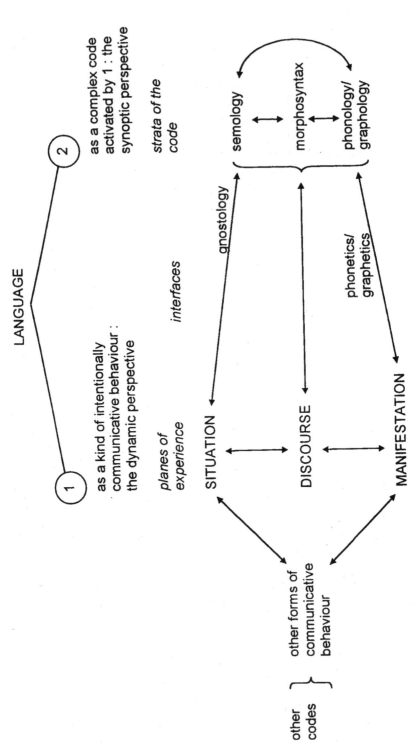

Figure 10.1 Communication linguistics: perspectives, planes of experience, strata of the code.

of experience which caters for the instantial aspect of 'content substance' in Hjelmslev's terms. Generalizations, abstractions, are now assigned to the *gnostology*, the message interface between situation and code in which both instantial and codal matters of our knowing are related. It is clearly the *locus* for knowledge taxonomies (see Lockwood 1972/83:Chapter 5) and the 'base' predications associated with them (cf. Johannesson 1980 in which propositions are seen as part of semological networks, and whose semological stratum embraces the gnostological). It is also the domain of encoders' and decoders' relevant general and specific message potential, message creating environments, the macro- and the micro-environments for communication. These are called respectively, the communicating community context (CCC) and the *generic situation* (GS). The CCC is described along dimensions of *temporal, geographical, social* (including the ideological and political) and *individual provenances*. This macro-environment places the inter-communicators as regards when in human history they are communicating, where they are communicators, in what sociopolitical-economic system they are communicating, who they are as communicating persons. The GS, the micro-environment, is describable according to the *experience, medium, personal* and *functional relationships* of the intercommunicators: what aspect(s) of real or imaginary life are they communicating; how they are communicating (language or some other communicative code and, if language, spoken or written and so on); who they are to each other as inter-communicators in terms of relationships such as familiarity and power; and why they are communicating. The CCC construct generalizes, and the GS particularizes the knowledge that is relevant to the understanding of how messages have their origin, are transmitted, and more or less received and interpreted. Of course, caution is necessary in the use of the term 'message'. Minimally distinguishable are the addressers' message, the message received by the addressee, and what might be called the 'viable' message, those meanings which are retrievable by third parties who share the code and a generalized, relevant situational knowledge. The third is the one that most appropriately concerns the discourse analyst.

For a message to be transmitted (i.e. encoded, manifested, decoded) a code has to be activated and that code not only transmits ideational and interpersonal components of message, it also contributes *textual* or discoursal meaning. This is an instance of organizational meaning in the wider communicative sense. All means of communication contribute meaning by way of their organizational potential. This is one reason (the recognition of discourse as process is another) why we cannot see situation and language in any crude deterministic way. As Angus McIntosh put it (1965), sometimes situation is a dog which wags a linguistic tail; sometimes language is a dog which wags a situational tail. The relationship is mutual, reciprocal, dialectical rather than deterministic. A text is a component in its own context of situation (Firth 1957).

The study of the linguistic code is the *synoptic* perspective on language. Here we are concerned with modelling the linguistic resources of a speech community, the ideational, interpersonal and textual resources which allow the speakers of a language to discourse: that is, to encode, manifest and decode meanings by way of a language. As in most current models the code is seen as tri-stratally organized in a realizatory cycle (see Halliday 1979): *semology* (a language's 'meaning' resources), realized by *morphosyntax* (its 'wordings') realized by *phonology/graphology* (its ' soundings' or 'signings'). The reasons why we depart from the more orthodox systemic labels for the strata (or 'levels' as they used to be called) I have stated elsewhere (Gregory 1984a).

Discourse, the activation of the code in situation, is manifested in either those audible sound waves we call speech sounds or those visible marks on a surface we recognize as writing or print. What are manifested are instances of message realizing discourse, stretches of linguistic activity (i.e. codal activations) which are acceptable as more or less communicative wholes. The more usual systemic term *text* is reserved for the physical records of linguistic exchanges of meaning.

In Figure 10.1 manifestation is connected, by way of other forms of communicative behaviour and their codes, to situation. This is a reminder that language is not the only means by which meanings are manifested and exchanged in communication situations.

In this framework the planes of experience of language as activity and the strata of the language as code are intimately interrelated. This is not a competence-performance dichotomy but a code *and* behaviour perspective. Discourse, for example, is not only essentially activity, and instantial: it is also, to the extent that it is encoded and decoded, transitionally codal for the interlocuters even if its codality escapes description and prediction.

The planes and the strata are also distinguished, however, because my collaborators and I are attempting to avoid linguocentricity, particularly the 'grammar'-centricity of the last 25 years. As our prime interest is in discourse as the linguistic exchange of meanings in context we want a framework which can, at least potentially, relate language communication to other forms of communication which manifest messages in situation, so that the statements we make in linguistics reflect on communication as a general human social characteristic which is best viewed as regards both its dynamic and synoptic features and the relationship between them.

Phase

The key construct for the analysis of a particular discourse is that of *phase* (see Gregory 1981/1982, 1984a, 1984b; Gregory and Malcolm 1981; Malcolm 1983, 1984a, 1984b; Asp 1983; Young 1984). It is a construct which relates language activity which is dynamic to the synoptic language code. Phase characterizes stretches within discourse (which may be discontinuously realized in text) exhibiting their own significant and distinctive consistency and congruity in the selections that have been made from the language's codal resources: its semological, morphosyntactic and phonological resources for encoding and decoding ideational, interpersonal and textual meaning (see Halliday 1973, 1978).

An account of the particular descriptive procedure used in the study of these discourses will serve to clarify how the phasal analysis part of the framework operates in discourse description.

The text is recorded on filing cards, one sentence per card. The structure of each is morphosyntactically analysed at the ranks of sentence, clause and group. The analysis is recorded as a tree diagram. A systemic feature description is retrievable from the structural analysis.

Why these three units? The sentence is important because its obligatory structural element (the Propositional element realized by independent clauses) and the optional Link, Attitudinal, Topic and Vocative elements allow the user not only to realize a semological proposition but also to link it to previous discourse, and to attitudinalize it, topicalize and assign its relevance to an interlocuter (see Gregory 1983, 1984b). The clause in English is, of course, crucial. When independent it realizes a semological *proposition* which is simultaneously a *predication* (a process and attendant role(s)/a predicate and its argument(s)) realized by the morphosyntactic *transitivity* system, a *speech function* (statement, question, command, etc.) typically realized by the *mood* system, and a *message organization* with its focus (message starting point) realized by *theme*, and with points of *prominence* (message highlights) realized by marked theme (preposed or predicated) and/or by the phonologically realized *new* in the tone group or groups which realize it. Dependent clauses, with the notable exception of a class used in reported speech, lack speech-function mood contrasts, and realize semological predications, not propositions. They do, however, have their points of focus and prominence.

Groups (phrases) are important because they are the typical morphosyntactic locus of conceptual realization, of our cognitive segmentation of experience. Nominal groups realize the participants and referents for the discourse and are also the frequent realizatory source of many identificatory, classificatory and attributive relations, sometimes by way of action and mental predications (e.g. *the broken window, the forgotten regiment*). Prepositional groups are frequent realizations of temporal and spatial locational information; verbal groups of different types of process and their related aspectual, modal and temporal features. If the texts under examination were in a highly inflected language, or by an author such as Gerard Manley Hopkins or James Joyce, then the structural analysis would be richer if it was consistently extended to the word rank, but that has not yet been found necessary in the description of discourse in contemporary English made within the framework.

On the syntactic diagram, the semological information (roles, process types, speech functions, focus and prominence) are imposed for each proposition and predication, indicating non-isomorphism where this is necessary. The card is also used to record inter-sentential discourse information: the membership of items in event, locational and attitudinal chains, and matters of ellipsis, substitution and endophoric, exophoric and paraphoric reference (see Halliday and Hasan 1976). Where and when appropriate, phonological and phonetic information can be added at the bottom; Figure 10.2 is an example of a card from the Hemingway analysis.

This tri-functional information (ideational, interpersonal and textual) is the basis for the phasal analysis. The information is also multi-stratal to ensure renewal of connection, but that which is semological is considered most important because it is the semantically richest stratum of the code.

It has already been pointed out that phase characterizes those stretches of text in which there is a significant measure of consistency and congruity in what is being selected from each of the three metafunctional resources of the language. The problem arises as to how to judge 'significance'. The conduct of the analysis at different degrees of delicacy (see Halliday 1961) is an attempt to alleviate this problem. Judgements can be checked and rechecked as the analyst

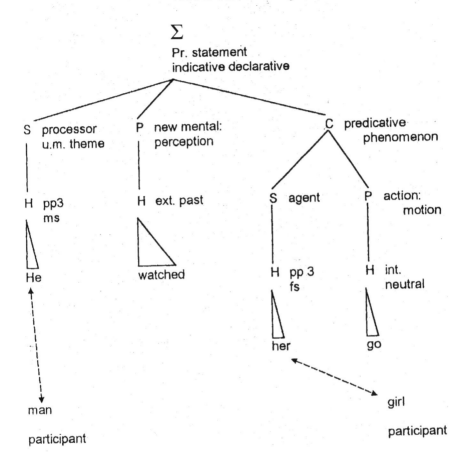

Figure 10.2 Description card

increases or decreases detail. What are termed *transitions* in and out of phases are indicated by a marked change in choice from one or more functional components or a backward and forward functional relevance.

Because of its tri-functional basis, phase can be thought of as a very delicate statement of *register* (see Gregory and Malcolm 1981). However I think it best to reserve register for Halliday's more abstract use of the term as 'the configuration of semantic resources that the members of a culture typically associate with a "situation type"' (Halliday 1978:111; the term 'situation type' is close to what here is called generic situation). Phase and transition are then free to be used to capture the dynamic instantiation of micro-registerial choices in a particular discourse (see Gregory 1984a).

The point has to be made that this framework does not recognize any dichotomous relationship between micro- and macro-analysis, quite the contrary. It is not a question of micro- or macro-analysis; it is a matter of micro- and macro-analysis. To preserve viability there has to be a renewal of connection between any macro-statement and the micro-analysis, and the micro-analysis is most fruitfully conducted if it keeps an eye on the questions macro-analysis tries to answer.

Furthermore, phase is quite deliberately presented as a 'soft' rather than a 'hard' category. It is itself non-codal, though based on codal information; it is non-predictive, a descriptive strategy with which to map the realization of message on the discourse plane of experience; it is a heuristic to find out what happens in the activation of code in situation. As has been noted, it is used in analysis with 'staged' delicacy. Varying degrees of differentiating detail are employed in order to catch measures of similarity and dissimilarity amongst different parts of the instance of discourse. So the discourse is characterized in its particularity and its generality.

In 'Text semantics and clause grammar', Halliday (1981) presented the independent clause as itself a type of mini-discourse having a significant measure of ideational, interpersonal and textual completeness. With this I am in accord, and so the analysis' maximum delicacy does not usually recognize as a phase or subphase a stretch of language smaller than the independent clause. Such stretches are able to be handled within the codal description.

A comprehensive phasal analysis of 'The Sea Change'

In the least delicate description of Hemingway's 'The Sea Change', the following four phases, discontinuously realized, are distinguished on the basis of their ideational, interpersonal and textual inner-consistency: the Man–Girl Conversation Phase (M in Figure 10.3); the Narrative Phase of events and participants in the bar (N); the Barman–Client Phase (B) and the Phil–Barman Conversation Phase (P). There are 176 syntactic sentences in the text: two of these primary phases account for the discourse meaning of 159 of them. The Man–Girl Conversation is realized by 117 sentences and indeed can be read and decoded itself as a story, and the Narrative Phase by 42 (the Barman–Client Conversation by 9, and Phil and the Barman by 8). At this degree of generalization the phases are more instantiations of register than of micro-register. They correlate with reasonably distinct generic situations and so reflect reasonably major distinctions in the experience, medium, personal and functional

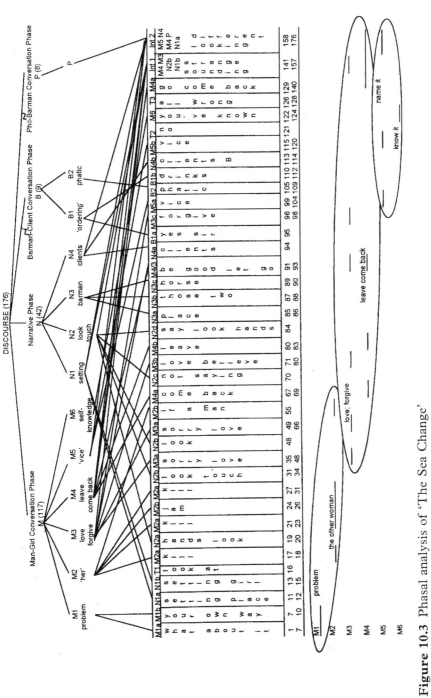

Figure 10.3 Phasal analysis of 'The Sea Change'

relationships in the generic situation, both the authorial and the inter-story one.

If, however, we are concerned with the discourse as process, we have to be more delicate in our phasal distinctions in order to see how these major components or *primary* phases interweave, and what internal variety they have. This leads to the delineation of more delicate phases (*secondary* phases, *tertiary* phases and transitions). The phasal relationship can then be charted as in Figure 10.3 to show communicative movement, the dynamic instantiation of registerial and micro-registerial options to manifest/realize message in situation. Later the extent to which this sort of analysis reveals and reflects what is normally called discourse structure will be discussed briefly. At the secondary degree of delicacy, six phases are recognized within the Man–Girl Conversation: M1 to M6 in Figure 10.3. They are given labels such as *problem* (M1), *her* (M2), *love-forgive* (M3), *leave-come back* (M4), *vice* (M5), *self-knowledge* (M6); but it must be noted that these labels are meant to serve as convenient memory devices. They are not intended to suggest, as some of them seem to, that phase is purely an ideational matter; the criteria for their recognition are tri-functional, but it is often easier to find a short ideational label than an interpersonal or a textual one.

There are four secondary phases within the Narrative Phase: N1 *setting*, N2 *looking and touching*, N3 *the barman*, N4 *the bar clients*. The Barman–Client conversation has two phases: B1 *ordering*, B2 *phatic*. The Phil–Barman Conversation is not subdistinguished; it operates within the second of the two phases which are called Integrative Phases (Int 1, Int 2) and recognized on the tertiary (maximum) delicacy line of the chart.

The first Integrative Phase (sentences 141–157) combines elements of the conversational M3 (*love-forgive*) and M4 (*leave-come back*) with the narrative N2 (*looking and touching*) and the girl's appearance part of the first narrative phase (N1b *setting*). The new narrative element is *sounding strange*. The second Integrative Phase (sentences 158–176) has the Phil–Barman Conversation (P) integrated with an echo of M5 (*vice*), N3 (*the barman*), N4 (*clients*) and an oblique but important reference to the man's tan mentioned in N1a. Talk about leaving (M4) has become narrative action. The new component narratively and chronologically is *looking different*.

The most delicate phasal analysis, already referred to, into M1a, M1b, M4a, M4b, N1a, N1b, etc. is on the third line of the chart (Figure 10.3). It plots the sequence of phasal occurrence and the sentences involved are recorded by number at the foot of the column.

So this description organizes, on the criterion of tri-functional consistency and congruity, 176 sentences (the most inclusive unit of the syntax, the minimum codal realization of discourse) in terms of 35 most delicate phases and three transitions, which are in turn organized in terms of fifteen phases at mid-delicacy and four at the least delicate. This type of analysis and display constitutes the central component of what is called *discourse plot*.

Phasal distinction

An examination in some detail of selected secondary, tertiary phases and transitions will clarify the criteria used in determining phasal boundaries.

Phase M1, *problem* (1–10), is the presentation of a conversation in the quoted, or Direct Speech, form with the verbalization process realization *say*. There are eight turns: #1, 3, 5 and 7 are assigned, explicitly or implicitly, to the participant identified as *the man*; #2, 4, 6 and 8 explicitly to the other participant, *the girl*. *The man* is identified as sayer only in #1; *the girl* is identified in all her turns. In 2, 4, and 6 this is by *said the girl*, but in turn 8 she is identified in the non-marked and sentence final form *the girl said*. This may be a marker of prominence and be related to what Fleming (1978a, b) calls the *ranking* of participants in this opening phase of the discourse. In this quoted presentation of speech, the quotatives (e.g. *said the girl*) give no other systematically potential information either ideationally (e.g. *quickly*, realizing manner) or interpersonally (e.g. *unfortunately*, realizing writer's attitude). This is a characteristic of the primary Man–Girl Conversation Phase. But, interestingly, *seriously* is used as an adjunct of both *the man's* and *the girl's* saying at the climactic point of the First Integrative Phase (sentences 154, 155).

Textually, this secondary phase is characterized by exophoric reference (*it*) and by verbal and clausal ellipsis (*I can't, I won't, you did*). The verbal and clausal ellipsis of *can't* and *won't* is unfulfilled. The phase opens with *All right*, an assent sentence linker which usually presupposes a previous communicative event. The *All right* in the sixth turn is an assent link used to end discussion prior to changing it ideationally and indeed, in this instance, interpersonally.

Interpersonally, there is, throughout phase M1, a *you and I* relationship and ten of the eleven speech functions are statements. There are also the negative ability/intentional modalities *can't* and *won't*, and *mean* is used twice in a speaker's interpretation of the other speaker.

Ideationally what is realized is largely non-specific as a result of the exophoric reference and unfulfilled ellipsis. Two people are talking, a man and a woman, and they are contradicting each other about something, or some event, or some state of being. They have a problem.

More delicate analysis distinguishes this secondary *problem* phase M1 into tertiary phases M1a and M1b. The change comes after the fifth turn, *You mean you won't.* The *it* of M1a (*What about it?*) is not identifiable with the *it* of M1b (*You have it your own way*); the first could refer to an event centred around either an action or a mental process rather than a thing or a state of being. The girl's response is *I can't*, and *I* could be realizing either agent or mental processor. The *it* of *have it your own way* can also mean one thing in the girl's utterance and another in the man's response; idiomaticity may be involved here. These tertiary phases are also distinguished ideationally and interpersonally. The *you* and *I* reference of M1a is to the girl; in M1b it is to the man, and M1b is without modality in the verbal group.

The first Narrative Phase, sentences 11–15, N1 *setting*, follows. This stretch of text is sufficiently different from what precedes and follows it, and has enough internal functional consistency and congruity to be recognized as a phase. Textually (with ideational implications) there is no direct or indirect speech presentation, and no inter-sentential ellipsis, although there is clausal ellipsis in the last sentence. References are all fulfilled. Theme selections are unmarked and the phonologically realized *new* would, in reading aloud, naturally occur towards the end of information units. There is no inter-sentential explicit or implicit conjunction (see Martin and Rothery 1981).

Interpersonally, the independent clauses are all indicative declarative mood. There is third person reference throughout, and the *you* and *I* of the opening phase has become *these two... together* and *both*. There are no modalities and no attitudinals.

Ideationally, a third participant is introduced, the barman. Location, both temporal (*It was early... It was the end of summer...*) and spatial (*café... at a table in the corner... in Paris*), is the main meaning of the transitivity system choices in the clauses of the first two sentences. They do, however, realize two other predications with the couple as participants in apparent action processes: as agents to *sit* and patients to *tan*; but these predications also have relational meaning: the first locational, the second attributive (see Gregory 1982–1983 for the specifics of predicational structures). These two sentences (#11 and 12) realize a subphase (N1a) of the first narrative phase: *setting of participants* (N1). The next graphological sentence (three syntactic sentences in this analysis) is recognized as another subphase at tertiary delicacy (N1b) with the function of *setting: the girl*. Four paratactically related propositions establish her appearance in terms of her suit, her skin, her hair and her forehead; and substantive, attributive and adverbial modification appears for the first time: *tweed... smooth, golden brown... blonde... short... beautifully away*.

The next sentence, the last of the graphological paragraph, is recognized as the first transition in the discourse: *The man looked at her*. The morphosyntagmeme *look + particle* is a recurrent feature of the second Narrative Phase which is discontinuous and interrupts the second, third and fourth secondary phases of the Man–Girl Conversation, and occurs again in the first Integrative Phase. The Second Integrative Phase, the last in the discourse, has *look + out, + back, + in, + into*.

One of the features of *look + particle* is that sometimes it is the morphosyntactic realization of a process with action (or material) characteristics to the fore (e.g. *he looked over the wall*), at others of a process dominated by mental characteristics of perception or cognition (e.g. *he looked at the painting thoughtfully*; *he looked into the matter*). I suggest that this multivalence helps the sentence *The man looked at her* operate transitionally in this discourse. It is preceded by a description of the girl's appearance which would lead one to tend towards a perception analysis. On the other hand, the man addresses her immediately after he has looked at her which suggests the action of raising the eyes to an addressee (he looks down at her hands three lines later). The past tense form of *look* preserves the multivalence because it is not aspectualized and so is unmarked as regards duration of the process.

The transition is into the second Man–Girl phase which provides the important information (missing from the first) that the problem is a love triangle, and that the third party is a woman; the affair is lesbian, and the man's present reaction is to kill *her*.

I draw attention now to two key secondary phases of the Man–Girl Conversation which, intertwined with a Narrative Phase (N2) concerned with the looking of the participants at each other, the offering of hands and touching (forms of non-linguistic communication), and a Narrative Phase (N3) concerned with the barman's indifference to them, occupy most of the middle of the story, and are echoed in the culminative Integrative Phases. The first of these two key phases to occur is the *love-forgive* phase (M3) in which the girl's turns are initiating, and express her sorrow for the situation, her love for the man, and request trust and forgiveness. The man's turns are responsive. Their use of reference makes them dependent upon hers. They express bitterness: *Yes, this proves it* (41); *That's funny... Trust you. That's really funny* (59, 60, 61); *Let's not talk rot* (72). The second to occur is the *leave-come back* phase (M4). This, too, is initiated and reinitiated by the girl: *I'll come back if you want me* (67) and *it breaks my heart to go off and leave you* (80). These two phases (M3 and M4 combine, after the Barman Narrative Phase (N3), in the question exchange:

> *Couldn't you just be good to me and let me go?* (91)
> *What do you think I'm going to do?* (92)

This is followed by the tertiary Narrative Phase (N4a) which records the arrival of the clients, and the Barman–Client conversational fragment *Yes, sir*. There is then a return to the girl's demand for forgiveness (expressed in questions), and for the first time she raises the question of self-knowledge: *You don't think things we've had and done should make any difference in understanding?* (98). One notes declarative mood with question intonation indicated, and the referential vagueness of *thing*, *have* and *do*. The man's response to this which initiates the secondary phase (M5 *vice*) raises the analytical matter of *intertextuality* (Lemke 1985).

The passage the man cannot quote is from the fifth section of the Second Epistle of Pope's *An Essay on Man* concerned with *How odious Vice is in itself, and how we deceive ourselves into it*. The actual words are:

> Vice is a monster of so frightful mien,
> As, to be hated, needs but to be seen;
> Yet seen too oft, familiar with her face,
> We first endure, then pity, then embrace.

The man (*Poor old Phil*) may not remember the words; however, like P. G. Wodehouse's Bertie Wooster he can't quote but has the gist of it. The phase this establishes is interrupted by the conversational phase between the barman (now identified as James) and the clients (B2, B1b), and by a short recurrence of the client's Narrative Phase (N4b) following the barman's *Trust me* (ironic in light of the Man–Girl Conversation): *The two at the bar looked over at the two at the table, then looked back at the barman again. Towards the barman was the comfortable direction.* Then phase M5 returns with the girl's continued (or is it resumed?) discussion of calling it *vice* without mentioning the word. However, N4b, as a narrative about the clients, meets none of the criteria for recognition as a transition although it does 'fit' where it occurs. It has little in common in its functional systemic selections with what precedes it or follows it, but what it does do is function as a *bridge* between two discourse-created instances of two different generic situations: the one at the bar which has given rise to the conversation about the barman's weight and the mixing of drinks, and the one that is related to the ongoing conversation between the man and the girl at the corner table. It creates this bridge in two sentences which realize five locational roles in the predicational semology: three dynamic locatives, two static locatives: *at the bar... over at the two at the table... back to the barman... towards the barman.* Communicatively, it can be thought of as a linguistic narrative equivalent of cross-switching in visual media.

The second transition, properly so called, occurs at the end of the *vice* phase (M5b) and before the *self-knowledge* phase (M6). The man says: *That's the name for it. (120) 'No' she said. 'We're made up of all sorts of things. You've known that'.*

The *No* is considered to be a transition because it functionally relates in different ways to the phases which precede and follow it. As a negative polarity realization it is elliptically related to the previous clause so that it can be decoded: *No, that's not the name for it* (anaphoric meaning within the textual function). There is then an expectation that this will be followed by a counter-assertion: *X is the name for it.* But what does follow it is a proposition in an implicit causal relation to the negation. So we can also decode: *No, that's not the name for it, because we're made up of all sorts of things* (cataphoric meaning within the textual function with logico-experiential implications).

The transition is into the *self-knowledge* phase (M6), which is a prime example of Hemingway's ability to involve us as decoders because of his inexplicitness as encoder:

> *We're made up of all sorts of things. You've known that. You've used it well enough.*
> *You don't have to say that again.*
> *Because that explains it to you.*
> *'All right,' he said. 'All right.'*

Lexical, and in Pike and Pike's use of the term (1982), *referential* starvation characterizes this phase. Quite what the *that* is, in a particular sense, that the man has *known*, we are not told; nor can we be specific as regards what *use* or *it* refer to. The *it* in *Because that explains it to you* we can decode as both the particular relationship and the kind of relationship she is having with the other woman. What remains tantalizingly unclear is what he has known and used. Does it perhaps relate to the earlier sentence in M3c (98): *You don't think the things we've had and done should make any difference in understanding?*

The phase ends: *'All right,'* he said. *'All right.'* And then there is the third transition: *You mean all wrong. I know. It's all wrong.* This is considered a transition because it makes use of the non-complementary functional relationships between *All right* (assent or evaluation) and *all wrong* (evaluation only) in order to move from one phase of discourse to another.

The transition is into a tertiary phase (M4c) of the *leave-come back* secondary phase which ends with the man's *Go on then* which is in marked contrast to his previous responses in other occurrences of this phase, and is the turning point of the story.

There follow the two Integrative Phases that complete the discourse. I have already outlined their constituent and contrastive components. Intertextuality is again relevant, this time to the body of Hemingway's work. The literary critic Robert P. Weeks (1962:12) discussing one type of Hemingway's ideal scenes, one which ends his short stories: 'The Killers', 'A Clean Well Lighted Place', 'The Capital of the World', and five of his six novels, writes:

It is the scene in which the hero has finally been cornered, but as he gallantly suffers his defeat he is not alone; he is in the presence of others who either do not even notice him, or if they do are unaware of his ordeal and the gallantry with which he endures.

Weeks considers that this particular type of scene is obviously deeply meaningful for Hemingway. I suggest that this ideal scene is certainly the scene of the second Integrative Phase (158–176); and to an extent, of the first Integrative Phase (141–157) too, if one contrasts the man's utterances with the girl's, and takes note of Hemingway's uncharacteristic use of comments on a character's phonation. It is to the man, the hero, that the voice sounds and is recognized as strange; on the other hand, *She could not believe him but her voice was happy.*

The title, 'The Sea Change', like many titles in the short story genre can operate as a decoding key, a point of entry and a point of return. Part of its intertextuality is Shakespeare's play *The Tempest* in which the phrase first occurred in print. Ariel sings (I. i. 394–401, *Oxford Shakespeare*, ed. Gregg):

> Full fathom five thy father lies,
> Of his bones are coral made;
> Those are pearls that were his eyes;
> Nothing of him that doth fade,
> But doth suffer a sea-change:
> Sea-nymphs hourly ring his knell;
> Hark now I hear them – ding, dong bell.

In *The Tempest* virtually all characters suffer or have suffered, literally and metaphorically, a *sea-change*, which has meant that their lives change or have changed considerably, and with a certain suddenness. In virtually all cases it could be argued that something is learnt in the change.

There is, of course, change in Hemingway's story, experiential and interpersonal change for the two principal characters. The man begins by wanting to solve the problem by killing 'the other woman' and ends by saying *Go on, then* (140). . . *And when you come back tell me all about it* (148); the girl works hard to get 'permission' to go, taking the dialogic initiative, but she is surprised when she gets permission to go and come back: *Really?* (141) . . . *Not really. Oh you're too sweet. . . You're too good to me* (146–148). . . *You want me to go?* (154).

James, the barman, does not change. For him, the man remains a tanned young man who *must have had a very good summer* (176). He has seen *many handsome young couples break up* (88). But then he, in Pike and Pike's referential hierarchy terms, is one of the *cast* of the story who is essentially a *prop* (Pike and Pike 1982:325).

Textually, in the discourse organization of the message, there is a change too. The man and the girl are in focus throughout; the message is about them, but the girl has overall prominence (i.e. more information is given about her) until the final two long Integrative Phases where the man is both in focus and prominent and she has left the story.

However, the importance to the discourse plot of the Man–Girl Conversation Phase can hardly be underestimated. The graph at the foot of Figure 10.3 indicates its pervasiveness. It also plots the discontinuous occurrence of each of its secondary phases, and groups together, in overlapping sequence, M1 and M2, then M3 and M4, and then M5 and M6. This suggests, perhaps, that a degree of descriptive generalization between what here were recognized as primary and secondary delicacy might have had value. One could say that the dynamism of the dominant primary phase of the discourse (M) resides in the sequence of these pairs of secondary phases, the members of which are related in tension. The problem is the other woman and killing isn't really 'on'. To love and forgive means that the girl can leave and come back. To try to name it is to try to know it.

This type of patterning, together with the internally allusive Integrative Phases, is perhaps to be expected when a discourse has a single author, is within the short story genre, and is written within the CCC of the English-speaking world in the post-First World War period of the first half of the twentieth century.

The Sue–Kay tape: communicating community context and generic situation

The discourse of the Symposium tape and transcript is, of course, differently patterned as a consequence of its different generic situation and distinct CCC. It has two authors who are interlocutors. The experience they are relating could most generally be described as *making an audio-visual tape*. For one of the participants, it is making a tape to be transcribed, replayed and talked about by fourteen linguists from the United States, Canada, Australia and Great Britain. This is an experience relationship which is dependent on the macro-environment of the CCC of the penultimate decade of the twentieth century with a North American provenance, and a social structure which has an educating, educated middle class with access to conference and research funding. Such an experience demands a topic or topics; people do like to talk about something, and talking about having to talk so that an audio-visual tape can be made is likely to run out of steam after a while. An experience of one of the interlocutors, an imminent operation, provides a topic which, in the least delicate analysis, also supplies a label for one of the discourse's primary phases. The experience of an imminent operation can provide grist to a linguistic mill because the communicators are active in a socio-cultural context which includes 'nose jobs' done for medical and/or cosmetic reasons, a context of insurance and hospital consultation, a context in which ear-nose-and-throat specialists and plastic surgeons are distinguished. Many of our contemporaries living in other parts of the world would not share such knowledge and the gnostological connections would not be made.

Their medium relationship is face-to-face, spontaneous speech interchange in the presence of camera and microphone. The personal relationship of the interlocutors is friendly and familiar; they evidently share contexts of experience and memory (K's involvement with soap operas for example, 129–145, and they both know who *Jim* is, 362). Interactively the personal relationship coexists with a functional relationship. In this situation S takes the role of interviewer and K of interviewee. They share the function of producing discourse which can be recorded: The text begins with S: *What I would like to find out more about is your operation ... that you are having* and ends thus: S: *I think we're finished ...* K: *OK ...* S: *Let's call it 'The End'.*

The transcript is headed *Conversation (Interview) between Sue and Kay. Interview* is an accurate indication of an aspect of the functional relationship which tempers the medium relationship of conversing. In the data that my colleagues and I have examined, conversation is typically marked by a genuine sharing of topic initiation and the linguistic space between the speakers. The experiences reflected in the fields of discourse in conversation do not usually suggest a fixed agenda. But, given the functional relationship of interview, the norm is a relatively fixed, circumscribed field agenda and an imbalance between the interlocutors. One asks the questions; the other gives the answers. The interviewer is engaged in dialogue; the interviewee in dialogue and monologue; the interviewee is the one who talks the most. And so it is in this text. S, the interviewer, has only two short monologues, one about her own automobile accident (169–175) and the other is the narrative of the problem child with the relative who studied Eastern mysticism (199–209). K, on the other hand, monologues frequently while S makes encouraging noises. So this text can be described as a cooperative discourse, induced extrinsically, rather than as a typical instance of the 'noises we make with our faces in order to live'. These features make the text no less interesting for the discourse analyst, and are reflected in the partial phasal analysis summarized in Figure 10.4.

The Sue–Kay tape and transcript: phasal analysis 1–150

This analysis covers the first 150 lines, approximately 40 per cent of the total text. At the least delicate stage of the analysis, the opening portion of discourse is considered one primary phase: *the operation*. At that degree of generalization it might be accompanied by phases such as *K's future* and *S's story* in a complete analysis of the transcript. As a primary phase it is characterized ideationally by a string of lexical items realizing participants and processes in the experience of the medical environment and of reaction to that

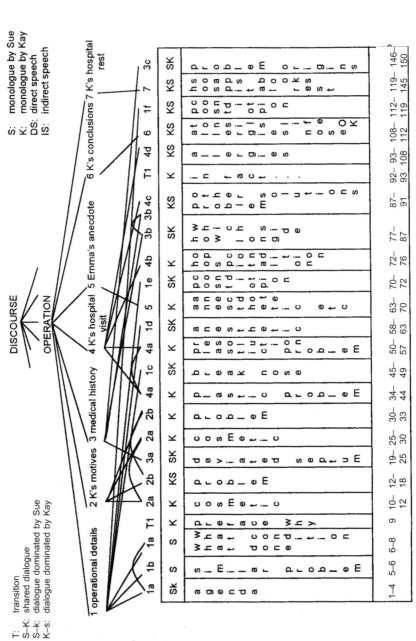

Figure 10.4 Partial phasal analysis of Sue-Kay tape

environment. Interpersonally (with textual consequences) it is marked by questions from S and responses from K. Indeed this phase is the expected registerial realization of the generic situation as it has been described above. The dynamics of its realization in discourse are best shown at the next two degrees of delicacy.

At mid-delicacy seven secondary phases are recognized in the portion of the text analysed: #1: *operation details*; #2: *K's motives for the operation*; #3: *history of the medical problem*; #4: *K's hospital visit*; #5: *Emma's anecdote about anaesthesia*; #6: *K's conclusions*; #7: *K's hospital rest*.

Secondary phase #1 *operation details*, is a phase initiated and re-initiated by S, except for its seventh textual occurrence when K briefly reinitiates it. Its phasal consistency becomes apparent if one reads through its occurrences consecutively, ignoring discontinuity in its instantiation.

1a (1–4)	S: *(sort ha-S) What I would like to find out more about is your operation … that you are having.* K: *My nose operation.* S: *Yes, your nose operation.*
1b (5–6)	*You see, I have a similar problem and I've been postponing doing something about it for a very long time,*
1a (6–8)	*so tell me what you're having done an' … what condition you're gonna be in when you're having it done.*
1c (45–49)	S: *Do they have to break your nose to correct your deviated septum?* K: *They may have to … they may not. But they do have to completely alter … inside … at least … they still have to change the whole shape, so I'm sure they're going to do something sort of drastic.*
1d (58–63)	S: *And what are … are they going to put you to sleep when you have it done? … or do you have to be awake, while its being done?* K: *Well, normally you're awake, and … if I understand it correctly they're gonna do it under general anesthetic, so that's OK … so I'll be asleep.*
1e (70–72)	S: *And how long afterwards are you going … to be black and blue, or …?* K.: *I don't know.*

And then K initiates;

> K: *I'm gonna look black and blue, though...when I come*
> *out of this operation*
> S: *Probably pretty swollen?...* ⌈ *all through* ⌉
> 1f   K: ⌊ *that's right ...* ⌋
> (112–119) *that's right so I have my sunglasses ready...*
> S: *Yes, big ones that come...*
> K: *Yes*

This secondary phase is characterized interpersonally by Sue as dialogic initiator. She gives directives realized, after an initial declarative clause stating discourse intention (*What I would like to find out more about is your operation*), by an imperative (*so tell me*), and then by polar and WH interrogatives.

Ideationally, the initial non-specific action process realization in *What you are having done* is then spelt out by specific action processes: *break, correct, put to sleep*. The initial attributive question (*What condition you're going to be in*) is made specific in the *black and blue* question. The syntax is that which realizes future events and states. Textually, this phase is dialogic not monologic. It reflects S sticking to her agenda as interviewer.

The first transition (9) precedes the next secondary phase, #2: *K's motives for the operation*. There is a *transition out*: *Well, maybe I should preface this thing*. The modalities (*well, maybe, should*), the particular mental process of verbalization (*preface*), and the combination of specific reference and lexical non-specificity (*this thing*) prepare for the *transition in*, the appositional, *why I want it done*. The sequent phase (10–18, 25–33) deals with the 'why' of the experience as opposed to the 'whats' raised by S in #1, and is monologic rather than dialogic. It is characterized by mental processes of reaction with speaker as processor, and key lexical items *cosmetic* and *problem*, both of which are given prominence phonologically and lead to the distinction at the next degree of delicacy, of 2a, *cosmetic motive* (10–12, 25–30), and 2b, *problem motive* (12–18, 30–33). The *problem* tertiary phase is distinguishable through its verbalization of past events and direct and indirect speech presentation.

The first textual occurrence of phase #2 is interrupted, after each tertiary phase has been introduced, by S's initiation of secondary phase #3 , the *medical history* (19–25, 77–88). Like #1 it is initiated and reinitiated by S and is dialogic, but unlike that phase, and unlike K's treatment of the problem in her *motives* phase, phase #3 is concerned with the past history of the medical problem and its recognition. This emerges from S's opening 'double-barrelled' questions in each occurrence of the phase:

3a: *Didn't you notice you had a deviated septum? ... that you couldn't breathe through the side, one side of your nose?* (19, 22–23; polar interrogative)

3b: *How long have you not been able to breathe out of .. is it the ... which side of the nose can't you breathe out of?* (77, 78; a temporal durative WH interrogative; a polar interrogative started but not completed; then a distinguishing WH interrogative).

3c: *So how long have you had this? ... has it been since you were a kid?* (146, 147, a temporal durative WH interrogative, then specified as a polar interrogative).

K's responses in these occurrences of phase #3 have their own pattern:

3a: *No, I mean everything else is crooked an' stuff* (20–21)
     No, so I thought, I mean there are other things wrong with me, so I figured, like, well, that was just ... natural (24, 25)

3b: *I mean, I just ... always thought that that's ... the way ... people breathed* (81, 82)

3c: *I don't know* (148)

After these responses she moves, each time, into one of her monologic phases characterized textually by her use of the conjunction *so* for her own several purposes. The first time she moves back into her *motives* phase #2, with a *so* and a *but, so ... but I always wanted a nice nose* (25–26). This phase is then succeeded by phase #4, *K's hospital visit* (34–44, 50–57, 72–76, 87–91, 93–108).

Ideationally, phase #4 has a new setting, *the hospital*, and a new participant *they* which textually becomes *he* and then *him: ...and they said 'sure you've got a real problem' ...* (34–35) *So, uh mm, he said he couldn't do plastic surgery. So ... in the conversation with him, I just said ...* (41–42). I understand that it is the same participant, institutionalized at first (*they*), then individualized. Textually, this phase is strongly marked by Direct Speech presentation of dialogue.

S interrupts the phase (cohesively, of course, on account of the broken nose reference) with a resumption of secondary phase #1 (*operation details*): *Do they have to break your nose ... ?* (1c, 45). But K soon returns to her hospital visit phase #4 with *so .. uh, .. so I got around it by saying, 'well, listen ... is it going to be straightened?'*

(50–51). This *it* refers back to the problem of getting her nose 'fixed', in both senses of the term, cosmetic and medical, by a surgeon who only wants to fix it in one sense. K ends this monologue phase with what appears lexically, syntactically and phonologically to be a 'sign off': *so he did consent to it then, so .. I'm gonna get this new nose* (56–57).

S keeps the interview and the recording going by reinitiating the operation details phase in terms of the type of anaesthetic (1d, 58–63), and then K launches a new monologic phase, #5, *Emma's anecdote* about doctors and anaesthetics. It, characteristically, has its snatch of direct speech. S returns to the operation details with her *black and blue* question (1e, 70–72) and in her response K returns to her hospital visit conversation with the surgeon (4b, 72–76). S reinitiates the history of the medical problem phase (3b, 77–87). K moves from that back to her hospital visit (4c, 87–91), and then makes an explicit transition (*I was so desperate ... I even went in for*, etc., 92–93) into a new subphase of her hospital visit phase (4d, *allergies* 93–108).

This is followed by a pause and a listing summary from K which is sufficiently different linguistically to be recognized as a new secondary phase (#6, *K's conclusions*, 108–112):

K: ... so if I get my allergies taken care of, my nose fixed, .. keep my
   tonsils, I think ... I think life can be ok! (short giggle-K) ..
K: ⎡ and then maybe ...   ⎤
S: ⎣ This is gonna be a big year ... ⎦
K: ... also get a good nose ... yeah.

This could well have brought the interview to a close, but it is now K who keeps text going by taking S's operation phase *black and blue* question and then initiating a new phase, #7, *K's hospital rest* (119–145), which is more like 'free' conversation than an interview-conversation. K emerges as a jester and S overlaps her cooperatively. Although there is a brief return to phase 3 (3c, 146–150) and the origins of the problem, the interlocutors are, from this point on, free from the constraints of the extrinsic generic situation, with its experience topic 'operation', and its interview function. They are less dependent on a question and answer framework; they make their own contributions, and the agenda is less fixed. The linguistic dog begins to wag the situational tail.

Concluding remarks

Within communication linguistics, phasal analysis is offered as an alternative (some might want to see it as a complement or supplement) to existing methods of handling discourse in a constituent structure way. Pike and Pike (1982) and Longacre (1976) see discourse as the upper level (or rank) of their grammatical hierarchy. In Pike's terms, the Man–Girl Conversation Phase in 'The Sea Change' would probably be seen as *nuclear*. But I should not want to see the two Integrative Phases as in any way *Marginal* or *Peripheral*. There may be, of course, a problem of terminology involved. One has to remember that, for Pike, marginal does not necessarily mean optional. Possibly Pike and Pike's referential hierarchy analysis (1982:321–358, see also Pike 1981) would yield descriptions with some similarities to those presented here, but I have not yet seen applications of it to discourses such as Hemingway's, or the Sue–Kay interview conversation.

Jean Ure's analysis of a Short Short Story in her forthcoming introduction to systemic linguistics (*Patterns and Meanings*) is very close to what my collaborators and I are doing in phasal analysis. Her text is Beatrix Potter's 'The Story of a Fierce Bad Rabbit' which is seventeen sentences long. On the basis of a tri-functional description of the sentences and clauses in the text she reveals and demonstrates a structure of Prelude – Part I: the Good Rabbit – Part II: The Episode of the Man with a Gun – The Climax – Conclusion. However, I have avoided, in the analysis of both the story and the interview, giving structure type labels to the phases. This is because I am unconvinced that discourses have a hierarchic constituent structure in the same way as a clause or tone group has. Furthermore, structural labels for discourse in common use, such as Orientation, Complication, Resolution, etc. tend to reflect on discourse as organization, rather than discourse as the realization of ideational and interpersonal message, which is the major concern of phasal analysis. Insofar as there are, in the registers associated with certain generic situations, common principles of organization in terms such as those mentioned above, they can be handled distinctly from phasal analysis and then correlated with it. Such principles of organization I consider *discoursal schemes* reflective of an aspect of the functional relationship of the generic situation (narrative, expository, etc.), and are a component of the textual or enabling function of language. It is not yet evident that all generic situations have clear schemes associated with them, and it is important not to overestimate their significance as regards the exchange of messages, or see them as determining. K at the beginning of the interview presents her motives for the operation (9–18) essentially in terms of an expositional scheme, and at the end (309–318) returns to the matter in terms of a narrative scheme with an imagined incident. However it is surely important to recognize that at one degree of delicacy these two passages realize the same phase, and that the expositional subphase has narrative touches (the dialogue with *my friend who's a nurse*). The variation of scheme can be related to another aspect of the functional relationships between speakers: the good advice known to many speakers that if you're going to say the same thing again, say it differently.

Beekman, Callow and Kopesec (1981) have asserted that meaning in discourse is 'packaged' for encoding and decoding ease. Phase is my packaging concept for discourse because I cannot analyse discourse as packaged in a Chinese box way. Discourse is more like a conveyer belt (in the case of dialogue often two conveyor belts) moving different but related packages, and the packages are 'message' packages rather than packages of linguistic material. So please note that the phasal analysis charts (Figures 10.3 and 10.4) are not meant to show a hierarchy of units, of elements in the structure of one unit filled by units of lesser extent. The scale of abstraction that lies behind the trees is that of *delicacy* not *rank* (see Halliday 1961). Phasal analysis distinguishes and plots similarities and differences of meaning, from the general to the particular, in the continuum of communication; it strives to leave the continuum more or less intact. It seeks to characterize discourse as process rather than as object. And this is as necessary for a text by a single author, such as a short story, as it is for an interchange between speakers in a conversation-interview. In either case phasal analysis can form a basis for the renewal of connection with conceptual or gnostological analysis, a basis for the investigation of how speakers construct reality.

References

Asp, Elissa (1983) The dynamics of discourse: an analysis of Dylan Thomas' 'Memories of Christmas. Unpublished honours thesis, English Department, Glendon College, York University, Toronto.

Asp, Elissa (1984) Metaphor and the nominal group: beyond the lexicon. Paper presented to the Annual Spring Colloquium, Applied Linguistics Working Group, Glendon College, York University, Toronto.

Asp, Elissa (1985) The communicative functions of metaphor: a cognitive, cultural and linguistic catalysis. Unpublished Master's thesis, York University, Toronto.

Asp, Elissa (1992) Natural language and human semiosis: a socio-cognitive account of metaphor. Unpublished Ph.D. dissertation, York University, Toronto.

Beekman, J., Callow, J. and Kopesec, M., (1981) *The Semantic Structure of Written Communication*. Dallas: Summer Institute of Linguistics.

Enkvist, N. E., Spencer, J. and Gregory, M. (1964) *Linguistics and Style*. London: Oxford University Press.

Firth, J. R. (1957) *A Synopsis of Linguistic Theory 1930–1955*. Oxford: Philological Society.

Fleming, Ilah (1978a) *Field Guide to Communication Situation, Semantic and Morphemic Analysis*. Mimeo, Dallas: Summer Institute of Linguistics.

Fleming, Ilah (1978b) Discourse from the perspective of four strata. *The Fifth Lacus Forum 1978*, Columbia, SC: Hornbeam Press, 307–317.

Gregory, Michael (1965) Old Bailey speech in *A Tale of Two Cities*, *Review of English Literature*, 6(2) New attitudes to style, 42–55.

Gregory, Michael (1967) Aspects of varieties differentiation. *Journal of Linguistics*, 3:177–198.

Gregory, Michael (1972) English patterns. Mimeo, Glendon College York University, Toronto.

Gregory, Michael (1974) A theory for stylistics exemplified: Donne's 'Holy Sonnet XIV'. *Language and Style*, 8(2):108–118.

Gregory, Michael (1978) Marvell's 'To His Coy Mistress': the poem as a linguistic and social event. *Poetics*, 7(4):351–362.

Gregory, Michael (1980) Language as a social semiotic: the recent work of M. A. K. Halliday. *Applied Linguistics*, 1:174–811.

Gregory, Michael (1981/1982) Linguistics and theatre: Hamlet's voice: aspects of text formation and cohesion in a soliloquy. *Linguistics and the Humanities Conference*, University of Texas, Arlington, and *Forum Linguisticum*, 7(2)(1982):107–122.

Gregory, Michael (1982a) The nature and use of meta-functions in systemic theory: current concerns. *Eighth Lacus Forum 1981*, Columbia, SC: Hornbeam Press, 67–74.

Gregory, Michael (1982b) Static and dynamic aspects of linguistic description. Paper presented to the *Annual Meeting of the Michigan Linguistic Society*.

Gregory, Michael (1982/1983) assisted by K. Malcolm, Notes on communication linguistics. Mimeo, Glendon College York University, Toronto.

Gregory, Michael (1983) Clause and sentence as distinct units in the morphosyntactic analysis of English and their relation to semological propositions and predications. *Ninth Lacus Forum 1982*, Columbia, SC: Hornbeam Press, 262–271.

Gregory, Michael (1984a) Towards 'communication' linguistics: a framework. In *Systemic Perspectives on Discourse, Vol. 1: Selected Theoretical Papers from the 9th International Systemic Workshop*, ed. by J. Benson and W. Greaves, Norwood, NJ: Ablex, 119–134.

Gregory, Michael (1984b) Propositional and predicational analysis in discourse description, *Tenth LACUS Forum 1983*, Columbia, SC: Hornbeam Press, 315–321.

Gregory, Michael and Carroll, Susanne (1978) *Language and Situation: Language Varieties and Their Social Contexts*. London: Routledge & Kegan Paul.

Gregory, Michael and Malcolm, Karen (1981) Generic situation and discourse phase: an approach to the analysis of children's talk. Mimeo, Applied Linguistics Research Working Group, Glendon College, York University, Toronto.

Halliday, M. A. K. (1961) Categories of the theory of grammar. *Word*, 17(3):241–292.

Halliday, M. A. K. (1973) *Explorations in the Functions of Language*. London: Edward Arnold.

Halliday, M. A. K. (1978) *Language as Social Semiotic: The Social Interpretation of Language and Meaning*. London: Edward Arnold.

Halliday, M. A. K. (1979) Modes of meaning and modes of expression: types of grammatical structure and their determination by different semantic functions. In *Function and Context in Linguistic Analysis: Essays Offered to William Haas*, ed. by D. J. Allerton, Edward Carney and David Holdcroft, Cambridge: Cambridge University Press, 57–79.

Halliday, M. A. K. (1981) Text semantics and clause grammar: some patterns of realization. *Seventh Lacus Forum 1980*, Columbia, SC: Hornbeam Press, 31–59.

Halliday, M. A. K. and Hasan, Ruqaiya (1976) *Cohesion in English*. London: Longmans.

Hemingway, Ernest (1987) The Sea Change. In *The Complete Short Stories of Ernest Hemingway*, The Finca Vigia Edition, New York: Charles Scribner's Sons, 302–305.

Johannesson, N.-L. (1980) On fictive sentence analysis. In *Papers in Cognitive-Stratificational Linguistics*, ed. by James E. Copeland and Philip W. Davis, Houston: Rice University Studies, 75–99.

Lemke, J. L. (1985) Ideology, intertextuality and the notion of register. In *Systemic Perspectives on Discourse, Vol. 1: Selected Theoretical Papers from the 9th International Systemic Workshop*, ed. by J. Benson and W. Greaves, Norwood, NJ: Ablex, 275–294.

Lockwood, David (1972/1983) *Introduction to Stratificational Linguistics*. New York: Harcourt, Brace, Jovanovich, and author's revisions, 1983.

Longacre, R. E. (1976) *An Anatomy of Speech Notions*. Lisse: Peter de Ridder Press.

McIntosh, Angus (1965) Saying, *Review of English Literature*, 6(2) New Attitudes to Style, 9–20.

Malcolm, Karen (1983) The paragraph: what is it? Some traditional and contemporary proposals. *Ninth Lacus Forum 1982*, Columbia, SC: Hornbeam Press, 382–389.

Malcolm, Karen (1984a) Communication linguistics: a sample analysis. In *Systemic Perspectives on Discourse, Vol. 2: Selected Applied Papers from the 9th International Systemic Workshop*, ed. by J. Benson and W. Greaves, Norwood, NJ: Ablex, 136–151.

Malcolm, Karen (1984b) Different approaches to the description of casual conversation, *The Tenth Lacus Forum 1983*, Columbia, SC: Hornbeam Press, 349–355.

Malcolm, Karen (1985) The dynamics of casual conversation: from the perspective of communication linguistics. Unpublished Ph.D. dissertation, York University, Toronto.

Martin, J. R. and Rothery, J. (1981) Writing project report no. 2. *Working Papers in Linguistics*, University of Sydney.

Pike, K. L. (1981) *Tagmemics, Discourse and Verbal Art*. Ann Arbor: Michigan Studies in the Humanities.

Pike, K. L. and Pike, E. G. (1982) *Grammatical Analysis*, (revised edn) Dallas: Summer Institute of Linguistics.

Ure, J. (in preparation) *Patterns and Meanings: An Introduction to Systemic Linguistics*. Manuscript.

Weeks, Robert P. (1962) *Ernest Hemingway: A Collection of Critical Essays*. Englewood Cliffs, NJ: Prentice Hall.

Young, Lynne (1984) Discourse analysis within the framework of communication linguistics. Paper presented to the *18th Annual TESOL Conference*, Houston.

Young, Lynne (1987/1988) *Language as Behaviour, Language as Code: A Study of Academic English*. Unpublished Ph.D. dissertation, Katholieke Universiteit, Leuven, 1987 and Amsterdam: Benjamins, 1988.

11

Some Aspects of Coherence in a Conversation

Peter H. Fries

Introduction

All linguists who investigate spoken or written texts deal explicitly or implicitly with the issue of coherence in the texts which interest them. Do the parts of the text 'fit together so well that it is clear and easy to understand'? (Sinclair 1987:264). Often this issue is dealt with simply by assumption. In such an approach, texts which are encountered in natural interaction simply *are* coherent. However, we can problematize this issue by asking the following basic question about our texts:

What, if anything, makes this text coherent?

One way of interpreting this question is to understand it as addressing the ultimate causes of coherence in a text. This interpretation of the question leads us into a consideration of the social and psychological factors which were relevant as this text was being produced. This interpretation of the question often leads linguists to a mental model of coherence such as that used by Givón and his associates (Gernsbacher and Givón 1995). Without wishing to contradict what they say, I would like to propose a more socially based approach. In this view, the cause of the coherence of a text lies in the social interaction which it encodes. That is, texts are coherent because people are interacting coherently together. This socially based approach to the causes of the coherence of text leads us outside the text to questions about the interactive context such as:

What participants were involved in the interaction?
What were they doing together?
What were the relations between the participants?
What was the role of language in the interaction?

These are the sorts of questions discussed by Halliday, Hasan and others under the headings of Contextual Configuration, Field, Tenor and Mode, and other related concepts.

A second way of interpreting the question understands it as addressing the issue of what features in the language of a text indicate that it is coherent. This interpretation leads to a detailed study of the language of the text, examining various features to see how they fit together to form a coherent whole. Here one talks about the structure of the text, the use of various cohesive devices, patterns in the occurrence of other language features, etc.

The two interpretations of this question cannot be addressed independently, however, for one entails a study of social action and the other a study of the ways these social actions are encoded in language. One cannot discover social actions except by examining the traces they leave in actual behavior. On the other hand, one cannot really understand the details of the language used in a text without trying to interpret them in terms of their relations to the social actions. This chapter will discuss the coherence of a text (a discussion between two people in which one participant describes an upcoming operation she will have in the near future). Although the focus of this chapter will be on the language of this text, let us begin with a few comments about the relevance of social interaction to the coherence of text and specifically the interactive context in which this text was produced.

Coherence and social interaction

General issues

As was said above, the social interaction which is encoded in the text is the basic source of the coherence of the text. As long as the participants are able to refer the language to some understandable social interaction, they will perceive the text as coherent. Indeed, it is not necessary that the interactants even have a common language. They simply need to be able to figure out what is taking place at the time. A dramatic example of this is the 'monolingual demonstration' which Kenneth Pike developed to illustrate techniques of linguistic analysis (Pike 1981). It was based on his early experiences as a missionary in southern Mexico when he began work in his village, having no translator and no language in common with the inhabitants. In this demonstration, Pike was provided with an informant who spoke a language that Pike did not know or know about. Pike would speak only in a Mexican Indian language which he knew, and the informant would speak only in his (or her) native language. Pike would create situations to which the informant would respond and this would provide Pike with clues as to what the language used by the informant meant. For example, at the beginning of the demonstration Pike would greet the informant. If the informant responded with language, Pike assumed it was a greeting, and would try to repeat what that person said and would transcribe it. Later in the interaction, Pike might hold up a leaf and then record what the informant said. Then he would get the informant's reaction to two leaves. Later a stick and two sticks, etc. Gradually Pike would learn the language and by the end of an hour would know the basics of the sound system, a core of the grammar and a little vocabulary. This technique worked because Pike was able to structure the situation in such a way that even though he and his informant began by speaking totally different languages, they both were able to guess relatively accurately what the other was doing and saying. The result was that together they produced coherent text. Of course, Pike and his informant had to guess about the meanings that the other was expressing, and such guesses were not always correct, but usually any major problems in understanding resolved themselves in the 45 minutes reserved for work with the informant.

Of course, the guesses each made about the other were not always accurate. Pike described in conversation two occasions in which he was unsuccessful in learning and analysing the language. In the first, the informant came in with special ideas of what was happening (i.e. special ideas as to the Field). He thought that the demonstration was some sort of intelligence or psychological test. As a result, he gave unpredictable answers to the various stimuli Pike gave. For example, when Pike held up one flower, the informant said something such as 'It's pretty.' While when Pike held up two flowers the informant said 'They're pink.' Pike was justifiably unable to discover patterns in what the informant said. The other case where Pike failed was an instance where the informant did not talk (i.e. remained silent) for roughly the first 40 minutes. Apparently he was an Australian aborigine (I do not know which specific group), and in his culture it was impolite to talk to someone one did not know. It was necessary to wait an appropriate time. Both of these failures illustrate the critical importance of the participants' conception of the nature of the interaction which is taking place at the time to the text.

My discussion of Pike's monolingual demonstration focusses

primarily on the Field, but it should be obvious that Tenor and Mode are also important to the construction of coherence in these conversations. Pike and his informants each had to assume that the other was sensible and had some discernible purpose in the interaction. Further, in the situation which Pike constructed, the language used was greatly dependent on the physical context. Clearly, all these assumptions are critical. If one participant considers the other as not thinking rationally, then whatever that participant says will not be interpreted.

I recall a case in which my wife's family was visiting her elderly grandfather (commonly called 'Pops'). The visit began with everyone sitting in the living room and Pops taking part to some extent in the conversation. Eventually Pops tuned out, and the conversation continued without him. Then suddenly, he said very loudly 'You don't have to take that from them!' We were unable to see how this was relevant to our conversation, and indeed I was struck by the fact that the conversation of the others continued as if he had not said anything. The noise he produced raised no more reaction than a conversation overheard from the next room. It simply was not regarded as language worth interpreting, though it was clearly understandable. Rather, as someone later commented, this was Grandfather off in his own world.[1] A second example of the same sort of phenomenon occurs when some people read poetry produced by computer. A significant number of people simply will not try to interpret such texts because they do not consider the producer to be capable of producing language with purpose behind it. These two examples have one thing in common: the language produced – that is, the text – is not treated as coherent, not because of some lack in the linguistic features, but rather because the listeners do not believe the producer is producing coherent text – i.e. what is said is not seen as relevant to some ongoing interaction. Provided that the listeners believe that the producer is engaging in rational, purposeful interaction, they will go to great lengths to interpret what is said and done. A number of people (particularly Hasan in Cloran, Butt and Williams 1996) have pointed out the efforts people make to interpret language which they believe is coherent. Witness also the lengths some people go to interpret the language of non-native speakers.

The social interaction in the 'nose job' text

Let us now turn to the social situation encoded in the 'nose job' text .

In this conversation there are two participants. They seem to be socially equal; however, one has assumed the role of questioner or interviewer, and in so doing, has temporarily assigned the role of expert and interviewee to the other. The activity in which the two are engaged is one of exchanging information. The setting is informal, involving face-to-face communication using spoken language. The interaction is achieved primarily through language, thus the text is constitutive rather than ancillary. The coherence of this conversation results in part from the fact that the participants maintained a relatively consistent functional context throughout the conversation.

Of course, the value of discussing the context of the conversation lies in our ability to use that description to explain various features of the language of that conversation and how it is to be interpreted. We should expect to find that the context affects the nature of the language produced down to the smallest detail. Thus the informal setting leaves traces throughout the language used by the speakers. For example, the combination of the lexical items and the grammatical constructions used are often marked for an informal colloquial style. (E.g. *great* (13), *stuff* (21, 29), *I mean* (20, 24, 43), *I figured* (25), *listen* (14, 50) *whacking* (67), etc.) Even the rhythms and intonation can be seen as demonstrating an informal setting. Thus in line 4, Sue repeats what Kay said in line 3 almost exactly, and she does this using almost the same intonation contour and the same rhythm (with extreme length on the syllable *nose*) that Kay used. This almost exact repetition of wording, intonation and rhythm seems to be quite unlikely to occur in a formal setting (say an interview with a representative of an insurance company).

An analysis of features in the language of the text

A clear implication of the discussion in the last paragraph is that when we turn to the second interpretation of our basic question ('What features of the language of this text indicate that it is coherent?') we find that *every* feature of language is relevant to the coherence of this text. There are no special 'coherence-making' features of language as opposed to features of language which do something else. We might well view much of the coherence of a text as the result of principled co-occurrence restrictions, where the principles relate features of the socially relevant context (field, tenor and mode) to linguistic features. Now obviously, when we wish to examine the features of a text which indicate that it is coherent, we cannot discuss every feature of the language of the text. We can only examine those features of the language of the text which help us understand those aspects of the text which interest us.

Types of information expressed

Admitting that any choice of features to analyse is at heart arbitrary, let us now turn to the analysis of the conversation to examine it for traces of coherence. Because of limitations of time and space, only the first 57 lines were chosen for analysis. This portion of the conversation was chosen because it constituted a relatively independent, unified portion of the text. On one level of interpretation, this segment constitutes a narrative. One can see this in the fact that most of the grammatically dominant verbs are verbs which describe actions and events. They are either material processes or verbal processes in the simple past tense.[2] Thus, events receive a kind of grammatical prominence which is not given to other types of information. Other types of information are present, however. Table 11.1 presents an analysis of the non-rankshifted clauses classified into four categories of information, based on three structural features: (a) the structure of the clause, (b) the process type encoded and (c) the internal structure of the verbal group.[3]

Table 11.1 Incidence of clauses assigned to each type of information

Category	Definition	Number of instances
Events	Material, behavioral or verbal processes in the simple past	28
Potential events	Questions, negations, commands, statements concerning events with future reference	33
Setting	Relational processes with no evaluational component in the complement structures such as *be _ for some time*	23
Evaluation	Relational processes with cognitive or evaluational component in the complement	3

Of course these three features do not occur alone. While each category was defined primarily by reference to features of the clause structure and the verb forms, other features of language correlate with these three features. For example, the conjunctive relations which link the various categories of clauses to their contexts differ. As a result, the overt markers of these conjunctive relations will differ. Thus, *so* occurs within the first 57 lines of the conversation a total of 18 times (excluding two occurrences in which it was repeated as part of a filled pause and one instance in which it occurred in a partial sentence which was impossible to classify). Of these 18 occurrences, 14 introduced clauses which had been categorized as actions, 3 introduced clauses categorized as potential actions, and 1 introduced a clause categorized as a setting. Similarly, *well* occurred a total of 13 times in the first 57 lines. Of these 13 occurrences, 8 introduced clauses categorized as potential actions, 4 introduced clauses categorized as setting, and 1 occurred in a context which was not categorizable. All three instances of I *mean* within the first 57 lines of the conversation introduce clauses categorized as setting. (Compare Schiffrin 1987.)

Correlation of information type with clause and sentence Theme

Turning to thematic structure, we again find a non-random distribution of Theme types in the clause categories proposed. Halliday (1967, 1970 and 1985/1994) defines the Theme as part of clause structure. In English, Theme is realized by being placed first in the clause. The Theme includes everything 'up to (and including) the first constituent of the clause which derives from transitivity' (Halliday 1985/1994:53). The meaning of Theme is 'the ground from which the clause is taking off' (Halliday 1985/1994:38). (Also see Halliday 1967:212, and 1970:161; Fries 1995; Matthiessen 1995 for similar descriptions.) In the first 57 lines of the conversation, about two-thirds of the Themes of the clauses refer to people. Clearly, people are being used as the points of departure of the messages of this section of the conversation, and the effect of this is to make references to people a major contributor to the method of development (in the sense of Fries 1981) of this section of the conversation. Again, however, these Themes are not distributed randomly in the four categories of clauses proposed above. Table 11.2 shows the distribution of Theme types in these four categories of clauses.

Event clauses use only person or time as Theme. Themes referring to things and facts are concentrated in clauses classified as settings. Or, to view it another way, though Themes referring to things and facts make up only 16 per cent of the total number of Themes in the first section of the conversation, they provide almost one-half of the Themes of the clauses which have been classified as settings.

Table 11.2 Distribution of Theme types in clauses of each information type

Information type	Theme type				Total
	Person	Non-person			
		Time	Thing	Other	
Event	26	2	0	0	28
Potential event	21	0	2	10	33
Setting	11	0	8	4	23
Evaluation	1	0	2	0	3
Total	59	2	12	14	87

Of course, one can say that the figures on thematic content and conjunctive relations largely reflect the nature of the content of the clauses classified in these four categories. And of course that is true. However, it should be noted that many of these figures are not automatic. There is no particular reason that virtually only clauses classified as events should be introduced by *so* or that *well* should occur predominantly within clauses classified as potential actions. As a result, distributional facts such as these must be interpreted as partially reflecting and partially constructing the functioning of the various categories of clauses in this section of the conversation. For example, if we remember that over two-thirds of the clauses which contain *so* are grammatically dominant, we may wish to say that *so* is being used here as a means of segmenting the information conveyed into manageable chunks. (Schiffrin 1987 finds a similar phenomenon in the dialogs she analyses, pointing out that the causal meaning of *so* can be subordinated to its function as a marker of discourse function. Indeed she describes the use of *so* in one of the conversations she analyses in the following terms: 'Thus *so* marks the main portion of the answer – but not of an explanation.')

Let us continue a few more steps in the discussion of Theme. First, very few Themes of the clauses of the first 57 lines of the conversation are not also Subjects. We have already shown the distributions of the various types of information in the Themes of the clauses. These figures would be changed very little if we considered only those Themes which were also Subjects. We have already discussed in the preceding paragraphs some of the significance of the ordinary patterns of thematic content. Of the Themes which are Subjects, the only one which is out of the ordinary pattern occurs in line 1. The conversation begins with a thematic equative (a pseudo-cleft construction):

L1   *What I would like to find out about* is your operation ... that you are having.

A thematic equative is a focus construction which implies the existence of other possibilities but excludes these from consideration (see Greenbaum and Quirk 1990). Further, the wh- clause in thematic equatives regularly has the function of presenting Given information – that is, information which is presented as if known by the listener. The effect of placing this construction as the initial sentence of the conversation is to imply that this is not really the beginning of the conversation. (See Quirk 1978 for a similar point about lyric poetry.) One might reconstruct the conversation which preceded the recorded conversation as roughly 'Let's get together for this taping session. It won't be a big deal. I'll just ask you some questions about some things.' The critical point of this reconstruction is, of course, the fact that the specific subject matter of the questions is left vague. The first sentence of this conversation is then used to specify exactly what the subject matter will be.

There are two instances of clauses in which the Themes have been dissociated from the Subject. Both of these clauses are event clauses.

LL 33–34   *so .. so, when* I went to the hospital this time, ...
LL 42–44   *so, in the conversation with him,* I just said 'well, I mean, I don't want to go pay someone else a second time to break my nose again ... to do this.

The example from lines 33–34 begins with conjunctive *so* and the wh- item *when*. Since these elements are required to occur initially in their clause, their status as Theme is of minimal significance and in fact, the Theme includes the Subject. The example from lines 42–44, on the other hand, contains the Theme *in the conversation with him,* which is not required to be thematic. This Theme is a temporal item, and that temporal placement (which seems to imply that Kay did not return to the topic of paying for a second nose operation immediately after the surgeon refused her request the first time) is being used as a basis for the interpretation of the rest of the clause.

Now let us move from the discussion of Themes of clauses to Themes of clause complexes. It has been useful in the analysis of texts to trace the information content of the initial constituents of independent conjoinable clause complexes. These consist of an independent clause, together with any subordinate material (clauses, adverbs, etc.) dependent on it. Clause complexes which consist of two independent clauses are excluded from consideration here because of the restrictions on the ordering of the clauses.[4] Looking at independent conjoinable clause complexes entails deciding whether *so* is a subordinating or a coordinating conjunction. First it should be noted that *so* seems to be used in at least two ways in this text. On the one hand, it is used with a fairly clear causal meaning as in the following examples:

LL 10–12   I'm sort of tired of everyone going like this to my nose, *so* I thought, well, . . . I would get it cosmetically changed, . . .

LL 25–27   . . . but I always wanted a nice nose, *so* .. I .. I had looked into, investigated, uh, getting this thing fixed.

LL 48–49   . . . they still have to change the whole shape, *so* I'm sure that they're going to do something sort of drastic, . . .

On the other hand there are a number of instances in which the causal meaning is absent or very weak. For example:

LL 5–6   I have a similar problem and I've been postponing doing something about it for a very long time, *so* tell me what you're having done . . .

LL 41–42   . . . he said he couldn't do plastic surgery. *So*. . . . in the conversation with him, I just said, . . .

Instances of *so* with weak or no causal meaning are taken to be coordinating conjunctions similar in force to the continuative conjunctive adverbs *now*, and *well*, etc. (see Halliday and Hasan 1976) and so are considered to begin independent clauses.[5] The instances of *so* which had a stronger causal sense are also considered to be coordinating conjunctions as far as the analysis of Theme is concerned, because of their effect on the potential ordering of constituents; they cannot precede both the constituents which they relate. That is, while sentences such as *I like it, so I'll buy it* are possible, sequences such as *so I'll buy it, I like it* are not.[6] This resembles the distributional properties of *and* and *but* more than it does the distributional properties of *because* and *if*.[7] Once all instances of *so* were included among the coordinating conjunctions, there were only five independent conjoinable clause-complexes in this text.

LL 31–33   [and someone also this summer told me that, uh mm that he had the operation done, and that] *you* really should get it done, because you can breathe better and all sorts of things, . . .

LL 33–34 *so .. so, when I went to the hospital this time,* I just inquired, ...

LL 40 *... once they were going to break my nose,* lets do everything ...

LL 42–44 *well .. I mean, I* don't want to go pay someone else ... a second time to break my nose again ... to do this, ...

LL 45–46 *Do they* have to break your nose to correct your deviated septum?

The example from lines 33–34 is an event. The time setting is thematic and is used as the take-off point of the message of the clause complex. It places the remainder of this clause-complex and the next several (almost to the end of the text portion under discussion) in time. The Theme of the example from line 40 expresses an assumed situation which is being used as the basis for an argument in favor of the action expressed in the main clause of the complex. These two examples recall Thompson (1983:7)[8] which uses the following terms to describe the difference between the effects of putting purpose clauses initially in sentences in which they occur and putting them elsewhere.

I suggest that an initial purpose clause provides a framework within which the main clauses can be interpreted, and that it does this by its role as a link in an expectation chain. That is:

1. The environment, including the text itself as well as the knowledge which the reader brings to it, creates a set of *expectations.*
2. Within this set of expectations a problem arises.
3. The purpose clause names this problem and raises further expectations about its *solution.*
4. The following material fulfills these expectations by providing the solution.[9]

In none of the remaining three examples – in which the subordinate clause is not thematic – does the information provided in the subordinate clause set up Thompson's 'framework within which the main clause can be interpreted'. The example from lines 45–46 ends with a purpose clause, and clearly, this purpose clause describes a goal to be achieved. However, this goal is not being used to describe a problem which arises out of the expectations aroused by the previous text and which the main clause is intended to solve. Indeed, in lines 45–46 *to correct your deviated septum* simply refers to a notion that has been repeatedly mentioned earlier in the discourse.

The ordering of constituents in this sentence is not merely a matter of old information occurring first. Both breaking the nose and correcting the deviated septum are in the attention of both parties here. The focus of the question is on the relation between the two acts. If the new–old distinction were the major influence here, either order of the independent and subordinate clauses should be equally acceptable:

> Do they have to break your nose to correct your deviated septum?
> To correct your deviated septum, do they have to break your nose?

The second version seems noticeably less likely in this context. Again, this is the case, because *to correct your deviated septum* does not describe a problem which everything else is oriented toward solving.

It was said earlier that the first 57 lines of the conversation constituted a narrative. However, the events of this narrative are not very interesting. They are not interesting to the analyst, since they consist primarily of *I said, he said, I thought*, etc. A preliminary indication that the narrative is not all that interesting to the participants in the conversation is the fact that fewer than one-third of the clauses in this section of the conversation are devoted to events. Clearly the participants spend considerably more time and effort on non-events. Finally, though Sue does not react to or question what is said very often in this section of the conversation, she never reacts to or questions anything that has been categorized as an event. Thus, the content of what was said, the settings and the evaluations seem to be more important to her.

Content-oriented analysis of coherence: cohesive harmony

Let us turn now to a more content-oriented analysis of the first 57 lines of the conversation. Most extended coherent texts take some topic and develop it in some way. An adequate analysis of such a text should capture such topic-centered development. Thinking intuitively, a topic-centered text should have relatively many messages which involve the same (small set of) participant(s) – the topic. Further, the messages of the topic-centered text should all revolve around a small set of ideas. How can one capture such topic-centeredness? Hasan (1983) and Halliday and Hasan (1985/1989) have developed a technique of measuring the coherence of a text which Hasan refers to as 'cohesive harmony'. As a first step one can examine the various chains of coreferential items in the text. Coherent texts regularly contain a limited set of referents which recur throughout the text. Each chain of references to an entity or group of entities can be called an identity chain. The number of the identity chains in a text will provide a first measure of how many referents play a prominent role in the text. (Does the text centre around a single main topic or do several topics enter into the text?) As a second level of analysis we can examine the words used in the text, noting how words of similar meaning are distributed in chains throughout the text. Chains of lexically related words are called 'similarity chains'. Finally we can look at the similarities among the messages of the text. This is done by examining interactions among the various chains in the text. Two chains interact if and only if the same experiential relation holds between them in at least two clauses. The analysis of chain interaction will provide a measure of how much repetition of similar ideas the text provides.

Identity chains

In the case of the section of the text analysed here, several referents seem to recur more than the others, but they occur with radically different frequencies. The asymmetry in the relations between the two participants in the conversation is reflected in the tremendous difference in number of times they are referred to in the first 57 lines of the text. Kay is referred to directly 60 times and indirectly (either by being included in a generic reference or by reference to a contrasting person) 6 times. Sue, on the other hand, is referred to only 8 times, and of these, 4 occur in instances of *you see*, a phrase which is not used with its full lexical meaning, and has the flavor of a conjunctive. Even Kay's nose seems more important to the conversation than Sue, since it (or some portion of it) is referred to directly a total of 13 times, and indirectly another two times (through mention of *other things* and *everything else*). Noses (or parts of noses) in general are referred to directly another 4 times. Two other chains of coreferential items which are important in this segment of text are chains of references to the doctor or doctors (23 references) and to Kay's nose operation and the specific processes which are part of the operation (26 clear references, and another 20 slightly problematic references).

Lexical sets and similarity chains

A second step toward a more content-oriented analysis is to examine the vocabulary of the text for groups of words which have similar meanings. As a first approximation, words whose meanings are related by a semantic relation involving synonymy, antonymy, hyponymy (the relation involving a class and its members) or meronymy (the relation involving a whole and its parts), will be considered to be similar in meaning and will be said to belong to the same lexical set. The lexical sets which result from grouping the words of the first 57 lines of the text on this basis are given in List 11.1.

List 11.1 Lexical sets

---

1. operation, operated, plastic surgery.
2. operation, operated, fix, fixed, correct.
    alter, change, changed.
    file down, break, straighten, straightened.
3. nose, septum.
4. side, part, inside, shape.
5. problem, wrong, natural, condition.
6. conversation, tell, told, said, saying, inquired, consent, preface, listen.
7. investigated, looked into, inquired, find out.
8. get, got, had, have, 've got, wanted [= possession].
9. get, getting, have, having, want, wanted [= causative].
10. straight, crooked, deviated.
11. figured, thought.
12. nice, funny.
13. cosmetic, cosmetically, look [= appear].

The term *operation* is obviously central to this segment and much of the vocabulary found in List 11.1 can be seen to be oriented around that concept. The *American Heritage Dictionary* defines *operation* as 'any procedure for remedying an injury, ailment, or dysfunction in a living thing' (Morris 1978). This definition explicitly mentions four major factors and implies a fifth: an operation is a (1) *procedure* which has a (2) *corrective* (3) *purpose*, and that purpose involves some (4) *injury* or *dysfunction*. Implicit in this definition is the fact that (5) *some part of the body* is involved.[10] List 11.2 shows the centrality of operation for this text in the fact that the text contains vocabulary that is oriented around each of these five major parts of the definition.

The vocabulary items in List 11.2 seem to constitute an example of a concept of association which Hasan has developed (personal communication) in which a key lexical item (*operation* and *operated*,

List 11.2 Terms from List 11.1 which associate directly with parts of the definition of the term *operation*

1.	**PROCEDURE:**	alter, change, changed, correct. file down, break, straighten, straightened.
2.	**PURPOSE:**	why, reasons.
3.	**CORRECT:**	fix, fixed, correct.
4.	**DYSFUNCTION:**	couldn't breathe [through nose], deviated septum. problem, wrong, natural, correct. deviated, straight, crooked. plastic surgery, cosmetic, cosmetically, nice, look funny.
5.	**BODY PART:**	nose, side, inside, part, shape.

in this text) names a recognizable social situation and 'all those lexical items which can be seen as names of the elements of the situation named by the key term are said to be in association with it'. But clearly, even the list provided here does not exhaust the list of terms which can be seen to be related in some way to the concept of operation, for a number of words name activities which are often associated with operations, though they do not literally 'name an element of the [operation] social interaction'. Such terms are associated via collocation with the term 'operation'. These added terms are provided in List 11.3.

List 11.3 Terms regularly associated with *operation*

1.	[operation]	medical, nurse,[11] hospital.
2.	[operation]	condition.
3.	[operation]	insurance, pay, money.
4.	[operation]	postponing.
5.	[operation]	investigated, looked into, find out, inquired.
6.	[operation]	consent.

Vocabulary items which are not directly related to the medical world, but which are semantically related to the terms which we have already said are so related can also be seen to be relevant to the coherence of the text. These words are given in List 11.4 (words from List 11.3 are included in brackets at the left of each line).

List 11.4 Terms indirectly associated with *operation*

1.	[pay]	trade
2.	[money]	art work
3.	[consent]	ok, well.
4.	[change]	new
5.	[nose]	breathe

Clearly, a large proportion of the nouns, verbs, and adjectives of this portion of the text can be seen as related (sometimes more directly as in List 11.2, sometimes less directly as in List 11.4) to the general concept of 'operation'. If we add to this group the number of words which are concerned with the conversation itself (see List 11.1, lexical set 6) and those terms which refer to one or another of the major participants (Sue or Kay), it is clear that we have accounted for a very large proportion of the vocabulary (both in terms of the word tokens and word types which occur) of this segment of the conversation. Virtually all of the nouns, verbs, and adjectives which occur more than once in this segment of the conversation are mentioned in the above four lists.

Chain interactions

While we have shown that the vocabulary of this conversation is largely derived from a few consistent fields of activity, we have not shown that this text develops a topic to any degree. To show this, one must examine the messages of the text for similarities and differences. Is some entity or small set of entities regularly referred to throughout this section of the dialog? Are similar things said about these entities? The investigation of the chain interactions is intended to explore this issue.

Table 11.3A shows a simple interaction involving several chains. The columns in the table represent chains – either identity chains (columns 1, 3, and 4) or similarity chains (column 2). Each row represents a message. Typically a message is realized as clause, as in the first four rows of Table 11.3A, but occasionally a message is realized in some other way. Thus the bottom row of Table 11.3A is actually a nominal group which realizes a message. The same syntagmatic relation holds between the members of the various columns in each of the messages from the text. Thus in each of the messages on this table, the filler of column 1 may be seen to possess an attribute which is described in either column 3 or column 4. That

Table 11.3A Chain interactions in a section of the 'nose job' text

Line #	Carrier	Relation	Attribute	
	Kay	Poss.	Problem	Deviated septum
13	I	had	problem	
14	you	've got		deviated septum
19	you	had		deviated septum
35	you	've got	problem	
45	your	[*have*]		deviated septum

is, a Carrier–Attribute relation holds between these columns in each of the messages in the table. Column 2 is a lexification of that attributive relation. Note that the relation is usually marked by a specific word in this table, but that in line 45 (the nominal group) that relation is not lexified. However, the absence of a specific lexical item to mark that relation should not be taken to imply that the relation does not exist. That is, the genitive *your* in *your deviated septum* implies that 'you have a deviated septum'. As a result, a word has been supplied in this row of Table 11.3A to show that an attributive relation holds between *your* and *deviated septum*, but it has been italicized and placed between square brackets to show that *have* did not occur in the original text. In Table 11.3A and in following tables, words which have been omitted through the grammatical process of ellipsis have been supplied and marked with brackets but not italicized. Bold indicates syllables which received tonic prominence. In Table 11.3A, *problem* and *deviated septum* have been placed in separate columns, because at first glance there is no obvious general linguistic means of linking the two. Yet, anyone who reads or hears this conversation knows that the second is a more specific description of the first. Are there any indications in the language of this conversation which support that interpretation? There are at least two. First, *deviated* seems to have bad associations. One deviates from the good and the true, not from the false. (*Longman's Dictionary of Contemporary English*, for example, defines *deviate* in the following terms: 'to be different or move away (from an accepted standard of behaviour, or from a correct or straight path'. Note also the associations with related words such as *deviant*.) Thus, it is perfectly conceivable that something which deviates would constitute a problem. Second, lines 13–14, in which *deviated septum* is introduced, recapitulate lines 12–13 with specifics added.

LL 12–13   And then **some**one told me that I **had** a problem …
LL 13–14   My **friend** who is a **nurse** said, '**lis**ten, **you've** got a deviated **sep**tum.

Why is this recapitulation necessary? The answer lies in the presence of the dramatic prominence of *had*, the lack of prominence of *problem*, and the evaluation together with extreme vagueness inherent in the word *problem*. Evaluations are regularly associated with details which provide the basis for the evaluation. Further, in this context, it is clear that *had* receives tonic prominence because the polarity of the verb is important. The lines which lead up to lines 12–13 are given below.

LL 10   **first** of all, I want it for cos**met**ic reasons …
LL 11–12   … so I **thought, well** … I would get it cos**met**ically changed,
LL 12–13   and then **some**one told me that I **had** a problem …

The concept of a problem has already been introduced by Sue in line 5, and so it is being treated as Given. Kay seems to assume that cosmetics is not a real problem, though it is still part of the similarity chain of possible reasons for surgery. An opposition is therefore set up in this text between a medical problem (i.e. a real problem) and a cosmetic problem. Kay can therefore be seen to start her narration with the attitude of 'I don't have a problem'. Lines 12–13 introduce the idea that she had a problem (and was surprised by that fact). But she has left her listener in the dark about the nature of that problem. Therefore lines 13–14 answer the question 'What problem is it?' with 'it's a deviated septum'. Note that the first syllable of deviated is salient, though it is not a tonic syllable. In this text, then, *a deviated septum* is being treated as a hyponym of *problem*.

This interpretation of *cosmetic* as non-problem is reinforced by the treatment of *plastic surgery* when that phrase is introduced later in the text.

LL 35   '**Sure, you've** got a real **prob**lem
LL 36   Let's just fix that **nose** right up.'
LL 36–38   But **I** wanted, … you see, **then** I had to figure out how to get plastic **surg**ery done .. **al**so.

Several items in lines 36–38 (the use of *but*, the prominence of *I*, *then*, and *plastic surgery*, and the devoting of a full information unit to *also* in line 38) all signal that Kay considers the cosmetic surgery to be an addition and a separate issue. Of course, anyone familiar with our culture would know that because of the policies of insurance companies, plastic surgery is a separate issue from corrective surgery. My point here, however, is that very specific features of the language tell us a great deal about the world that Kay is representing through her language, and these features limit the kinds of knowledge we may reasonably use as we interpret this text.

Given that the deviated septum can be seen as Kay's problem, Table 11.3A can then be reworked as Table 11.3B.

Table 11.3B Chain interactions in a section of the 'nose job' text: revised and expanded

Line #	Pol.	Kay	Sue	Relation	Problem	
					Quality	Thing
5			I	have	problem	
13		I		**had**	problem	
14		**you**		've got	deviated	**sep**tum
19		you		had	deviated	septum
20–21					**croo**ked	**ev**erything else
24					**wrong**	**oth**er things
25–26		I		**wan**ted	nice	nose
35		you		've got	**prob**lem	
45		your		[*have*]	deviated	septum
50–51	Q				**straight**ened	it
51	**yes**				[straightened]	[it]
51–52	Q				what about[12]	**this** part
53–54					all straight	**that**
54					**fun**ny	**this**
54–55	Q				**straight**en up	**that**
55	O.K.				[straighten up]	[that]
57		I		'm gonna get	[new]	this **new** nose

Table 11.3B is more than merely a reworking of Table 11.3A. Additional rows have been added to account for additional clauses. A column has been added for Sue, representing an identity chain which contrasts with Kay's. The fourth column sometimes divides into two: the second subcolumn represents some part of the nose, or body which has an attribute, while the first subcolumn represents the attribute that nose part or body part has. Note also that these attributes all revolve around some problem. *Deviated*, *wrong* and *crooked* indicate the presence of the problem, while *straightened* and *nice* indicate the absence of that problem. Although *natural* (line 25) belongs to the same lexical set as *problem*, and *wrong*, it is not

included in this table as part of the interaction with these other chains, since in this sentence it seems to be an attribute of not breathing through your nose rather than an attribute of the nose (or part of the nose) itself. *What about* (line 51) is included as part of the lexical set, since it seems to be used in this sentence to question whether a particular part of the nose will be straightened.

Tables 11.4–11.6 provide similar analyses of other portions of this segment of the text.[13]

The first two columns in Tables 11.3B, 11.4, and 11.5 indicate messages which contain modal verbs or adverbs, and polarity items,[14] respectively. The frequency with which these items occur in these messages, and particularly the frequency with which these items occur with tonic prominence, is related to the fact that this portion of the conversation revolves around three polar questions:

Does Kay have a problem?
Will she get the operation done?
Will the doctor do the operation as she wishes?

Tables 11.3B–11.6 each demonstrate some portion of the interactions among chains in this text. The messages presented in each table are partially similar, and thus, the tables can be taken as a measure of the repetitiveness of the text. Each table can be viewed as presenting a message paradigm, in which the interpretation of any single message is partially determined by the interpretations of the other messages on the table. It should be emphasized here, however, that these are not merely four unrelated tables. The tables themselves overlap and are structurally related. Thus, the *deviated septum* in Table 11.3B is the same as that in Table 11.4, and is a meronym of *nose* in Table 11.4. The people in Tables 11.3B and 11.4 are the same people. Clearly these two tables interweave by sharing chains. Tables 11.4 and 11.5 are even more closely interlocked and could have been combined. Table 11.6 looks quite different from Tables 11.3B, 11.4 and 11.5, but even here the speakers are the same people who are involved on the other tables. Furthermore, Table 11.6 is structurally related to the other tables, in that Table 11.6 contains (verbal or mental) processes which project some content, while the other tables generally present the sayings or thoughts that are projected by the processes in Table 11.6. Of course, Table 11.6 is not the only table to be linked structurally to others. The various messages of the text are related conjunctively,[15] and many of these conjunctive relations link messages from different paradigms. Thus these four message paradigms are intimately related both in content and in their

Table 11.4 Chain interactions concerning *operation*

Line #	Modal	Polar.	Kay	Dr.	Other	Cause	Nose	Operation
2			you		're having		**nose**	operation
3			my				**nose**	operation
4			your					operation
6–7			you			're having		**what** done
8			you			're **having**		it done
9			I			want		it done
10			I			want		it
11–12	would		I			get	it	changed
16	can	Q	I			get	my **nose**	operated on
27			[I]			getting	this thing	fixed
28	**could**	n't	I		[get]		this thing	fixed]
30			I				it	changed
31					**he**	had	nose	*operation* done
32	**should**/**really**	you			get			it done
36	Let's		['s]				that **nose**	fix up
37–38			*I*		to get			plastic surgery done
41	could	n't		he				do plastic surgery
45–46		Q		[they]			deviated septum	to correct
55–56			I		wanted			all . . . done

Table 11.5 Chain interactions emphasizing details of the procedure

Line #	Modal	Polar.	Kay	Doctors	Procedure	Nose
11–12	would		I		changed	it
29–30			I		**changed**	it
40				they	**break**	my nose
40			's	's	do **everything**	
41			I	you	do it	
41	**could**	n't		he	**do** plastic surgery	
43–44				s.o. **else**	to **break**	my nose
45–46	**may**	Q		**they**	have to break	your nose
47	may	**not** **do**		they	have to [break]	[your nose]
47				they	[have to break]	[your nose]
47				they	have to alter	**inside** *of your nose*
48–49				they	have to change	**shape** *of your nose*
49	**sure**			they	do something **drastic**	
50–51		Q			be **straight**ened	it
51		**yes**			[be straightened]	[it]
51–52		Q			what about	**this** part
52–53	**could**	**OK**		you	file down	that
53	[could]			[I]	[file down]	[that]

Table 11.6 Chain interactions emphasizing verbal processes

Line #	Sayer			Say	Receiver		Content
	Kay	**Dr.**	**Other**	**Say**	**Sue**	**Kay**	**Content**
6–8	*you*			**tell**	me	'...'	
9	I			**pre**face			why I ...
11–12	I			thought			...
12–13			**s.o.**	told		me	-that ...-
13–14			**friend**	said			'...'
16	I			said			'...'
17–18			she	said			'...'
24	I			thought			
25	I			figured			-...-
29–30	I			thought			-...-
30	I			thought,			
31–33			s.o.	told		me	-that ...-
35–36		they		said			'...'
38–41	I			said			- ... -
41		he		said			-...-
42–44	I			said			'...'
44		he		said			'...'
50–51	*I*			saying			'...'
51		he		said			'...'
51–53	I			said			'...'
52–53		you		said			-...-
53		he		said			'...'
53–55	I			said			'...'
55		he		said			'...'

structural relations.[16] This point can be emphasized by one last example which involves a sequence of three sentences which either belong to or refer to three different paradigms.

> LL 55–56 ... that's **all** I **wan**ted done **any**way, as far as plastic surgery's concerned,
>
> LL 56–57 so he **did** con**sent** to it then
>
> L 57 so .. I'm gonna **get** this new nose.

In the sentence from lines 55–56 (from Table 11.4) *that* refers to what the Doctor has agreed to do, and *all* and *done* refer to the process of the nose operation as Kay wants it. As a result, we can see that in lines 55–56 Kay expresses the identity of what she wants with what the Doctor is willing to do. This identity is emphasized by the tonic prominence placed on *all* and *wanted*. In the sentence in lines 56–57, Kay refers, through the metalinguistic term *consent*, to what the Doctor did through his speech; that is, *consent* refers to what the Doctor achieved by saying 'OK' etc. in the previous lines. *It* refers to the nose operation as Kay wants it. The tonic prominence on the tense carrier *did* emphasizes the polarity of the clause. *So* and *then* link 56–57 to 55–56 as consequence to cause. Finally, the sentence in line 57 draws the consequence, signaled by *so*, that Kay will acquire a new nose. The salient word *new* is closely related to terms such as *change*, *alter*, etc. (as consequence to cause) which have been used to describe the process of the operation (Table 11.4). *Get* in the sense of acquire is also closely linked to the notion of possession from Table 11.5. Because of the close lexical ties to both the terms of Table 11.3 and Table 11.4, line 57 seems quite appropriate as a summation of what has been said before.

Conclusion

Now let us return to the question with which we began. 'What makes this text coherent?' The first section discussed part of our answer. This text is coherent because it is perceived as being produced by two competent people who are interacting with one another in understandable ways.

The next section focussed on the second part of our answer.[17] That is, coherent texts typically contain a good deal of partial repetition. Few real texts do not contain such repetition expressed or at least implied. For example, chains of anaphoric reference typically occur within most natural texts. But the discussion of Tables 11.3–11.6 would seem to emphasize the *repetition* part of the phrase *partial repetition*. Actually the word *partial* is equally important. It is not true that the ideal – the maximally coherent – text is one which repeats itself exactly n-times. There should be change and development as well. In fact, this happens even when the repetition is almost exact repetition. The repetition in the first exchange illustrates this point very well.

L 3   My **nose** operation.
L 4   Yes, your **nose** operation.

In spite of the fact that the line 4 comes very close to an exact repetition of line 3, the two play quite different roles in the conversation. As she says line 3, Kay has obviously been taken by surprise. We can interpret her line as partly an outburst directed toward herself and partly as a request for confirmation directed toward Sue. Certainly Sue interprets it as a request for confirmation, and in her line provides that confirmation. However, that is not all she does, for she does so by repeating Kay's phrase with a rendition which is so close to that of Kay's that it is impossible not to think of it as a partial mimicking of her outburst. Thus, Sue's contribution is more than just a confirmation, it is also a bit of good-humored teasing.[18]

One might well ask what role does knowledge of the world play in this framework? The answer is, of course, that it is quite important. Certainly listeners use their knowledge of the world and how we interact with it to interpret this conversation and to figure out why certain things are said. For example, all of us who know about insurance know that insurance companies only pay for certain types of operations. The notion of schema has been introduced to account for the ability of people to fill in ideas which are missing from the text and to use these ideas in the interpretation of the text. However, people have a vast, perhaps unbounded, number of schemata available to use as they read and listen, only a limited number of which are appropriate to any given text. How do language users determine which schemata are relevant and which are not? Or, to pose a related problem: how do people with different schemata communicate? Most of the time the schemata leave traces in the text. We use these artifacts to reconstruct the schemata which were used as the text was produced. We do not necessarily have to have all the relevant schemata already formed before we approach a text in order to understand it. If this were necessary, there would be no learning through language.

Notes

1. This reaction is to be contrasted with a later interaction within the family. In this case, Pops was visiting my wife's father in his house. At a point late in the afternoon Pops became tired and began to suggest that we go home so that he (Pops) could take a nap. It was with great difficulty that the family was finally able to persuade Pops that it was he who was the visitor and who had to go home. In this case, his contributions to the conversation were taken as coherent, but wrong because they were based on false assumptions.
2. See Halliday (1985/1994) or Matthiessen (1995) for an explanation of process types and of other technical concepts such as Theme.
3. The categorization used here is based on the approach initially described in Grimes (1975), and later adapted and developed by Longacre (1981, 1983/1996, 1989, 1990).
4. For the purposes of identifying Themes, the conjunction is considered

to be a part of the following clause. Therefore, a combination of two independent clauses will occur in only one order. That is, a sequence such as *he played the piano and he sang*, is possible, while a sequence such as *And he sang, he played the piano*, is not. Of course this analysis leaves open the question of why a given chunk of information is placed first in such a combination of independent clauses. Although the answer to this question must consider the textual function of the clause-complex in its context (e.g. to explain why a given context requires *he came but he didn't say anything* rather than *he didn't say anything but he came*), it must also consider implications for the experiential aspect of language as well. Thus the difference between *he took poison and he died* and *he died and he took poison* does not derive solely from the function of the two clause-complexes in their respective contexts, but also involves relations among the 'real world' events being represented. This sort of change of experiential information conveyed does not seem to be involved with thematic changes within independent conjoinable clause-complexes, and therefore the relations within independent conjoinable clause-complexes have been analysed separately.

5. Note that in some cases these weak causal instances of *so* begin punctuated sentences and link these sentences to the preceding context. This distribution resembles the distributional properties of the conjunctive adverbs. Of course, the punctuation was added in the transcription, and was not in the oral language, but even so, it represents something of the interpretation of at least one listener – the transcriber. In fact, it probably represents the interpretations of a number of listeners, since all the participants were asked to examine a draft of the transcription to discover places of disagreement.

6. Note that *so* with the meaning of 'purpose' is excluded from this statement. Thus, *so the paint will dry more quickly, we'll use a dehumidifier*, is not relevant.

7. Greenbaum and Quirk (1990:254) quite properly point out that so lies 'on the gradient between the "pure" coordinators and the "pure" subordinators'. The analysis used here is not intended to contradict theirs. Rather, when one considers those features of *so* which are most relevant to thematic structure, the matter being considered here, *so* acts like a coordinating conjunction rather than a subordinating one.

8. See also Bäcklund (1989) for a similar description of initial purpose clauses – but one which is more descriptive of the functions of Theme in general, since it allows for the possibility of initial infinitive clauses (i.e. functioning as Theme) which convey new information.

9. Emphasis in the original.

10. The fifth factor is sometimes made explicit by definition writers. See, for example, the definition in *The Longman Dictionary of Contemporary English*: '6. med the cutting of the body in order to set right or remove a diseased part'.

11. *Nurse* seems to occur by chance here, since there is no direct grammatical connection to *hospital, operation,* etc. However, there is a strong textual reason that *nurse* occurs where it does. The person referred to is cited as a source of information about a medical problem. Indeed, this marks the first time that a medical term is used to describe the problem. Therefore that person's medical knowledge, as certified by her being a nurse, is directly relevant to the point of the conversation. Note that, in a similar way, the second unnamed source of information about the operation is certified as knowledgeable by mentioning that he had undergone the operation and so had personal experience of it.

12. While the phrase *what about* does not describe a quality, itself, it constitutes a focus question which in this context requires as answer the providing of a quality. (*It will be/won't be straightened.*)

13. Ideally these tables would be presented as one large table which would show the entire set of chain interactions. These chain interactions have been separated simply for ease of presentation on the page.

14. Polarity items not only include words such as *not*, but also whether the message as a whole constitutes a polar interrogative. Polar interrogatives are indicated by Q on the tables. *Sure*, from line 35 and the tonic prominence on *had* in line 13, should probably also be included as polarity items in Table 11.3B. They have not been included, in the one case, because the interpretation of *sure* is not unambiguous, and in the other case, because it is difficult to represent in a table such as this.

15. For reasons of space, no attempt has been made to present a systematic analysis of the conjunctive relations which hold between the various messages of the text. Clearly they are an important aspect of the coherence of the text, and must be considered. We have chosen to focus on other aspects of the coherence of this text here because they are less familiar, not because they are of particularly greater importance. See Martin (1992) for a discussion of conjunction within a larger framework. Martin (Undated), Figure 13 provides a conjunctive analysis of a portion of the text considered here.

16. This discussion should not be interpreted to imply that the signals of coherence are limited to those messages which have been placed on one of the various tables so far. All the messages in this conversation may reasonably be examined with respect to how they relate to the rest of the conversation.

17. Two other parts of the answer to this question should be mentioned here, although this chapter has not addressed them. First, this text is coherent because it hangs together structurally. It has structure as a whole, moving from part to part. This movement takes place on a large-scale level such as might be revealed by a generic description such as ones discussed in Hasan (1978) and Halliday and Hasan (1980, 1985/ 1989), or a phasal description such as the one presented in Gregory

(2001) and Gregory and Malcolm (1981). The text has structure on a lower level as well, with the movement provided by the conjunctive relations which hold between the various parts of the text.

A second part of the answer which has not been addressed in this chapter is the intertextual relations and axiological values brought to bear in the production and interpretation of the text. This factor has been addressed in the chapters by Lemke and Thibault in this volume.

18. The discussion of movement here has referred specifically to movement within the features of language of the text. In fact, at least two issues are relevant here. First, it is necessary to notice that even exact repetition of wording recontextualizes each occurrence so that even where the exact same thing is said several times (e.g. A rose is a rose is a rose) there is 'movement'.

Second, there is the interesting question of the degree to which movement in the social interaction which is being enacted through language (i.e. the contextual configuration) is required as well. To put it in non-technical language, can participants in a conversation leave that conversation having exactly the same relation with which they started it? Surely, most satisfying conversations involve some progress or change. (I have bought my oranges, or I have touched base with old friends, etc.) Whether such 'progress' should be discussed in ways similar to those developed for the discussion of the language of texts is a question which is yet to be considered. My point here is that both in the discussion of the features of the language of the texts and in the discussion of the factors controlling the nature of texts there is a need to discuss both a static aspect (involving repetition in texts and stasis in contexts) and a dynamic aspect (involving change in both texts and the contexts in which they are produced).

References

Bäcklund, I. (1989) To sum up: initial infinitives as cues to the reader. In *Proceedings from the Fourth Nordic Conference for English Studies, Helsingør, May 11–13, 1989*, ed. by Graham Caie, Kirsten Haastrup, Arnt Lykke Jakobsen, Jørgen Erik Nielsen, Jørgen Sevaldsen, Henrik Specht and Arne Zettersten, Department of English, University of Copenhagen, 289–302.

Cloran, Carmel, Butt, David and Williams, Geoffrey (eds.) (1996) *Ways of Saying, Ways of Meaning: Selected Papers of Ruqaiya Hasan*. London: Cassell.

Fries, Peter H. (1981) On the status of theme in English: arguments from discourse. *Forum Linguisticum*, 6:1–38.

Fries, Peter H. (1995) Patterns of information in initial position in English. In *Discourse and Meaning in Society: Functional Perspectives*, ed. by Peter H. Fries and Michael Gregory, Norwood, NJ: Ablex, 47–66.

Gernsbacher, Morton Ann and Givón, Talmy (1995) *Coherence in Spontaneous Text.* Amsterdam: John Benjamins.

Greenbaum, Sidney and Quirk, Randolph (1990) *A Students' Grammar of the English Language.* London: Longman.

Gregory, Michael (2001) Phasal Analysis within Communication Linguistics: Two Contrastive Discourses. (Chapter 10, this volume.)

Gregory, Michael, and Malcolm, Karen (1981) Generic situation and discourse phase: an approach to the analysis of children's talk (mimeo).

Grimes, Joseph (1975) *The Thread of Discourse.* The Hague: Mouton.

Halliday, M. A. K. (1967), Notes on transitivity and theme in English: Part 2. *Journal of Linguistics,* 3:177–274.

Halliday, M. A. K. (1970) Language structure and language function. In *New Horizons in Linguistics,* ed. by John Lyons, Baltimore, MD: Penguin, 140–165.

Halliday, M. A. K. (1985/1994) *An Introduction to Functional Grammar.* London: Arnold.

Halliday, M. A. K. and Hasan, R. (1976) *Cohesion in English.* London: Longmans.

Halliday, M. A. K. and Hasan, R. (1980) *Text and Context,* Sophia Linguistica 6. Tokyo: Sophia University.

Halliday, M. A. K. and Hasan, R. (1985/1989) *Language, Context, and Text: Aspects of Language in a Social-Semiotic Perspective.* Oxford: Oxford University Press.

Hasan, Ruqaiya (1978) Text in the systemic-functional model. In *Current Trends in Textlinguistics,* ed. by Wolfgang U. Dressler, Berlin: Walter de Gruyter, 228–246.

Hasan, Ruqaiya (1983) Coherence and cohesive harmony. In *Understanding Reading Comprehension: Cognition, Language and the Structure of Prose,* ed. by James Flood, Newark, DE: International Reading Association, 181–219.

Longacre, Robert E. (1981) A spectrum and profile approach to discourse analysis. *Text,* 1:337–359.

Longacre, Robert E. (1983/1996) *The Grammar of Discourse.* New York: Plenum.

Longacre, Robert E. (1989) Two hypotheses regarding text generation and analysis. *Discourse Processes,* 12:413–460.

Longacre, Robert E. (1990) *Storyline Concerns and Word Order Typology in East and West Africa. Studies in African Linguistics,* Supplement 10. Los Angeles, CA: Department of Linguistics, UCLA.

Martin, James (1992) *English Text: System and Structure.* Philadelphia: John Benjamins.

Martin, James (undated) Lexical cohesion, field and genre: parceling experience and discourse goals. Unpublished manuscript.

Matthiessen, Christian (1995) *Lexicogrammatical Cartography: English Systems.* Tokyo: International Language Sciences Publishers.

Morris, William (1978) *The American Heritage Dictionary*. Boston: Houghton Mifflin.

Pike, Eunice (1981) *Ken Pike: Scholar and Christian*. Dallas: Summer Institute of Linguistics.

Pike, Kenneth (1967) *Language in Relation to a Unified Theory of the Structure of Human Behavior*. The Hague: Mouton.

Proctor, Paul (ed.) (1978) The *Longman Dictionary of Contemporary English*. London: Longman.

Quirk, Randolph (1978) Focus, scope, and lyrical beginnings. *Language and Style*, 11:30–39.

Sinclair, John (1987) *The Collins COBUILD English Language Dictionary*. London: Collins.

Schiffrin, Deborah (1987) *Discourse Markers*. Cambridge: Cambridge University Press.

Thompson, Sandra A. (1983) Grammar and written discourse: initial vs. final purpose clauses in English. *Text*, 5:55–84.

Appendix: Conversation (Interview) between Sue and Kay

(Videotaped and audiotaped at Rice University, 11/3/83)

[Brackets indicate simultaneous conversation. Laugh indications immediately following a word begin on that word.]

1	**Sue:**	(snort ha-S) What I would like to find out more about
2		is your operation . . . that you are having.
3	**Kay:**	My nose operation.
4	**S:**	Yes, your nose operation (giggle-S)
5		You see, I have a similar problem and I've been postponing
6		doing something about it for a very long time, so tell me what
7		you're having done an' . . . what condition you're gonna be in when
8		you're having it done.
9	**K:**	Well, maybe I should preface this thing, why I want it done.
10		First of all, I want it for cosmetic reasons. I'm sort of tired
11		of everyone going like this to my nose, so I thought, well, . . . I
12		would get it cosmetically changed, and then someone told me that
13		I had a problem, you see. That was great! My friend who is a
14		nurse said, 'listen, you've got a deviated septum.'
15	**S:**	(sympathetic laugh)
16	**K:**	I said, ah, does that mean I can get my nose (giggle-S) operated on?
17		Will someone else pay for it? She said, 'sure, it's a medical
18		problem an' they'll . . .'
19	**S:**	Didn't you notice, you had a deviated septum?
20	**K:**	No, I mean, everything else
21		⌈ is crooked an' stuff, you can't even (?) . . ⌉
22	**S:**	⌊ . . . ⌋
		that you couldn't breathe through the
23		side, one side of your nose?
24	**K:**	No, so I thought, I mean there are other things wrong with me,

25   so I figured, like, well, that was just ... natural, so ... but I
26   always wanted a nice nose, so .. I .. I had, uh, looked into,
27   investigated, uh, getting this thing fixed. But it was a long
28   time ago, so I couldn't do it. And it was just time and money
29   and all that other stuff. So then I thought, well, ... its about
30   time I changed it. I got new insurance, you see, so I thought,
31   well, .. and someone also this summer told me that, uh mm
     that he had the
32   operation done, and that you really should get it done,
33   because you can breathe better and all sorts of things, so .. so,
34   when I went to the hospital this time, I just inquired, and
35   they said, 'sure, you've got a real problem. (small sympathetic
36   laugh-S) Let's just fix that nose right up!' But I wanted, ...
37   you see, then I had to figure out how to get plastic surgery
38   done .. also. So I said, well, I can trade art work (small laugh-
39   S) .. uh .. (small laugh-K) extra, or I give em money ...
     anything, that
40   once they were going to break my nose, let's do everything
     ...
41   why do it twice? So, uh mm, he said he couldn't do plastic
     surgery.
42   So ... in the conversation with him, I just said, 'well .. I
43   mean, I don't want to go pay someone else ... a second time
     to
44   break my nose again, .. to do this,' and so he said, 'well .. '
45 **S:** Do they have to break your nose to correct your deviated
46   septum?
47 **K:** They may have to .. they may not. But they do have to
     completely
48   alter .. inside ... at least ... they still have to change the whole
49   shape, so I'm sure that they're going to do something sort of
     drastic,
50   so .. uh, .. so I got around it by saying, 'well, listen ... is it
     going
51   to be straightened?' you see and he said, 'yes.' I said, 'well,
     what
52   about this part, you said that you could file that down a little
53   bit.' He said, 'well, .. ok (ha-K)!' I said, 'well, then, if that's
54   all straight, this is gonna look really funny. can you .. like
55   straighten that up?' And so he said 'well, ok.'. . and that's all I
56   wanted done anyway, as far as plastic surgery's concerned, so
     he

57   did consent to it then, so . . I'm gonna get this new nose.

58 **S:** And what are . . . are they going to put you to sleep when you

59   have it done? . . . or do you have to be awake, while it's being

60   done?

61 **K:** Well, normally you're awake, and . . if I understood it

62   correctly, they're gonna do it under general anesthetic, so

63   that's ok, . . so I'll be asleep . . . But, uh, my friend, Emma,

64   said that all the doctors, when they get their noses fixed, or,

65   corrected, then they want to be put asleep, you see (long ha-K),

66   but they tell these patients, 'this is nothing' (sympathetic laugh-

67   S), . . except that you see this hammer (long ha-K) whacking your

68   face, and that's sort of traumatic. So . . Emma told me not to get it

69   done under . . uh . . local, cause it will hurt, and uh, . . so?

70 **S:** And how long afterwards are you going . . . to be black and blue,

71   or . . ?

72 **K:** I don't know. I asked him if I could teach on the following

73   Monday, since the operation is on Thursday, . . Would I be ok? . .

74   and he said, 'yes', but he said, 'you won't be able to

75   breathe out of your nose' . . so . . but he said uh, 'you haven't

76   been able to breathe anyway (giggle-K), so why not?'

77 **S:** How long have you not been able to breathe out of . . is it is it the . .

78   which side of the nose can't you breathe out of?

79 **K:** This side . .

80 **S:** Out of your right side?

81 **K:** Uh hum it's just collapsed . . . I mean, I just . . . always thought that

82   that's . . . the way. . people breathed, . . you know, sort of less (low

83   ha-K), . . just use your mouth a lot . . . to breathe , . .

84 **S:** Uh huh, yeah (giggle-K) . . . right (sympathetic giggle-S)! . .

85 **K:** Right, so . . . I think it's . . . the problem, they say, is that you

86   get a lot of colds, . . stuff like that, and, . . . and, uh, I'm tired of

87   colds. In fact I said if this doesn't work, I want my tonsils

88   out . . . if that doesn't work, maybe a big pipe (giggle-K),

89 S: Just . . .

90 K: ⌈ That's right! . .   ⌉
91 S: ⌊ Irrigation system . . . ⌋

92 K: In fact I was so desperate to sort of get rid of colds and
93   coughing and all that other stuff, that I even went in for . . . new
94   allergy tests, . . so on the same day that I scheduled my operation
95   I had sixty-two shots up my arm, . . . to see what I was allergic
96   to . . and . . . you know, I just really want to breathe . .
97 S: Did they tell you what you were allergic to?
98 K: All sorts of stuff . .
99 S: Have you gotten . . .
100 K: Yes, I'm . . . but I'm a good allergy patient.
101 S: They can treat every one of the allergies, . . huh? . .
102 K: Yes, after having all these diseases, you see,
103   tuberculosis, all that other stuff, they said, that, . . .
104   'you're lucky' (low contained giggle-K), you see, . . 'because you can be
105   treated' and that's nice. I mean the fact that I can get shots and
106   that I don't have a problem . . . is sort of nice . . And my allergists
107   gave up on me back in Pittsburgh, because they can't do anything
108   anymore . . . all these molds and mildews and stuff . . . so if I get my
109   allergies taken care of, my nose fixed, . . keep my tonsils, I think . . .
110   I think life can be ok!
         (short giggle-K) . .   ⌈ and then, maybe . . .   ⌉
111 S: ⌊ This is gonna be a big year . . . ⌋
112 K: . . . also get a good nose . . . yeah . . . I'm gonna look black and
113   blue, though . . . when I come out of this operation.
114   . . . .
115 S: Probably pretty swollen? . . . ⌈   all through ⌉
116 K: ⌊ that's right . . ⌋
117   that's right so I have my sunglasses ready . .
118 S: Yes, big ones that come . . .
119 K: Yes, but I am sort of, . . I think I'm, I'm ready for this
120   operation, cause I need like three days in the hospital for
121   rest . . read cheap novels . . stuff like that . . so I'm up

122   for. . convalescing . . I won't give up
       my phone ⌐ number out ...   ⌐
123 S: ⌊ What kind of cheap⌋
124   novels are you going to read? . . Harlequin
125   romances or something like that . . to ...
126 K: Who knows? . . I think *The Nurses* . .
127 S: *The Nurses* (small laugh-S-giggle-K)
128 K: Yeah, ⌐ something definitely general . .
129 S: ⎮ In between soap operas on television? . .
130 K: ⌊   Well,
131   I don't like those soap operas, but I sort of ... I like
132   reading better than watching TV, I think, . . so, I, I would rather
133   read something like *General Hospital*, but in . . besides they can
134   ⌐be more graphic ...⌐
135 S: ⌊Big print . . and ...⌋
136 K: . . in those books . .
137 S: . . yes . .
138 K: . . and they don't really do all that stuff, so . . besides you have
139   to wait too long ... this way I can jump over paragraphs, you see,
140 K: ⌐and get . .
141 S: ⎮ . . find out what happens to . .
142 K: ⌊ . . the real good stuff . .
143 S: . . yeah . .
144 K: Instead of having to wait 'til tomorrow . . to get the
145   information.
146 S: So how long have you had this? . . has it been since you were
147   a kid?
148 K: . . I don't know. I, . . I swear it was when my brother, Jeff,
149   pushed me out of the bunkbeds when we were about . . two and three . .
150   y'see, ... I think I broke my nose then, but my mother ... maybe its
151   child abuse!
152 S: Child abuse (giggle-S then K), yes.
153 K: I don't know . .
154 S: Let's make this statement on (giggle-S then K) TV right
155   now (giggle S).
156 K: Thats right! so, uh ...
157 S: Broker is the victim of child abruse (ha-S) abuse ...

158 K: That's right, I mean, I wish I could just go in and get a
159   total body overhaul, I mean, I wish you could go in for sort of things
160   like that, but you have to be .. have aesthetic reasons, they have
161   to .. instead of saying, 'I don't like it,' .. it seems to me
162   that's enough ... I don't like my ankles, let's cut off ...
163 S: ⌈.. put in some new ones ..⌉
164 K: ⌊.. a few inches ...   ⌋
165   that's right! .. But now you have to have
166   really good reasons, so luckily with my nose, I've got a great
167   reason ... it happens to be, uh, physical, but luckily it fits in there,
168   you see ..
169 S: Yeah, I was always disappointed, I was in an automobile accident
170   about eight years ago and smashed ... my mouth, and ... when I was taken
171   to the hospital I didn't really realize what state I was in and
172   the plastic surgeon came in and completely reconstructed ... my
173   bottom lip, but had I known, what he was doing, I would have
174   asked to see a book of mouths (giggle-S, then K) first, and pick out
175   a new one ... I was tired of my old one ...
176 K: I hadn't thought of it like that. ...
177   Well, I, ... it's a good thing I don't like my nose, you see ..
178 S: I think your nose is perfectly fine ..
179 K: .. because you don't own it (sympathetic giggle-S) .. You
180   don't (giggle-K) have to look at it all the time. No, but it's like,
181   all crooked and stuff like that .. and it goes up, and I mean, I'm
182   thinking ahead ... when I'm forty ...
183 S: You mean it's not gonna go up anymore?
184 K: That's right! .. it's gonna come down ... a little bit. You see,
185   then I don't have to be a 'cute' forty-year-old, in a few years,
186   you see, it's gonna be like ...
187 S: This is gonna alter your appearance altogether ..
188 K: .. gonna alter my-whole-outlook-   ⌈on-life (giggle-K) ...⌉
189 S: ⌊.. your demeanor   ⌋
190 S: and presence and ... everything.

191 K: That's right, that's right, you never know … dates …

192   ⌈ and things like that …   ⌉

193 S: ⌊ personality (giggle-K), too, ⌋   who knows …

194 K: Right! yes. … Maybe more, .. higher enrollment (giggle-K) …

195 S: .. (giggle-S) higher enrollment in your classes ..

196 K: .. they're gonna come in and say, 'look at that

197   nose!' … anyway, I'm sort of excited about this, cause I waited a

198   long time …

199 S: There's some guy, we heard a story a couple of weeks ago,

200   Uh mm, .. of this this family … and there was a young child in the

201   family, a young boy .. and he was .. he was having tremendous

202   problems in school, he was a a very difficult child … he was too

203   active and he was always getting in trouble, and .. and, uh mm, a long

204   lost relative came into this family, and who had been to India

205   and studied with some of the Eastern mystics .. an' so he suggested to

206   this child that he stuff cotton up the right side of his nose ..

207   and so they stuffed cotton up the right side of his

208   nose (giggle/laugh-S) and his personality completely changed, he

209   became this very passive, nice docile child (giggle-S) …

210 K: (giggle-K) yeah, he had to sort of writhe on the floor for a while … he

211   couldn't breathe … poor guy! …. Well, uh, I, as a kid I used to

212   tape my nose down though .. every night I would get this masking

213   tape and I would put this tape on, you see …

214 S: Was that to change the shape of it?   ⌈ .. to flatten out your …? ⌉

215 K: ⌊ That's right,   ⌋

216   I thought it would hold it down, 'cause

217   everybody would go like this, you know, and say, 'oh, look at

218   that cute Broker nose,' … well they (long contained ha-K), you know,

219   like … they .. I wanted words like … beeyoudiful (sympathetic

220 giggle-S) ... gorges .. great .. not cute (laugh-K) ....

221 **S:** ... nstead of cute ..

222 **K:** So I learnt right off, that I've got to get a new nose ... but I

223 would last in bed for about ... ten minutes ... with this tape, you

224 see, and then I'd ...

225 **S:** .. then breathing became more important (sympathetic giggle-S) ..

226 **K:** .. whip it off ... I'm surprised I just didn't have little

227 welts going up my nose, but I just couldn't stand it, so .. you

228 can see, I ... I've thought about this for a while .. I mean .. even

229 though my mother complains, and says that it's, because I had to

230 blow my nose as a child ... my first reaction is ... why? .. you see,

231 and .. and their their response to me blowing my nose was .. uh .. stop

232 blowing it! just stop! .. it's all in your head. Course,

233 then I'd (laugh/giggle-K) try and I'd sort of be (giggle-K) this kid with ...

234 **S:** .. (sympathetic giggle-S) runny nose ..

235 **K:** That's right (ha-K)! ... that's right! .. and I would have to apologize

236 for blowing my (sympathetic giggle-S) nose ... I kept thinking, like, I'm

237 mentally deficient, because I'm blowing my nose ... and I know it sounds like

238 such a stupid subject, but those sort of things really sort of

239 last, you see, ... long enough ...

240 **S:** They really stay with you, .. that's .. yeah ..

241 **K:** That's right! ... long enough for me just to out of the blue ... to

242 have someone say, 'well, I had my nose operated on'. ... Why? .. you

243 know, 'because I had a deviated septum,' and then, I just .. it

244 sort of fired, it rekindled all that enthusiasm, and ... here I am!

245 **S:** Do you know what they have to do with a deviated septum? Do

246 they have to reconnect? Do they .. move ... it's cartilage, isn't

247 it, that they have to move over, so that it ... Do they have to

248		reconnect that to something .. that it has torn away from .. or s-?
249		Do you know what they are doing?
250	K:	Well, it seems to me, . . . and I must be totally, I'm hoping
251		I'm wrong, but I think they just take these poles and they just
252		sort of (giggle/laugh-K) . . . make . . .
253	S:	. . (sympathetic giggle-S) they violently knock your . . .
254	K:	. . thats right! I think they're .. basically it's like breaking
255		inside, I think . . . now . . . ⌈And the reason I don't kn- .. ⌉
256	S:	⌊.. but how do they set it again?⌋
257	K:	Well .. they pack it!
258	S:	. . oh, pack it . . .
259	K:	. . you see, they pack it .. and it resets . . . and so it's like . . .
260	S:	. . so that's why you can't breathe until they take out the
261		packing.
262	K:	. . that's right! .. you see, so that's the only problem I
263		foresee, is that I . . .
264	S:	You can't breathe for .. you have to breathe through your mouth ..
265	K:	Right! .. and the thing is that if you choke on food, I mean
266		you could die (sympathetic giggle-S) . . . all these years . . .
267	S:	Yes .. there's danger involved in this operation ..
268	K:	. . that's right! ..
269	S:	. . high risk (ha-S)! ..
270	K:	. . well, imagine this, I mean, all those years you've been
271		keeping yourself away from muggers, rapists, things like
272		that .. and then all at once you die, because you've got
273		⌈ a nose . . . ⌉
274	S:	⌊. . . choked on a piece of food (giggle-S) .. ⌋
275	K:	⌊ .. operation .. ⌋
276		I mean that's a real sort of ⌈a disgusting way to go . . . ⌉
277	S:	⌊You have to be very careful⌋
278		for a period of time . . . this is ..
279	K:	I mean it's Murphy's Law! I know that (small giggle-S) this could
280		possibly happen . . .
281	S:	. . . on chocolate mousse or (sympathetic giggle-S) something like that . . .
282	K:	. . that's right! .. and . . . besides, I can't taste anything, so at
283		least if I .. I can go to cheap restaurants now, because I can't
284		taste anything .. I could be eating dogmeat and it wouldn't

285   matter, because I can't taste it.
286 **S:**   mmm be an economical week!
287 **K:**   Right! I .. and, it might pay for my
288   operation (giggle/laugh-K&S), .. so .. I hope this ... this better be a good
289   nose that's all I can say! ...
290 **S:**   .. yeah, maybe you should look at a book of noses or something,
291   before you go in ...┌ he doesn't
292 **K:**   │ No, he doesn't want me to do that, ..
293 **S:**   └   want you to ...
294 **K:**   because then he's gonna feel like he's doing plastic surgery, you
295   see, I mean, ... I HAD a nose .. I could DRAW him a nose .. that I would
296   want; but then I may have to get other things done, too. I mean,
297   I do think ... that the curve and things of your nose sort of goes with the
298   rest of it ... like I .. if I had a real pointy nose, I'd have to
299   have half my chin taken off, you see, or something like
300   that (laugh/giggle-S), so (giggle-K) I can't be real radical about
301   this. I don't want someone looking at me, and saying,
302   oh, what's wrong with you,' you see, ... I just don't want them
303   to say, 'what a cute nose'. .... fact, I'd like them to drop the
304   subject (laugh/giggle-K, then sympathetic giggle-S) ...
305 **S:**   .. just not even notice your nose anymore ..
306 **K:**   Thats right .. just forget it ... so .. I don't know. That's about
307   the only operation I've had. I mean other than .. sort of foot
308   reconstruction, and .. but .. but that was a real physical
309   problem .. so this is the first time, and, and, and at .. at least
310   this time when people say, 'Why are you getting your nose
311   fixed?' .. as a female, they already think that it's because you
312   want a nice nose, you see. Well, they're right! (laugh-S), but but
313   but (giggle-K) I'm not gonna admit to that ... yeah .. so I
314   immediately say,   ┌'Ah, I can't
315 **S:**   └ I have a deviated septum ┘
316 **K:**   breathe (ha-S), I haven't been able to breathe for years' ... They say,
317   'Ah, that's a shame.' See, so it's nice ... maybe it's catholic

318   guilt ... something like that ..

319 S: It's gonna be a new experience. Probably for the first time in

320   your memory, you'll be able to breathe out of both nostrils? ..

321 K: Yeah .. I was hoping that my voice was gonna change, like, I'd

322   go really low or something ... that it would .. that I would sound

323   more like the way I hear it ... but .. uh .. after talking to, uh, Jim

324   and, .. he just said, 'Forget it!' It's not where voice comes from, or

325   whatever. Although he may be wrong! .. see ... I mean maybe he's

326   wrong ...

327 S: Hey, .. if you .. if these Eastern mystics are right, you see,

328   what they figure is it's right and left brain kind of stuff, so

329   that .. the air that goes into your right nostril controls your

330   left ... brain thinking ... which is your more analytical,

331   intellectual kind of stuff. And the air that goes in the left

332   side controls your right brain thinking ...

333 K: .. so the more the artistic side .. uh-oh!

334 S: Yeah,

335 K: ⌈ Uh oh!⌉

336 S: ⌊ so this ⌋ way your more intellectual side is going to

337   surface more ... right?

338 K: Oh God ... I'll (giggle-K)   ⌈be a Renaissance professor ...⌉

339 S: ⌊You're going to be a   ⌋

340   (giggle-S) Renaissance professor of art.

341 K: Thats right! .. and, you see, now that I only have a right

342   brain (giggle K&S), basically cause I'm not using the left one, right?

343   and ..

344 S: ⌈   ... a new dimension ...⌉

345 K: ... and, have you ever   ⌊book, *Drawing on the Right Side*⌋ read that

346   *of the Brain?*

347 S: .. Uh-uh ..

348 K: .. well, it's an ok book .. I mean, I wouldn't use it, uh .. it's

349   nice for evening reading, sometimes ... but, .. so I use my right

350   hand, see, and they do feel that you could use the right side of

351   your brain better ... and uh .. , so this way .. maybe I'll learn how to

352   use computer now .. maybe it will ...

353 **S:** ⌈ Right! .. it will open up   ⌉

354 **K:** ⌊ ... all make sense (low giggle-K) ⌋

355 **S:** a whole new (giggle-S) G world to you ..

356 **K:** Instead of saying—bashing in there—, 'Hey, you in there,

357   send up (low giggle-K) that information!,' or, 'Stop saying things like,

358   "doesn't compute", or whatever' (low giggle-K), ... you know ...

359 **S:** You'll invent the perfect one.

360 **K:** ... or when the paragraph goes off the page, when you're just

361   trying to type in that little bit of information, and I'm

362   screaming to Jim, 'it just left, I didn't do it (sympathetic

363   giggle-S)! I only wanted to put an "a" in there instead of an

364   "e", and he keeps saying, 'you have ... you know you are the

365   person in charge of this computer, an' it only listens to

366   whatever you punch in' ... but ... I know (low giggle-K) ... that ...

367 **S:** .. it has a mind of its own ..

368 **K:** .. that's right! ... so maybe if I get the left side working, I

369   won't have to be bashing on (giggle-K) the side of the computer ..

370 **S:** (sympathetic giggle-S) You won't have to be so. ... yes!

371 **K:** ... violent with it ..

372 **S:** violent with it, yes ..

373 **K:** ... or in lithography it's ... I won't say, 'Well, it's magic,'

374   while I'm teaching it, you see, .. not that it's chemistry, that

375   it's magic, so .. but if it doesn't work, I'll stuff the right side

376   (giggle K and S) of my, my nose with stuff, ok? .. so ...

377 **S:** You would just take it out at night to sleep ..

378 **K:** That's right!

379 **S:** (loud mock whisper) I think we've finished ...

380 **K:** OK.

381 **S:** Let's call it 'The End'.

Index